Turgot, Controller General, 97–104, 131, 134–37, 221, 237–38

Unwin, George, 143
Urban work force, 106–8
Usher, Abbot, 119–20

Valor Ecclesiasticus, 17
Voltaire, 62

War of the Austrian Succession (1740–48), 181
War of the Grand Alliance against France (1688), 188
War of the Spanish Succession, 40
Webb, Beatrice, 154
Webb, Sidney, 154
Weingast, Barry, 188, 219
Weir, David, 75
Westminster Company soap monopoly, 147
Whig oligarchy, 39. *See also* British Parliament
Wittfogel, Karl, 48–49

|  |  |
|--:|:--|
| Compositor: | Impressions |
| Printer: | Edwards Brothers, Inc. |
| Binder: | Edwards Brothers, Inc. |
| Text: | 10/13 Aldus |
| Display: | Aldus |

*Receveurs generaux des finances,* 167
Renfort, M., 99–100
*Rentes perpetuelles,* 175
*Rentes viagères,* 190
Rents: accessed through property rights, 10; dissipated in Parliament/Crown competition, 156–57; institutionalization of competition for, 222–23; protecting monopolies for, 145–46. *See also* Monopolies; Property rights (France)
Reputation mechanism, 115–16; repeat play, 170
Revolutions: link between privilege and, 236–40; theory of state breakdowns and, 227; violence of peasant, 63–68. *See also* French Revolution
Ricardo, David, 12
Richelieu, Cardinal, 39, 170
*The Rise and Decline of Nations* (Olson), 114
Roche, Daniel, 106
Royal Battery Works, 142–43
Royal charters, 149. *See also* Monopolies
Rudé, Georges, 82–83, 106, 111

Saint-Simon, duc de, 195
Say, Jean-Baptiste, 181, 192
Schaeper, Thomas, 27
Scott, James, 68
*Secrétaires du roi,* 172–74
"The *secrétaires du roi:* Absolutism, Corporations, and Privilege under the *ancien régime*" (Bien), 172
Senac de Meilhan, Gabriel, 201
Settlement Act of 1662, 157
Seven Years' War (1756–63), 181, 183
Six Corps, 124
Skocpol, Theda, 227
Slave trade, 30n, 31
Smith, Adam, 62, 74–75, 81–82, 141, 181
Society of the Mines Royal, 146
South Sea Bubble (1721), 53n

Star Chamber, 155
Starchmakers' Company, 147
*States and Social Revolutions* (Skocpol), 227
Statute of Artificers, 154–55
Statute of Laborers (1349–51), 16
Statute of Monopolies (1623–24), 149–50
Subsistence ethic, 68–71
*Sur les administrations provinciales* (Tocqueville), 237
*Syndics,* 121–24, 126

Talleyrand, Charles de, 229
Tallow Chandlers' Guild, 150
Tavannes, M. le comte de, 99
*Taxation populaire,* 83–84
Tax farms, 35, 37, 167, 205, 235
Tax system (England): compared to French, 216; monopoly charges as part of, 149; used to back public debt, 191
Tax system (France): bureaucracy of general farms within, 167; compared to English, 216; *droits de halle* within, 71; evolution of, 18–19; income redistribution through, 106; merchant dependence on, 35; peasant poverty stimulated by, 61–62; privilege status within, 186, 237; proposed reforms of, 181, 199–200
Terray, Abbé Joseph-Marie, 33, 49, 52–53, 201
Thompson, E. P., 83, 111
Tilly, Charles, 84, 111
Tobacco excise bill of 1733, 42
Tocqueville, Alexis de, 76, 185–86, 233, 235, 237
Tollison, Robert, 151, 156
Tour du Pin, M. de la, 101
Trading privileges (France): awarded by monarchy, 28–29; granted by controller general, 33; La Rochelle, 30n, 31. *See also* Merchants (French)
*Trésor royale,* 174
*Trésoriers receveurs,* 122

Pamphlet literature *(continued)* attacking fiscal policy, 180–81; cites England as fiscal example, 185, 197; on fiscal policy through democracy, 182, 194; promoting Estates General, 196. *See also* Old Regime France

Parlements: appointments to, 24; Burgundy granted a, 15; control over grain supplies by, 96–98; fiscal reform blocked by, 185; impact on market of, 6, 70–73; opposition to new trading jurisdictions by, 29; refusing to release guild debts, 137; resistance to recording of property by, 17

Patronage system (England): function of corruption within, 229–30; function of cronyism within, 47; of monarchy, 44–45; of Whig oligarchy, 39

Patronage system (France): economic privileges through, 9–10, 28–33, 234–35; function of cronyism within, 47–48; of guilds, 118–19; industrial policies and, 119–21; of king's financial ministers, 49; social differentiation due to, 236–40

*Payeurs*, 122

*Pays d'états*, 199

Peasant culture (France): burdened by absolutism, 226–27; capitalism as threat to, 63–68; economic/political impotence of, 61–63, 238; evolution of individualistic norms in, 75–76; impact of local economic control on, 71–74; subsistence ethic (moral economy) of, 68–71, 77. *See also* Collective violence

Pin industry, 141–45, 158

Pitt, M., the younger, 193

Plumb, J. H., 44, 153

*Point de banqueroute* (Brissot de Warville), 196

Political authority (England): dispersed through Parliament, 214, 224–25, 228; establishment of, 14–16; of monarchy, 44–45; rural basis of, 108

Political authority (France): absolutism causes demise of royal, 205–7, 214, 219–20; economic consequences of splintered, 18–20; Fronde rebellion as conflict over, 39; link between wealth and, xiii; obstacles to centralized, 14–15; urban basis of, 108

Political favor. *See* Cronyism

Political instability: due to cronyism, 220–23; link between economic rights and, 10–11; link between redistribution and, 22–23, 213–14

Political modernization, 229–32, 241–46

Political stability: cronyism and, 220–23; in England/France, 230–33; facilitated by Parliament, 225–29

Pontchartrain, Controller General, 48

Popper, Karl, xv, 52, 183

Portland, earl of, 147

*Pot de vin*, 49

Price, William Hyde, 147–49

Private bills, 41–42

Privileges. *See* Patronage system (France)

Property rights (England): cataloging of, 17; enclosure acts and, 244

Property rights (France): of corporate groups, 238; cronyism and the defense of, 245; defense of, by French Crown, 56–57, 176, 203; impact on economic efficiency of, 56–57; lack of comprehensive record of, 17; and loyalty-based cronyism, 4–5; market assumptions regarding, 3–4; Old Regime restrictions on, 5–10; peasantry collective, 65–68. *See also* Rents

Public debt (England), 189–92, 197, 210

Public relief (France), 104

Quo Warranto survey of 1272, 17

competitiveness in, 155–59; link between political instability and, 10–11, 241–46; mercantilist policies of, 34–37; nationalism of, 117–21; Old Regime restrictions on, 5–10; as politically allocated right, 3; regulated trade within, 28, 127–29; seeds of peasantry revolution within, 61–67; threats to moral economy of, 82–86. *See also* Guilds (France); Industrial policies (France)

Mazarin, Cardinal, 39, 48

*Mémoires* (duc de Saint-Simon), 195

Mercantilism. *See* Guilds (England)

Merchants (English): credit exchanges by, 92–93; grain market operations of, 92–93. *See also* Elites (England)

Merchants (French): government control of, 34–35; granted *accredités*, 71; guild regulations over, 127–33; as special interest groups, 23. *See also* Elites (France); Trading privileges (France)

*Mercuriales*, 96

Ministers (English): corruption of, 50; lobbying directly to, 42; political power of, 214; support to parliamentary review, 34

Ministers (French): autonomy of, 32–33, 215, 218–19; clientele of, 49; economic *dirigisme* by, 50–51; reliance on familial loyalties by, 217–18; venality of, 39–40

Mirabeau, comte de, 206

Mollien, Count Nicolas-François, 49, 201

Monopolies: attempt by pin industry to create, 141–45; decline of, 155–59; enforcement of, 147–49; JPs' regulation enforcement of, 151–54; jurisdiction competition over, 149–51; protection of, 145–47. *See also* Market system (England); Market system (France)

Moral economy: pre-industrial, 82–86; of subsistence ethic, 68–77

Morril, John, 153
Mousnier, Roland, 219

Nairac, Jean-Baptiste, 30–31
Namier, Sir Lewis, 45, 50
Navigation Acts (England), 53–54
Necker, Jacques, 33, 136–37, 168, 181, 201, 204–5, 221
Nemours, Pierre-Samuel du, 107
Newcastle, duke of, 39
"New Draperies" industry, 151
Norman conquest (1066), 16

Old Regime France: administrative structure of, 23–29; cronyism and fall of, 233–36; economic cost of court of, 38; economic restrictions of, 5–10; failure of fiscal reform in, 203–7; famine plot rumors within, 52–54; fiscal crisis (1787) of, 186–87; fiscal irresponsibility in, 163–65, 180–81; fiscal state policy in, 183–86; government compared to England, 214–17; grain policies of, 86–88; impotence of peasants within, 61–63; link between collective violence and food policy of, 108–10; market development in, 155–59; obstacles to political authority in, 14–15; property rights allocation/enforcement in, 4–6; public financial sentiments prior to fall of, 194–98; redistribution politics in, 54–56; *rentes perpetuelles* (government bonds) of, 175; social differentiation within, 236–40; trading companies of, 34–37; as unable to adapt to modernization, 219–20, 231–33, 241–46; vulnerability to urban disaffection of, 106–8. *See also* Pamphlet literature; Peasant culture (France)

Olson, Mancur, 87, 114–15, 239
Ormesson, Intendant, 49
Outhwaite, R. B., 94

Pamphlet literature: attacking bankruptcy/interest rates, 197–98;

Interest groups (France) *(continued)* 48; impact on redistribution by, 21–23; merchants as special, 28–29; monarchy insulated from, 23; privileges granted by controller general to, 33; profiting from market imperfections, 13; urban residents as, 106–8. *See also* Elites (France)

Interest rates: corporate institutions linked to, 168; impact of funded public debt on, 189–90; impact of economic uncertainty on, 181; pamphlet attacks against, 197; on private vs. public loans, 169–70

"Intermediate system," 137n

James I (England), 146–48, 151
James II (England), 153–54
Jews: and corruption, 229; and guilds, 130
*Jugement impartial sur les questions principales qui intéressent le tiers-état* (Ducloz-Dufresnoy), 208
Justices of the peace (JPs): creation and functions of, 16–17; James II's purge of, 153–54; regulation enforcement by, 151–53, 156–57
"Just price" concept, 83–84

Kaplan, Steven, 52, 92–93, 95, 105–6
Keynes, John Maynard, 246
King's Council (Conseil d'état du roi): described, 23n; dismantling of, 30, 230–31; expropriation of rights by, 6–7; legislation process within, 41–42; mandates free grain trade, 100–101

Labrousse, C. E., 70
La Rochelle, 30–31
Law, John, 36, 181, 184, 195
Lefebvre, Georges: discovery of peasant revolution by, 62–63; on peasants as semi-subsistence producers, 69–70; on social significance of food riots, 111; traces violence of peasant revolution, 63–68

*Lettres de maîtrises*, 123–24
*Lettres patentes*. See *Arrêts*
Lobbying (England): directly to ministers of state, 42; increased public information due to, 54; obstacles to, 41–45; to British Parliament, 33–34
Lobbying (France): changed by French Revolution, 31; of Colbert's family/cronies, 40; by guilds, 114–15; of merchants to monarchy, 28; process of, 214–15
London Goldsmith's Company, 154
London Silkweavers' Company, 151
Long Parliament, 149. *See also* British Parliament
Louisiana Trading Company, 37
Louis XIV (France): elites socially controlled by, 38, 221; government organization under, 23, 25, 33, 175, 215, 218, 230; legacy of social disintegration of, 234–36, 239
Louis XV (France), 215
Louis XVI (France), 19, 208, 215
Lüthy, Herbert, 190
Lydsey, Mr., 142–43

*Manufacture royale*, 118
Market system (England): corruption/cronyism as contracts within, 46–47, 222–23, 229–30; development of competitive, 155–59; evolution of pin makers within, 141–45; government role in redistribution of, 21–22; historical evolution of, 3–4; political modernization mechanisms and, 241–46; transformations within, 10–11
Market system (France): corruption/cronyism as contracts within, 46–47; government role in redistribution of, 21–23; historical evolution of, 3–4; impact of absolutism on, 56–57; impact of capitalism on, 63–68; impact of collective credit on, 116–17; impact of government fiscal policy on, 180–81; impact of local control over, 71–74; lack of

ment financial views prior to, 194–98; impact on lobbying by, 31; role of peasantry in, 62–63, 226–27. *See also* Revolutions
The Fronde (1652), 19, 39, 234
Furet, François, 183

Gegie générale, 174
General Chamber of Manufactures, 32n
General farms, 167
Generalities, 15
George III (England), 45
Girdlers' Company, 141
Glorious Revolution of 1688, 17, 153–54
Grain market (England): bounties granted for, 51–52; evolution of, 92; impact of credit regulations on, 92–93
Grain market (France): Burgundy's regional intervention in, 97–104; impact of expanded flour trade on, 97; lack of storage facilities and, 105–6; price determination within, 104–5
Grain price policies (England): impact of stable wheat price on, 91; moral economy and, 85–86; politics of, 93–95
Grain price policies (France): described, 86–88; moral economy and, 85–86; politics of, 95–97; urban bias of, 106–8
Grain riots: as collective action, 81–82, 84; origins of English, 88–89; origins of French, 87–89; social significance theories on, 111
Great Council of Commerce, 24–25
*Greffiers*, 122
Guilds (England): denied rural production jurisdiction, 150–51; impact of corruption on, 229; replaced by free trade, 140–41; restricted by common law courts, 149, 154–55. *See also* Market system (England)

Guilds (France): abolition and revival of, 133–39; absolutism control over, 121–27, 157; claims over rural production by, 150; demands for regulated trade by, 127–33; economic nationalism of, 117–21; origins of, 115–17; structural reforms of, 113–15; zero-sum mentality of, 235–36. *See also* Market system (France)
The Guinée company, 36

Haberdashers' Company, 141
Halstead, Mr., 143
Heckscher, Eli, 148–49, 152, 154, 156
Henri IV (France), 24
Hill, Christopher, 140
Hundred Rolls, 17

Income redistribution policies: corruption as part of England's, 51–52; of early modern England/France, 54–56, 213–14, 223–25; impact on French aristocracy of, 37–40; impact of interest groups on, 21–23; taxation/feudal dues as, 106–7
"The Inconvenience of Feudal Dues," 74
Industrial policies (France): Colbert's direction for, 119–20; privileges as strategy of, 120–21
Information: British Parliament access to, 11n; British use of public, 55–56; cronyism promoted by private, 47–48; cronyism threatened by public, 233n; held by *fermiers généraux*, 185; impact of lobbying on public, 54; impact on market rights of, 6; lack of French public access to, 218–19, 233; limitations of shared guild, 138–39
Interest groups (England): impact on redistribution by, 21–22; political cooperation among, 216. *See also* Elites (England)
Interest groups (France): "bureaucratic capitalism" of ministerial,

England *(continued)*
  38–39; path to stable public finances in, 187–94; political authority within, 14–17; redistributive politics in, 54–56; state finance policy in, 183–86. *See also* British Parliament
English Civil War (1641–49), 140, 143
English Crown: economic competition between Parliament and, 156–57; intervention in pin industry by, 142–45; limited industrial regulation jurisdiction of, 149–51; political jurisdiction of, 16–17; purge of JPs by, 153–54; Stuart model of favoritism by, 38–39. *See also* British Parliament
*Entraves*, 84–85
Estates General (1789): and the primacy of social issues, 207, 228, 239–40; difficulty of consensus within, 17; economic privilege disbursement function of, 9–10, 186; monarchy calls for, 182; pamphlet support for, 196–97

Famine plots, 52–54
Farrer, Thomas, 92
Ferme des postes, 174
Ferme générale, 49, 181–82, 185, 201–2
*Fermiers généraux. See* Financiers (French)
Feudalism: English institutions characterized by, 14; impact of dues on market, 74; increased French hostility to, 69
Financiers (French): aristocracy membership of, 202; definition of, 168; evolution of mini-society of, 170; fiscal failures (1787) of, 187; function of private/public, 168–70; privileges as *fermiers généraux*, 167; royal prosecutions against, 170–72; syndication of, 174; trading companies directed by, 34–37
Fiscal reform failures, 203–7

Fiscal stability: comparison of England/Old Regime, 187–94; Crown's absolutism impact on, 183–86; link between democracy and, 181–83; Old Regime/English failures at, 163–65; promotion of Estates General for, 196–97; ties between quest for equality and, 207–10. *See also* Credit exchanges (France)
Fleury, Joly de, 98–99, 204
Flour trade, 97. *See also* Grain market (France)
Fouquet, Nicolas, 40, 171, 174
France. *See* Old Regime France
French aristocracy. *See* Elites (France)
French monarchy: *arrêts* as expression of authority of, 23; calls for constitutional, 197–98; communal rights/property ensured by, 67; concessions to urban constituencies by, 106–8; contract "discretion" of, 170–72, 177–78; control over aristocracy social success by, 38, 234–35; corporate control of "discretion" by, 172–75; currency reform by, 171; economic privileges disbursed by, 9–10, 28–33; financial reform failure of, 176–77; lack of fiscal credibility of, 183–86; link between corporate institutions and, 165–68; loss of authority over fiscal policies, 207–10; mercantilist policies of, 34–37; political concessions granted by, 15–19; promotion of elite cliques by, 234; protection of property rights by, 56–57; *rentes perpetuelles* (government bonds) sold by, 175; restructures debt, 200–203; sale of new guild offices by, 121–27, 163; security for loans to, 168–70. *See also* Absolutism
French Revolution: cronyism role in causes of, 233–36; economic measures of, 30; financial conditions prior to, 198–200; fiscal policies as cause of, 180–83, 207–8; govern-

Court of Exchequer, 154
*Court Society* (Elias), 38
Credit exchanges (England): establishment of public debt in, 189–92, 210; flexibility of, 92–93; impact of Bank of England on, 187–89; history of irresponsibility of, 163–65
Credit exchanges (France): demands for corporate governance of, 172–75; development of public, 175–76; evolution of corporate society for, 165–68; function of financiers within, 168–70; guilds denied, 133; history of irresponsibility of, and impact of, 163–65, 180–81; mini-society of financiers within, 170; monarchy default of, 170–72; reform failures within, 176–77, 203–7; vulnerability of, 93. *See also* Fiscal stability
Cromwell, Oliver, 147, 149
Cromwell, Richard, 147
Cronyism: autocratic regime maintenance of, 5, 231; described, xii–xiii, 10; as distinct from corruption, 45–47; fall of Old Regime and, 233–36; information as critical to, 47–48; political instability due to, 220–24. *See also* Corruption
Crozat, Antoine, 36–37
Currency reform, 171
Custom of London, 154–55

Democracy: fostered by eighteenth-century English corruption, 226; legitimacy of constitutional, 219–20; link between fiscal stability and, 181–83, 194; pamphlet literature promoting, 185, 196–97
Desmaretz, Nicholas, 40, 48
Dessert, Daniel, 39–40, 164
Deveau, Jean-Michel, 30–31
Dickson, P. G. M., 188
Discretion, definition of, 170
Doomsday Inquiry, 17
*Droit de visite*, 123
*Droit social*, 64

*Droits*, 123, 136
*Droits de halle*, 71
Ducloz-Dufresnoy, Charles Nicole, 193, 208
D'Umons, Nicoud, 197
Durand, Yves, 202
Dutch pin industry, 141–45

Economic nationalism, 117–21
Economic system. *See* Market system (England); Market system (France)
Ekelund, Robert, 151, 156
Elias, Norbert, 38, 234, 236, 239
Elites (England): access to authority through Parliament, 228; Parliament policies supported by, 55–56; political cooperation among, 216–17; relationship between English Crown and, 16. *See also* Interest groups (England)
Elites (France): *fermiers généraux* made up of, 202; hostilities between peasant and, 61–77; impact of cronyism on, 221–22; impact of redistribution policies on, 37–40; of La Rochelle, 30–31; local jurisdiction of, 15–16; market privileges granted to, 18–19, 71–74; merchants as, 28–29; monarchy's promotion of distrust among, 234–36; as open to capitalism, 64–66; political cliques among, 216, 238; social status bestowed by Crown on, 38, 234–35; tax-exempt status of, 186, 237. *See also* Interest groups (France)
Enclosure movement, 51–52
England: available mechanisms for modernization of, 229–33, 241–46; corruption within eighteenth century, 45–46; development of competitive markets in, 155–59; episodes of fiscal irresponsibility in, 163–65; establishment of public debt in, 189–92, 210; failure of mercantilism in, 158; government compared to France, 214–17; grain export bounties in, 90; grain riots of, 88–89; monarchy favoritism in,

British Parliament *(continued)*
    monopoly unsupported by, 143–45; political authority of and through, 17, 214, 228; provisioning contracts awarded to, 50; role in economic concessions by, 21–22; support of elites for, 55–56; vote corruption within, 46. *See also* England; English Crown
Bubble Act of 1720, 157
Bureau of Commerce, 25
"Bureaucratic capitalism," 48
*Bureaux des finances*, 167
Burghley, Lord, 153
Burgundy: grain shortage in, 97–104; granted a *parlement*, 15
Bushell, Thomas, 146–47

*Cahiers de doléance* (1789), 29–30
Calonne, Charles Alexandre de, 33, 198–99, 204, 221
Capitalism: grain riots as response to, 84; as threat to peasant culture, 63–68
Cardiganshire mines, 146–47
Chamber of Accounts, 206
Chamber of commerce, 29–30
Chambre de justice, 170–71, 196
Charles I (England), 142–43, 147, 151–52
Charles II (England), 143, 147
Charles VI (France), 18
Charlesworth, Andrew, 88
Clavière, Etienne, 197
Clay, C. G. A., 156
Coats, A. W., xiv
Cobb, Richard, 106
Cobban, Alfred, 69
Cockayne Project of 1614, 148
Colbert, Jean-Baptiste: allows financiers to direct trading companies, 34; bureaucratic capitalism of, 48; collaboration with provincial business people, 25; industrial policy of, 119–20; promotion of guild nationalization by, 117; replaces Fouquet, 174; venality of, 39–40
Cole, Charles Woolsey, 120

Collective violence: grain riots as, 81–82; Old Regime food policy and, 108–10; origins of peasant revolution, 62–63; as response to threatened moral economy, 82–86. *See also* Peasant culture (France)
*Le Commerce rochelais face à la Révolution* (Deveau), 30
*Commissaires*, 126–27
Common law courts (England): guilds restricted by, 149, 154–55, 156; investment incentives of, 5n; ruling on monopolies by, 146, 149–50
*Confrèrie*, 123, 136
Conseil d'état du roi. *See* King's Council (Conseil d'état du roi)
Conseil royale des finances, 24
Constituent Assembly (France): abolishes chambers of commerce, 30; economic priorities of, 31; struggle for financial control, 206–7
Constitutional Settlement of 1689, 192
Contracts: monarchy "discretion" regarding, 170–72, 177–78, 218; problems with transaction, 4; reputation mechanism of guilds for, 115–16
Controller general (France): British Parliament as equivalent to, 44; function and power of, 26, 32–33, 217; increasing vulnerability of, 215–16, 223; personal gain from office of, 40
Corporate institutions (France): demands for regulations through, 172–75; development of, 165–68. *See also* Credit exchanges (France)
Corruption: of eighteenth-century England, 50–52, 225–26; as form of income transfer, 45–46, 213–14; French executive perceived as corrupt, 216; link between modernization and, 229–30; vs. cronyism, 46
Council of Commerce, 25–26, 32
Council of Finance, 25, 32–33

# Index

Absolutism: cronyism resulting from, 231; destroys royal authority, 205–10; elites as victims of, 234–36; failures of, 228–29; of French monarchy, 117, 133–39, 157, 214, 217n; French peasantry burdened by, 226–27; lack of moral leadership within, 218; possibility of national bank under, 195. *See also* French monarchy
Administration des domains, 174
Aftalion, Florin, 206
Amelot, Jean-Antoine, 99
Anglo-French trade treaty of 1713, 42
Antoine, Michel, 23, 25, 32, 41, 219
D'Argenson, Marquis René-Louis, 26, 218
*Arrêt du conseil* (1754), 98
*Arrêt du conseil* (1773), 102–3
*Arrêts:* bankruptcy interpretation of 1788, 201n; on commission tutelage over guilds, 126; to declare free trade (1775), 53; functions of, 23, 41–42; issued by Council of Finance, 32–33; outlining Bureau of Commerce functions, 25; prohibiting Dijon grain exports, 98–99
Assembly of Notables (1787), 198–200, 206
*An Atlas of Rural Protest in Britain* (ed. Charlesworth), 88

*Auditeurs*, 122, 124
*Auneurs de drap*, 122

Bank of England (1689), 181, 187–89
Bankruptcy: *arrêt* (1788) interpreted as, 201n; French monarchy restructuring to avoid, 200–203; promoted as solution to fiscal crisis, 206–7
Bartlett, Sir Thomas, 141–42
Bernard, Samuel, 29
Bien, David, 172, 237
Board of Trade, 43
Bohstedt, John, 89
Boissonnade, Prosper, 119
Bonaparte, Napoleon, 193
Bosher, J. F., 187
Brienne, Loménie de, 199–201, 204
Brissot de Warville, Jacques, 196–97
British Parliament: agrees to funded public debt, 189–91; control over guilds by, 155–59; demands for annual budget by, 204–5; economic competition between crown and, 156–57; economic deal-making within, 11–12, 216; income transfer facilitated by, 51–52, 223–25; industrial licenses originating in, 33–34; JP commissions replaced by, 153; legislative process in, 41–45; monopolies as source of revenue for, 147, 149; pin makers'

271

———. *Did British Capitalism Breed Inequality?* New York: Collier Macmillan, 1985.
Williamson, Oliver. *The Economic Institutions of Capitalism.* New York: Free Press, 1985.
Winiecki, Jan. "Are Soviet-Type Economies Entering an Era of Long-term Decline?" *Soviet Studies* 38, no. 3 (July): 325–48.
———. "Soviet-Type Economies: Considerations for the Future?" *Soviet Studies* 38, no. 4: 543–61.
Wittfogel, Karl August. *Oriental Despotism: A Comparative Study of Total Power.* New Haven: Yale University Press, 1957.
Wolf, Eric. *Peasant Wars of the Twentieth Century.* New York: Harper & Row, 1969.
Woronoff, Denis. *L'Industrie sidérurgique en France pendant la Révolution et l'Empire.* Paris: Editions de l'Ecole des hautes études en sciences sociales, 1984.

Valfons, Charles, marquis de. *Mémoires sur le XVIII<sup>e</sup> siècle: Souvenir de marquis de Valfons.* Paris, 1906.

Vann, James Allen. *The Making of a State: Württemberg, 1593–1793.* Ithaca, N.Y.: Cornell University Press, 1984.

Veitch, John M. "Repudiations, Defaults and Confiscations by the Medieval State: The Italian Bankers in England, 1270–1345." *Journal of Economic History* 46, no. 1 (March 1986): 31–36.

Véri, abbé de. *Journal de l'abbé de Véri.* 2 vols. Paris: J. Talandier, 1928–30.

Voltaire [F.-M. Arouet]. *Philosophical Letters.* Translated by Ernest Dilworth. Macmillan, 1985.

Vuitry, A. D. *Le Désordre des finances et les excès de la spéculation.* Paris, 1885.

Walter, John, and Keith Wrightson. "Dearth and the Social Order in Early Modern England." In *Rebellion, Popular Protest and the Social Order in Early Modern England,* edited by Paul Slack. Cambridge: Cambridge University Press, 1984.

Webb, Sidney. *English Local Government from the Revolution to the Municipal Corporations Act: The Manor and the Borough.* New York: Longmans, Green, 1908.

Weber, Max. *General Economic History.* Translated by Frank Knight. New York: Greenberg, 1927.

Weingast, Barry R. "The Economic Role of Political Institutions." MS. Stanford University, 1992.

———. "Institutional Foundations of the 'Sinews of Power': British Financial and Military Success Following the Glorious Revolution." Mimeographed. Hoover Institution, Stanford University, 1991.

Weir, David. "Tontines, Public Finance, and Revolution in France and England, 1688–1789." *Journal of Economic History* 49 (1989): 95–124.

———. "Life under Pressure: France and England, 1670–1870." *Journal of Economic History* 44 (March 1984): 27–47.

———. "Markets and Mortality in France, 1600–1789." MS. Yale University, 1984.

Weir, David, and François Velde. "The Financial Market and Government Debt in France, 1750–1793." Unpublished paper, 1989.

White, Lynn, Jr. *Medieval Technology and Social Change.* London: Oxford University Press, 1962.

Williams, Dale. In *An Atlas of Rural Protest in Britain, 1548–1900,* edited by Andrew Charlesworth. Philadelphia: University of Pennsylvania Press, 1983.

Williams, E. N., ed. *The Eighteenth-Century Constitution: Documents and Commentary.* New York: Cambridge University Press, 1960.

Williamson, Jeffrey. "Debating the British Industrial Revolution." *Explorations in Economic History* 24 (1987): 269–92.

Terray, Joseph-Marie. *Compte rendu au roi (sur l'état des finances en 1775)*. N.p., 1775.
Thomas, Peter D. G. *Lord North*. London: Penguin Books, 1976.
———. *The House of Commons in the Eighteenth Century*. Oxford: Oxford University Press, 1971.
Thompson, E. P. "The Moral Economy of the English Crowd in the Eighteenth Century." *Past and Present* 50 (1971): 71–136.
———. *The Making of the English Working Class*. New York: Vintage Books, 1963.
Tilly, Charles. *The Contentious French*. Cambridge, Mass.: Harvard University Press, 1985.
———. *As Sociology Meets History*. New York and London: Academic Press, 1981.
———. "Food Supply and Public Order in Modern Europe." In *The Formation of National States in Western Europe*, edited by Charles Tilly. Princeton, N.J.: Princeton University Press, 1975.
Tilly, Charles, and David S. Landes. *History as a Social Science*. Englewood Cliffs, N.J.: Prentice-Hall, 1971.
Tilly, Louise A. "Food Entitlement, Famine, and Conflict." In *Hunger and History: The Impact of Changing Food Production and Consumption Patterns on Society*, edited by Robert I. Rotberg and Theodore K. Rabb. Cambridge: Cambridge University Press, 1985.
———. "The Food Riot as a Form of Political Conflict in France." *Journal of Interdisciplinary History* 2 (1971): 23–58.
Tocqueville, Alexis de. *The Old Regime and the French Revolution*. 1856. New York: Anchor Books, 1955.
Tracy, James D. *A Financial Revolution in the Habsburg Netherlands: Renten and Rentiers in the County of Holland, 1515–1565*. Berkeley and Los Angeles: University of California Press, 1986.
Turgot, Anne-Robert-Jacques, baron de l'Aulne. *Oeuvres de Turgot*, edited by Gustave Schelle. 5 vols. Paris: Alcan, 1913–23.
———. "On the Municipalities." In *Oeuvres de Turgot*, edited by Gustave Schelle, 4:568–628. Paris: Alcan, 1913–23.
———. *Oeuvres posthumes de M. Turgot, ou Memoir de M. Turgot sur les administrations provinciales*. Lausanne, 1787.
Unwin, George. *The Guilds and Companies of London*. London: Methuen, 1908.
———. *Industrial Organization in the Sixteenth and Seventeenth Centuries*. London: Cass, 1957.
Uselding, Ed P. "English Open Fields as Behavior toward Risk." In *Research in Economic History: An Annual Compilation*. Oxford: Oxford University Press, 1976.
Usher, Abbot Payson. "Colbert and Governmental Control of Industry in Seventeenth-Century France." *Review of Economic Statistics* 16 (1934): 237–40.

1700–1790." In *Work in France,* edited by Steve Kaplan and Cynthia J. Koepp. Ithaca, N.Y.: Cornell University Press, 1986.

Shepsle, Kenneth. "Representation and Governance: The Great Legislative Trade-Off." *Political Science Quarterly* 103, no. 3 (1988): 461–84.

Skocpol, Theda. *States and Social Revolutions.* New York: Cambridge University Press, 1979.

Skocpol, Theda, Peter Evans, and Dietrich Rueschemeyer, eds. *Bringing the State Back In.* New York: Cambridge University Press, 1985.

Smith, Adam. *An Inquiry into the Nature and Causes of the Wealth of Nations.* 1776. London: Adam, Black, & Longmans, 1850.

Smith, Vera. *The Rationale of Central Banking and the Free Banking Alternative.* Reprint. Indianapolis, 1990.

Soboul, Albert. "The French Rural Communities in the Eighteenth and Nineteenth Centuries." *Past and Present* 10 (1956): 78–96.

Solnon, Jean François. *La Cour de France.* Paris: Fayard, 1987.

Sonenscher, Michael. *Work and Wages: Natural Law, Politics, and the Eighteenth-Century French Trades.* Cambridge: Cambridge University Press, 1989.

——. *The Hatters of Eighteenth-Century France.* Berkeley and Los Angeles: University of California Press, 1987.

Soto, Hernando de. *The Other Path.* New York: Harper & Row, 1989.

Stevens, John. *Observations on Government, Including Some Animadversions on Mr. Adams Defence of the Constitutions of Government of the United States and of Mr. De Lolme's Constitution of England, by a Farmer of New Jersey.* New York: W. Ross in Broad Street, 1787.

Stevenson, John. "Food Riots in England, 1792–1818." In *Popular Protest and Public Order: Six Studies in British History, 1790–1920,* edited by R. Quinault and J. Stevenson. London: George Allen & Unwin, 1974.

——. "The Moral Economy of the English Crowd." In *Order and Disorder in Early Modern England,* edited by A. Fletcher and John Stevenson. Cambridge: Cambridge University Press, 1985.

Stigler, G. J. "The Theory of Economic Regulation." *Bell Journal of Economics and Management Science* 2 (Spring 1971): 211–40.

Stourm, René. *Bibliographie historique des finances au dix-huitième siècle.* Paris: Guillaumin, 1895.

——. *Les Finances de l'ancien régime et de la Révolution: Origines du système financier actuel.* 2 vols. Paris: Guillaumin, 1885.

Strayer, Joseph. *On the Medieval Origins of the Modern State.* Princeton, N.J.: Princeton University Press, 1970.

Supple, B. E. *Commercial Crisis and Change in England, 1600–1642: A Study in the Instability of a Mercantile Economy.* Cambridge: Cambridge University Press, 1970.

Taylor, George. "The Paris Bourse on the Eve of the Revolution, 1781–1789." *American Historical Review* 67, no. 4 (July 1962): 951–77.

———. *Paris and London in the Eighteenth Century*. New York: Viking Compass Edition, 1973.
Ruhlmann, Georges. *Les Corporations, les manufactures, et le travail libre a Abbeville au XVIII<sup>e</sup> siècle*. Paris: Recueil Sirey, 1948.
Rupnel, Gaston. *La Ville et la campagne au dix-septième siècle: Etude sur les populations du pays dijonnais*. Paris, 1922.
Saint-Jacob, Pierre de. *Les Paysans de la Bourgogne du nord au dernier siècle de l'ancien régime*. Dijon, 1960.
Saint-Simon, Louis de Rouvroy, duc de. *Mémoires*, edited by A. de Boislisle. Vol. 37. Paris: Nouvelles éditions, 1925.
Say, Jean-Baptiste. *Traité d'économie politique, ou simple exposition de la manière dont se forment, se distribuent, et se consomment les richesses*. Paris: Crapelet, 1803.
Schaeper, Thomas J. *The French Council of Commerce, 1700–1715: A Study in Mercantilism after Colbert*. Columbus: Ohio State University Press, 1983.
Schneider, Robert A. *Public Life in Toulouse, 1463–1789: From Municipal Republic to Cosmopolitan City*. Ithaca, N.Y.: Cornell University Press, 1989.
Schultz, T. *Transforming Traditional Agriculture*. New Haven: Yale University Press, 1964.
———, ed. *Distortions of Agricultural Incentives*. Bloomington: Indiana University Press, 1978.
Schumpeter, Elizabeth Boody. "English Prices and Public Finance, 1660–1822." *Review of Economic Statistics* 20 (1938): 21–37.
Schumpeter, Joseph. "Capitalism." *Encyclopædia Britannica*, vol. 4, s.v. Reprinted in *Essays on Economic Topics of Joseph Schumpeter*, edited by Richard V. Clemence. Port Washington, N.Y.: Kennikat Press, 1969.
Schwartz, Robert M. *Policing the Poor in Eighteenth-Century France*. Chapel Hill: University of North Carolina Press, 1988.
Scott, James, Jr. *The Moral Economy of the Peasant: Peasant Rebellion and Subsistence in Southeast Asia*. New Haven: Yale University Press, 1974.
Scott, W. R. *The Constitution and Finance of English, Scottish, and Irish Joint Stock Companies to 1720*. 3 vols. Cambridge: Cambridge University Press, 1910–12.
Selton, Reinhard. "Evolution, Learning, and Economic Behavior." *Games and Economic Behavior* 3 (1991): 3–24.
Senac de Meilhan, Gabriel. *Considérations sur les richesses et le luxe*. Amsterdam, 1787.
Sewell, William H. *Work and Revolution in France: The Language of Labor from the Old Regime to 1848*. Cambridge: Cambridge University Press, 1980.
Shepherd, Edward J. "Social and Geographic Mobility of the Eighteenth-Century Guild Artisan: An Analysis of Guild Receptions in Dijon,

Putnam, Robert D., Robert Leonardi, and Raffaella Nanetti. *Governance and the Civic Community*. Princeton, N.J.: Princeton University Press, 1992.
Quiggin, John. "Scattered Landholdings in Common Property Systems." *Journal of Economic Behavior and Organization* 9 (1988): 187–201.
Rebillon, Armand. *Recherches sur les anciennes corporations ouvrières et marchandes de la ville de Rennes*. Paris, 1902.
Richard, Guy. *Noblesse d'affaires au XVIII$^e$ siècle*. Paris: Colin, 1974.
Riker, William H. "Civil Rights and Property Rights." In *Liberty, Property, and the Future of Constitutional Development*, edited by Ellen Frankel and Howard Dickman. Albany: State University of New York Press, 1990.
——— . "Political Science and Rational Choice." In *Perspectives on Positive Political Economy*, edited by James E. Alt and Kenneth A. Shepsle. New York: Cambridge University Press, 1990.
Riley, James. *The Seven Years War and the Old Regime in France*. Princeton: Princeton University Press, 1986.
Roche, Daniel. *The People of Paris*. Translated by M. Evans. Berkeley and Los Angeles: University of California Press, 1987.
Romano, R. *Commerce et prix du blé à Marseille au XVIII$^e$ siècle*. Paris: S.E.V.P.E.N., 1956.
Root, Hilton L. "Challenging the Seigneurie: Community and Contention on the Eve of the French Revolution." *Journal of Modern History* 57 (1985): 652–81.
——— . "Institutions, Interest Groups and Authority in Ancien Régime France." *French History* 6, no. 4 (1993): 1–24.
——— . "The 'Moral Economy' of the Pre-Revolutionary French Peasant." *Science and Society* 54 (1990): 351–61.
——— . *Peasants and King in Burgundy: Agrarian Foundations of French Absolutism*. Berkeley and Los Angeles: University of California Press, 1987.
Rosenberg, Nathan, and L. E. Birdzell. *How the West Grew Rich*. New York: Basic Books, 1986.
Rosenthal, Jean-Laurent. "Credit Markets and Economic Change in Southeastern France, 1630–1788." *Explorations in Economic History* 30 (April 1993): 129–57.
Rowan, Herbert. *The King's State: Proprietary Dynasticism in Early Modern France*. New Brunswick, N.J.: Rutgers University Press, 1980.
Rudé, Georges. *The Crowd in History: A Study of Popular Disturbances in France and England, 1730–1848*. New York: Wiley, 1964.
——— . *The Crowd in the French Revolution*. London: Oxford University Press, 1959.
——— . *Europe in the Eighteenth Century: Aristocracy and the Bourgeois Challenge*. London: Sphere Books, 1974.

Phillips, J. A. *Electoral Behaviour in Unreformed England*. Princeton, N.J.: Princeton University Press, 1982.

Plumb, J. H. *England in the Eighteenth Century, 1714–1815*. Harmondsworth: Penguin Books, 1950.

———. "Robert Walpole's World: The Structure of Government." In *Aristocratic Governance and Society in Eighteenth-Century England: The Foundations of Stability*, edited by Daniel A. Baugh. New York: New Viewpoints, 1975.

———. *Sir Robert Walpole: The Making of a Statesman*. London: Creeset Press, 1956.

Polanyi, Karl. *The Great Transformation*. Boston: Beacon Press, 1957.

———. *Primitive, Archaic, and Modern Economies*. Boston: Beacon Press, 1971.

Polanyi, Karl, Conrad Arensberg, and Harry Pearson, eds. *Trade and Markets in the Early Empires*. Chicago: Free Press, 1957.

Ponko, Vincent, Jr. "Norman Scott Gras and Elizabethan Corn Policy: A Re-examination of the Problem." *Economic History Review* 17 (1964): 32.

Popkin, Samuel L. *The Rational Peasant: The Political Economy of Rural Society in Vietnam*. Berkeley and Los Angeles: University of California Press, 1979.

Popper, Karl. "Normal Science and Its Dangers." In *Criticism and the Growth of Knowledge*, edited by Imre Lakatos and Alan Musgrave. New York: Cambridge University Press, 1970.

———. *The Open Society and Its Enemies*. 2 vols. New York: Harper & Row, 1963.

———. *The Poverty of Historicism*. London: Routledge & Kegan Paul, 1957.

———. "Predictions and Prophesy in the Social Sciences." In *Conjectures and Refutations*. 2d ed. New York: Harper & Row, 1965.

Posner, Richard. "Theories of Economic Regulation." *Bell Journal of Economics and Management Science* 2 (Spring 1971): 3–21.

———. "A Theory of Primitive Society with Special Reference to Law." *Journal of Law and Economics* 23 (1980): 1–53.

Pospisil, Leopold. *Kapauku Papuans and Their Law*. New Haven: Yale University Press, 1958.

Postlethwayt, Malachy. *The Universal Dictionary of Trade and Commerce*. 4th ed. Reprint. 2 vols. New York: A. M. Kelley, 1971.

Price, Jacob M. "The Excise Affair Revisited: The Administrative and Colonial Dimensions of a Parliamentary Crisis." In *England's Rise to Greatness, 1660–1763*, edited by Stephen Baxter. Berkeley and Los Angeles: University of California Press, 1983.

Price, William Hyde. *The English Patents of Monopoly*. New York: Houghton Mifflin, 1906.

North, Douglass C., and R. P. Thomas. *The Rise of the Western World: A New Economic History.* Cambridge: Cambridge University Press, 1973.

North, Douglass C., and Barry R. Weingast. "Constitution and Commitment: The Evolution of Institutions Governing Public Choice in Seventeenth-Century England." *Journal of Economic History* 49 (1989): 803–32

Nye, John. "The Myth of Free Trade Britain and Fortress France: Tariffs and Trade in the Nineteenth Century." *Journal of Economic History* 51 (1991): 23–46.

Nye, Joseph S. "Corruption and Political Development: A Cost-Benefit Analysis." *American Political Science Review* 61 (1967): 417–27.

O'Brien, Patrick, and Caglar Keydor. *Economic Growth in Britain and France 1780–1914: Two Paths to the Twentieth Century.* London: George Allen & Unwin, 1978.

Olson, Alison G. "The Board of Trade and London-American Interest Groups in the Eighteenth Century." In *The British-Atlantic Empire before the American Revolution,* edited by Peter Marshall and Glyn Williams. Totowa, N.J.: Frank Cass, 1980.

Olson, Mancur. *The Logic of Collective Action.* Cambridge, Mass.: Harvard University Press, 1965.

———. *The Rise and Decline of Nations.* New Haven: Yale University Press, 1982.

———. "Towards a Unified View of Economics and the Other Social Sciences." In *Perspectives on Positive Political Economy,* edited by James E. Alt and Kenneth A. Shepsle. New York: Cambridge University Press, 1990.

Ordeshook, Peter C. "The Emerging Discipline of Political Economy." In *Perspectives on Positive Political Economy,* edited by James E. Alt and Kenneth A. Shepsle. New York: Cambridge University Press, 1990.

Ormrod, David. *English Grain Exports and the Structure of Agrarian Capitalism, 1700–1760.* Hull: Hull University Press, 1985.

Outhwaite, R. B. "Dearth and Government Intervention in English Grain Markets, 1590–1700." *Economic History Review,* 2d ser., 34 (1981): 389–406.

Passet, René. *L'Industrie dans la généralité de Bordeaux sous l'intendant Tourny: Contribution à l'étude de la décadence du système corporatif au mileu du XVIII$^e$ siècle.* Bordeaux and Paris: Editions Bière, 1954.

Peck, Linda Levy. "Corruption and Political Development in Early Modern Britain." In *Political Corruption: A Handbook,* edited by Arnold J. Heidenheimer, Michael Johnston, and Victor T. Levine. New Brunswick, N.J.: Transaction Publishers, 1989.

Peter, Daniel. "Les Manifestations paysannes en Alsace du nord durant l'été 1799." *L'Alsace au coeur de l'Europe révolutionnaire* 116 (1990): 39–56.

Morellet, André, abbé. *Réflexions sur les avantages de la libre circulation.* Geneva, 1758.
Morineau, M. "Budgets de l'état et gestion des finances royales en France au dix-huitième siècle." *Revue historique,* October–November 1981: 289–337.
Mousnier, Roland. *The Institutions of France under the Absolute Monarchy, 1598–1789: The Organs of State and Society.* Translated by Arthur Goldhammer. 2 vols. Chicago: University of Chicago Press, 1979.
———. *La Vénalité des offices sous Henri IV et Louis XIII.* Paris: Presses universitaires de France, 1945.
Namier, Sir Lewis. "The Social Foundations." In *Aristocratic Goverance and Society in Eighteenth-Century England: The Foundations of Stability,* edited by Daniel A. Baugh. New York: New Viewpoints, 1975.
———. *The Structure of Politics at the Accession of George III.* 1929. 2d ed. New York: St. Martin's Press, 1957.
Necker, Jacques. *Compte général des revenues et des dépenses fixes au 1$^{er}$ de mai 1789.* Paris: Imprimerie royale, 1789.
———. *Compte rendu au roi, par M. Necker, directeur général des finances, au mois de janvier 1781.* Paris: Imprimerie du cabinet du roi, 1781.
———. *De l'administration des finances de la France.* N.p., 1784.
———. *Dernières vues de politique et de finance, offertes à la nation française par M. Necker.* Geneva, 1802.
———. *Discours prononcé par M. Necker, premier ministre des finances, à l'Assemblée nationale, le 24 septembre 1789.* Toulouse: Pijon, 1789.
———. *An Essay on the True Principles of Executive Power in Great States.* London: G. G. J. and J. Robinson, 1792.
———. *Lettre de M. Necker au roi.* Utrecht, 1782.
———. *Mémoire de M. Necker, le premier ministre des finances, envoyé à l'Assemblée nationale, et lu dans la séance du samedi 6 mars 1790.* Paris: Baudouin, 1790.
———. *State of the Finances of France Laid before the King.* London: G. Kearsly et al., 1781.
———. *Sur l'administration de M. Necker.* Paris: Hôtel de Thou, 1791.
Nef, John U. *Industry and Government in France and England, 1540–1640.* Ithaca, N.Y.: Cornell University Press, 1969.
Nigeon, René. *Etat financier des corporations parisennes d'arts et métiers au XVIII$^e$ siècle.* Paris: Editions Rieder, 1934.
North, Douglass C. "Institutions." *Journal of Economic Perspectives* 5 (1991): 97–112.
———. *Institutions, Institutional Change, and Economic Performance.* New York: Cambridge University Press, 1990.
———. "Is It Worth Making Sense of Marx?" *Inquiry* 29 (1990): 57–63.
———. *Structure and Change in Economic History.* New York: Norton, 1981.

McCahill, Michael. *Order and Equipoise: The Peerage and the House of Lords.* London: Royal Historical Society, 1978.
McCloskey, Donald N. *The Applied Theory of Price.* 2d ed. New York: Macmillan, 1985.
———. *Econometric History.* London: Macmillan Education, 1987.
———. "Economics as an Historical Science." In *Economic History and the Modern Economist*, edited by William N. Parker. Princeton, N.J.: Princeton University Press, 1987.
———. "The Industrial Revolution, 1780–1860: A Survey." In *The Economics of the Industrial Revolution*, edited by Joel Mokyr. Totowa, N.J.: Rowman & Allenheld, 1985.
———. "The Open Fields of England: Rent, Risk, and the Rate of Interest, 1300–1815." 1988. Forthcoming in *In Search of Historical Markets*, edited by David Galenson.
———. "The Persistence of English Common Fields." In *European Peasants and Their Markets: Essays in Agrarian Economic History*, edited by William Parker and Eric Jones. Princeton, N.J.: Princeton University Press, 1975.
Meuvret, J. "Les Crises des subsistances et la démographie de la France de l'ancien régime." *Population* 1 (1946): 643–50.
———. "Demographic Crisis in France from the Sixteenth and Eighteenth Centuries." In *Population and History*, edited by David Glass and D. E. C. Eversley. London: E. Arnold; Aldine, 1965.
———. "Géographie des prix des céréales et les anciennes économies européennes: Prix méditerranéens, prix continentaux, prix atlantiques à la fin du 17$^e$ siècle." *Revista de economica* 4, no. 2 (1951): 97–104.
Meyssonnier, Simone. *La Balance et l'horloge: La Genèse de la pensée libérale en France au XVIII$^e$ siècle.* Paris: Les Editions de la passion, 1989.
Miller, J. *The Pragmatic Economy: Liberal Reform and the Grain Trade in Upper Normandy, 1750–1789.* Durham, N.C.: Duke University Press, 1987.
Mokyr, Joel. "Demand vs. Supply in the Industrial Revolution." *Journal of Economic History* 37 (1977): 981–1008.
———. "Has the Industrial Revolution Been Crowded Out? Some Reflections on Crafts and Williamson." *Explorations in Economic History* 24 (1987): 293–319.
———. "The Industrial Revolution and the New Economic History." In *The Economics of the Industrial Revolution*, edited by Joel Mokyr. Totowa, N.J.: Rowman & Allenheld, 1985.
Montyon, Antoine-Jean-Baptiste Robert Auget, baron de. *Particularités et observations sur les ministères des finances de France les plus célèbres, depuis 1660 jusqu'en 1791.* Paris: Le Normant, 1812.
Moore, Barrington, Jr. *Social Origins of Dictatorship and Democracy: Lord and Peasant in the Making of the Modern World.* Boston: Beacon Press, 1966.

———. *Les Paysans de Languedoc*. Paris: Mouton, 1966.
Lever, Evelyne. *Louis XVI*. Paris: Fayard, 1985.
Levi, Margaret. *Of Rule and Revenue*. Berkeley and Los Angeles: University of California Press, 1988.
Levi, Margaret, and Stephanie Todd. "The Introduction of the Income Tax in Eighteenth-Century Britain." Paper given at the Social Science History Association Meeting, November 1985.
Lévy, Claude-Frédéric. *Capitalistes et pouvoir au siècle des lumières*. 3 vols. Paris: Mouton, 1969.
Linguet, Simon-Nicolas-Henri. *Du commerce des grains*. Paris, 1788.
Lipton, M. *Why Poor People Stay Poor: Urban Bias in World Development*. Cambridge, Mass.: Harvard University Press, 1979.
Loewenstein, Karl. *British Cabinet Government*. London: Oxford University Press, 1967.
Luce, R. Duncan, and Howard Raiffa. *Games and Decisions*. New York: Wiley, 1957.
Luethy, Herbert. *La Banque protestante en France, de la révocation de l'Edit de Nantes à la Révolution*. Vol. 2. Paris: S.E.V.P.E.N., 1961.
Maillard, Jacques. *Le Pouvoir municipal à Angers de 1657 à 1789*. 2 vols. Paris: Presses de l'Université d'Angers, 1984.
Major, J. Russell. *Representative Government in Early Modern France*. New Haven: Yale University Press, 1980.
Mann, Michael. *The Sources of Social Power*. Vol. 1. New York: Cambridge University Press, 1986.
Margairaz, Dominique. "Les Dénivellations interrégionales des prix de froment en France, 1756–1870." Thèse du 3$^e$ cycle, Université de Paris I. 1982.
———. *Foires et marchés dans la France*. Paris: Editions de l'Ecole des hautes études en sciences sociales, 1988.
Marion, Marcel. *Dictionnaire des institutions de la France aux XVII$^e$ et XVIII$^e$ siècles*. Paris: A. Picard, 1923. Reprint. New York: Burt Franklin, 1968.
———. *Histoire financière de la France depuis 1715*. Paris: Rousseau, 1927.
———. *Machault d'Arnouville: Etude sur l'histoire du contrôle général des finances de 1749 à 1754*. Paris: Rousseau, 1892.
Markovitch, Tihomir. *Histoire des industries françaises: Les Industries lainières de Colbert à la Révolution*. Paris: Librarie Droz, 1976.
Mathias, Peter, and Patrick O'Brien. "Taxation in Britain and France, 1715–1810: A Comparison of the Social and Economic Incidence of Taxes Collected for the Central Governments." *Journal of European Economic History* 5, no. 3 (1976): 601–50.
Mauss, Marcel. *The Gift*. Chicago: Free Press, 1954.
Mayhew, David. *Congress: The Electoral Connection*. New Haven: Yale University Press, 1974.

Kaye, Harvey J. *The British Marxist Historians: An Introductory Analysis*. Cambridge: Polity Press, 1984.
Kennedy, W. *English Taxation, 1640–1799: An Essay on Policy and Opinion*. New York: A. M. Kelley, 1964.
Kindleberger, Charles P. *A Financial History of Western Europe*. London: George Allen & Unwin, 1984.
Krishna, Vijay. "The Folk Theorem for Repeated Games." Harvard Business School Working Paper 89-003, 1988.
Kuczynski, Marguerite, and Rinald L. Meek, eds. *Quesnay's Tableau economique*. London: Royal Economics Society, 1972.
Kuhn, T. *The Structure of Scientific Revolutions*. Chicago: University of Chicago Press, 1970.
Kydland, F. W., and Prescott, E. C. "Rules, Rather Than Discretion: The Inconsistency of Optimal Plans." *Journal of Political Economy* 85 (1977): 473–91.
Labrousse, C. E. *La Crise de l'économie française à la fin de l'ancien régime et au début de la Révolution française*. Paris: Presses universitaires de France, 1944.
———. *Esquisse du mouvement des prix et des revenus en France au XVIII$^e$ siècle*. 2 vols. Paris: Dalloz, 1932.
———. "Prix et structure régionale: Le Froment dans les régions françaises de 1782 à 1780." *AHES* (1939).
Lacour-Gayet, Robert. *Calonne: Financier, réformateur, contrerévolutionnaire, 1732–1802*. Paris: Hachette, 1963.
Lambert, Sheila (Lady Elton). *Bills and Acts: Legislative Procedure in Eighteenth-Century England*. Cambridge: Cambridge University Press, 1971.
Landau, Norma. *The Justices of the Peace, 1679–1760*. Berkeley and Los Angeles: University of California Press, 1984.
Laugier, Lucien. *Turgot ou le mythe des réformes*. Paris: Albatros, 1979.
Lefebvre, Georges. "The Place of the Revolution in the Agrarian History of France." Translated and reprinted in *Rural Society in France*, edited by Robert Forster and Orest Ranum. Baltimore: John Hopkins University Press, 1977.
———. *The Great Fear of 1789: Rural Panic in Revolutionary France*. Translated by Joan White. New York: Vintage Books, 1973.
———. "La Révolution française et les paysans." *Annales historiques de la Révolution française*. 1933. Reprinted in *Cahiers de la Révolution française*. 1934. Reprinted in *Etudes sur la Révolution française*. Paris: Presses universitaires de France, 1963.
———. *Les Paysans du nord pendant la Révolution française*. Reprint. Paris: Bari, 1959.
Le Roy Ladurie, Emmanuel. "Les Comptes fantastiques de Gregory King." *Annales: Economies, sociétés, civilisations* 23 (1968): 1086–1102.

Horwitz, Henry. *Parliament, Policy and Politics in the Reign of William III*. Manchester: Manchester University Press, 1977.

Hufton, Olwen. "Social Conflict and the Grain Supply in Eighteenth-Century France." *Journal of Interdisciplinary History* 14 (1983): 303–32.

Hughes, E. *Studies in Administration and Finance, 1558–1825, with Special Reference to the History of the Salt Tax in England*. Manchester: Manchester University Press, 1934.

Hunt, Lynn. *Revolution and Urban Politics in Provincial France*. Stanford: Stanford University Press, 1978.

Huntington, Samuel. *Political Order in Changing Societies*. New Haven: Yale University Press, 1968.

Hurstfield, Joel. *Freedom, Corruption, and Government in Elizabethan England*. Cambridge, Mass.: Harvard University Press, 1973.

Hyams, Paul. "The Origins of a Peasant Land Market in England." *Economic History Review* 23 (1970): 18–31.

Jacquart, Jean. *La Crise rurale en Ile-de-France, 1550–1670*. Paris: Armand Colin, 1974.

Jones, E. L. "Agriculture 1700–80." In *The Economic History of Britain since 1700*, edited by Roderick Floud and Donald McCloskey. Cambridge: Cambridge University Press, 1981.

Jouvencel, Henri de. *Le Contrôleur général des finances sous l'ancien régime*. Paris: Larose, 1901.

Jouvenel, Bertrand de. *Sovereignty: An Inquiry into the Political Good*. Chicago: University of Chicago Press, 1957.

Kadish, Alon. *Historians, Economists, and Economic History*. London: Routledge & Kegan Paul, 1989.

Kaiser, Thomas. "Money, Despotism, and Public Opinion in Early Eighteenth-Century France: John Law and the Debate on Royal Credit." Work in Progress, University of Arkansas, Little Rock.

Kaplan, Steven Laurence. *Bread, Politics and Political Economy in the Reign of Louis XV*. 2 vols. The Hague: Martinus Nijhoff, 1976.

———. "Les Corporations, les 'Faux Ouvriers,' et le Faubourg Saint-Antoine au XVIII$^e$ siècle." *Annales: Economies, sociétés, civilisations* 43 (1988): 353–78.

———. *The Famine Plot Persuasion in Eighteenth-Century France*. Philadelphia: American Philosophical Society, 1982.

———. "The Luxury Guilds in Paris in the Eighteenth Century." *Francia* 9 (1981): 257–98.

———. *Provisioning Paris: Merchants and Millers in the Grain and Flour Trade during the Eighteenth Century*. Ithaca, N.Y.: Cornell University Press, 1984.

———. "Réflexions sur la police du monde du travail, 1700–1815." *Revue historique* 529 (1979): 17–78.

Hartwell, R. M. *The Industrial Revolution and Economic Growth*. London: Methuen, 1971.
Harvey, P. D. A., ed. *The Peasant Land Market in Medieval England*. Oxford: Oxford University Press, 1984.
Hayek, F. A. "History and Politics." In *Capitalism and the Historians*. Chicago: University of Chicago Press, 1954.
Heckscher, Eli F. *Mercantilism*. New York: Macmillan, 1955.
Heilbroner, Robert L. *The Making of Economic Society*. 7th ed. Englewood Cliffs, N.J.: Prentice-Hall, 1985.
―――. *The Worldly Philosophers: The Lives, Times, and Ideas of the Great Economic Thinkers*. 6th ed. New York: Simon & Schuster, 1986.
Henneman, J. B. *Royal Taxation in Fourteenth-Century France: The Captivity and Ransom of John II, 1356–1370*. Philadelphia: American Philosophical Association, 1976.
―――. *Royal Taxation in Fourteenth-Century France: The Development of War Financing, 1322–1356*. Princeton, N.J.: Princeton University Press, 1971.
Hennet, Le Chevalier. *Théorie du crédit public*. Paris, 1816.
Herold, Christopher J., ed. *The Mind of Napoleon*. New York: Columbia University Press, 1955.
Heumann, P. "Un Traitant sous Louis XIII: Antoine Feydeau." *Revue d'histoire moderne* 1938: 5–45.
Hicks, John. *A Theory of Economic History*. New York: Oxford University Press, 1969.
Hilaire-Perez, L. "Invention and the State in Eighteenth-Century France." *Technology and Culture* 32, no. 4 (October 1991): 911–31.
Hill, Brian W. *Robert Harley: Speaker, Secretary of State, and Premier Minister*. New Haven: Yale University Press, 1988.
Hill, Christopher. *The Century of Revolution: 1603–1714*. London: Nelson, 1961.
Hirsch, Jean-Pierre. "Négoce et corporations." In *La Révolution française et le développement du capitalisme*, edited by Gérard Gayot and Jean-Pierre Hirsch. Lille: Revue du nord, 1989.
Hirschman, Albert. *Exit, Voice, and Loyalty: Responses to Decline in Firms, Organizations, States*. Cambridge, Mass.: Harvard University Press, 1970.
Hobsbawm, E. J. "Class Consciousness in History." In *Aspects of History and Class Consciousness*, edited by Istvan Meszaros. London: Routledge & Kegan Paul, 1971.
Hodges, Richard. *Primitive and Peasant Markets*. Oxford: Basil Blackwell, 1988.
Hoffman, Philip. "Institutions and Agriculture in Old Regime France." *Politics and Society* 16 (1988): 241–64.
Homer, Sidney. *A History of Interest Rates*. New Brunswick, N.J.: Rutgers University Press, 1963.

Gallagher, Mark. *Rent Seeking and Economic Growth in Africa*. Boulder, Colo.: Westview Press, 1991.

Garden, Maurice. *Lyon et les Lyonnais au XVIII<sup>e</sup> siècle*. Paris: Les Belles Lettres, 1970.

Gauthier, Florence. *La Voie paysanne dans la Rèvolution française: L'Exemple Picard*. Paris: François Maspero, 1977.

Gauthier, Florence, and Guy-Robert Ikni, eds. *La Guerre du blé au XVIII<sup>e</sup> siècle*. Paris: Les Editions de la passion, 1988.

George, Peter, and Muir Dickson. *The Financial Revolution in England: A Study in the Development of Public Credit, 1688–1756*. New York: St. Martin's Press, 1967.

Goldstone, Jack A. *Revolution and Rebellion in the Early Modern World*. Berkeley and Los Angeles: University of California Press, 1991.

Gomel, Charles. *Histoire financière de l'Assemblée constituante*. 2 vols. Paris: Guillaumin, 1896.

Goodwin, Albert. "Calonne, the Assembly of French Notables of 1787 and the Origins of the *revolte nobiliaire*." *English Historical Review* 61 (1946): 329–77.

Goubert, Pierre. *Beauvais et le Beauvaisis de 1600 à 1730*. Paris, 1960.

Grange, Henri. *Les Idées de Necker*. Paris: Klincksieck, 1974.

Granovetter, Mark S. "The Strength of Weak Ties." *American Journal of Sociology* 78 (1973): 1360–80.

Gras, N. S. B. *The Evolution of the English Corn Market*. Cambridge: Cambridge University Press, 1915.

Grief, Avner, Paul Milgrom, and Barry Weingast. "The Merchant Guild as a Nexus of Contracts." *Journal of Political Economy*, forthcoming.

Griffin, Keith. *The Political Economy of Agrarian Change: An Essay on the Green Revolution*. Cambridge, Mass.: Harvard University Press, 1974.

Gruder, Vivian. "A Mutation in Elite Political Culture: The French Notables and the Defense of Property and Participation, 1787." *Journal of Modern History* 56 (December 1984): 598–634.

Guery, Alain. "Les Finances de la monarchie française sous l'ancien régime." *Annales: Economies, sociétés, civilisations* 33 (1978): 216–39.

———. "Le Roi dépensier: Le Don, la contrainte, et l'origine du système financier de la monarchie française d'ancien régime." *Annales: Economies, sociétés, civilisations* 39 (1984): 1241–69.

Harris, Michael, and Allan Lee. *The Press in English Society from the Seventeenth to Nineteenth Centuries*. London and Toronto: Fairleigh Dickinson University Press, 1986.

Harris, Robert D. *Necker and the Revolution of 1789*. Lanham, Md.: University Press of America, 1986.

———. *Necker: Reform Statesman of the Ancien Régime*. Berkeley and Los Angeles: University of California Press, 1979.

Eggertsson, Thrainn. *Economic Behavior and Institutions*. New York: Cambridge University Press, 1990.
Egret, Jean. *Necker, ministre de Louis XVI*. Paris: H. Champion, 1975.
———. *La Pré-Révolution française, 1787–1788*. Paris: Presses universitaires de France, 1962.
Ekelund, Robert B., and Robert D. Tollison. *Mercantilism as a Rent-Seeking Society: Economic Regulation in Historical Perspective*. College Station: Texas A&M University Press, 1981.
Elias, Norbert. *La Société de cour*. Translated by Pierre Kanntzer. Paris: Calmann-Lévy, 1974.
Epple, Denis, and Chester Spatt. "State Restrictions on Local Debt: Their Role in Preventing Default." *Journal of Public Economics* 29 (1986): 199–221.
Faure, Edgar. *La Disgrâce de Turgot*. Paris: Gallimard, 1961.
Fenoaltea, Stefano. "Authority, Efficiency, and Agricultural Organization in Medieval England and Beyond: A Hypothesis." *Journal of Economic History* 35 (1975): 693–718.
———. "Risk, Transactions Costs, and the Organization of Medieval Agriculture." *Explorations in Economic History* 13 (1976): 129–51.
———. "Transactions Costs, Whig History, and the Common Fields." *Politics and Society* 16 (1988): 171–240.
Flandrin, Jean-Louis. *Families in Former Times*. Cambridge: Cambridge University Press, 1976.
Fletcher, Anthony. *Reform in the Provinces: The Government of Stuart England*. New Haven: Yale University Press, 1986.
Fogel, Robert William, and G. R. Elton. *Which Road to the Past? Two Views of History*. New Haven: Yale University Press, 1983.
Foncin, Pierre. *Essai sur le ministre de Turgot*. Geneva: Slatkine-Megariotis Reprints, 1976.
Forbes, W. *Memoirs of a Banking House*. Edinburgh, 1859.
Forbonnais, François Véron Duverger de. *Examen des avantages et des desavantages de la prohibition des toiles peintes*. Marseilles: Chez Carapatria, 1755.
———. *Principes et observations économiques*. Amsterdam, 1767.
Fortunet, Françoise. *Charité ingénieuse et pauvre misère: Les Baux à cheptel simple en Auxois aux XVIII$^{eme}$ et XIX$^e$ siècles*. Dijon: Editions universitaires de Dijon, 1985.
Frank, Robert H. *Choosing the Right Pond: Human Behavior and the Quest for Status*. New York: Oxford University Press, 1985.
Fudenberg, Drew, and Eric Maskin. "The Folk Theorem in Repeated Games with Discounting and with Incomplete Information." *Econometrica* 54 (1986): 533–54.
Galbraith, John Kenneth. *Economics in Perspective: A Critical History*. Boston: Houghton Mifflin, 1987.

———. *Louis XIV prend le pouvoir*. Paris: Editions complexe, 1989.
———. "Pouvoir et finance au XVIIᵉ siècle: La Fortune du cardinal Mazarin." *Revue d'histoire moderne et contemporaine* 23 (1976): 161–81.
Deveau, Jean-Michel. *Le Commerce rochelais face à la Révolution: Correspondance de Jean Baptiste Nairac*. La Rochelle: Rumeur des âges, 1989.
Dewald, Jonathan. *Pont-St-Pierre, 1398–1789: Lordship, Community, and Capitalism in Early Modern France*. Berkeley and Los Angeles: University of California Press, 1987.
Deyon, Pierre, and Philippe Guignet. "The Royal Manufactures and Economic and Technical Progress in France before the Industrial Revolution." *Journal of European Economic History* 9 (1980): 611–32.
Dickson, Peter George Muir. *The Financial Revolution in England: A Study in the Development of Public Credit, 1688–1756*. New York: St. Martin's Press, 1967.
Dietz, Fredrick C. "English Public Finance and the National State in the Sixteenth Century." In *Facts and Factors in Economic History: Articles by Former Students of Edwin Francis Gay*. 1st ed. Cambridge, Mass: Harvard University Press, 1932.
Dowell, S. *A History of Taxation and Taxes in England from the Earliest Times to the Present Day*. 6 vols. 3d ed. London: F. Cass, 1965.
Doyle, William. *The Origins of the French Revolution*. Oxford: Oxford University Press, 1980.
———. "The Prices of Offices in Pre-Revolutionary France." *Historical Journal* 27, no. 4 (1984): 831–60.
———. *The Parlement of Bordeaux and the End of the Old Regime, 1771–1790*. New York: St. Martin's Press, 1974.
———. "Was There an Aristocratic Reaction in Pre-Revolutionary France?" *Past and Present* 57 (1972): 97–123.
Duby, Georges. *Warriors and Peasants: The Early Growth of the European Economy*. Translated by Howard B. Clarke. Ithaca, N.Y.: Cornell University Press, 1974.
———. *Rural Economy and Country Life in the Medieval West*. Translated by Cynthia Postan. New York: Columbia University Press, 1968.
Du Pont de Nemours, Pierre-Samuel. *The Autobiography of Du Pont de Nemours*, edited by Elizabeth Fox-Genovese. Wilmington, Del.: Scholarly Resources, 1984.
———. *Oeuvres politiques et économiques*. Vol. 4. Nendeln: KTO Press, 1979.
Durand, Yves. *Les Fermiers généraux au XVIIIᵉ siècle*. Paris: Presses universitaires de France, 1971.
———. *Finance et mécénat: Les Fermiers généraux au XVIIIᵉ siècle*. Paris: Hachette, 1976.
Durandeau, Joachim. *La Révolution en Bourgogne 1789: Les Châteaux brûlés*. Dijon, 1895–1901.

Coleman, D. C. "Politics and Economics in the Age of Anne: The Case of the Anglo-French Trade Treaty of 1713." In *Trade, Government and Economy in Pre-Industrial England,* edited by D. C. Coleman and A. H. John. London: Weidennfeld & Nicolson, 1976.

Collé, Charles. *Journal et mémoires.* Paris: Firmin Didot, 1868.

Colley, Linda. *In Defiance of Oligarchy: The Tory Party, 1714–1760.* Cambridge: Cambridge University Press, 1982.

Collins, James B. *Fiscal Limits of Absolutism: Direct Taxation in Early Seventeenth-Century France.* Berkeley and Los Angeles: University of California Press, 1988.

Compere-Morel, Adeodat Constant Adolphe. *Grand dictionnaire socialiste du mouvement politique.* Paris: Publications sociales, 1924.

Coornaert, Emile. *Les Corporations en France.* Paris, 1941.

Cooter, Robert. "Inventing Property: Economic Theories of the Origins of Market Property Applied to Papua New Guinea." Working Paper. University of California, Berkeley, 1989.

Coquereau, Jean Baptiste Louis. *Mémoires concernant l'administration des finances sous le ministère de M. l'abbé Terray, contrôleur général.* London: Adamson, 1776.

Crafts, N. F. R. "British Economic Growth, 1700–1850: Some Difficulties of Interpretation." *Explorations in Economic History* 24 (1987): 245–68.

Crouzet, François. *De la supériorité de l'Angleterre sur la France: L'Economique et l'imaginaire, XVII$^e$–XX$^e$ siècles.* Paris: Perrin, 1985.

Cruickshank, Eveline. "Ashby v. White: The Case of the Men of Aylesbury, 1701–1704." In *Party and Management in Parliament, 1660–1784,* edited by Clyve Jones. New York: St. Martin's Press, 1984.

Dahlman, C. *The Open Field System and Beyond.* Cambridge: Cambridge University Press, 1980.

Dakin, D. *Turgot and the Ancien Regime in France.* London: Methuen, 1939.

Darby, Henry Clifford. *An Historical Geography of England before A.D. 1800.* Cambridge: Cambridge University Press, 1936.

Dardel, Pierre. *Commerce, industrie, et navigation: Rouen et Havre au XVIII$^e$ siècle.* Rouen: Société libre d'émulation de la Seine-Maritime, 1966.

Dent, Julian. *Crisis in Finance: Crown, Financiers and Society in Seventeenth-Century France.* New York: St. Martin's Press, 1973.

Depitre, Edgard. *La Toile peinte en France au XVII$^e$ et XVIII$^e$ siècles.* Paris: Marcel Rivière, 1912.

Dessert, Daniel. *Argent, pouvoir et société au grand siècle.* Paris: Fayard, 1984.

———. "Finances et société au XVII$^e$ siècle: A propos de la Chambre de justice de 1661." *Annales: Economies, sociétés, civilisations* 29 (1974): 847–71.

Casaux, M. de. *Reflexions sur la dette exigible et sur les moyens proposés pour la rembourser 1789*. Paris, 1790.
Chapuisat, Edouard. *Necker: 1732–1804*. Paris: Librarie du Recueil Sirey, 1938.
Charlesworth, Andrew, ed. *An Atlas of Rural Protest in Britain, 1548–1900*. Philadelphia: University of Pennsylvania Press, 1983.
Chartre, J. A. "The Marketing of Agricultural Produce." In "Agrarian Change," bk. 2 of *1640–1750*, vol. 5 of *Agrarian History of England and Wales*, edited by Joan Thirsk. Cambridge: Cambridge University Press, 1985.
Chassagne, Serge. "La Diffusion rurale de l'industrie cotonnière en France, 1750–1850." *Revue du nord* 61 (1979): 32–40.
Chaunu, Pierre. "L'Etat." In *Histoire économique et sociale*, edited by Fernand Braudel and C. E. Labrousse. Paris: Presses universitaires de France, 1977.
Chaussinaud-Nogaret, Guy. *Les Financiers de Languedoc au XVIII$^e$ siècle*. Paris: S.E.V.P.E.N., 1970.
Chazal, M. L. *L'Abbé Terray: Contrôleur général des Finances*. Paris: Batignoles, 1847.
Chevrier, G. *Remarques sur l'introduction et les vicissitudes de la distinction du "jus privatium" et du "jus publicum" dans les oeuvres des anciens juristes françaises*. Paris, 1952.
Clark, J. C. D. *Revolution and Rebellion: State and Society in England in the Seventeenth and Eighteenth Centuries*. New York: Cambridge University Press, 1986.
Clay, C. G. A. *Economic Expansion and Social Change: England, 1500–1700*. Vol. 2, *Industry, Trade, and Government*. New York: Cambridge University Press, 1984.
Clément, Pierre, and Alfred Lemoine. *M. de Silhouette, Bouret les derniers fermiers généraux: Etudes sur les financiers du XVIII$^e$ siècle*. Paris: Didier, 1872.
Coase, R. H. "Durability and Monopoly." *Journal of Law and Economics* 15, no. 1 (April 1972): 143–50.
Coats, A. W. "Explanations in History and Economics." *Social Research* 56 (1989): 345–46.
Cobb, Richard. *The Police and the People: French Popular Protest, 1789–1820*. London: Oxford University Press, 1970.
Cobban, Alfred. *A History of Modern France, 1715–1799*. 3 vols. Harmondsworth: Penguin Books, 1957.
———. *The Social Interpretation of the French Revolution*. Cambridge, Mass.: Cambridge University Press, 1964.
Coke, J. "The Debate between the Heralds of England and France." In *Tudor Economic Documents*, 3:6. London: Longmans, 1924.
Cole, Charles Woolsey. *Colbert and a Century of French Mercantilism*. 2 vols. New York: Columbia University Press, 1939.

Brewer, John. *The Sinews of Power: War, Money, and the English State, 1688–1783*. New York: Knopf, 1989.

Bridbury, A. R. "Markets and Freedom in the Middle Ages." In *The Market in History*, edited by B. L. Anderson and A. J. H. Latham. London: Croom Helm, 1986.

Britnell, Richard H. "The Proliferation of Markets in England, 1200–1349." *Economic History Review* 34 (1981): 209–21.

Bruguière, Michel. "L'Aristocratique Descendance des affairistes de la Révolution." In *Pour une renaissance de l'histoire financière XVIII$^e$–XX$^e$ siècles*. Paris: Comité pour l'histoire économique et financière de la France, 1991.

———. *Gestionnaires et profiteurs de la Révolution: L'Administration des finances françaises de Louis XVI à Bonaparte*. Paris: Olivier Orban, 1986.

———. *Pour une renaissance de l'histoire financière XVIII$^e$–XX$^e$ siècles*. Paris: Comité pour l'histoire économique et financière de la France, 1991.

Buchanan, James M. "The Domain of Constitutional Economics." *Journal of Constitutional Political Economy* 1 (1990): 1–18.

———. *Liberty, Market, and State*. New York: New York University Press, 1986.

Buchanan, James M., and Gorden S. Tulluck. *The Calculus of Consent*. Ann Arbor: University of Michigan Press, 1962.

Buxton, Sydney Charles. *Finance and Politics: An Historical Study, 1783–1885*. 2 vols. London: J. Murray, 1888.

Calonne, Charles Alexandre. *De l'état de la France, présent et à venir*. 4th ed. London and Paris: Laurent, 1790.

———. *Discours prononcé de l'ordre du Roi et en sa présence par M. de Calonne, contrôleur général des finances, dans l'Assemblée des notables, tenue à Versailles, le 22 février 1787*. Versailles: Pierres premier imprimeur ordinaire du Roi, 1787.

———. *Réponse de M. de Calonne à l'écrit de M. Necker, publié en avril 1787; contenant l'examen des comptes de la situation des finances, rendus en 1774, 1776, 1781, 1783, & 1787: Avec des observations sur les résultats de l'Assemblée des notables*. London: Spilsbury, 1788.

Cameron, W. J. "Lobbying by the White Paper Makers, 1690." In *Seventeenth-Century Economic Documents*, edited by Joan Thirsk and J. P. Cooper. Oxford: Clarendon Press, 1972.

Caple, Jeremy. "North Midlands: August and September 1756." In *An Atlas of Rural Protest in Britain, 1548–1900*, edited by Andrew Charlesworth. Philadelphia: University of Pennsylvania Press, 1983.

Carra, Jean Louis. *M. de Calonne tout entier, tel qu'il s'est comporté dans l'administration des finances, dans son commissariat en Bretagne*. Brussels, 1788.

Bloch, Marc. *The Historian's Craft*. New York: Vintage Books, 1953.
Bohstedt, John. *Riots and Community Politics in England and Wales, 1790–1810*. Cambridge, Mass.: Harvard University Press, 1983.
Bonney, Richard. *The King's Debts: Finance and Politics in France*. Oxford: Clarendon Press, 1981.
Bordes, Christian, and Jean Morange, eds. *Turgot: Economiste et administrateur*. Paris: Presses universitaires de France, 1982.
Bosher, J. F. "French Administration and Finance." In *The New Cambridge Modern History*, vol. 7, edited by A. Goodwin. Cambridge: Cambridge University Press, 1965.
———. *French Finances, 1770–1795: From Business to Bureaucracy*. Cambridge: Cambridge University Press, 1970.
———, ed. "*Chambres de justice* in the French Monarchy." In *French Government and Society, 1500–1800: Essays in Memory of Alfred Cobban*. London: Athlone Press, 1973.
Bossenga, Gail. "City and State: An Urban Perspective on the Origins of the French Revolution." In *The Political Culture of the Old Regime*, edited by Keith M. Baker. Vol. 2 of *The French Revolution and the Creation of Modern Political Culture*. London: Pergamon Press, 1987.
———. "From Corporations to Citizenship: The *bureaux des finances* before the French Revolution." *Journal of Modern History* 58 (1986): 610–42.
Bourgeon, J. L. "Colbert et les corporations: L'Exemple de Paris." In *Un Nouveau Colbert*, edited by Roland Mousnier. Paris: Editions SEDES/CDU, 1985.
Boutier, Jean. "Jacqueries en pays croquant: Les Révoltes Paysannes en Aquitaine (décembre 1789–mars 1790)." *Annales: Economies, sociétés, civilisations* 34 (1979): 760–86.
Bouton, C. *Solidarities and Tensions in Ancien Regime France: Rural Society Confronts the Subsistence Crisis in 1775*. Binghamton, N.Y.: SUNY, 1985.
Braudel, Fernand P. *L'Identité de la France*. Paris: Arthaud & Flammarion, 1986.
———. *The Structure of Everyday Life*. 3 vols. New York: Harper & Row, 1981–1982
Braudel, Fernand P., and F. Spooner. "Prices in Europe from 1450." In *The Cambridge Economic History of Europe*, vol. 4, edited by E. E. Rich and C. H. Wilson. Cambridge: Cambridge University Press, 1966.
Brenner, Robert. "The Agrarian Roots of European Capitalism." In *The Brenner Debate*, edited by T. H. Aston and C. H. E. Aston. Cambridge: Cambridge University Press, 1985.
Breton, Albert. "Representative Governments and the Formation of National and International Policies." *Revue économique*, no. 2 (March 1981): 356–73.

Beaumont, Déon M de. *Pour servir à l'histoire générale des finances.* 2 vols. London, 1758.
Becker, Gary S. "A Theory of Competition among Pressure Groups for Political Influence." *Quarterly Journal of Economics* 98, no. 371 (1983): 371–400.
Beik, William. "Etat et société au XVIIe siècle: La Taille en Languedoc et la question de la rédistribution." *Annales: Economies, sociétés, civilisations* 39 (1984): 1270–98.
Bell, Daniel. "Models and Reality in Economic Discourse." In *The Crisis in Economic Theory,* edited by Daniel Bell and Irving Kristol. New York: Basic Books, 1981.
Bendix, Reinhard. *Max Weber: An Intellectual Portrait.* New York: Doubleday, 1960.
Bergin, Joseph. *Cardinal Richelieu: Power and the Pursuit of Wealth.* New Haven: Yale University Press, 1987.
Berry, R. Albert, and William Cline. *Agrarian Structure and Productivity in Developing Countries.* Baltimore: Johns Hopkins University Press, 1979.
Biddick, Kathleen. "Medieval English Peasants and Market Involvement." *Journal of Economic History* 45 (1985): 823–31.
Bien, David. "The Army in the French Enlightenment: Reform, Reaction, and Revolution." *Past and Present* 85 (1979): 68–98.
———. "Offices, Corporations, and a System of State Credit: The Uses of Privilege under the Ancient Regime." In *The French Revolution and the Creation of Modern Political Culture,* edited by Keith M. Baker. London: Pergamon Press, 1987.
———. "Manufacturing Nobles: The Chancelleries in France to 1789." *Journal of Modern History* 61 (1989): 450–86.
———. "La Réaction aristocratique avant 1789: L'Exemple de l'armée." *Annales: Economies, sociétés, civilisations* 29 (1974): 23–48, 505–34.
———. "The *secrétaires du roi:* Absolutism, Corporations, and Privilege under the *ancien régime.*" In *Vom ancien régime zur französischen Revolution: Forschungen und Perspektiven/De l'ancien régime à la Révolution française: Recherches et perspectives,* edited by E. Hinrichs. Göttingen: Vandenhoeck & Ruprecht, 1978.
Binney, John, ed. *British Public Finance and Administration, 1774–1792.* Oxford: Oxford University Press, 1958.
Binswanger, H., and M. Rosenzweig. "Contractual Arrangements, Employment and Wages in Rural Labor Markets: A Critical Review." In *Contractual Arrangements, Employment and Wages in Rural Labor Markets in Asia,* edited by H. Binswanger and M. Rosenzweig. New Haven: Yale University Press, 1984.
Blaug, Mark. *Economic History and the History of Economics.* New York: New York University Press, 1986.

Argenson, René-Louis, marquis d'. *Considérations sur le gouvernement ancien et présent comparé avec celui des autres états suivies d'un nouveau plan d'administration.* 2d ed. Amsterdam, 1784.

Ashton, T. S. *An Economic History of England: The Eighteenth Century.* London: Methuen, 1955.

Axelrod, Robert. "The Emergence of Cooperation among Egotists." *American Political Science Review* 75 (1981): 306–18.

Bacquié, Franc. *Les Inspecteurs des manufactures sous l'ancien régime, 1669–1792.* Paris: Hachette, 1927.

Bailly, Antoine. *Histoire financière de la France, depuis l'origine de la monarchie jusqu'à la fin de 1786.* Paris: Moutardier, 1830.

Baker, Keith M., ed. *The French Revolution and the Creation of Modern Political Culture.* 3 vols. London: Pergamon Press, 1987.

Baker, T. H. *Records of the Seasons: Prices of Agricultural Produce and Phenomena Observed in the British Isles.* London: Archon Books, 1883.

Barbier, Edmond-Jean-François. *Journal d'un bourgeois de Paris sous le régime de Louis XV.* 4 vols. Paris: Renovard, 1847–56.

Bardhan, Pranab K. *Land, Labor, and Rural Poverty: Essays in Developmental Economics.* New York: Columbia University Press, 1984.

Barnes, Donald Grove. *History of the English Corn Laws.* London: Routledge & Sons, 1930.

Barro, Robert. "Recent Developments in the Theory of Rules versus Discretion." *Economic Journal* 96 (1986 suppl.): 23–37.

Barzel, Yoram. *Economic Analysis of Property Rights.* Cambridge: Cambridge University Press, 1989.

Bates, Robert H. "A Critique by Political Scientists." In *Politics and Policy Making in Developing Countries: Perspectives on the New Political Economy*, edited by Gerald M. Meier. San Francisco: International Center for Economic Growth, 1991.

———. "Lessons from History, or the Perfidy of English Exceptionalism and the Significance of Historical France." *World Politics* 15 (1988): 499–516.

———. *Markets and States in Tropical Africa: Political Base of Agricultural Policies.* Berkeley and Los Angeles: University of California Press, 1981.

———. "Some Conventional Orthodoxies in the Study of Agrarian Change." *World Politics* 11 (1984): 234–254.

———, ed. *Toward a Political Economy of Development: A Rational Choice Perspective.* Berkeley and Los Angeles: University of California Press, 1988.

Bates, Robert, and Donald Lien Da-Hsiang. "A Note On Taxation, Development, and Representative Government." *Politics and Society* 14, no. 1 (1985): 53–70.

Bayard, Françoise. *Le Monde des financiers au XVII$^e$ siècle.* Paris: Flammarion, 1988.

# Works Cited

ARCHIVAL SOURCES

AN   Archives nationales
BN   Bibliothèque nationale

SECONDARY SOURCES

Abel, Wilhelm. *Agrarkrisen und Agrarkonjunktur im Mitteleuropa vom 13. bis zum 19. Jahrhundert.* Berlin: P. Parey, 1966.
——. *Agricultural Fluctuations in Europe from the Thirteenth to the Twentieth Centuries.* Translated by Olive Ordish. New York: St. Martin's Press, 1980.
Aftalion, Florin. *L'Economie de la Révolution française.* Paris: Hachette, 1987.
Alan, Robert. "The Efficiency and Distributional Consequences of Eighteenth-Century Enclosures." *Economic Journal* 92 (1982): 937–53.
Amsden, Alice. "Taiwan's Economic History: A Case of Etatisme and a Challenge to Dependency Theory." In *Toward a Political Economy of Development: A Rational Choice Perspective,* edited by Robert Bates. Berkeley and Los Angeles: University of California Press, 1988.
Antoine, Michel. *Le Conseil du roi sous le régime de Louis XV.* Paris and Geneva: Libraire Droz, 1970.
——. *Le Gouvernement et l'administration sous Louis XV: Dictionnaire biographique.* Paris: Editions du CNRS, 1978.
——. "La Monarchie absolue." In *The Political Culture of the Old Regime,* edited by Keith M. Baker. Vol. 2 of *The French Revolution and the Creation of Modern Political Culture.* London: Pergamon Press, 1987.

nomic theory, Lord Keynes noted, "is a method rather than a doctrine, an apparatus of the mind, a technique of thinking, which helps its possessor to draw correct conclusions."[8] Although it is beyond the means of a single author to be a specialist in all the issues raised here, I hope a useful way of thinking that can be applied to specific examples, according to the different background and perspective of readers, has been illustrated. Indeed, that approach may be more useful for some topics than for others. It is my hope that readers will be able to go further in drawing implications relevant to their special areas of interest.

[8] John Maynard Keynes, "Introduction," Cambridge Economic Handbook Series, quoted in Albert Breton, "Representative Governments and the Formation of National and International Policies," *Revue économique*, no. 2 (March 1981): 356–73.

rights can be negotiated so that society may capture the gains from new technology and markets.

The consequences of the different methods early modern French and English governments used to reduce the impediments to exchange and to determine the contractual parameters for trade are a central concern of this book. It is assumed that government's ability to provide society with the institutions necessary for individuals to trade to an efficient point—the point at which all welfare-enhancing trades were completed—was essential to European economic expansion. Economic activity is not frictionless or without costs. The frictions involved in most economic activity—transaction costs, uncertainty, and information asymmetry—may explain the contractual relationships that shape the evolution of society. Put differently, the need to cope with trading frictions and transaction costs is an important motivation for individuals to enter into contracts, both privately and with their government or king. The costs and the contracts designed to cope with trading frictions evolved differently in England compared to France, and as a result Old Regime England and France represent two rival paths to economic and political modernization. The great success of French absolutism lay in its unification of the politically fragmented French nation. The liberation of market forces was the great success of England's parliamentary regime. This liberation occurred because political markets evolved in which inefficiencies in the original allocation of property rights could be corrected by trade rather than by revolution. Where trade was not possible, corruption allowed those with the higher-valued usages to outbid the holders of inefficient property rights. Corruption thus created an auction market for property rights when face-to-face exchange in Parliament failed. The French system of centralized control institutionalized cronyism, which reduced both corruption and trade. Cronyism nevertheless provided sufficient security of property rights to allow for the level of investment needed to sustain growth.

One final caveat cannot be stated too forcefully. This analysis represents an effort to understand the economic logic underlying the evolution of Old Regime institutions. From this understanding, I have tried to extrapolate an analysis of the possible and probable costs those institutions imposed on society. In calculating those costs, many hypotheses have been presented whose validity has yet to be tested. The research needed to fully evaluate the costs of organizing the economic systems of early modern France and England will require the work of scholars needing many more pages to report their findings. This book represents a tentative first step toward understanding the origins of Old Regime institutions, the incentives that produced them, and their probable costs to the economy. Eco-

The English enclosure acts provide a good example of the negotiation and liquidation of traditional property rights so that gains can be captured from the expansion of market relations. The gains from the negotiations could be captured by the lords in the form of higher rents, which could then be taxed by the king. The contractual solution required to facilitate enclosures was too costly to be negotiated locally because it required procedural regularities whose standardization and enforcement had to be predetermined. In England this could be done by parliamentary initiative because the king's property rights were not jeopardized. In France, such agreements required the king's consent and participation because he claimed that common fields and rights were ultimately a grant from the king and belonged to future generations as well as to the present one. The rights were protected by royal officials because the revenues they produced were linked to royal tax collection. The efficiency gains to enclosure in France were not easy for the king to capture, since the noble landlords who might benefit most from the enclosure often claimed tax exemptions.[5]

The Old Regime in France did not produce political institutions that could capture and reallocate the efficiency gains of redefined property rights or abolished privileges. An institution or set of rules was needed to provide privileged elites with equity stakes in the efficiency gains that would have resulted from property-rights reform, as well as ex-post assurance that the rights would not be violated or confiscated.[6] The failure to devise such a set of rules was owing to the central role of the king, upon whom the creation of such an institution would have depended. The king would not be a party to institutional changes that might even temporarily reduce the flow of revenues to the Crown's coffers.

A simple but powerful lesson can be drawn from the political failure of the French Old Regime: the formation of political markets that allow all social assets or property rights to be traded, transferred, and made liquid is essential to the survival of a regime.[7] The system of economic trade ultimately depends on the degree to which politically contracted property

---

[5]See Hilton L. Root, *Peasants and King in Burgundy: Agrarian Foundations of French Absolutism* (Berkeley and Los Angeles: University of California Press, 1987), ch. 4.

[6]Similarly, the American Civil War might have been avoided if the North could have devised a method to reimburse Southern landlords for their slaves. The failure to come up with a contract ensuring subsequent enforcement of such a contract prevented a peaceful resolution of the conflict.

[7]Of course, commodifying everything runs into social and normative barriers. Constitutions must determine what can and cannot be commodified. Political markets must be restricted by a constitution that defines fundamental and inalienable rights.

tinual interaction. As markets expand, trade with strangers increases in importance and the social networks sustained by the expectation of repeated interaction diminish in importance. New institutions to reduce uncertainty in exchange are needed to regulate the anonymous trade that develops. Local elites increase their control over the market in the name of policing or providing necessary services, such as safeguarding property rights and enforcing contracts. This allowed elites to increase their bargaining power vis-à-vis the peasantry, making it more costly for peasants to participate in market transactions. The beneficial effects of markets can be restricted when market officials are capable of collusion to capture monopoly rents and when unequal bargaining strength allows unequal access to resources, capital, and information. Although lower information costs, economies of scale, and improved enforcement of contracts all indirectly contributed to the well-being of the peasantry, the more conspicuous benefits tended to accrue to those groups who typically devised the rules to restrict the market access of weaker parties. The growth of markets did not automatically produce uneven distributional consequences; rather, the institutions devised to govern markets produced inequalities. The collusion or monopoly power of the elites to whom the original property rights were allocated permitted the transfer of income away from the peasants to urban merchants or seigneurial elites.[4] Creating monopoly benefits for themselves, local elites limited the effectiveness of the markets they supervised. Efficiency losses occurred when peasants responded by resisting participation in markets.

Markets often originated as grants by the king to the nobility or the towns in exchange for loyalty or revenue. The exchange or elimination of these property rights did not occur, since in the absence of compensation for the expected value of the rents they were due over time, the elites would not relinquish rights once granted. A wealthier society would have resulted if peasant production had been fully integrated into the market system. When the potential benefits of markets to the peasants in the form of higher income and reduced uncertainty cannot be fully captured, peasants limit their participation in markets. French society was poorer because there was no market for political contracts allowing elites to negotiate the liquidation of their property rights over market governance.

---

[4]Political influence and the formation of cartels provided early modern elites with advantages they were unable to procure by competitive production strategies. The eighteenth-century grain bounties that protected large British estates during a period of declining grain prices are an excellent example of how elites dominated because their economic interests were backed by the coercive authority of the state.

work on such issues. Although a few important preliminary forays have been made by economic theory into those domains, a dialogue between economists and cultural historians is necessary in order to develop a more complete understanding of the relationship of the economic system to other domains of social behavior.[3]

By far the most important caution that needs to be stated is the role played in this book by market analysis and market terminology. The argument here contrasts sharply with the neoclassical view that extols government inaction. It does not endorse the idea that the government that governs least is best, or that markets will solve all problems if only government would stand aside. Markets depend on rules that are politically determined. Government was involved in the considerable economic growth of England and France during the eighteenth century as arbiter of disputes and defender of property rights. In both nations competitive markets required the construction of jurisdictions that resisted capture by cartels of private groups whose local authority obstructed the formation of national and international markets. Here England was more successful than France in combining local economic decision making with free national markets. In France rights to participate in the market system were transferred to the center, but local obstacles to the distribution of goods and services were not entirely eliminated.

Because expansion of markets seems to intensify inequality in traditional societies, the view that markets are the source of social inequality and injustice finds much support. Linking the observed inequality with the growth of markets, however, confuses the impact of markets with the conditions under which markets evolve and ignores the role of politics on the governance of markets.

Increased specialization as a result of the expansion of trade beyond the village or region and the division of labor are two conditions universally acknowledged by economists to increase productivity. By increasing the number of trading partners, however, market expansion also greatly increases uncertainty. Dense social networks enforce informal rules in traditional societies, thereby reducing the uncertainties of trade and the costs of transacting; however, these norms depend upon the expectation of con-

---

[3]Most notable among attempts to translate insights about culture into terminology understood by economists are Douglass C. North, *Structure and Change in Economic History* (New York: Norton, 1981), 45–59. North has tried to reintroduce ideology in a way that would be consistent with economic theory, but it is too early to tell whether the effort will inspire successful work along this line. Also see Robert H. Frank, *Choosing the Right Pond: Human Behavior and the Quest for Status* (New York: Oxford University Press, 1985).

# 11 Caveat Emptor
## Markets and History

The source material upon which this book is based was collected primarily from French sources. In effect it offers a view of France in an English mirror, much in the spirit of the eighteenth-century French political economists, who similarly contrasted the two nations in order to highlight particular characteristics of French economic organization. They believed that much can be learned about a particular nation by using a common methodology to study others. Only a partial coverage of the economy is offered; an assessment of the level of production and a comparison of relative growth rates are not attempted. This, then, is not a book about the relative retardation of French industrial and agricultural development. Debates concerning measurement and calculation that such a study would entail are outside of the scope of this analysis.[1] Nor do I venture into questions of family or domestic organization or demography.[2] Instead, the emphasis is on the motivations underlying institutional innovation in Old Regime France and England and on the centrality of political arrangements in determining economic outcomes. This perspective has permitted the exploration of how the institutions developed to sustain intertemporal trades in political markets influenced variations in the public policies of Old Regime France and England.

Between structure and individual action is a domain governed by symbols, rhetoric, and ideology. A more complete explanation of the transition to industrial society depends on incorporating the ideas of scholars who

---

[1]See Patrick O'Brien and Caglar Keydor, *Economic Growth in Britain and France, 1780–1914: Two Paths to the Twentieth Century* (London: George Allen & Unwin, 1978).
[2]See Jack A. Goldstone, *Revolution and Rebellion in the Early Modern World* (Berkeley and Los Angeles: University of California Press, 1991).

They did not identify the Crown or its government with any broader public interest that was worth defending. Once assembled, the national community did not view the regime as having something greater than the sum of individual interests to offer. So it was that what had taken the kings of France so many generations to build could disappear in the twinkling of an eye.

sector was legally isolated and forced to operate informally. Since the administrative structure of the Old Regime had become autonomous, composed of offices that had become private property, which the state could no longer afford to buy back, institutional gridlock resulted.

Mancur Olson has studied the effects of distributional coalitions on political life. As groups begin to distinguish themselves from one another by highly nuanced codes of behavior, they become increasingly castelike, and political life becomes increasingly divisive.[58] Louis XIV's legacy to the eighteenth century was a society in which privilege incited social disintegration. The status quo established by the Sun King's reforms still reigned on the eve of the Revolution. Each group was willing to support limits on the privileges of the others, while unwilling to be dominated or lose place to some other social subset. Groups would not tolerate the loss of even a ceremonial privilege and were too preoccupied with their own particular privileges to speak for the regime when it was in trouble. Ties of collaboration within and among the social orders were ruptured; civic solidarity was fractured. Groups that viewed each other as adversaries could not represent the nation, since efforts at reform were viewed as a challenge to social equilibrium. No one branch of the government was strong enough to impose reforms on any other branch, and the king was no longer in a position to risk losing the support of a group like the clergy or the nobility by hazarding radical change. "Like boxers frozen in a stand-off, none of the privileged groups dared change position for fear that the slightest change in attitude would compromise its privileges or benefit its rivals," Elias writes. "Unlike a boxing match, however, there was no referee who could separate the boxers in order to continue the match."[59]

In its hour of need, the Old Regime could find few defenders. "Nowhere else in the world were citizens less inclined to join forces and stand by each other in emergencies," Tocqueville observes.[60] Instead of uniting to defend the structure that provided their rents and privileges, the elites of Old Regime France regarded the privileges of adjacent groups with resentment. Each group came to the Estates General in 1789 with the goal of defending its exemptions from unreimbursed loss, but no group was prepared to defend the system itself. In other words, the elites who benefited from the redistributional game did not enjoy the blessings of class consciousness.

---

[58]Mancur Olson, *The Rise and Decline of Nations: Economic Growth, Stagflation, and Social Rigidities* (New Haven: Yale University Press, 1982), 47–53.
[59]Elias, *Société de cour*, 314–15.
[60]Tocqueville, *The Old Regime and the French Revolution*, 77.

Turgot's testimony can be explained by the fact that in a centralized, autocratic regime, strategic or cooperative interactions are not observed among different social groups, because no one finds that his own interests or choices depend on the choices of any other individual or group. No group in Old Regime France had an incentive to bargain with other groups. One consequence of the absence of strategic interaction was that no group had a coherent vision of the distributional system of which it was a part. Instead, the relationship among the different groups was governed by resentment of one another's privileges, while each jealously guarded its own. Norms and networks of civic engagement between and among members of the various elites were shattered during the process by which the Crown became the guarantor of civic order. The vote by the third estate of Brittany against the *vingtième* (a tax on all individuals regardless of status) in 1752 was an example of the inability to cooperate to achieve long-term goals. Just like the first and the second, the third order voted against the tax, fearing an increase in its taxes, thinking only in terms of protecting its own privileges. No leader emerged within Brittany's third estate with the foresight to realize that it would be beneficial to the group if the *vingtième* was approved, because it would mean submitting the privileged first and second estates to the same taxes as the third.

The economic expansion of the eighteenth century further contributed to the tension. Mobility certainly increased during the century, especially at the very top of the social hierarchy, where wealthy financiers intermarried with members of the old aristocracy.[56] Nevertheless, the groups excluded from the power monopoly also grew in strength during the Old Regime. Despite the accession of newcomers, the growing demand for privilege created by the century's rapid economic expansion was not met.[57] The demands of peasants for access to the surpluses generated by markets were unsatisfied. The formal sector could not grow fast enough to absorb the growing informal sector. One barrier to reform came from the existence of property rights that had reinforced the power of corporate groups. Because of the Crown's support of the guilds, the new proto-industrial

---

[56] Brugière cautions that the majority of the children of financiers did not conclude prestigious marriages with the old nobility; most married in their milieu of origin. Only the children of several very significant financiers were able to marry into the upper aristocracy, but those financiers were already in the king's direct service. See Michèle Brugière, "L'Aristocratique Descendance des affairistes de la Révolution," in *Pour une renaissance de l'histoire financière XVIII$^e$–XX$^e$ siècles* (Comité pour l'histoire economique et financière de la France, 1991), 312–25.

[57] See David Bien, "Manufacturing Nobles: The Chancelleries in France to 1789," *Journal of Modern History* 61 (1989): 450–86.

their inflexible sources of income, prevented a nonviolent transformation of the institutions by the voluntary limitation of privileges."[52]

In Old Regime France, no two industries or imports were taxed the same way, no two provinces or social groups paid the same taxes or held the same privileges. Residents of Paris had privileges in relationship to residents of other cities; the bourgeoisie of La Rochelle had little in common with the bourgeoisie of Toulouse. David Bien has suggested that differences among members of the nobility may have been more intense than those between the nobility and other social groups.[53] Since "differentiation had taken place within each of these three classes, with the result that each was split up into a number of small groups almost completely shut off from each other, the inevitable consequence was that, though the nation came to seem a homogeneous whole, its parts no longer held together," Tocqueville notes.[54] In his memoir *Sur les administrations provinciales*, published posthumously in 1787, Turgot commented on the consequences of this atomization of society into self-regarding clans:

> The cause of the evil, sire, stems from the fact that your nation has no constitution. It is a society composed of different orders badly united, and of a people among whose members there are but very few social ties. In consequence, each individual is occupied only with his own particular, exclusive interest; and almost no one bothers to fulfill his duties or to know his relationship to others. As a result, there is a perpetual war of claims and counterclaims, which reason and mutual understanding have never regulated, in which Your Majesty is obliged to decide everything personally or through your agents. Everyone insists on your special orders to contribute to the public good, to respect the rights of others, sometimes even to make use of his own rights. You are forced to decree on everything, in most cases by particular acts of will, whereas you could govern like God by general laws if the various parts composing your realm had a regular organization and clearly established relationship.[55]

---

[52]Ibid., 316. One difficulty was that the various privileged orders possessed assets in the form of offices and fiscal privileges that could not easily be negotiated in a new order.
[53]See David Bien, "La Réaction aristocratique avant 1789: L'Exemple de l'armée," *Annales: Economies, sociétés, civilisations* 29 (1974): 23–48, 505–34, and "The Army in the French Enlightenment: Reform, Reaction, and Revolution," *Past and Present* 85 (November 1979): 68–98.
[54]Tocqueville, *The Old Regime and the French Revolution*, 137.
[55]Anne-Robert-Jacques Turgot, *Oeuvres posthumes de M. Turgot, ou Memoir de M. Turgot sur les administrations provinciales* (Lausanne, 1787), 9; reprinted in Pierre-Samuel du Pont de Nemours, *Oeuvres politiques et économiques* (Nendeln: KTO Press, 1979), 4:159.

mentality of their membership has never been doubted. No historian has yet found evidence of guild spokespeople subscribing to a belief in the benefits of a competitive order. The zero-sum mentality also had its parallel in politics in the emphasis on court etiquette and on place, which implied that a change in the rights attributed to one group altered its relation to rival groups. Where hierarchy is carefully articulated, any loss of professional status is keenly felt socially, since each improvement in rank of one group or individual diminishes the status of another. For example, the eighteenth-century financial elites bitterly opposed reforms limiting their control over the kingdom's finances because they did not want their status diminished in relation to old landed families.

A society divided into closed self-regarding groups was the result of Louis XIV's policies. "The fact is that the reinforcement of the existing differences and rivalries, especially among the elites and within them, and between the different rungs of the hierarchy was one of his fixed maxims as a ruler," Norbert Elias explains. "It is quite obvious that these differences and petty jealousies between the most powerful elite groups in the realm were among the basic preconditions for the abundance of power held by the king and denoted by the term 'absolutist.' "[51] After Louis's death, the exploitation of social mobility was more influenced by the internal power struggles of the court than by the king's discretion. In conclusion, Elias emphasizes that, despite the decline in the Crown's capacity to manipulate the social hierarchy, becoming accustomed to imposed standards of behavior reinforced by dependence and subjugation contributed to transforming tensions and conflicts among groups into a relationship of permanent hostility. Keenly aware of differences and unable to forget past rivalries, the elites could not close ranks to protect the system that ensured their status.

## PRIVILEGE AND REVOLUTION

The economic theorists of the eighteenth century recognized the enormous burden the proliferation of privilege placed on the state. But programs for reform never enjoyed wide support within the elites because the beneficiaries of the monopolies had no common spokesperson. Another fundamental problem was that no institution existed in which privileged groups could negotiate with one another or with the groups excluded from power. Elias explains that the leading groups or monopoly elites of the regime had become imprisoned by the institutions that maintained their privileged positions. "Their incapacity to look at their own dysfunction, along with

---

[51]Elias, *Société de cour*, 52.

Louis XIV encouraged the formation of an elaborate and highly articulated distributional hierarchy. Alongside the pyramid of nobles, he constructed a pyramid of bourgeois offices, many bestowing nobility, that produced great rivalry among members of the elite. The nobles were further divided by rivalry between robe and sword. The nobility of the robe monopolized the hereditary civil offices in the superior courts. The nobles of the sword dominated rural property, owning special monopolies on peasant production and consumption, as well as monopolizing many posts in the army, the Church, and the diplomatic corps. The king maintained his distance from the two groups and exploited their rivalry to assert his own authority, which was enhanced by adherence to the principle that differences in rank depended ultimately on the king's discretion; he claimed the right to limit the mobility of his subjects no matter how powerful they were. As a further challenge to the old nobility's social status, the king sponsored many new monopolies on the kingdom's financial resources, the most important of which was tax farming.

The middle classes were as "eager to secure preferential treatment . . . as any noble to retain his privileges," Tocqueville noted.[49] At the summit of the post-feudal distributional hierarchy stood the tax farmers. Further down were the non-noble owners of offices, many of which bestowed fiscal privileges. These were followed by wealthy members of the bourgeoisie who possessed monopolies on production in the new trades, on procurement for the army, and in the international trading companies. Still lower down the chain were the guild masters granted monopolies on artisanal production.[50] The vast majority of the population, who could not play the rent-seeking game because they were unable to find an appropriate form of organization, were left out of this distributional hierarchy. Peasants were by far the largest segment of this group.

The redistributive tradition consummated by the reforms of Louis XIV transformed economic and social organization into a zero-sum game. In economic life, a zero-sum mentality was fostered by mercantilism, which assumes that the total sum of wealth cannot be increased. Since one individual's gain was another's loss, mercantilism incited social resentment. The political system provided a strong incentive for merchants to seek excess profits through rent seeking. Merchants during the Old Regime invariably professed to be free traders, except when it concerned the restrictions on trade that protected them. As for the guilds, the zero-sum

---

[49]Ibid., 136.
[50]Like the other privileged groups, the Catholic Church, too, had its monopoly: that over belief. In exchange for tax exemptions, the Church supported absolutism, giving its benediction to divine right monarchy.

234 / *Hypotheses and Conclusions*

According to Norbert Elias, the fragmentation of society into self-regarding groups was a deliberate consequence of royal policy.[46] Louis XIV initiated the policy to prevent a collusion of social forces that could pose a threat to the monarchy. As a child, Louis XIV had observed that, when able to surmount their aversion for each other, the nobility of the sword and the magistrates of the robe could join forces and challenge the king. To prevent a repeat of rebellions such as the Fronde, Louis attempted to use social stratification and the control over definitions of social mobility as instruments of domination. He consciously cultivated the differences between orders and social levels and established court etiquette that reinforced the differences.[47] To establish the primacy of vertical ties to the Crown, the French monarchy systematically promoted mutual distrust among the kingdom's elites so that the Crown was the arbiter of disputes and information.

Tocqueville pointed out that members of the landed nobility were the first victims of the Crown's effort to become the sole determinant of social status. The Crown ruled that a royal charter was needed to bestow nobility on a family regardless of its status in provincial society; even the most notable families had to show justification of their titles and privileges. To accommodate the king, many noble families had to purchase titles to permit them to enjoy the privileges they were accustomed to exercising by tradition. Louis XIV invited the great families of the realm to Versailles, where court life became an elaborate ritual of hierarchy, in which the privileged few could carry the king's candle to bed, hand him his spoon at dinner, and carry his nightshirt to his dressing room. Underlying the ritual lay fierce competition for sinecures, posts in the army and in the church, and, occasionally, access to commercial or industrial patents of monopoly and shares in the tax farms. Consumed by the competition for access to the spoils of government, the nobility lost the habit of thinking of society as a whole, or of leading society. Partly in consequence, the nobles, who were among absolutism's first victims, were similarly to be among the first victims of the Revolution.[48]

---

outpouring of publications to commemorate the Revolution's 200th anniversary, I know of no article or book that addresses the reasons of the Old Regime's sudden collapse. Yet recent history, the fall of the Marcos regime in the Philippines and that of the shah of Iran, suggests that the sudden collapse of an authoritarian regime merits direct scholarly attention.

[46]Norbert Elias, *La Société de cour*, trans. Pierre Kamitzer (Paris: Calmann-Levy, 1974).

[47]Montesquieu too saw the Crown's ability to manipulate social stratification as a key to the success of absolute government in France.

[48]Tocqueville, *The Old Regime and the French Revolution*, 86.

generated a greater public awareness of, and commitment to, the political process.[44]

## CRONYISM AND THE FALL OF THE OLD REGIME

Tocqueville was one of the few writers on the French Revolution to ask why the Old Regime collapsed so suddenly. Why did the elites who enjoyed its many benefits not come to its defense in its hour of need? He sought the answer in an analysis of the links between the administrative traditions of the Old Regime and the revolutionary condition that caused its demise. Tocqueville speculated that the Old Regime's administrative traditions had split society up into "small, isolated, self-regarding groups." This fragmentation, Tocqueville believed, was responsible for what he considered to be one of the three great anomalies leading to the outbreak of the French Revolution—namely, why the monarchy, which had weathered so many storms in the past, collapsed so suddenly and catastrophically.[45]

---

[44]Individuals in both England and France sought public knowledge in order to enjoy private advantage. Government remained arcane, obscure, and private in France, whereas in England, information about it was more widely available. The larger the governing circle, the more difficult it is to guard secrets. In the seventeenth century, few government papers or committee reports were available to the public in England. By the early eighteenth century, a journal called the *Votes*, intended initially for the MPs, was being distributed to the general public (a thousand copies were sold). It provided only a minimum of information, but other sources became available in the 1740s, when journals previously available only in manuscript were published. After 1767, the publication of a separate series of collected parliamentary reports appeared while Parliament was actually in session. See Brewer, *Sinews of Power*, 227. Interested parties in England thus had access to material for which there was no equivalent in France, where such information had to be secured through family membership.

Information about government is one of cronyism's greatest enemies. One reason the much greater cronyism of the late seventeenth century had less direct consequences for the duration of ministerial tenures was that little information was publicly available. The governing circle was much narrower and more tightly drawn during the seventeenth as compared to the eighteenth century. The greater role of the *parlements* during the late eighteenth century also contributed significantly to the dissemination of information about cronyism. In fact, the *parlements* may have exaggerated the venality of eighteenth-century ministers to a public whose tolerance of cronyism had fallen. An understanding of the growing intolerance of cronyism and an insistence on distinguishing the private from the public were essential to the development of a democratic culture in early modern France and England.

[45]Alexis de Tocqueville, *The Old Regime and the French Revolution* (1856; New York: Anchor Books, 1955). The other two main aims of Tocqueville's study were to explain why the Great Revolution appeared first and foremost in France and secondly why the Revolution "presented itself as an almost natural outcome of the very social order it made such haste to destroy." Oddly, the third question has received the least attention from scholars of the French Revolution. In the great

flict and compromise in which various interested parties participated. An important feature of that process, lacking in France, was the ability of parties to negotiate and trade votes and rights directly. Vote trading did not necessarily lead to more efficient economic decisions, but it did lead to greater stability, which is, after all, an important component of growth. One of absolutism's greatest failures was its inability to discriminate between public expenditure and the private purses of the king and his financial officials; conversely, this distinction was one of Parliament's greatest successes. The French royal administration was open to the constant suspicion of malfeasance by the public. The English political system took an additional step forward in combining the needs of social with economic modernization by providing participation beyond the village and beyond the clan to social groups throughout the social hierarchy and the kingdom. Finally, the party organization generated by Parliament allowed more general interests to transcend those of individual, family, and clan.[41] Parliament was thus able to claim more credibly than the institutions of French absolutism that its interests were the public interest, and, as a result, it was able to "increase the mutual trust prevailing at the heart of the social whole."[42]

Lacking a commitment to broad philosophical ideals, however, eighteenth-century English politics often seems less innovative than French politics. The edicts of French kings often took the form of philosophical treatises articulating abstract rights and policies, in which the public interest was stated in ideal values such as natural law, justice, or right reason. Rooted in issues of immediate concern, English political debates were focused on remedies to particular problems rather than on the platitudes about free markets characteristic of French edicts and legislative processes.[43] Similarly, the programs of English political parties had little to offer in the way of philosophical merit, although perhaps more to offer as a source of practical enthusiasm. One could identify oneself as a Tory or a Whig without subscribing to an abstract philosophy. Even though the issues that dominated parliamentary debates were narrow, they may have

---

[41]Even J. H. Plumb, who emphasizes the clannish and factional nature of English politics, concludes: "Both houses of Parliament contained a number of pressure groups, bound closely by family as well as political ties. Their attempts to secure or retain office clutter the history of the eighteenth century with trivial detail and obscure the deeper issues which were involved" (*England in the Eighteenth Century*, 41).

[42]Bertrand de Jouvenel, *Sovereignty: An Inquiry into the Political Good* (Chicago: University of Chicago Press, 1957), 123.

[43]The petitions from the provincial *parlements* and estates to the king were encased in abstractions about rights and principles of economics.

government credibility in the long run, they undermined their power.[38] With the council's demise, the monarchy was left with no single institution that could be identified with the national interest.

With the goal of promoting modernization, the defenders of absolutism rejected parliamentary government to avoid the patronage, influence peddling, and compromise they thought were characteristic of party politics. France's bureaucratically organized system of governance, with its differentiated structure and merit system of promotion, was, they believed, a more logical and efficient tool for implementing modernization. However, the French kings' efforts to insulate government from social forces made their government less stable than the parliamentary system they eschewed.

Contrary to the hopes and predictions of its advocates, absolutism did not facilitate social and economic change; instead, it resulted in cronyism. The distribution of rents on the basis of personal loyalty prevents conflicts from being mediated and thus produces pressures for constant changes in regime. Moreover, the role of discretionary government in promoting cronyism prevented the emergence of more abstract and universal loyalties to the state.[39] The power of the unelected executive branch of the French government to redistribute the national income to private individuals made the Old Regime prone to revolutionary upheaval.[40]

Although Old Regime centralization in France exhibits many important features of political modernization, particularly structural differentiation and the rationalization of authority, it seems that England's more pluralistic and feudal polity was more flexible. That greater adaptability had several facets. Being less capable of supporting commercial or industrial monopolies and of disbursing sinecures and pensions to particular families, parliamentary regulation did not encourage internecine rivalries between elite clans. Parliamentary decisions were the outcomes of a process of con-

---

[38] One consequence of too much discretion concentrated in a single place was ministers who were cut off from discussion and debate with their colleagues.
[39] Joseph Strayer remarks that the most important test of the development of the state occurs when there is "a shift in loyalty from family, local community, or religious organization to the state and the acquisition by the state of a moral authority to back up its institutional structure and its theoretical legal supremacy. At the end of the process, subjects accept the idea that the interest of the state must prevail, that the preservation of the state is the highest social good. But the change is usually so gradual that the process is hard to document; it is impossible to say that at a certain point on the time scale loyalty to the state becomes the dominant loyalty" (*On the Medieval Origins of the Modern State* [Princeton: Princeton University Press, 1970], 9–10; for his definition of the state, see 3–19).
[40] See Hernando De Soto, *The Other Path* (New York: Harper & Row, 1989), 189–231.

of England, then, suggests that political development does not necessarily mean rational, honest government.[35] Nor does the prevalence of corruption suggest the absence of a "developed" society.[36]

## POLITICAL STABILITY IN ENGLAND AND FRANCE

Despite its commitment to national goals and to drawing politics out of the decision-making process, the French legislative system had the reverse effect. Although committed to the rationalization of authority, Crown policies intensified government dependence on clique and family. The new elite of civil servants of the French bureaucracy was caught up in the clientele and patronage systems of the past. Instead of regional integration, absolutism embedded regional privilege. Instead of promoting national consensus, the political process in France intensified mistrust and hostility among conflicting groups. Groups clung to their particular privileges because there was no open format to trade privileges and rights with other regions or groups.[37] Thus, the institutions of absolutism did not meet the needs for personal identity, social welfare, and social advancement created by the century's rapid economic development, greater wealth, and broader markets.

Louis XIV made an effort to identify the interests of the nation with the King's Council, which acquired its legitimacy as an embodiment of the national will during his reign. By the late eighteenth century, however, the King's Council had become a fiction. Once denied the veneer of disinterest provided by the notion that government decisions originated in council, government actions seemed less legitimate, since they appeared to express the will of an individual rather than an institution. By establishing their autonomy and independence from the council, the king's ministers may have increased their authority in the short run, but by weakening

---

[35] One of the most unstudied topics in European economic history is how the corrupt state was changed into a strong, uncorrupt liberal state. How were morals strengthened in the higher strata? How did the elites of Victorian England come to internalize conceptions of public interest? One element of this change was the transformation of customary bribes into legalized fees. John Brewer suggests that an open political culture that internalized integrity was perhaps being nurtured in eighteenth-century England; the outcome was "the creation of sophisticated 'interests' whose political conduct was, in turn, informed by the open and accountable political system in which they operate" (Brewer, *The Sinews of Power: War, Money, and the English State, 1688–1783* [New York: Knopf, 1989], 249).

[36] Scholars are much further from possessing a standard of political development or modernization than they are from a common definition of economic development.

[37] Despite the East India Company's strong webs of patronage, Pitt's reforms subjected the company to greater government regulation in 1784.

because elements of centralization and decentralization were not coordinated. The absence of facilities for bilateral and multilateral bargaining among different social and political units was to prove fatal.

Having placed all power to settle disputes in the hands of the king, the Old Regime did not develop institutions capable of supporting the complex bargaining needed to adjudicate differences among competing interest groups. As Talleyrand put it: "France seemed to be made up of a certain number of societies with which the government bargained. In this way, it kept each one under control using the credit that it had. Then the government turned to another, dealing with it in the same way. How could such a state of things continue?"[33]

The practice of resolving conflicts by separate negotiations with each group was inadequate in 1789 when the complexity of the trading necessary to achieve parity among the various groups required face-to-face negotiations among those groups.

## CORRUPTION AND MODERNIZATION

As argued in chapter 3, one of the crucial distinctions between English and French modernization is that between corruption and cronyism. Corruption is a competitive form of rent seeking, while cronyism is a monopolistic form. Cronyism throve in France because of the French king's relatively unrestricted power to allocate favors to his supporters. We tend to view both as economically wasteful, politically destabilizing, and destructive of government capacity. Yet in chapter 7 we saw that corruption may not necessarily be a hindrance to economic growth and progressive social change. It contributed to the decline of mercantilism in England and may also have had positive political consequences in helping to overcome divisions in the British ruling elite that might have otherwise produced destructive conflict.[34] Any English person possessing the capital could bribe an official, but to get the same advantages in France one needed connections, which presupposed family ties to influential courtiers. The history

---

[33]Talleyrand quoted in Jean-François Solnon, *La Cour de France* (Paris: Fayard, 1987), 523.

[34]The slow speed of parliamentary action may have increased the incentive for corrupt behavior. Analysts of political modernization in the developing world have observed that when officials attempt to avoid responsibility for policy decisions in a bureaucratic regime, corruption may help to cut excessive red tape. See Joseph S. Nye, "Corruption and Political Development: A Cost-Benefit Analysis," *American Political Science Review* 61 (1967): 417–27. Scholars have observed that corruption allowed European Jews to gain access to the political decisions necessary for them to provide their skills. Because of corruption, however, they were further isolated from the respect needed to enter the mainstream.

present in eighteenth-century France. Lacking, however, were the institutional mechanisms needed for complex, face-to-face bargaining among privileged members of the elites. Absolutism's greatest political achievement—the king as arbiter of conflict among groups and regions—prevented necessary, direct negotiations between groups and regions. Here again comparison with the parliamentarianism of England is particularly relevant. Parliament provided the English elites with the means to resolve conflicts such as the fiscal crisis caused by the American War. In fact, English elites took upon themselves a large share of the burden of paying for the war precisely to avoid precipitating a social crisis. Resolving the fiscal crisis within Parliament, where the masses were not represented, prevented the mobilization of popular discontent and the creation of a general crisis. As a result, public disturbances in England, such as the frequent grain riots, did not have the same impact that disturbances had in France, where the regime was weakened by its inability to resolve the dispute among the elites and the provinces. The important point was that the political machinery available to the British prime minister, William Pitt, allowed him to resolve England's fiscal crisis within the existing institutional structure. The French kings did not have the means to resolve the 1789 debt crisis without calling the Estates, drawing participants into a debate in which fiscal issues were secondary to social privilege.

The key component accounting for the British Parliament's contribution to eighteenth-century stability was not more democratic representation or more socially equitable policies than those emanating from the French executive. We have seen that in many respects Parliament offered public policies that were less democratic and less fair in their redistributive consequences than those issued by the French bureaucracy.[32] When comparing Old Regime England and France, the critical difference for stability goes beyond the extent of democratic consent or franchise to the mechanisms available to French elites to resolve the fiscal crises and implement complex, simultaneous bargaining among groups and regions. Absolutism represented a failure of bureaucratic administration

---

[32]It has not been the purpose of this analysis to assert that parliamentary regimes are inherently more stable than authoritarian regimes. The literature on stability and parliaments is in its infancy, and recent events in eastern Europe will certainly help expand it. Comparative history can make crucial contributions to the literature, but the key variables for such comparisons have yet to be identified. Although France was relatively democratic and had a national assembly in the nineteenth century, revolutionary turmoil occurred, and the ensuing Fourth Republic, also relatively democratic, was likewise unstable and unable to resolve crucial issues.

the Revolution, the masses of the people, and social issues more generally, are not emphasized. Instead, the analysis here concentrates on institutional arrangements and conflicts among elite groups. The bankruptcy of the state, which resulted in the loss of the central government's coercive capabilities, permitted popular unrest to snowball into revolutionary upheaval. What was unusual in 1789 was the state's inability to limit the impact of familiar outbreaks of collective resistance, such as grain riots. Access to or possession of resources, social solidarity, bargaining power, and perceptions of the probability of success all contributed to collective action. However, the inability to resolve the fiscal crisis with the available institutions for conflict resolution was crucial and becomes all the more striking when one considers how much the French elite had to lose if the crisis expanded to include the demands of the populace.

In *States and Social Revolutions,* Theda Skocpol presents a case for the causes of state breakdowns that parallels the argument being presented here. Skocpol argues that three of the great revolutions of modern times—the French, Russian, and Chinese—were precipitated by state breakdowns. In these revolutions, the state collapsed because internal contradictions prevented it from coping with exogenous shocks, such as the appearance of a dangerous military competitor. Unable to obtain political and economic concessions from dominant social groups, the autocracy fell apart, opening the way for social-revolutionary transformations, initiated by revolts from below. To explain the institutional rigidity and failure of the state-sponsored reform movements that often preceded state breakdowns, Skocpol focuses on "the political capacities of landed upper classes as these were shaped by the structures and activities of monarchical bureaucratic states."[31] Thus, in Skocpol's treatment, the law of increasing misery did not lead the exploited to overthrow the state. Misery and class conflict were endemic among pre-industrial popular classes. Anomic factors such as riots or demonstrations, Skocpol suggests, played their world historic revolutionary role only once the forces of state breakdown had materialized.

As we have seen in previous chapters, both the awareness that reform was necessary and the economic expertise to guide the reforms were

---

peasant collective action both before and during the Revolution, see Hilton L. Root, *Peasants and King in Burgundy: Agrarian Foundations of French Absolutism* (Berkeley and Los Angeles: University of California Press, 1987).
[31]Theda Skocpol, *States and Social Revolutions* (New York: Cambridge University Press, 1979), 47, 50.

the fact that English political parties paid for votes rather than extracting them by force, threat, or fraud may have advanced the cause of popular democracy.[28] The process of buying votes led to broader participation in politics and precipitated the breakdown of traditional family-based patronage systems. By reducing group pressures for policy changes, corruption tended to create stability. He who corrupts a judge or a customs official may identify with the institutions he is corrupting. That a landlord would expect his tenants to vote on his behalf might seem corrupt to us, but it was instrumental in creating political coherence in a traditional society. The handing out of bribes or local offices may have humanized the state for a village farmer, encouraging identification with the activities of the national government.[29] Electoral corruption permitted newly enfranchised groups to use their voting powers to acquire something useful, such as a job in the civil service. There was no similar method of bringing national politics into the small towns and villages of France. Participating in elections might make a wealthy peasant in England feel he had a role to play in the formation of the national government, but a village leader in France had no institutional link to the national policymaking process. He did not share the interests of the groups responsible for important national political decisions. To the extent that British elections offered concrete payoffs to participants, they may have generated more commitment to electoral procedures in national politics than in France.

Readers will observe that the French peasantry appears in only one of this book's chapters. Contemporary observers generally agreed that the peasantry bore the burden of absolutism but received few of the benefits. As a group, the peasants were organizationally too weak to impose demands for redistributive benefits upon the polity. It is also suggested in this analysis that the peasantry's direct influence on the outbreak of the French Revolution was less decisive than previous accounts have suggested.[30] Because of a focus on the fiscal crisis that precipitated

---

[28]See J. A. Phillips, *Electoral Behaviour in Unreformed England* (Princeton: Princeton University Press, 1982).
[29]Studies of contemporary American politics confirm this observation. David Mayhew reports candidates with bases in "the traditional parts of the old machine ... seldom take positions on anything (except for roll calls), but devote a great deal of time and energy to the distribution of benefits. On the other hand, congressmen with upper-middle class bases ... tend to deal in positions" (Mayhew, *Congress: The Electoral Connection* [New Haven: Yale University Press, 1974], 74).
[30]The French Crown's reinforcement of the village community resulted in a higher level of successful collective action by the peasantry in France than in England. For a discussion of how village communities in Burgundy provided a base for

the state, albeit fewer lasting loyalties among individual families.[26] Parliament was also a public forum for bargaining and compromise among groups with conflicting objectives. For example, pin makers and haberdashers might desire different import and export schedules. In Parliament they might be able to achieve a compromise and benefit from political decisions that accommodated the interests of both groups. In this sense, the possibility of face-to-face negotiating in Parliament created incentives for a pattern of political behavior that emphasized consensus over command in the resolution of conflicts. A more open and stable relationship among conflicting interests may have resulted, and a format for trading policy preferences allowed for gains from trade. Moreover, Parliament displayed the policy preferences of its constituents. The French Crown was constrained in its ability to determine the preferences of constituent groups, which is one reason the king focused on the interests of a few or one at a time. While negotiating in Parliament did not necessarily lead to more efficient economic outcomes, it reduced factional friction. A similar ability to aggregate interests and reconcile political differences was absent in the French polity.

As a way of understanding the different redistributive outcomes of parliamentary versus autocratic governments, we might reflect on the fact that to achieve redistribution, many more bargains have to be struck under a parliamentary than under an autocratic regime. As a result, the potential net return to an interest group is lower, because the cost of passing the necessary regulations will consume many of the potential rents. In other words, the transaction costs of acquiring monopolies are higher under a parliamentary regime, so that potential returns on rents are lower. This, however, may not necessarily reduce the lobbying activity among pressure groups and may expand the numbers of participants, lowering the cost to any one participant.

## PARLIAMENT, THE PEOPLE, AND STABILITY

The high point of corruption in English public life is generally considered by English historians to have occurred during the eighteenth century.[27] Most notable was widespread electoral corruption. Ironically,

---

[26]Mark Granovetter, "The Strength of Weak Ties," *American Journal of Sociology* 78 (1973): 1360–80.
[27]Corruption has not escaped the attention of English historians. See, e.g., Hurstfield, *Freedom, Corruption and Government*; Linda Levy Peck, "Corruption and Political Development in Early Modern Britain," in *Political Corruption: A Handbook*, ed. Arnold J. Heidenheimer, Michael Johnston, and Victor T. Levine (New Brunswick, N.J.: Transaction Publishers, 1989).

Whereas MPs had to build coalitions with rival groups in order to be effective, French pressure groups could depend on their relations with the bureaucrats and ministers who were the direct decision makers. Linkages among French families and particular members of the bureaucracy or a ministry much more reliably secured preferential treatment than were efforts by English clans to influence parliamentary decisions. The nature of English parliamentary institutions made it more costly for networks of kin to use government regulations to divert income to family members.

By contrast with the disintegrative effects of exclusionary French-style cronyism, the parliamentary system of wealth redistribution may have had an integrative effect, extending benefits more broadly across the political elite. Although cliques and factions were equally active in the politics of both nations, the emergence of political parties in England had the effect of reducing the direct impact of cliques on policymaking.[24] As a result, the benefits of government economic regulation were divided among a wider elite, and the dissemination of spoils was not rooted in the kinship system. Because of this mutual trust and social cooperation, a well-developed sense of civic duty characterized the English ruling class. Parliament became the focal point of a civic community capable of both sustaining informal cooperation and uniting in the face of an outside threat. That unity was elevated to the status of a principle in the philosophy of Burke. Competitive rent seeking open to all members of the elite was the hallmark of this British civic tradition.

When compared to French absolutism, the British parliamentary regime seems to have been more capable of accommodating several of the political and social needs that arose during modernization. The greater accountability of the parliamentary regime provided the basis for a political culture that was more open to achievement-based, merit-oriented norms. These norms were more universalistic than those based on birth and political competition between competing clans characteristic of French court politics.[25] Broader access to political authority led to more abstract loyalties to

---

40). Although rarely accomplished in England, it was achieved on average every four years in eighteenth-century France.

[24]The emphasis on Tory survival and persistence in Linda Colley's *In Defiance of Oligarchy: The Tory Party, 1714–1760* (Cambridge: Cambridge University Press, 1982) corrects the earlier view that Tory influence died with the Hanoverian succession.

[25]Necker thus went back to the idea of using administrators who were *commis* and almost functionaries rather than royal officeholders who owned their offices. Necker brought about the victory of bureaucracy over aristocracy, yet the victorious bureaucracy was still staffed by clients devoted to patrons. See Mousnier, *Institutions of France*, 2:213.

associated with cronyism—political instability. Frustrated by their inability to gain access to rents, excluded groups may disrupt the political system by the dissemination of anti-government propaganda, vilification of regime leaders, palace coups, and finally revolution. The fall of *contrôleurs généraux* during the Old Regime can be understood as a series of palace coups. A cottage industry of regime vilifiers proliferated in France during the late eighteenth century, contributing to the impression of general moral decay and impending doom. The resulting increase in instability prejudiced investments in favor of short-term projects. Cronyism inflicted its greatest harm on the economy by shortening investment horizons.

In the standard economic models of rent seeking, the costs over time of different types of rent seeking are not considered. Nor do theoretical grounds exist to assign different welfare consequences to various forms of rent seeking, of which cronyism may be one. Standard economic arguments do not assume external effects on the political system: the political system continues as is despite the action of rent seekers. Although welfare differences between the results of different forms of rent seeking are not significant in a static economic sense, cronyism may be worse than other forms of redistribution because it undermines the political and legal system that makes economic trade possible. Welfare losses also occur when feasible trades are not consummated because individuals do not trust the justice system to enforce contracts.

## REDISTRIBUTION AND PARLIAMENT

English historians generally view eighteenth-century British politics as struggles between rival clans and families. Indeed, just as in France, English family groups coalesced around their chosen leader and jockeyed for control of the administration.[22] However, controlling the administration was not sufficient. Even a majority in Parliament was not a reliable instrument for redistributing the nation's income to one's friends and relations.[23]

---

[22]"Political society was, of course, extremely intimate and inbred and this, as well as the intrigue for place and the control of influence, led to the development of clans as well as factions," remarks J. H. Plumb. "For a member, like Joseph Ashe in 1710, to have fifty relatives who were MPs was a commonplace. At the head of clans there was usually a peer who aspired and intrigued for ministerial office, and his standing was measured by the number and reliability of the relatives he controlled" (Plumb, *England in the Eighteenth Century, 1714–1815* [Harmondsworth: Penguin Books, 1950], 41). Nevertheless, Plumb cautions there were deeper issues involved.

[23]Plumb explains how eighteenth-century politicians of the opposition might "exert all their skill to win over patrons of importance, then to provoke a ministerial crisis, and in the resulting intrigue to capture the treasury, a manoeuvre of great strategic and tactical complexity, frequently attempted and rarely achieved" (ibid.,

got which benefits. It became more difficult for the Crown to shroud its deals in secrecy during the eighteenth century. As wealth and education became more common among the population, more individuals felt excluded from the benefits. The growing sense of exclusion gave opposing groups specific grievances and a generalized sense of being deprived of access to power.

Where cronyism thrives, the decisive elites are loyal to particular ministers in power rather than to the regime itself. By contrast, the parliamentary pattern of redistribution, characterized by cooperation based on informal arrangements among interest groups, generates relatively greater legitimacy. The elite continues to benefit regardless of who comes to power, and as a result it remains more loyal to the regime. Parliament, an institution that could mediate conflicts between rivals in the competition for political and economic rents, was crucial to political stability in early modern England. Greater informal cooperation among political actors resulted. Greater stability allows for lower interest rates, which in turn result in a higher percentage of long-term as opposed to short-term investments, thus expanding the threshold of economic possibilities.

The different ways in which competition for rents were institutionalized under the two regimes generated important variations in economic performance. Under mercantilist regimes, government controls generated two basic economic costs: (1) deadweight losses from monopolies and inefficient regulations that prevented efficient allocation of resources through competition, and (2) rent-seeking costs incurred in the pursuit of monopolies or other redistributive benefits, whether by individuals or by groups. Rent-seeking costs reflect a net loss to society, inasmuch as resources are diverted from productive investments to rent extraction. In a world in which groups have to outbid one another to acquire rents or redistributive goods, rent-seeking costs might conceivably be greater than in an environment in which only a limited elite can acquire such goods. Thus, in the quest for redistributional goods, cronyism is not by definition more prone to economic waste (once the sunk costs of becoming a crony are taken into account) than is competition for rents under a parliamentary regime. In fact, cronyism may actually waste less social capital than competitive rent seeking under a parliamentary regime, because direct competition for rents is reduced. In short, when many groups are allowed to bid for rents, they may waste more total resources in pursuit of those rents than would be wasted under a regime that does not encourage competitive rent seeking. Hence, there may be less direct economic waste when only the relatives of a particular minister can obtain a particular monopoly or property right.

While excluded groups may expend resources unproductively in their pursuit of rents, there is another, perhaps more important, class of costs

sentiment among the losers. By splitting society into winners and losers, cronyism increased instability in the long run. A key appointment or a construction contract delivered to a family member had few systematic rules to follow.[20] Cronyism thus bore the threat of deteriorating into rivalry as disappointments led to internecine feuds. Court cases between rival clans of financiers fill the judicial archives of the Old Regime. To restrain the disruptive effects of court cases between rival financial clans, the king ruled that all cases concerning his finances had to be settled in his courts or council.[21] The emergence of collective liability for financiers was another means of restraining the effects of conflicts among financiers.

Cronyism at the highest levels of government was a potent source of resentment, which worked to undermine public support for the government. The activities of controllers general perceived as opportunistic, such as Desmaretz or Terray, left the nation feeling it had been looted. While reneging on commitments to creditors, officeholders, and bondholders, both controllers general and their cronies made fortunes that aroused enormous resentment among the general population and among the courtiers excluded from the governing clique. For the sake of the argument here, a distinction must be made between reneging—which was publicly mandated—and the private corruption of individual ministers. Despite his efforts at fiscal reform, Calonne was despised because he was thought to have lined his own pockets and those of his cronies. In contrast, although unpopular among many courtiers, Necker and Turgot enjoyed relative public support because they were viewed as incorruptible and above cronyism.

Although cronyism drew small influential groups together into networks of mutual interest and obligation, it also fostered a collective interest in maintaining secrecy and excluding outsiders. Feelings of exclusion were perhaps less widespread before Louis XIV brought the kingdom's elites to the court, where attention could be more closely focused on which groups

---

[20]Despite the relative infrequency of exchange between members of different clans, the dowry, by providing a permanent and significant bond, played a crucial role in maintaining intergenerational continuity within the elite. To further ensure the continuity of the elite, the dowry was exempt from legal seizure; in the case of bankruptcy it could not be assigned. The practice of giving dowries meant that the terms of exchange between families were worked out in advance. However, a transaction that cannot soon be repeated contains a strong incentive for parties to maximize returns as in a one-period game. Hence, while playing a critical role in maintaining stability, dowries could not ensure against the breakdown of cooperation among rival families.

[21]In England, by contrast, disputes concerning financiers could be settled by a theoretically independent judiciary.

out a publicly accepted constitution that defines the rights of subjects, each individual or subgroup has to determine the legal and moral boundaries of its relationship to the sovereign on its own. By contrast, the existence of a bill of rights allows aggrieved citizens to appeal to common principles in order to mobilize support, which in turn increases the likelihood of a collective response to violations of the rights of a few.[19] Because there was no universally acknowledged constitution in France, the Crown could violate the rights of the few without risking the ire of the many. The constraints on the Crown's behavior could then be set by the Crown's dependence on a particular group's support. Upon taking office, Louis XVI agreed to desist from arbitrary behavior, like declarations of bankruptcy and abrogations of habeas corpus. Nevertheless, subjects still feared the Crown's temptation to act in an arbitrary manner. As observed in chapter 8, despite the French Crown's claims to avoid arbitrary behavior in general, its promises were not seen as credible in the absence of binding institutions that could apply sanctions to the Crown. The perception that the Crown's incentive to protect its subjects' property was questionable made it more costly for the Crown to contract loans. The absence of a constitution also meant that the Crown could not be restrained from promoting preferred private interests at the expense of others. That no institutional mechanism existed to restrain the Crown from offering special privileges to clients and cronies increased divisiveness and resentment, thereby undermining the legitimacy of government.

## CRONYISM AND POLITICAL STABILITY

The prevalence of cronyism led to rivalry among potential recipients, to factional conflict, to grudging commitments from the winners, and to re-

---

(mimeo, Hoover Institution, Stanford University, July 1991), which forms the basis of the following discussion. Without a constitution, a sovereign could violate the rights of subsets of the society without fearing the loss of broad support. A constitution facilitates coordination of the separate judgments of a large body of individuals. The existence of a constitution increases the ability of citizens to consolidate reaction by increasing the possibility of reaching a collective judgment. Policing a sovereign is more difficult when disagreement arises over the constitutionality of an action. A constitution will also be less effective if it does not pertain to all citizens equally, since then the government can discriminate against minorities whose political support it does not need. For a copy of the British Bill of Rights, see E. N. Williams, *The Eighteenth-Century Constitution: Documents and Commentary* (New York: Cambridge University Press, 1960), 26.

[19]"Indeed, on close examination 'the constitution' resolves itself into no more than a large number of men making claims about what the constitution is," remarks J. C. D. Clark, who vehemently rejects the importance of the Constitutional Settlement of 1688 (*Revolution and Rebellion*, 90). Of course it is easier to agree on standards than to agree on how a standard applies to a particular issue at hand.

department; all sharing of authority stopped."[15] Michel Antoine has argued that the majority of decisions made by the finance ministry were not even reviewed by the controller general but were the products of a single intendant of finance acting on his own.[16] Roland Mousnier observes:

> During the seventeenth and eighteenth centuries we see a gradual intensification of processes which began in the preceding centuries and led to the development of absolutism, or, rather, to increasing bureaucratic centralism, which was confused with absolutism. We witness a gradual shift from orders issued as personal letters to orders couched in the form of anonymous memoranda, from authenticated open letters to sealed letters not authenticated by any regular procedure, from verification by the Grande Chancellerie to verification by specialized bureaus, and from decisions made in council, at least in principle, to more or less openly avowed individual decision-making.[17]

This discretion contrasted with the increasingly bureaucratic structure of authority required to manage government bureaus. In the absence of a set of predictable political procedures, the Crown's decisions seemed arbitrary.

Barry Weingast points out that in determining a citizen's or a parliament's judgment about the constitutionality of a government's behavior, the existence of a bill of rights, or lack thereof, can have an important influence on a society's capacity for collective action and resistance.[18] With-

---

[15] René-Louis d'Argenson, *Considérations sur le gouvernement ancien et présent comparé avec celui des autres états suivies d'un nouveau plan d'administration* 2d ed. (Amsterdam, 1784), 13, 163. Argenson's father (1652–1721) had been *lieutenant de police* of Paris and *garde de sceaux* during the reign of Louis XIV.

[16] As proof of how meetings of the council became a fiction, Antoine provides examples where over one hundred decisions were issued by the council on days when the council did not meet ("Monarchie absolue," 398).

[17] Roland Mousnier, *The Institutions of France under the Absolute Monarchy, 1598–1789: The Organs of State and Society*, trans. Arthur Goldhammer (Chicago: University of Chicago Press, 1979), 2:238. "During the two centuries we are examining, however, the number of orders issued under the secret seal or over the king's signature alone continued to increase, as did the importance of the subjects treated in this way; the form of these orders shifted from that of a letter to that of an official report. In other words, the work of government and administration was increasingly done not by councils but by individuals working alone in offices dealing individually with their subordinates and private individuals from whom they received information and to whom they issued orders. They examined the files and made decisions on their own. This was what the parlements characterized as 'ministerial despotism' " (ibid., 244).

[18] See Barry R. Weingast, "Institutional Foundations of the 'Sinews of Power': British Financial and Military Success Following the Glorious Revolution"

teenth century by inhibiting the association of universalistic, achievement-oriented norms with the state.[13]

Drawing the distinction between obligation to the state and obligation to family members, an important component of successful modernization, was further stymied by the official rhetoric of divine right monarchy. The king claimed the right to rule the state as a father would his family; the nation's resources were his patrimony. He further claimed not to be subject to human institutions.[14] Being above the law meant that contracts between the king and his subjects were difficult to enforce legally, creating additional risks for the government's creditors, an extra cost that revealed itself in the interest rates paid by the state when it attempted to contract loans or sell annuities. So long as the Crown's commitments were dependent upon its discretion alone, it could only reduce the cost of credit transactions and increase the amount of liquidity in the economy by depending on intermediaries. While the delegation of finance to corporate intermediaries expanded credit and liquidity in the economy as a whole, the property rights assigned to the groups restricted necessary institutional reforms.

Another area in which absolutism failed to provide the moral leadership essential in modernization involved the distinction between private and public expenditures. Ministers personally used a percentage of the funds they handled as the king's representatives. For example, an intendant might set aside public money for the marriage of his daughter. Failing to distinguish between private interests and public welfare, the government found it hard to mobilize confidence in its conduct of public business.

Public access to information about how government decisions were made and the economy was regulated was lacking in France. Ministerial discretion meant that each bureaucrat decided largely according to his own pleasure how to rule in the domain under his authority. Was it not France that Marquis René-Louis d'Argenson (1694–1757) referred to when he spoke of a monarchy "ruled by five or six ministers who act without agreement, and what is even worse, without knowing what the others have ordered, lacking familiarity with each other's principles and without knowing what has been prescribed"? Argenson viewed the king as responsible for this breakdown of cooperation between various members of the government; "Under Louis XIV our government was arranged according to a new system, the absolute discretion [*volonté*] of the ministers of each

---

[13]See Samuel Huntington, *Political Order in Changing Societies* (New Haven: Yale University Press, 1968), 32–39.
[14]Michel Antoine, "La Monarchie absolue," in *The Political Culture of the Old Regime*, ed Keith M. Baker (London: Pergamon Press, 1987), 3–24.

In England, offices were never for sale, yet political power could be bought by nouveaux riches (West Indies planters, Anglo-Indian nabobs). Paradoxically, in France one could literally buy an office, yet the offices did not bring political power; networks of connections and wealth were crucial in penetrating government bureaus.[12] While exercising absolute power in theory, in reality the most powerful individual in the French administration, the controller general, depended upon his personal connections with private networks of financiers for the funds needed to run the government. The success of absolutism in rewarding ministerial favorites engendered bitter rivalries among members of the elite and intensified resentment by dividing the decisive elites into winners and losers, ins and outs. Although the centralization of the French Old Regime reduced the cost of negotiating with the king, it increased the costs of negotiating among themselves for private groups.

Specifying the regime-specific variations in the institutionalization of competition for rents will help unravel some of these paradoxes.

## ABSOLUTISM, CRONYISM, AND THE FRENCH STATE AS AN ABSTRACTION

The lack of accountability of France's principal government officials permitted a system of patronage to develop in which narrow, redistributive coalitions flourished, held together by family ties (see chapter 8 for discussion of the economic logic of these connections). The king's ministers depended upon the loyalties of particular families, clans, or cronies, and, with few exceptions, were unable to generate broadly based national or public support. This reliance on familial loyalties during a period of rapid economic expansion split the society into groups that regarded one another with suspicion. When members of a society depend on marriage or close personal ties to finance their long-term investments, liquidity will be reduced, the number of transactions will be diminished, and economic activity will contract. In addition, the primacy of clique and family conflicted with political modernization and economic expansion during the eigh-

---

[12] The French monarchy created a political system that by comparison with England's did not allow new groups or interests to gain access to state power. The government's inability to assimilate Protestants was perhaps the most striking example of the closed character of the regime. Necker, despite his prominence in international banking circles and his appointment as financial minister, was barred from meetings of the king's council because he was not Catholic. Wealthy families could buy into the political sphere with the purchase of offices, but this means of accommodating new groups was inadequate. First, there were never enough offices. Second, the offices rarely carried real political or administrative authority.

roughly twenty months.[10] What had changed to account for the greater vulnerability of controllers general to "public opinion"? Especially curious is the fact that ministerial discretion increased at the very point when private groups seem to have captured the principal governmental bureaus, including finance.

In both nations, bribery and maneuvering behind the scenes pervaded government. Despite widely known corruption, however, the appearance of legitimacy had an important role in empowering the British Parliament, while the decisions that emanated from the French executive were perceived as illegal and corrupt, although the actual activities of the French ministers were hidden from the public eye and tangible evidence of government corruption was less abundant in France.

Tax policy too was riddled with paradoxes. The English were able to tax a larger percentage of national production than could the French. However, because much of the revenue raised by the English government came in the form of excise taxes and tariffs, the English complained less about the weight of taxes than did the French, who were taxed at proportionally lower rates.

Despite the tendency of the French elite to become more homogeneous in the late eighteenth century, rivalry still stifled the cooperation needed to make necessary reforms. Theoretically, all subjects were equal before the French king, yet decision-making power was circumscribed by cliques. Although the English elites were divided into interest groups, they were able to cooperate in achieving a parliamentary consensus on major policy issues. Relatively broad interests of the nation were more frequently represented in governmental decisions, because Parliament provided an institutional forum in which English interest groups could reach a consensus.[11]

---

[10]Turgot (1774–76), Clugny (May–October 1776), Taboureau des Réaux (October 1776–June 1777), Necker (1776–81), Joly de Fleury (1781–83), D'Ormesson (April–October 1783), Calonne (1783–87), Bouvard de Fourqueux (1787), Laurent de Villedeuil (1787), Lambert (1787–90), and we should also add Brienne, who had the power of controller general without the title from 1787 to August 1788, and Necker's second term in the office from September 1788 to September 1790. See Marcel Marion, *Dictionnaire des institutions de la France aux XVII$^e$ et XVIII$^e$ siècles* (Paris: A. Picard, 1923; repr., New York: Burt Franklin, 1968), 144.

[11]Even more curious, we learn from Michael W. McCahill that the House of Lords "often effectively represented the interests of localities and individuals despite the absence of a democratic mandate" (*Order and Equipoise: The Peerage and the House of Lords, 1783–1806* [London: Royal Historical Society, 1978]). Nevertheless, while arguing for their continued importance, McCahill does not see the lords as dominating the Commons.

dependent on one or two central agencies, so that the forces of political persuasion could more economically be focused on the appropriate central structure. Not only was power concentrated at the national center in Old Regime France; tasks within the central structure were also highly specialized. From the time when Louis XIV set the precedent of working independently with each ministry, thereby eliminating the threat of rivalry from a prime minister, the ministries grew ever more autonomous.[5] In the absence of a prime minister to coordinate all administrative affairs and implement consistent policies, the increasing autonomy of individual ministries meant an increasing susceptibility to the campaigns of pressure groups such as the financiers. This increasing susceptibility in turn reduced the security of ministerial tenure. Louis XIV never dismissed a minister on account of public opinion and hoped to endow his successors with the institutional means to resist similar pressures.[6] Yet less than fifty years later, Louis XV remarked, "I appoint the controller general; public opinion dismisses him."[7] During his fifty-four-year reign, Louis XIV had five controllers general, which averages out at almost eleven years per minister, each of whom either died in office or left of his own will.[8] By contrast, nine controllers general were appointed between 1745 and the death of Louis XV in 1774, averaging just over three years per ministry.[9] From the beginning of Louis XVI's reign to the calling of the Estates General, there were ten finance ministers, the average length of service dropping to

---

*Governmental Politics,* ed. Fred I. Greenstein and Nelson W. Polsby (Reading, Mass.: Addison-Wesley, 1975), 171–228.

[5] As an example of how the principle of absolutism was passed down through the administrative hierarchy, Alfred Cobban tells how Louis XV found cabriolets in the streets of Paris disruptive. "If I were Lieutenant of Police I would ban cabriolets," he said; but, Cobban continues, "he was merely king, and his only sanction was to dismiss an official who refused to carry out his wishes" (Cobban, *A History of Modern France, 1715–1799* [Harmondsworth: Penguin Books, 1957], 1:30).

[6] Before Louis XIV there was considerable ministerial instability. On the campaign of opposition to d'Hemery and the campaign for the restoration of La Vieuville, at the beginning of and during the Fronde, see Richard Bonney, *The King's Debts: Finance and Politics in France* (Oxford: Clarendon Press, 1981).

[7] Antoine-Jean-Baptiste Robert Auget de Montyon, *Particularités et observations . . . depuis 1660 jusqu'en 1791* (Paris: Le Normant, 1812), 388.

[8] Colbert (1661–83), Le Pelletier (1683–89), Phelypeaux (1689–99), Chamillart (1699–1708), and Desmaretz (1708–15). Considerable uncertainty surrounds the departure of Chamillart, who claimed to have left of his own will. Significant changes occurred after his departure, suggesting that he may have been prompted to leave the finance ministry. He did, however, remain in the government.

[9] Machault d'Arnouville (1745–54), Moreau de Séchelles (1754–56), Peirenc de Moras (1756–57), Boullongne (1757–59), Silhouette (March–November 1759), Bertin (1759–63), L'Averdy (1763–68), Mayon d'Inmvau (1768–69), Terray (1769–74).

redistribution that flourished in England to a much greater extent than in France. Although both political systems produced socially inequitable outcomes, important differences between the two nations' political institutions led to differences in political stability.

## A COMPARISON RICH IN PARADOX

The contrast between the French and English systems of government is rich in paradox. In France, discretion was concentrated in several government bureaus with highly differentiated functions. The French ministers were empowered to make wholesale reforms but could not remain in office once their zeal for reform was revealed. In England, power was dispersed in Parliament, where reforms could be blocked at many levels, yet adjustments were enacted with greater success than in France. Moreover, legislation enacted by Parliament was usually implemented, whereas the will of the much stronger executive in France was less frequently carried out. A significant implementation gap existed under absolutism. The king issued edicts pertaining to the entire nation, and instruments of coercion were mobilized, but the Crown's subordinates, even those directly subject to absolutism's command structure, did not implement reforms that conflicted with short-term tax collection. There were no legal limits on the French king's power or, by extension, that of his ministers, yet time and time again his ministers succumbed to cabals within the court, instrumented by individuals and groups that possessed no legal or formal means of influencing government decisions. In England, the king, and by implication the executive, admitted that "we at no time stand so highly in our estate royal as in the time of parliament."[2] Despite the legal limits on the Crown's power imposed by Parliament, the English king managed to maintain his position and policies. It seemed to many contemporaries that George III's ministers were more powerful and more likely to be obeyed than the unaccountable and theoretically stronger ministers of the French king.[3]

In contrast to those in England, French lobbyists could take a far more streamlined course.[4] A client of the French government might be wholly

---

[2]Joel Hurstfield, *Freedom, Corruption and Government in Elizabethan England* (Cambridge, Mass.: Harvard University Press, 1973), 43. Margaret Levi makes this same point in *Of Rule and Revenue* (Berkeley and Los Angeles: University of California Press, 1988), 95–144.
[3]This perception underlies the revisionist writings of J. C. D. Clark, *Revolution and Rebellion: State and Society in England in the Seventeenth and Eighteenth Centuries* (New York: Cambridge University Press, 1986), 68–91, 120–63.
[4]For a summary of the political science literature on interest group behavior, see Robert H. Salisbury, "Interest Groups," in *Handbook of Political Science: Non*

# 10 Modernization, Revolution, and the State

One of the underlying intuitions of this analysis is that the ability of a society to develop mechanisms that institutionalize trust, credibility, and monitoring is critical to the process of modernization. Such institutions are necessary to sustain intertemporal trades in both political and economic markets.[1] We shall now set aside consideration of the economic institutions necessary to achieve growth and concentrate on political institutions and practices. The ability of an economy to encourage the investment needed to sustain long-term economic growth ultimately depends on the sustainability of political contracts. If each new prince or minister overturns the contracts of his predecessor, a society will sustain only short-term investments, and economic growth will be stifled.

In both France and England in the early modern period, private groups benefited from the use of political means to redistribute the nation's income, inasmuch as the principal governing institutions became centers for the disbursement of patronage. In France, the principal redistributive mechanisms were tax farming, the granting of industrial and commercial monopolies to preferred businesses, and the distribution of sinecures, army commissions, and procurement contracts to preferred courtiers.

Redistribution of France's income was carried out by the executive authority of the King's Council, whose functional counterpart in England was Parliament. Parliamentary redistribution, by contrast, benefited more broadly defined social groups than those relatively smaller clans in France clustered around individual ministers. Corruption was another form of

---

[1]*Intertemporal* refers to trade that requires trust between parties who come together for the sole purpose of trade. Public goods needed to sustain trade include institutions that ensure contract enforcement by a neutral third party, such as a judicial system independent of political authority.

# 5
## HYPOTHESES AND CONCLUSIONS

best-informed with the most foresight, it seemed that French kings were in a far better situation than the English. The French financiers had cultivated all the trappings of solidity and permanence; they built the most ostentatious quarters in the most fashionable sections of the capital and behaved as if they had been around since the beginning of the monarchy, marrying into the most illustrious and oldest of France's noble families. Nevertheless, possessing new fiscal technology, Britain's financial system rapidly shifted the ground beneath what seemed to be one of Europe's most enduring edifices—the French fiscal establishment.

Competition between France and the other European states was critical in precipitating the preferences for institutional change within France. The decentralized competition among European states dramatically rewarded nations for successful organizational innovations and just as dramatically penalized those nations whose organizational structure lagged. The rise of Britain's funded public debt presented an alternative that ultimately invalidated the French system. In the absence of a central authority that could impose uniform governance on the entire continent, there was no way to prevent an interloper from introducing a more efficient method of public finance that disrupted the entire international system. The diffusion of diverse fiscal institutions among rival European states meant that the splendid structure built by the Old Regime kings had to be torn down. It was invalidated by an upstart, Britain, which during the seventeenth century had hardly seemed worth taking into account.

nation's debt. French kings recognized the need to develop more effective sources of credit because, during the eighteenth century, the ability to borrow at low cost had altered the proportion of national wealth needed to support the military force required by Europe's diplomatic and commercial rivalry.[72]

In effect, taking into account their preference for giving up as little control as possible, we can look on the Old Regime French kings as having created the most efficient system possible. Viewing monarchy as a firm, a king could obtain financing by issuing either debt or equity. If he issued debt and did not go bankrupt, he stayed in command. Using a parliament to finance the state is a way of creating equity, but it cedes control of the firm to the shareholders. This is in effect what happened in England, where the king, having lost control of the state to his shareholders, was put on salary. Considering the institutional constraints with which it was forced to comply, the English monarchy had reached the limit of its ability to raise funds on its own; the constitutional crisis and defeat in the Civil War that ensued left the Crown with no alternative but to increase equity. The French king was more successful, in that he did not have to convoke a representative body; increasing his debt rather than his equity allowed him to stay owner of the firm. To seventeenth-century observers, even the

---

[72]The thesis of this chapter is neatly summarized by Jean-Baptiste Say, who wrote:

> Where power rests in the hands of a single man, the government has difficulty in enjoying great credit. It cannot offer the good will of the monarch for security. Under a government where legislative power rests in the people or in their representatives, one has an added guarantee; the interests of the people who are creditors as individuals and at the same time debtors of a nation, and who can only receive what is due them in their first role if it is paid in their second. This single consideration can lead one to presume that at a time when nothing great is achieved except at great cost, and when great costs can only be supported by loans, representative governments will make marked progress in the political system (in Europe, in general) because of their financial resources, independent of all other circumstances.
>
> (Say, *Traité d'économie politique*, 2:526–27)

For an example of the credit advantages of parliaments, see James D. Tracy, *A Financial Revolution in the Habsburg Netherlands: Renten and Rentiers in the County of Holland, 1515–1565* (Berkeley and Los Angeles: University of California Press, 1986). Tracy contrasts the insolvent Spanish Crown's dependence on enormous short-term debts at high interest rates with the Dutch system based on long-term loans guaranteed by public authorities. The Dutch withstood the superior resources of Philip II's Spain because they could borrow at moderate interest rates a sum equivalent to twelve times their annual revenue. A representative assembly of the county (the Estates of Holland) accepted collective responsibility for the loans and voted taxes on which the loans were secured.

law, the delegates transformed the political debate and set the stage for drastic solutions. Ducloz-Dufresnoy accurately depicted the danger in a pamphlet entitled *Jugement impartial sur les questions principales qui intéressent le tiers-état* [An Impartial Assessment of the Third Estate's True Interests], in which he cautions the third estate to avoid "the dangerous principles in the works lately published." The only issues the third estate should discuss with the privileged orders were "the subsidies or impositions necessary to restore public order, the choice of impositions, the manner of distributing them and the rules needed to ensure that their proper use is respected." Concentrate on consolidating the nation's debt and respect the fundamental order of the kingdom, he cautioned. Raising the question of legal equality would invite disaster.[70]

Louis XVI's vacillating character must bear some of the blame for the Crown's failure to resolve the fiscal crisis before it provoked a social revolution. The king seemed incapable of making a decision or of taking a position. Under pressure he abandoned each one of his ministers, undermining his own credibility and that of the negotiating process. At several stages of the crisis a more decisive king might have imposed a settlement.

While the personalities involved played a role, the evolution of financial intermediation, the technology of contractual relations in Old Regime France, followed a generally consistent pattern. Under the Old Regime an important constraint on the expansion of state power and economic growth was the need to devise institutions that could restrain and compensate for the Crown's discretionary authority over fiscal and monetary policy. The need to design mechanisms to enforce commitments—to make the government's repayment promises credible—was the driving force behind the evolution of corporate institutions (see chapter 8). A regime of privileged corporations throve under absolutism and had the effect of economizing on the costs of gaining credible commitments from the monarchy.[71] Parliamentary institutions eventually replaced the institutions of absolutism because they made possible credible commitments from government at an even lower cost to the general population. Expanding upon this insight offers a possible explanation for the French Crown's inability to negotiate a peaceful transition from corporate to parliamentary management of the

---

[70]Charles Nicole Ducloz-Dufresnoy, *Jugement impartial sur les questions principales qui intéressent le Tiers-Etat* (Paris: Chez Clousier, 1788). BN, L39b 762. Citing Montesquieu, he reminds the third estate not to lose sight of the nobility's role of defending the nation from the despotism of ministers.

[71]Depending on one's point of view, the entire system of financial intermediation developed by the Crown can be viewed as either a transaction cost or an economizer of transaction costs. On transaction costs, see Oliver E. Williamson, *The Economic Institutions of Capitalism* (New York: Free Press, 1985).

irritated an even smaller percentage of the assembly members' constituents. Aftalion also reports that certain deputies considered that the continued existence of the king's debts would highlight the Crown's dependence on the Constituent Assembly and thus reinforce its power. He speculates that perhaps only the desire not to let the Crown off the hook for its previous engagements prevented the deputies from indulging in their hostility to the world of high finance.[69]

## CONCLUSION

Because the French king could not solve the nation's fiscal problems, he ended up with a social crisis. By calling the Estates General, the king invited individuals into the political debate for whom fiscal and economic matters were secondary. In the king's address to the Constituent Assembly, he emphasized the need to settle the fiscal crisis. However, social and legal inequalities seemed more pressing by far to the delegates. The very first question of importance discussed by the assembly, that of suffrage (vote by head or by order), was linked to legal and social status. Had the king acted earlier, he might have avoided such issues, and the reform of the nation's political institutions might have been guided by fiscal considerations.

The quest for equality before the law desired by many of the third estate's delegates and that of fiscal stability desired by the king and his ministers could have produced very different constitutional outcomes. Fiscal stability could have been achieved without broad democratic participation in the political process. Equality before the law could have been achieved without representative institutions. If the monarchy's political power had been absolute in reality, it might have been able to complete the social and legal revolution it had begun without making political concessions to either the elites or the populace. The Crown, however, was too dependent on the financiers to steer an independent course, and too dependent on the sale of privilege to establish the principle of the equality of all citizens before the law. Instead, the Crown reinforced privilege and inequality by exchanging tax-exempt offices for short-term revenue. The assembly's efforts to unravel the web of privilege and exemptions woven by the Crown led to increasingly radical measures. In one sense, the French Revolution began once the debate in the assembly shifted from fiscal to social and juridical reform. Introducing the issue of equality before the

---

[69]Florin Aftalion, *L'Economie de la Révolution française* (Paris: Hachette, 1987), 84–85. In May 1794, thirty-six *fermiers généraux* were arrested; twenty-eight of them were subsequently executed. Their estates were confiscated for the benefit of the Republic. See also Chaussinaud-Nogaret, *Financiers de Languedoc*, 266.

*fermiers généraux* opposed such measures, and they were not alone in their hostility to them. As already noted, the unification of the Treasury under the Crown's direction did not appeal to the Assembly of Notables. Who could trust greater centralization if it were carried out under the auspices of a king whose principal ministers were viewed as rogues? Informed members of the public insisted on the need to subject economic policy to public discussion and to design institutions that would limit the Crown's discretion in matters of finance.[66]

Restricting the king's control over government finance was one of the first and most consistently implemented reforms carried out by the Revolutionary government. From the outset of the Revolution, the Constituent Assembly fought the Crown for control of government finance.[67] It set up the Treasury as an alternative to the Department of Finance, which remained under the king's control. On July 17, 1790, the assembly transferred to the Treasury the government bureaus authorized to make payments, so that the Department of Finance could no longer distribute funds without the assembly's jurisdiction. By the autumn of 1790, the assembly's Committee on Finance assumed full control over the nation's finances by dismantling the Department of Finance. As a final step toward the establishment of full legislative control over the Treasury, the assembly suppressed the Chamber of Accounts by decrees of September 17 and 29, 1791. The Crown was left with virtually no leverage over state finances.[68]

This concern to assume control over the nation's finances was not matched by a concern for responsible finance. Before embarking on a course of monetary irresponsibility, many of the representatives in the Constituent Assembly argued that bankruptcy was a socially equitable solution to the nation's fiscal problems. The comte de Mirabeau argued eloquently that only a minority of the population, the rich, would be affected. Many in the assembly, like Mirabeau, reasoned that a bankruptcy would only fall on the rich, since they held the debt. Bankruptcy further presented itself as way of settling scores with the capitalists for their past sins and excessive profits. Why not sacrifice this minority for the good of the larger number? Florin Aftalion speculates that bankruptcy was avoided because the creation of the *assignat* offered a politically safer solution: it

---

[66] An extensive pamphlet literature proliferated during the 1780s that solicited public support against the threat of an impending royal bankruptcy. Brissot, Clavière, and Mirabeau were noted authors of such pamphlets.

[67] Contemporaries often referred to the Constituent Assembly as an "assembly of the nation's shareholders."

[68] See Charles Gomel, *Histoire financière de l'Assemblée constituante* (Paris: Guillaumin, 1896).

Finance ministers could not be expected to pursue policies that would terminate the financiers' control over the nation's financial system without sacrificing their ability to act as intermediaries between the financiers and the king. At best, the so-called reforming ministers wanted only to increase royal control over the financiers. Even these controls were too radical to sell to their financial constituencies. The financiers opposed efforts at fiscal centralization because they considered it essential to conserve their personal discretion and to maintain secrecy in their affairs. Nor did they want the assets that they possessed in the form of offices to be terminated. Over the course of the eighteenth century, the syndicate of *fermiers généraux* had increased in independence and strength because greater public confidence in the tax farms increased their ability to borrow from the public. Because the Crown depended on the syndicate's advance payments on tax-farming contracts, the syndicate had sufficient leverage to prevail against government efforts to centralize finance.[65] As administrators of indirect taxes, the farmers general supplied the French government with more than 40 percent of its operating capital. By threatening to withhold advances and keeping monthly payments low, the farmers general could undermine public confidence in state credit. The leverage of this group prevented the Crown from pursuing radical reform.

In short, the irony of absolutism discussed in chapter 8 led to the demise of royal authority. Instead of creating institutions with which to negotiate for loans and taxes, the Crown circumvented public consent by relying upon private contracts with privileged special interest groups. Now the fiscal foundations of the Crown's absolute authority, its ability to rule without the consent of its subjects, was jeopardized by some of the very financiers and corporations it had used to evade direct accountability to the nation's creditors. The financial interests and groups that the king had built up were strong enough to block reforms that threatened their profits or their control over the kingdom's financial system. Financial families and corporations would not surrender the privileges they enjoyed without compensation. By threatening to withdraw financial support, they left the Crown with no alternative but to call the Estates General. The Crown was thus the victim of the very groups it had cultivated in order to avoid consulting with its subjects on fiscal policy.

The Crown's hopes of resolving the fiscal crisis by establishing greater central control over financial contracts were doomed from the start. The

---

[65]The *fermiers généraux* were not all-powerful. They could not prevent the government from attempting to eliminate internal tolls.

unified state budget would have been to increase the royal treasury's central control over finance. With the exception of Necker, none of the controllers general who served the Crown in the decade before the Revolution attempted to terminate the system of basing public credit on the private resources of the financiers entirely.[61] When Necker was replaced as controller general by Joly de Fleury (1781–83), the latter reported to the king on the need to reestablish the system of financiers that Necker had attempted to eliminate. He claimed that the public would not be well served by salaried officials, who "guided by no personal interest are less zealous in their work." Fleury insisted that the Crown was having difficulty raising funds because "the twelve administrators who were substituted for the forty-eight Receivers General [by Necker] sign these rescriptions, it is true, but they are not the guarantors of them. The people who lend their money want to have a rich guarantor behind the rescriptions."[62] Louis XVI's controllers general, including Calonne, who replaced Fleury, believed that maintaining the confidence of the investing public was most reliably ensured by the personal wealth of the financiers. Calonne did not produce a plan to eliminate the system of *caisses* and financiers.[63] He believed in basing royal credit upon the private credit of the financiers and tax farmers, and that the state's credit needed to be supported by groups of separate financiers acting as private business agents.[64]

Insistence upon greater public control over spending was ignored by the king's advisers. With the exceptions of Necker and Brienne, controllers general were chosen because they were influential figures among the financiers. (Necker's influence was among bankers rather than financiers.)

---

[61]The absence of a central treasury and reliance on private resources are not the same. One can have a decentralized public system or centralized private system like that of England. The line between public and private is not as clear-cut as one would like to think. Even today the low rates available to the U.S. government are owing to the liquidity and underwriting services provided by private intermediaries, all of whom are well capitalized.

[62]Joly de Fleury quoted in Bosher, *French Finances*, 175. Bosher explains that the *taille* was collected by *receveurs*, venal officers pledged to disburse funds according to a fixed timetable. *Rescriptions*, claims made on the *receveurs*, were owed to the Treasury and due a year later. The Treasury could sell these claims at a discount for cash, and the money was at the *receveurs'* disposal for the year. In addition, *receveurs* collected a commission, or *taxation*, on the sums collected. The *taxations* issued by the Ferme générale under the name of *billets* were sometimes known as "anticipation notes." A floating debt was created by allowing these notes, for which the *receveurs* were personally responsible, to be used by the government.

[63]Bosher calls these individuals "accountants." In French they were called *comptables*, which meant simply that they were personally accountable for the management of the king's funds.

[64]For a discussion of Calonne's view of reform, see Bosher, *French Finances*, 215–30.

of the sacredness of property than were the actions of the Constituent Assembly.[60]

## THE FAILURE OF REFORM IN FRANCE

Despite the increased emphasis on corporate liability and public responsibility, secrecy continued to characterize the French financial system at the end of the Old Regime. The French controller general still did not have a complete picture of national finance, since there was no unified Treasury. The financiers still maintained personal and discretionary relationships with each other and with the public. Many were paid fees by members of the public whom they served or were entitled to a portion of the public's funds they handled; some were even expected to draw revenues from their private investment of public funds.

By contrast, the British Parliament in the eighteenth century demanded an annual budget from the king that anticipated all receipts and expenditures. Parliament could thus predict and control spending and find the means to meet the king's demands. One way for the French to achieve a

[60] A number of French authors have suggested an additional reason why the monarchy avoided bankruptcy in 1778–89: whereas in previous crises the Crown had been able to generate public support for persecuting the financiers and repudiating its debt, by the late eighteenth century a broad segment of the population had invested in government securities and had a stake in preventing a royal bankruptcy. A royal declaration of bankruptcy, Brissot de Warville observes in his pamphlet *Point de banqueroute*, would be especially disastrous for the poor. This broad participation in government finance is confirmed by the research of the historian Daniel Roche, who found government *rentes* mentioned in the wills of relatively modest Parisians: "Rentes can be found everywhere.... With estates between 500 and 3,000 livres, journeymen, assistants, casual and manual workers, valets, lackeys and servants all had government bonds. ... In short, the Parisian servant became a rentier very early, and the wage earner who had made his fortune quickly followed suit" (Roche, *The People of Paris*, trans. M. Evans [Berkeley and Los Angeles: University of California Press, 1987], 82–83). "A larger percentage of the nation's wealth is now held by the populace in the form of money or in securities," Senac de Meilhan reflected in his book on state finance, *Considerations sur les richesses et le luxe*, written in 1787. Clavière calculated that there were about three hundred thousand state creditors. "These investors are found among all classes; the extreme subdivision of the nation's securities and the ease with which they can be bought and sold cause securities to circulate from the wallets of the wealthy, through the artisan's shops and even through the hands of servants, all of whom purchase securities to prepare for their retirements" (Clavière, *De la foi publique*). Subleases of tax farms were often broken down into very small denominations, so that tax-farming responsibilities penetrated the entire social system and a wide range of the population participated in tax farming. In Brittany, for example, the indirect tax farms were subleased parish by parish. For an example of how extensively taxes were subfarmed, see P. Heumann, "Un Traitant sous Louis XIII: Antoine Feydeau," *Revue d'histoire moderne* 1938: 5–45. I know of no study, however, that discusses this topic for the eighteenth century.

the vile bourgeoisie and were treated as quite distinct from the old aristocracy. During the eighteenth century, distinctions between the old aristocracy and the new financial elites had eroded, creating a more homogeneous elite.[57] Yves Durand found that, by the late eighteenth century, the *fermiers généraux* were culturally indistinguishable from the rest of the French nobility; only 10 percent of them were not aristocrats.[58] The strategy of dividing the elites, so effectively used by Louis XIV, was ineffective under Louis XVI. The Crown could no longer arouse the old aristocracy against the monied upstarts.

There is a second reason why it had become much harder to persecute individual financiers. Again Senac de Meilhan explains: "Things have changed. Administration has become a science of which the principles are better known. The various branches of the financial administration are more efficient." After 1770, financial administration was increasingly looked upon as a public activity to be managed by experts. The tax farms had become impersonal bureaucracies and were less easily associated with the fortunes of particular individuals. "Business is no longer concentrated within the small circle of people who once grew rich by public usury and who could dictate the laws in difficult times." Persecution of individual financiers was no longer a viable alternative. There was widespread public recognition that the financial system was in need of wholesale reform.

Protecting the integrity of the bargaining process was the third reason for avoiding the behavior of the past. The monarchy initiated and invited discussion with the nation's elites on the possibility of exchanging political authority for fiscal exemptions. If the Crown had resorted to another bankruptcy, it would have compromised its credibility, thereby undermining its ability to negotiate for the voluntary surrender of exemptions. The Crown needed to appear to be negotiating in earnest and convince property owners that for the first time the king had come to recognize the absolute property rights of his subjects.[59] The need to maintain the integrity of the negotiating process thus prevented the Crown from acting as it did in 1770, when it repudiated part of its debt. Ironically, the monarchy's actions at the end of the Old Regime were much more in accord with the principle

---

[57]"At the beginning of the century, the marriage of the count of Evreaux to the daughter of Crozat caused indignation; later, when the Mazade married Aumont, no one raised an eyebrow," notes Chaussinaud-Nogaret (*Financiers de Languedoc*, 250), who concludes that the financiers were fully integrated into the society of the Old Regime as allies of the aristocracy, spread throughout the robe (ibid., 271).
[58]See Yves Durand, *Les Fermiers généraux au XVIII$^e$ siècle* (Paris: Presses universitaires de France, 1971).
[59]By "absolute property rights," I mean the right to be paid interest at the time and in the manner stated in a contract.

had restructured a significant portion of its debt to head off a fiscal crisis under Abbé Joseph-Marie Terray, *contrôleur général* from December 1769 to August 1774. Twelve years later the government seemed careful to avoid similar tactics. Even though the fiscal crisis that led to the calling of the notables had begun in 1782, the chief minister, Brienne, waited until August 1788 to suspend payments on the debt.[53] Necker, who immediately replaced Brienne, reversed this policy and restored payments to the *rentiers*.[54]

Historians of Old Regime France continue to be perplexed by the Crown's efforts to avoid repudiating its debts, since it had resorted to repudiation so often before under similar pressures. Why did the king resist repudiation in 1788–89? Three reasons dominate. An especially important component of public opinion could no longer be mobilized to persecute the financiers. As financiers became increasingly leveraged, confidence increased; consisting more of claims holders, they became less distinct as a group. Gabriel Senac de Meilhan observed that the financial officials, no longer rogues but public servants, "are drawn to financial employments by their talents; and hold their posts in much the same way that magistrates and military officers hold theirs. Many financiers are related to great families: these talented individuals could have distinguished themselves in other careers; most have been carefully educated."[55] Similarly, Count Nicolas-François Mollien, who became minister of the Treasury during the Empire, commented that "the majority of *fermiers généraux*, through their culture, spirit, and the amenity of their habits, take their place among the highest ranks of French society. By the direction they have taken in their studies, they are better disposed to serve the state."[56] In the seventeenth century, the financiers were viewed as part of

---

[53]The infamous *arrêt* of August 16, 1788, has been too loosely interpreted as a bankruptcy, according to Bosher. "Only to believers in the traditional system of depending upon the private credit of accountants and tax farmers, admittedly the majority of observers in 1788, did this seem like bankruptcy" (Bosher, *French Finances*, 198). Bosher sees the edict as part of Brienne's efforts to suppress and consolidate financial offices and to nationalize the Treasury and the currency. "His suspension of payments was interpreted at the time as a royal bankruptcy; in fact it was a precocious attempt to replace private short-term credit with national or public credit" (ibid., 309).
[54]Salaried officers of the government and *rentiers* received three-fifths of the *gages* in treasury notes.
[55]Gabriel Senac de Meilhan, *Considerations sur les richesses et le luxe* (Amsterdam, 1787), 346–47, cited in *French Government and Society, 1500–1850: Essays in Memory of Alfred Cobban*, ed. J. F. Bosher (London, 1973), 38–39.
[56]Mollien quoted in Marcel Marion, *Dictionnaire des institutions de la France aux XVIIe et XVIIIe siècles* (Paris, 1923; repr., New York, 1968), 234.

sessed tax whose total amount would be determined by the needs of the state.[50] He presented more accurate estimates of the deficit and reiterated the government's commitment to restricting spending, but his proposals were also rejected. The notables wanted a unified Treasury—the centralization of all receipts and payments, so that it would be possible to know "the actual financial situation day by day, and, limiting the accounting to one source, all payments would be made into a single fund."[51] Furthermore, they demanded a record of the actual receipts and expenses for the current year and wanted to know all the financial details, such as the amounts of the pensions and subsidies the king provided his favorites, and even about abuses in the postal system. In addition, the notables wanted military reforms and control over the king's stables. Brienne was sympathetic to these demands and offered to work with the notables to economize. In the struggle against the deficit, the notables insisted on controls over future spending. They claimed that only active collaboration between the wealthy and the king could provide the accountability needed to restore confidence in state finances. However, Brienne was unable to provide the notables with sufficient political guarantees that investors would have the power to prevent the recurrence of future deficits and fiscal disorder. He decided to dismiss the notables on May 25, 1787, when it became clear that they would not agree to increased taxation without further concessions by the king.[52]

## BANKRUPTCY HAD BECOME UNTHINKABLE

With the failure of the notables to resolve the fiscal crisis, state bankruptcy seemed imminent; yet it did not occur. Earlier, in 1770, the government

---

[50] Brienne was responding to a request from the notables for a land tax that was reapportioned annually in proportion to the deficit.

[51] Egret, *Pré-révolution française*, 62.

[52] This account is based on Egret, *Pré-révolution française*. The notables refused to support tax reforms, arguing that since they were not a representative body, their consent was not binding on the nation. See Albert Goodwin, "Calonne, the Assembly of French Notables of 1787 and the Origins of the *revolte nobiliaire*," *English Historical Review* 61 (1946): 373. Vivian Gruder has argued that the notables repudiated the repartitional tax they had originally demanded because they desired to redefine political authority. In other words, their principal objective was to establish institutional restraints on "ministerial despotism." Gruder believes that opposition to the Crown by the privileged orders went beyond a narrow defense of fiscal privilege. Many notables were seeking institutional changes that would subject royal policy to a consensus-generating institution. See Gruder, "A Mutation in Elite Political Culture: The French Notables and the Defense of Property and Participation, 1787," *Journal of Modern History* 56 (1984): 598–634. This tendency is confirmed by John Markoff's work in progress on the Cahiers of the second estate.

general problems of administering the kingdom. One subject dominated the discussions: the deficit, which Calonne had made public for the first time in the nation's history.[48] Discussions among contemporaries regarding the reduction of the deficit and the reform of existing fiscal practices, however, often raised fundamental questions about the nature of government.

During the plenary session, Calonne presented six memoranda, which proposed two principal reforms. First was the establishment of a proportional tax to be paid in kind by all landowners. Second was the creation of provincial assemblies to assist the intendants with local administration in all the *pays d'election*. The assemblies would be consultative bodies, not administrative or legislative, and would participate in assessing local and royal taxes but not in policymaking. The *pays d'états* were excluded from the reforms essentially because local estates already facilitated bargaining agreements between the Crown and the provinces. The existence of such estates reduced the cost of borrowing to the king. The expectation of similar reductions in transaction costs was the principal reason the king was willing to authorize the creation of these consultative bodies throughout the kingdom. He clearly did not wish to share political power with them.

The Assembly of Notables failed to reach an agreement with the king. The notables seemed to approve the principle of equality of tax responsibility, but rejected the measures proposed by the Crown for the implementation of the reforms. Calonne's proportional tax ignored the fiscal privileges of individuals, corporate bodies, and provinces. Not surprisingly, the notables did not want to give up their fiscal privileges without compensation. Tax exemptions were, after all, a form of property that had either been inherited or purchased. Calonne's proposed provincial assemblies were rejected because they were perceived as having little real power, although the notables were being asked to surrender significant financial privileges. "If the assembly serves only to levy taxes . . . [it] will be compromised in the eyes of the nation," the prince de Beauvau warned his peers.[49] With his proposals defeated, Calonne was removed from office, and the assembly was disbanded.

Loménie de Brienne replaced Calonne as principal minister (1787–88), although he was not appointed controller general. An admirer of Necker, he made many concessions to the notables. Instead of the proportional tax of undetermined extent proposed by Calonne, Brienne proposed an as-

---

[48] It has been subsequently determined that Calonne's estimates were low.
[49] Jean Egret, *La Pré-révolution française, 1787–1788* (Paris: Presses universitaires de France, 1962), 62.

with those of our neighbors. Since all commerce depends on credit, the advantage is always with France's neighbors because the king pays from 5 to 12 percent; or even more, which is exorbitant."[44] To correct this lamentable situation, "Each state where receipts are not sufficient to pay the obligations it has contracted must act like a banker in the same situation. This banker is served by his good reputation: he floats his paper in the marketplace to get some money in order to fulfill his obligations by their due date. Good banking houses never lose on their paper; why should the state not follow suit? Because public capital costs too much in France. The government does not have the means to break even with its creditors." This should not be a problem, he adds: "The king's debt is that of the nation, so it is up to the nation to pay and for the king to supervise that it is paid." He goes on to advocate the creation of a national debt under the jurisdiction of the Estates or some body that represents the nation's credit holders.[45]

Finally, the calling of the Estates raised new hopes of the creation of a national bank. However, the new bank would have to distance itself from association with the failure of the Law system. As one pamphleteer pointed out, under Law, ministers had the capacity to increase the money supply without the public being able to know how much specie was in circulation. The public never knew either what, if anything, stood behind the bank notes in circulation.[46] This would be impossible under the new system, because the money could not be manufactured without the nation's consent. Under the new system, "the public would have nothing to fear, because the quantity of notes in circulation could never exceed the proportion determined by the nation. The two systems would be completely different. Under Law, the bank's notes were issued when the king was too young to know the interests of his people. The paper money I am proposing would be created by the nation and backed by it."[47]

## THE FINANCIAL PRECONDITIONS OF REVOLUTION IN FRANCE

On February 22, 1787, Controller General Charles Alexandre de Calonne (1734–1802) convened an assembly of the kingdom's notables to discuss

[44]P. L. B. W. K., *Mémoire pour l'establissement d'une caisse publique nationale ou française* (BN, L39 6536), 6.
[45]BN, L39b 6536:3.
[46]Nothing needs to stand behind a currency except the promise to accept it as payment for something such as taxes. Thus one never "knows" whether these promises will be kept in perpetuity; one can only have expectations.
[47]BN, L39b 6536. L39b 6539. 30 pages.

Brissot's ideas appeared in a number of other pamphlets as well. In support of the creation of a national debt placed under the supervision of the Estates General, Etienne Clavière (1735–93), another pamphleteer writing from England, related England's success in expanding public credit to the creation of the public debt: "On this island it is the people who spend; it is they who borrow; it is they who engage . . . unlike in France, where the Crown directly incurs the nation's financial obligations. In England the debt is guaranteed by the nation itself, which is solidly behind the expenses incurred by its Parliament." He reasoned that in England public spending expanded more than revenue as a result of the creation of the public debt. "While public spending has quintupled since the times of [Charles] Davenant [political economist, 1656–1714], the GNP has only increased in a ratio of 5 to 2."[42]

Another extensive study of public credit, undertaken by Nicoud D'Umons, concluded with a call for the establishment of a constitutional monarchy in which taxation and the creation of money would be in the hands of the Estates General. D'Umons wrote that public credit would not be established until some restraints were imposed on the Crown's discretion.

> If the public accords little confidence to royal notes, it is because the king alone stands behind them, and reasons of state can force him to delay payments. Confidence will be reestablished once, under sanction of the Estates General, a national bank is created that consolidates or reimburses the debt and offers the public notes of its own. The administration cannot achieve the solvency it needs by relying on individual [financiers] . . . but when the notes are solidly backed by a bank that represents the interests of all citizens, including the controller general and the king's ministers, then all fear and uncertainty will cease. One cannot expect fifty thousand individuals to compromise their fortunes and allow themselves to be seduced by the government.[43]

Many of the pamphlets written against bankruptcy linked the crisis in public credit to high interest rates and a commercial bankruptcy crisis. On the eve of the Revolution, contemporaries reported numerous private bankruptcies. One author noted: "Everyone is convinced that there is not enough specie in France, that interest rates are excessive in comparison

---

[42]Etienne Clavière, *De la foi publique envers les créanciers de l'état: Lettres à M. Linguet sur le N. CXVI de ses annales* (London, 1788). BN, L39b 516.
[43]Nicoud D'Umons, *Essai sur le crédit public* (Paris, 1789), 199–200. BN, L39 7148.

A new fiscal crisis raised the possibility of another royal repudiation. Opponents of absolutism hoped that Louis XVI would summon the Estates General to avoid a masked bankruptcy, involving employment of the Chambre de justice against financiers, or outright bankruptcy, which had been resorted to by earlier kings. Jacques Brissot de Warville (1754–93) was one of the many who wrote pamphlets to generate public support for summoning the Estates General. His first pamphlet, *Point de banqueroute,* written from London, advocated putting the Estates in charge of the nation's finances in order to restore public faith in the state's credit. "The Estates General can verify, determine, and grant taxes needed to cover it, and it can establish an administration designed to prevent forever the return of depredations [by the Crown]," he observed. To achieve these ends, he recommended that the Estates General demand that

1. The amount of the deficit be made public.
2. Taxes be levied only with the consent of the Estates.
3. A regular system of finances be established to avoid a return to the disorders of the past.
4. Its next meeting establish the amount of the deficit and the amount and the kind of taxes, as well as requiring free and open annual discussion of the nation's accounts.

In a second pamphlet, written from Paris in 1787, Brissot wrote that summoning the Estates and establishing constitutional principles

> should interest the creditors of the state no less than other citizens, since their investments would become more secure once the Crown's arbitrary powers were diminished. National bankruptcies would become increasing rare when perverse ministers found it less easy to borrow, to impose, and to waste, and if all were required to subject their accounts to the nation's scrutiny every year. Then wasteful measures would disappear, along with the shady maneuvers that accompany them; then the interest rate that the state's creditors receive would stay intact; the average citizen would pay less, and creditors would collect more easily. When the English Parliament registers a loan, it guarantees that the nation will pay the capital and the interest. It also certifies that the loan carries the nation's consent. Registration by Parliament is an order to each citizen to pay; it is the sign of good faith that money is advanced to the government. The nation's credit would be infallibly compromised in the eyes of foreigners should it appear that the loan was not consented to by the nation.[41]

---

[41]Jacques Brissot de Warville, *Point de banqueroute* (first part, London, 1787; second part, Paris, 1787). BN, L39b 6308.

Crown's ability to manage the nation's finances was widespread, especially since the king had altered the value of the currency forty-three times between 1689 and 1715.[38] What was to prevent him from annulling the bank's debts, confiscating its funds, or issuing money without limit? In his *Mémoires* (published for the first time in the late eighteenth century), the duc de Saint-Simon (1675–1755) suggested that the establishment of a national bank could only be of benefit "in a republic or a monarchy such as England, where finance is governed absolutely by those who furnish it, and who only furnish as much as they want to; or in a weak state rather than in an absolute state like France, where confidence is lacking since in cases of extreme necessity, such as those in which [Louis XIV] found himself in 1707, 1708, 1709, and 1710, a king, or in his name a mistress, a minister, or a favorite, could topple the bank by consuming its resources."[39]

To convince a largely skeptical French public that a national bank could indeed exist under conditions of absolutism, John Law argued that national economic expansion would benefit if all credit flowed from the king. The principal obstacle to economic growth, he believed, was that if left in private hands, gold and silver would not be employed in the public interest, inasmuch as private individuals tended to hoard the nation's supply of precious metals. To overcome this reluctance to invest, Law argued, an enlightened monarch could use his authority to guarantee that the nation's treasure would be circulated to promote industry and commerce. Moreover, an enlightened monarch could ensure that the bank honored its debts.[40] Nevertheless, under Law's directorship, the bank issued paper currency that quickly became worthless, leading to a massive state bankruptcy. The Law experiment was the point of reference for discussions in the late eighteenth century of the question of creating a national bank when hopes resurfaced that the king would call the Estates General.

---

[38] A. D. Vuitry, *Le Désordre des finances et les excès de la spéculation* (Paris, 1885), 156. Between 1726 and 1785, the value of currency was unchanged.

[39] Louis de Rouvroy, duc de Saint-Simon, *Mémoires*, ed. A. de Boislisle (Paris: Nouvelles éditions, 1925), 37:178–79. I would like to thank Thomas Kaiser for introducing me to these passages. See his "Money, Despotism, and Public Opinion in Early Eighteenth-Century France: John Law and the Debate on Royal Credit," *Journal of Modern History* 63 (March 1991): 1–28.

[40] See BN, *ancien* MS FR 7768, esp. folios 200–220, "Recueil de mémoires concernant la banque de Law (1716–1717)." Contemporaries generally believed that an absolute monarchy was incompatible with the creation of a national bank, because the government would be able to manipulate the currency or confiscate holdings with impunity. In BN *ancien* MS FR7774–79, "Mémoires sur le gouvernement en général et en particulier sur les finances vers 1726," there is further discussion of why a national bank would not function properly under absolutism.

thereby creates an unlimited surety resting on individual self-interest.[35]

Although documents have not been found that reveal in what terms the Old Regime French government understood England's fiscal advantages, French fiscal theorists of the late eighteenth century often compared the English and French systems.[36] French tracts of the late eighteenth century on political economy typically concentrated on why the English Crown did not resort to bankruptcy even in times of great fiscal distress and often warned of the reprehensible consequences that would follow a royal bankruptcy.

## FRENCH VIEWS OF GOVERNMENT FINANCES ON THE EVE OF THE REVOLUTION

A cost-benefit analysis of the net advantages of a parliamentary organization to government fiscal affairs can be found in a number of pamphlets published during the years 1787–88, when confidence in the Old Regime was eroding. A speculative boom that had begun in the early 1780s seemed ready to burst, and anxiety was widespread. Contemporaries complained of the exhaustion of credit and the proliferation of bankruptcies as loans bought on credit were called in. The panic in private finance paralleled the governmental crisis.[37] Pamphlets began to appear stressing that representative institutions would provide greater fiscal responsibility than could the institutions of absolutism. The fiscal advantage of representative institutions was not a new idea in French political discourse, but it could be stated with greater urgency in an environment of uncertainty, apprehension, and fear. As French people scrambled to safeguard their fortunes, the need for fundamental fiscal and related political reforms was no longer mere speculation.

The crisis of 1787 reopened public discussion of state finances for the first time since the Regency of 1715–20. During the Regency, the problems posed by the Crown's fiscal irresponsibility became the subject of heated public debate, focusing on the creation of a national bank that could issue paper money. England already had such a bank, but in France many believed that the necessary political conditions were lacking. Mistrust of the

---

[35]Conversation, December 1812, from *The Mind of Napoleon*, ed. Christopher J. Herold (New York: Columbia University Press, 1955), 94.
[36]The most statistically rigorous of these comparisons is located in BN, L76f 122 (unsigned), *Situation actuelle des finances de la France et de l'Angleterre* (Paris: Briand, 1789).
[37]George Taylor, "The Paris Bourse on the Eve of the Revolution, 1781–1789," *American Historical Review* 67 (1962): 951–77.

Charles Nicole Ducloz-Dufresnoy, one of France's most important fiscal theorists prior to the Revolution, understood the incentive structure of the English system in the terms presented here. "Ten or twelve months after the last peace there was general desolation in London and the fear that business would undergo an inevitable convulsion," he explained. "In the heat of this universal alarm, M. Pitt [the Younger] was placed at the head of finances."[33] Pitt declared war on the deficit rather than contemplate state bankruptcy. "To liquidate the debts, Parliament decided to increase its revenue by levying new taxes" advocated by Pitt, Ducloz-Dufresnoy noted. "In a word, to increase taxes to the level of expenses was the new plan, just as it had been the program of Pitt's successors under similar circumstances. The House of Commons understood the wisdom of this approach and adopted it. In 1786 Pitt received the payment for his courage when he was able to show the Commons that receipts and expenses were once again in tandem."[34]

Napoleon Bonaparte also understood the incentives of the English fiscal system. In a conversation he is reported to have said:

> In England everything is based on something imaginary. Her credit depends entirely on confidence, since she has no surety to cover it—although I admit that the English government has something better than that, since the individual fortunes are linked to that of the State. The system of successive loans, which continually tie the present to the past, in a manner compels confidence in the future. By giving every individual proprietor a stake in the wealth of the State, the government creates something better than a material surety, which it lacks; for it

---

[33] Charles Nicole Ducloz-Dufresnoy, one of the principal notaries of Paris, is outstanding among contemporary writers on finance for his grasp of practice and attention to detail. See BN, L39b 655, *Discours de M. Ducloz-Dufresnoy sur l'offre d'un crédit de six millions prêté au roi par la Compagne des notaires* (Paris: Clousier, 1788); BN, L39b 4227, *Reflexions sur l'etat de nos finances, a l'epoque du premier mai et du 18 Novembre, 1789* (Paris, 1790); BN, L39b 762, *Judgment impartial sur les questions principales qui interessent le tiers-état* (Paris, 1788); BN, L39b 6648, *Encore quelques mots sur les questions de savoir si le tiers-état peut être representé par des ordres privilégés* (Paris: Chez Clouzier, 1788); *Origine de la Caisse d'escompte, ses progrès, ses révolutions, au lettre de M. Ducloz-Dufresnoy, notaire à M. le comte de Mirabeau* (Paris, 1789); BN, L32b 3233, *Observations de M. Ducloz-Dufresnoy, sur l'état de finances* (Paris: Chez Clousier, 1790); BN, L39b 4083, *Observations rapides sur l'impossibilité d'adopter le plan de la municipalité de Paris, Calcul du capital de la dette publique, reflexions sur les causes de discrédit* (Paris, 1790).
[34] BN, L32b 3223, *Observations de M. Ducloz-Dufresnoy sur l'état des finances* (Paris: Chez Clousier, 1790), 20–21.

cipal force in the war, we shall not be hasty in attributing it entirely to the nature of her government. . . .

But another cause of the great credit of England is, undoubtedly, the public scrutiny to which the state of her finance is submitted. . . . The money lenders, being thus regularly informed of the balance between the receipts and disbursements, are not upset by chimerical suspicions and fears. . . .

In France, the state of Finances has constantly been made a matter of mystery.[29]

France's outstanding economist Jean-Baptiste Say, who was born twenty years before the Revolution, later echoed this thought in his authoritative fashion: "Public credit is the confidence that exists in the kings. . . . Credit rises to the highest degree [of confidence] only when the government by virtue of its structure cannot easily violate its promises, and when its resources are equal to its needs. It is for this last reason that public credit is weak where the financial accounts of a nation are unknown."[30]

By providing avenues for participation in the formation of government policy, the Constitutional Settlement of 1689 provided a way to reduce the costs to the state of gaining the cooperation of those members of the nation whose wealth and authority made them especially capable of helping the English king finance his state.[31] By contrast, the growth of state finance in France was restrained by the absence of a public institution bound by law to protect the interests of investors. When compared to the commitment technology of French absolutism—bilateral exchanges with royal financiers and corporations—the parliamentary institutions of England were relatively efficient at producing credible commitments from governments over time.[32]

---

[29]Jacques Necker, *State of the Finances of France Laid before the King* (London: G. Kearsly et al., 1781), 2–3.

[30]Jean-Baptiste Say, *Traité d'économie politique, ou simple exposition de la manière dont se forment, se distribuent, et se consomment les richesses* (Paris: Crapelet, 1803), 2:526.

[31]Many contemporary authors agreed that the English government gained credibility because it possessed a continuous institution that made its public debt credible. John Hicks makes a similar point in *A Theory of Economic History* (New York: Oxford University Press, 1969).

[32]One of the reasons constitutional monarchies replaced absolute monarchies in most of western Europe was that parliaments could borrow at lower interest rates than kings. See Herbert Rowan, *The King's State: Proprietary Dynasticism in Early Modern France* (New Brunswick, N.J.: Rutgers University Press, 1980). William and Mary's advisers recognized these advantages when offering proposals on how to raise the revenue necessary to contain French power. The ability to borrow liquid assets made possible the comparatively enormous state power of the western European democratic nations by contrast with eastern European countries.

and directly from repudiation, especially when the alternatives were the alienation of public authority or greater power for corporate groups or legislative bodies. In this sense, kings might have to sell the family jewels to support the state's debt, unlike representatives in a legislative body. At a time of financial exigency, an MP, as a government creditor, would prefer to increase taxes rather than default on obligations, since taxes were spread over a broader segment of the population than was the debt. The taxes an MP (or his constituents) might pay to support the nation's debt were likely to be smaller than the costs of defaulting. Moreover, MPs might also be indirectly hurt by repudiation, since friends and relatives might hold public securities. Certainly, an important part of a member's political support came from individuals who held portions of the debt.[28] Following the creation of a funded debt controlled by Parliament, English investors recognized that the government's incentive was to repay rather than renege, and hence interest rates no longer needed to reflect a default risk.

An additional advantage of establishing a public debt was that a legislative body did not have the same incentive as a king to withhold information about the state's debt. Information about the scale of revenues and services was needed in order for the public to assess the long-term ability of the government to service its loans from existing revenues. Such information was an investor's only way of judging the likelihood of a royal bankruptcy. In France, the fact that such information was not public knowledge diminished the government's credibility and increased interest rates. Necker made this same point in explaining England's financial advantages to the king in 1781:

> Indeed, if we fix our attention on the immense credit which is enjoyed by England, and which constitutes at this day her prin-

[28]On British finance in the seventeenth and eighteenth centuries, see Peter Mathias and Patrick O'Brien, "Taxation in Britain and France, 1715–1810: A Comparison of the Social and Economic Incidence of Taxes Collected for the Central Governments," *Journal of European Economic History* 5 (1976): 601–50; John E. D. Binney, *British Public Finance and Administration, 1774–1792* (Oxford: Oxford University Press, 1958); S. Dowell, *A History of Taxation and Taxes in England from the Earliest Times to the Present Day*, 3d ed. (London: F. Cass, 1965); Fredrick C. Dietz, "English Public Finance and the National State in the Sixteenth Century," in *Facts and Factors in Economic History: Articles by Former Students of Edwin Francis Gay*, 1st ed. (Cambridge, Mass.: Harvard University Press, 1932); W. Kennedy, *English Taxation, 1640–1799: An Essay on Policy and Opinion* (New York: A. M. Kelley, 1964); Sydney Charles Buxton, *Finance and Politics: An Historical Study, 1783–1885* (London: J. Murray, 1888); Elizabeth Boody Schumpeter, "English Prices and Public Finance, 1660–1822," *Review of Economic Statistics* 20 (1938): 21–37; E. Hughes, *Studies in Administration and Finance, 1558–1825, with Special Reference to the History of the Salt Tax in England* (Manchester: Manchester University Press, 1934).

bankers were not always able to collect the 4 to 5 percent in interest owed each quarter when the payments were due.[23]

French interest rates did decline after 1720. Lüthy provides examples of interest rates of 4 to 5 percent on bonds issued by the Crown but notes that the bonds generally sold at a 40 percent discount.[24] The Crown was legally restricted from increasing the rate over 5 percent and hence sold the perpetual bonds at a discount instead of adjusting the interest rate. Taking the discount into account, the real interest rate rose to 6.7 percent, more than twice the interest rate on English government bonds sold during the same period. The interest rates on the more popular *rentes viagères* (life annuities) varied from 8 to 10 percent amortized over fifteen to eighteen years.[25] Once we discount the effect of capital loss (capital effect) and compound the interest, at twenty years we get an interest rate of 6.7 on 8 percent *rentes viagères*.[26]

The relatively lower English interest rates suggest that the costs of government credit in England were diminished by the use of parliamentary institutions. A perpetual public body—rather than the individuals who comprised it or a monarch who was above the law—was responsible for repayment of these obligations. There were fewer incentives to default than for a king; the personal fortunes of individual MPs could not be served by repudiation: if Parliament chose to default, individual legislators did not come into the funds thereby conserved. Since MPs did not have as great an incentive as the king to default, the investing public could feel protected from arbitrary seizures of concentrated assets like those that had occurred in 1640 and 1672.[27]

As representatives of the government's creditors, members of Parliament had more to gain by increasing taxes to honor all debts than from repudiating part of the debt. By contrast, a king could benefit personally

---

[23] See Herbert Lüthy, *La Banque protestante en France, de la révocation de l'Edit de Nantes à la Révolution* (Paris: S.E.V.P.E.N., 1959), 2:180–81.

[24] Lüthy reports that *rentes perpetuelles* were negotiated at 50 percent of value in 1752 (ibid., 58).

[25] Life annuities appealed to investors without families, since they expired on the death of the lender.

[26] The "head," or person named on the annuity, would have had to live more than twenty years for the interest rate to surpass the real interest rates of the *rentes perpetuelles*. Over a thirty-year period, the real interest rate rose to 7.6 percent. If the head lived to age fifty, the interest rate rose to 7.9 percent. Interest rates of 10 percent, equivalent to a real interest rate of 9.19 percent over twenty years, were available to individuals over age fifty.

[27] "The royal creditors must have reflected that had their loans been 'on parliamentary security,' instead of being backed only by the Crown's promises, they would not have been repudiated" (Dickson, *Financial Revolution*, 45).

new system of government borrowing based on long-term loans,[20] as well as the establishment of a permanent national debt. Under the new system of borrowing, investors drew interest on their loans as long as they lived. The Bank of England was permitted to borrow money on security of Parliament, to deal in bullion and bills of exchange, and to act as pawnbroker. By the end of 1694, by leveraging liabilities to the public, the bank had advanced sums greater than its total capital to the state in the form of bills, which the Exchequer accepted in lieu of tallies used to pay government creditors. The Bank of England thus became indispensable to the government as a source of credit and a channel for making remittances to soldiers overseas. As the issue of bank notes grew and became standardized over the course of the eighteenth century, the bank's ties with the government became more intimate.

The next big step toward expanding the British government's creditworthiness—the creation of the funded debt—came in 1715. A political agreement with Parliament established that a specific loan had to be secured by Parliament's vote of a specific tax designed to fund the loan's repayment. As a result of Parliament's backing of the public debt, the interest rate on English government bonds fell from 10 percent in 1689 to 3 percent during the eighteenth century, greatly expanding the English government's capacity to use the nation's savings.[21] The lower interest rates reflected the fact that loan repayment had become more probable. In contrast, across the channel the French king paid interest rates (taking into account the discounted prices of *rentes* and life annuities) that greatly exceeded the interest rates paid by corporations and estates. In 1707, for example, Samuel Bernard agreed to supply 13.2 million livres in cash to pay French troops in the Spanish Netherlands, and an additional 6 million for troops in Spain. His contract stipulated payment in various forms, including the right to collect receipts from the taxes. Bernard's "fee" for supplying the loan was equivalent to an annual interest rate of 15 percent, and he was promised an additional 1,100,000 livres until the funds were repaid.[22] Herbert Luethy reports similar interest rates of 16–20 percent for loans made by Swiss bankers that same year (1706–7) but adds that the

---

[20]Dickson, *Financial Revolution*. This liquidity transformation also existed in France in the form of rescriptions, because most people held liquid short-term notes or zero-term notes (currency).

[21]The most significant indication of the success of parliamentary borrowing was that the public interest rate had fallen beneath private interest rates. Private interest rates in England were about 4 or 5 percent throughout the second half of the eighteenth century, while in France they varied from 5 to 12 percent.

[22]See Daniel Dessert, *Argent, pouvoir, et société au grand siècle* (Paris: Fayard, 1984), 194–95.

access to significant rents and subjected it to the criticism that it served a small elite of City bankers at the expense of national interests.[16] Barry Weingast explains that centralizing the kingdom's loan decisions in a single intermediary had an additional motivation: it allowed the Bank of England to enforce a credit boycott, greatly increasing the penalties the government would experience if it defaulted.[17] By reducing the likelihood of default, this arrangement increased the credibility of the government's commitments to the bank.[18]

Although the English may have disagreed about the merits of the Constitutional Settlement of 1688, few questioned its impact on public finances or on England's rise to power in the eighteenth century. Like numerous contemporary observers, the English financial historian P. G. M. Dickson notes that the government's increased power to borrow was essential to war financing. At the outset of the War of the Grand Alliance against France in 1688, the British Crown was able to borrow £1,000,000. By the end of the war in 1697, the government had borrowed nearly £17,000,000, and this was supported by a GNP estimated to have been no larger than £41,000,000.[19] Government debt grew from between 2 and 3 percent of the GNP to about 40 percent in fewer than ten years.

According to Dickson, this spectacular increase in war finance was brought about by the creation of the Bank of England, which permitted a

---

[16]P. G. M. Dickson reports that many contemporaries thought that the influence of wealthy citizens on the government was sinister. If a bank became a monopoly lender to Parliament, bankers would be able to dictate national policy in their interests. "It was alleged that the National Debt had been created to meet not an economic need, the need for greater revenue, but a political need: to secure for the political settlement of 1689 the support of powerful groups concerned in government loans" (Dickson, *Financial Revolution*, 17). The Bank of England was designed as an intermediary to float the government's loans, much as the U.S. Federal Reserve System does today in its open-market transactions, but it was not a part of the British government. Not being the actual lender, the bank thus lacked monopoly power to set unreasonably high interest rates. Loans and interest rates were determined by parliamentary legislation, and whether or not to subscribe to the loans lay in the discretion of individuals.

[17]International trading companies like the East India Company offered an alternative source of loanable funds, since they were not banks.

[18]This intepretation of how the bank functioned can be found in Barry Weingast, "Institutional Foundations of the 'Sinews of Power': British Financial and Military Success Following the Glorious Revolution" (mimeo, Hoover Institution, Stanford University, July 1991).

[19]Estimates of England's GNP are from Emmanuel Le Roy Ladurie, "Le Comtes fantastiques de Gregory King," *Annales: Economies, sociétés, civilisations* 23 (1968): 1086–1102. After England's entry into the war against France in 1689, public expenditure increased from under £2,000,000 a year to an average of from £5,000,000 to £6,000,000. See Dickson, *Financial Revolution*, 46.

sion, increasing direct taxes on the peasantry would have made taxes even harder to collect.[13] According to J. F. Bosher, investors would have rejected new loans and the *parlements* new taxes because both had lost confidence in the Crown's credit system. Despite the fact that the general tax farms had become more bureaucratic and operated more explicitly as public institutions, the Crown's solvency still depended upon the personal credit of its financiers. A series of financial failures occurred among some of the king's financiers during the first six months of 1787, and others were rumored to be on the verge of failure or to have difficulty finding credit. Furthermore, the fear that the general economic depression would diminish tax revenues and contribute to further failures among prominent financiers raised doubts about the solvency of the Crown.[14]

## PARLIAMENTARY INSTITUTIONS, THE PUBLIC DEBT, AND PUBLIC INTEREST RATES

The first step on the road to more stable public finances in Britain was the chartering in 1689 of the Bank of England with a monopoly on loans to the government, so that potential investors had no alternative.[15] Since the common law courts were independent of the Crown, the Bank of England could call upon them to block the government from seeking alternative credit sources. Small independent lenders were thus barred from competing among themselves or with the bank, leaving the Crown without alternative sources of funds. The ability to use the courts to prevent the Crown from seeking additional sources of credit gave the Bank of England

---

Coase, "Durability and Monopoly," *Journal of Law and Economics* 15 (1972): 143–49.

[13]On the economic recession, see C. E. Labrousse, *La Crise de l'économie française à la fin de l'ancien régime et au debut de la Révolution française* (Paris: Presses universitaires de France, 1944), 473.

[14]Bosher, *French Finances,* passim. "The simultaneous bankruptcies of de Baudard de Saint-James et de Megret de Secilly, in 1787, and that of Morquet, suis de le Normond, were the coup de grace to royal finances under Calonne" (Guy Chaussinaud-Nogaret, *Les Financiers de Languedoc au XVIII$^e$ siècle* [Paris: S.E.V.P.E.N., 1970], 249).

[15]By ordering in 1697 that henceforth all sums due the Crown must be paid through the Bank of England, the British government gave it a monopoly on holding state funds. It was also provided that no other bank could establish itself by act of Parliament. These privileges were renewed in 1742. The same legislation limited the liability of bank investors. "No act of the Governor and Company of the Bank of England was to subject or make liable to forfeiture the particular or private and personal property of any member of the corporation, a clause which bestowed on it the privilege of limited liability" (Vera C. Smith, *The Rationale of Central Banking and the Free Banking Alternative* [repr., Indianapolis: Liberty Press, 1990], 12–13).

fiscal imperatives underlying the Old Regime's political structure. The tax-exempt status of the French nobility, he argued, altered the evolution of France's political institutions and caused the great divergence in the institutional development of the two nations. Building upon Tocqueville's insight, the growing demand for representative institutions that preceded the French Revolution can be related to the imperatives generated by the government's fiscal crisis. Three questions arose out of that crisis: a social question, who would pay? a political question, who would decide? and a constitutional question, what mechanisms would be needed to coordinate the decision-making process? Had the Crown been willing to resolve these issues with the kingdom's notables, it might not have incurred the social upheaval that followed the calling of the Estates General. The discussions at the Estates General quickly focused on equality before the law, raising issues that went far beyond the need for equal responsibility for taxes and requiring far more radical solutions than those needed to solve the fiscal crisis.

## FISCAL CRISIS IN FRANCE

By the mid eighteenth century, both England and Prussia could challenge France's traditional hegemony in European politics because their governments could more efficiently harness the resources of their subjects than could the French. The relative efficiency of England's financial machinery allowed the magnitude of government borrowing in relation to national wealth to be much greater in England than in France. While the English were particularly successful at tapping capital reserves throughout Europe,[11] the French king had difficulty paying his creditors at home. With his ability to borrow in jeopardy, the king looked for new ways to increase his income. Expanding the existing fiscal structures, however, was not considered feasible. The king would have found little support from the *parlements* for the sale of new offices, since as officeholders the *parlementaires* were concerned that sales of additional offices would diminish the value of those already existing.[12] Because of a general economic reces-

---

[11]Foreign holdings of English government securities were considerable between 1723 and 1780. See P. G. M. Dickson, *The Financial Revolution in England: A Study in the Development of Public Credit, 1688–1756* (New York: St. Martin's Press, 1967), 311–12.

[12]Moreover, the king could not sell new offices at the price of his choosing. As a durable goods monopolist—the king was the sole creator of new offices—he was compelled to sell at the competitively determined rather than the monopoly price. When he increased the price of new offices, he had to compete with existing officeholders, who might sell existing offices if the price was high enough. See R. H.

Efforts to reform the fiscal system in France were blocked by the provincial *parlements,* whose consent was necessary to raise taxes. The monied groups that grew rich under the Crown's sponsorship were also an obstacle to reform. They would not, without compensation, surrender their control over the nation's fiscal resources and institutions. The kingdom's wealthiest families had invested heavily in the Ferme générale and had acquired privileges through the purchase of offices. They had thus acquired assets that could not easily be renegotiated under a new regime, since the Crown could not afford to buy back the privileges or portions of public authority alienated to individuals. Nor would the king have been capable of replacing the *fermiers généraux.* As information brokers they were indispensable to the Crown, inasmuch as they substituted for incomplete financial markets. Put differently, the king could not replace the *fermiers généraux* because they had information that no one else had. The investment they had made in information gathering allowed for the pricing of shares in the debt, thus creating a market in state debt.[10]

An analysis of the economic logic of England's fiscal organization can be found in the crisis years 1787–88, when a burgeoning pamphlet literature flourished in France. England was cited as an example of the ways in which representative institutions were more efficient than either individual financiers or corporate institutions in achieving credible commitments from the government. The literature addressed the investing public at large and rarely represented the opinion of established financiers. The French Crown's inability peacefully to reform the nation's financial structure reveals how the democratic implications of the fiscal or economic functions of representative institutions led to revolution.

To explain the decline of the Old Regime, Tocqueville emphasized the

---

century, owing in large part to the ability of corporate groups to attract funds from a wider segment of the public than could individual financiers. A more impersonal debt was created, with numerous small investors sharing the profits of financing the state by buying portions of the debt offered by the corporations. David Bien estimates that in the 1780s the corporations collectively supplied about one-third of the king's loans. The success of this system, which Bien calls the surrogate or functional equivalent of England's national debt, made bankruptcy and reform more difficult. See Bien, "Offices, Corporations, and a System of State Credit: The Uses of Privilege under the Ancient Regime," in *The Political Culture of the Old Regime,* ed. Keith M. Baker (London: Pergamon Press, 1987), 89–114. And see also id., "The *secrétaires du roi:* Absolutism, Corporations, and Privilege under the *ancien régime,"* in *Vom ancien régime zur französischen Revolution: Forschungen und Perspektiven / De l'ancien régime à la Révolution française: Recherches et perspectives,* ed. E. Hinrichs (Göttingen: Vandenhoeck & Ruprecht, 1978), 153–67.

[10]The *fermiers généraux* created a market that revealed information about state debt allowing for the pricing of shares to the debt.

government's fiscal credibility.⁶ The first public discussions of this problem occurred during the Regency, when, under the influence of John Law, the government tried to create a national bank in imitation of the Bank of England. The experiment failed, and it was not repeated during the Old Regime. The failure was itself the result of the Crown's claims to absolute power: the royal bank failed because of the Crown's inability to make credible fiscal commitments.

By the late eighteenth century, the failure of the Law system led many to argue that fiscal reform was impossible without the establishment of a representative body to inhibit the Crown's exercise of unfettered discretion in state financial matters. The theory elaborated in chapter 8 about the need for credible government commitments in financial matters helps to explain why a number of eighteenth-century observers believed that the creation of representative institutions would help the king establish credibility with those French whose opinions counted and whose resources were necessary to resolve the crisis at hand (see chapter 8). Many of the French government's financial problems arose from the difficulty of obtaining credible commitments from the Crown; they could not be resolved merely by reorganizing the Treasury or establishing a national bank.⁷ Like that of the French fisc, the management of the British fisc during this period was chaotic and inefficient,⁸ but because of the greater credibility of British government promises, that inefficiency did not have the same impact on interest rates. France's comparative disadvantage stemmed directly from the structure of its political institutions. Indeed, many contemporary French observers asserted that Britain's military success and consequent emergence as a world power were owing to its innovative financial organization and superior state finances. France could not emulate this success because the government was unable to tap its citizens' wealth as efficiently, either through taxation or by borrowing.⁹

---

⁶A declaration of March 28, 1765, forbade the publication of any writing or project concerning the reform or administration of finances.
⁷J. F. Bosher, *French Finances, 1770–1795: From Business to Bureaucracy* (Cambridge: Cambridge University Press, 1970).
⁸See ibid., 22–25, 42, on the success of Britain's parliamentary fiscal administration and the relative failure of the French Crown's fiscal administration. "The high rate of interest on the French debt was another clue to the fundamental differences between the administrative systems of the two countries. Those differences were sufficient to determine that in the decade between the peace of 1783 and the war of 1793, England would take one road to stronger public finances and France would take another," Bosher observes (ibid., 24).
⁹In the eighteenth century, the grouping of financiers into public corporations gave the French state a borrowing capacity it had not possessed in the seventeenth

Documents shedding light on the Crown's financial decision making have not been uncovered and perhaps never will be. In his many books on the French Revolution, François Furet has taught that we should distance ourselves from the explanations given by the actors themselves to understand the meaning of the events. The immediate and visible consequences may be in accord with their stated positions. History, like economics at its best, should look beyond the stated intentions of the participants and attempt to explain the underlying structure of incentives, as well as the hidden consequences and costs of decision making. As Karl Popper puts it, "the main task of the theoretical social sciences . . . is to trace the unintended social repercussions of intentional human action."[3]

## SUSTAINED POLARITIES: STATE FINANCE IN EARLY MODERN FRANCE AND ENGLAND

During the eighteenth century, even by our standards today, the governments of both England and France borrowed a large proportion of their gross national products.[4] It was nevertheless more costly for the French than the English to borrow. The English government was thus able to borrow a much larger percentage of national wealth, putting France at a comparative disadvantage in its competition with England. The competition peaked in the Seven Years' War, which produced a decisive English victory over France. The subsequent French commitment to the American War of Independence required a level of borrowing that the government was unable to support from current revenues. Nor could it find a way to raise taxes without major social and political reform.[5]

Despite the severe penalties that would inevitably follow direct criticism of the Crown's behavior, many in France acknowledged that the king's claim of absolute power—to being above the law—had undermined the

---

[3] Karl Popper, "Predictions and Prophecy in the Social Sciences," in *Conjectures and Refutations*, 2d ed. (New York: Harper & Row, 1965), 342.
[4] BN, L40b 2401. Using figures from Arthur Young, M. de Casaux estimated that the GNP of England was about 2,800,000,000 livres, of which the government paid 384,000,000 in interest to creditors—that is, "between 7 and 8 percent of total revenues" (Casaux, *Reflexions sur la dette exigible et sur les moyens proposés pour la rembourser 1789* [Paris, 1790], 21).
[5] James Riley has demonstrated in *The Seven Years War and the Old Regime in France: The Economic and Financial Toll* (Princeton: Princeton University Press, 1986) that the high interest rates that underlay the crisis of the 1780s had their roots in the 1760s. Riley is the first modern author to notice that no published authority of the eighteenth century recognized that restructuring the debt and reducing the costs of a possible bankruptcy might have helped the monarchy exit the crisis situation with less damage.

England), causing higher interest rates and reduced possibilities of credit. In the absence of a parliamentary system, the French increased royal credit by developing a corporate debt secured by the sale of offices and channeled through the tax farmers and urban guilds. As noted in the previous chapter, reinforcement of the corporations made it more costly for the Crown to renege on its creditors and thus had the salutary effect of restraining royal currency manipulation and bankruptcies. Nevertheless, by reinforcing the corporations, the Crown had created powerful vested interests in the tax system, making fundamental reform all the more difficult.

The links between representative government and fiscal stability were made public for the first time in a few pamphlets prior to the Revolution. At the time, the Crown was willing to accept and even to initiate discussions aimed at introducing a representative forum in the hope of resolving the fiscal crisis. The Crown's eagerness for discussion may be attributed to two motivations. First, the creation of representative institutions may have been viewed by the Crown as a way to circumvent the power of the financiers, especially the Ferme générale. Second, the Crown may have hoped that the nation's elites would ultimately surrender their fiscal exemptions in exchange for the right to be represented. To negotiate in good faith for the renunciation of exemptions, the Crown resisted declaring bankruptcy. The negotiations on ending fiscal privileges would have been doomed from the start if the Crown were unable to convince potential interlocutors of a commitment to respect the property of its subjects.

Direct negotiations with the nation's elites might have resulted in the creation of an aristocratic body like the British Parliament if the Crown had been willing to share its political authority. In any event, hoping it would be more accommodating than the influential elites had been, the king called a meeting of the Estates General.[2] The Crown welcomed the idea of members of the Estates General considering themselves the nation's representatives precisely because this might give that assembly the prestige needed to override the elites and local groups who opposed the elimination of exemptions. Failure to achieve a settlement with the financial interest groups, however, brought into the political debate participants for whom fiscal issues were secondary. The result was the French Revolution, which replaced one fiscal crisis with another. France continued well into the nineteenth century to lack banking and fiscal facilities similar in scope and capacity to those of the British.

[2]The Estates General was an assembly of the three orders, or estates, of the kingdom: the clergy, the nobility, and the third estate, or unprivileged classes. It was only summoned in times of difficulty, and its meetings had rarely led to fruitful results.

Did members of the French public value this promise of stability enough to accept the prospect of new taxes? Many pamphleteers expressed the concern that additional taxes without an end to governmental discretion and secrecy would do little to reduce the risks and uncertainty that kept interest rates high. In fact, interest rates stabilized briefly after the reinstatement of Necker in 1787 primarily because of his promise to pay creditors on time and in coin, unlike the previous finance minister, Loménie de Brienne, who proposed payments partly in paper to holders of government securities and offices.[1] The fiscal ideals of 1789 were monetary stability, the timely payment of interest, rules over discretion, and the reduction of uncertainty.

Although many members of the 1789 Constituent Assembly called for equal taxation across regions and social groups, this did not mean they wanted more taxation. During the Revolution an increase in taxation led to resistance in those regions where taxation had traditionally been low. While calling for a more equal distribution of the tax burden, many in France envisioned eliminating particularly unpopular taxes, including the salt tax, the tithe, and the internal tariffs and tolls. An end to the Ferme générale was also desired, as were cuts in government spending on the court. No consensus existed in 1789 in favor of increasing the government's ability to tax as a means of resolving the fiscal crisis. Both Adam Smith and Jean-Baptiste Say pointed out that the French Crown's ability to wage warfare was limited only by its ability to fund wars. Greater tax revenues might have meant longer wars, not greater fiscal and monetary stability.

## REPRESENTATIVE GOVERNMENTS AND FISCAL STABILITY

The collapse of France's disastrous experiment with the schemes of the Scots financier John Law in 1720 contributed to the French government's failure to institute paper money or establish a national bank. Conversely, the rise of the Bank of England and the fact that the principal British state creditors essentially controlled the government, and thus guaranteed the debt, gave England a considerable advantage in the War of the Austrian Succession (1740–48) and the Seven Years' War (1756–63). France's failures in these wars highlighted its lack of national representative government and inability to mobilize confidence among creditors (as compared to

---

[1] The crucial role of investor confidence is confirmed by David Weir's study of French and English interest rates, "Tontines, Public Finance, and Revolution in France and England, 1688–1789," *Journal of Economic History* 49 (1989): 95–124. Weir found that Controller General Terray's partial default in 1770 pushed rates upward until 1774, while English rates remained stable until 1776.

contrast, the lack of public information reduced liquidity and increased interest rates above the English levels. Moreover, because French bills were privately traded, any revelation of instability could have a domino effect—the result of incomplete financial markets and limited, asymmetrically distributed information about the kingdom's debts and assets. Uncertainty about some of the king's bankers quickly led to uncertainty about the entire financial system. Indeed, it was a default spiral that triggered the French Revolution.

## RULES OVER DISCRETION

To explain the fiscal origins of the French Revolution, historians have traditionally emphasized the central government's inability to raise taxes. The underlying reason was the unwillingness of key groups to endorse tax increases in the absence of stated rules of monetary and fiscal policy. Economists have given considerable attention in recent years to the question of economic uncertainty. Uncertainty raises the cost of acquiring capital and discourages investment, which in turn results in a lower level of output than might otherwise be possible. A major cause of uncertainty in Old Regime France was irresponsible government fiscal policy. The threat of late payment of interest, for example, continually hung over the heads of the holders of government securities and offices. Reduction of this uncertainty would have reduced interest rates and increased investment even given a constant but insufficient rate of taxation. French capitalists of the eighteenth century were well aware that uncertainty affects accumulation of capital by increasing interest rates. French industrialists did not invest in projects that their counterparts across the Channel would have pursued, because the higher French interest rates discouraged investment in all but the most profitable of enterprises. Government-guaranteed monopolies satisfied the highest requirements of profitability, whereas productive, unregulated enterprises might not. The government's fiscal irresponsibility thus burdened the nation's economic development.

In the years before the French Revolution, a burgeoning pamphlet literature expressed a clear preference for rules over discretion in government fiscal policy. The authors of the pre-revolutionary pamphlets hypothesized that greater certainty through limits on government fiscal discretion was the primary benefit that parliamentary institutions had brought to England. They enthusiastically endorsed the calling of the Estates General, inasmuch as it might remedy the regime's chronic financial uncertainty. The pamphlet authors affirmed that more public control over fiscal policy would impose restrictions on the previously unfettered fiscal discretion of government ministers.

# 9 The Fiscal Origins of Democratic Revolution

At the time when they were made, many of the vast political consequences of the French king's efforts to remain the central political deal maker were unforeseen. Compared to his English counterpart, it seemed to contemporaries that the French king was in the enviable position of bargaining from strength. A comparison of the two financial systems suggests another conclusion.

Financial institutions specializing in credit assessments were needed to reduce risk, since neither the French nor the English Crown could sell its debt in financial markets. The governments of both nations looked to financial intermediaries as substitutes for nonexistent markets. The intermediaries developed diversified portfolios of loans based on private spread and credit assessments, thereby reducing monitoring costs to the Crown. Fixed-interest debt forms or instruments were developed, supported by the collateral of the intermediaries. The system was buttressed by bankruptcy penalties, since the intermediaries could be held legally responsible for their debts. The similarity between the English and French systems of public finance ends there, however.

In England, a system evolved in which the king's creditors became holders of equity in the state. In France, shares in the royal debt were sold by intermediaries who traded on the presumption of privileged access to political decisions, which significantly enhanced their credibility as deal makers. The French king's intermediaries were private brokers of private information, and their assets and those of their clients were confidential; secrecy was essential to their deal-making role. The resulting information asymmetry put the entire financial system at great risk.

In England, the existence of publicly available information moderated the information asymmetry, thereby reducing interest rates. In France, by

to renege, and thereby the equilibrium interest rate, could be reduced by increasing the sanctions against default.[39]

When many of the corporate institutions became insolvent during the late eighteenth century, the king found he was unable to reform or eliminate them. As managers of the king's funds, the corporations were able to dominate the nation's financial resources. On the eve of the French Revolution, the corporations were thus able to impose their terms on the Crown and block efforts to overhaul the fiscal system.

---

[39] In his study of French finances during the Seven Years' War (1756–63), James Riley argues that the financial authorities late in Louis XIV's regime did not understand the system they administered. He observes that after 1725, royal officials "became convinced of the usefulness of paying the royal debt" and were more reluctant to exploit officeholders than before. Even after incurring "a burden of debt that could not be borne," methods of reducing interest payments—either through conversion, a partial debt repayment in paper currency, or a tax on debt service—were all rejected, however, by what Riley calls an inflexibly cautious financial administration. This bears out the expectation that increased corporate backing of the debt would reduce the temptation of royal officials to renege on their commitments to officeholders. Riley's position differs slightly from the one presented here in that he contends that the financial authorities were excessively cautious "because they did not possess an understanding of finance." See Riley, *Seven Years War*, 162–91.

his cooperation was necessary for the concept of corporate liability to become credible. Assurances of protection by the king's courts were needed in order for the public to believe in corporate solvency. The king's dependence on corporate groups may have evolved as part of an implicit understanding, never formally stated by the king or his officials. It was an understanding that may have benefited both sides, even though societal groups such as the financiers may have initiated the bargaining that led to the establishment of the corporate management of the king's debt.

## THE IRONY OF ABSOLUTISM

In sum, claiming full discretion, the king had less real power. Claiming to be above the law in fiscal matters made it more difficult for him to find business partners. The use of discretion reduced his payoffs in equilibrium because invoking absolute power destroyed royal credibility. Creditors took into account the king's reputation for repudiating debts and therefore demanded higher interest rates than would otherwise have been needed to elicit loans. Actually, because he was above the law, the king had to pay more for loanable funds than did his wealthy subjects. In short, the Crown had a problem asserting its credit because it had a history of reneging on commitments.

An attempt to resolve this dilemma was made by encouraging the growth of intermediary powers in the contracting of loans. Among the intermediaries the king called upon were the traditional corporations: the village communities, the guilds, and the provincial Estates. In return for official recognition and privileges, the corporate groups acted as bankers for the king. They increased the liquidity of the financial system by underwriting transferable securities. There was greater opportunity cost to the king if he defaulted on a group of financiers than on individual financiers. Individuals could more easily be replaced than a corporation that included hundreds of families. Thus, by diminishing the king's temptation to renege, the offices held by members of a corporation became more valuable than those belonging to isolated individuals. Because the offices were more valuable as sources of credit, the king was less likely to default.[38] Such additional discipline was beneficial to the king, because his temptation

---

[38]Consistent with my predictions, William Doyle has argued that "the overall trend was for office prices to rise" during the second half of the eighteenth century. I would like to determine if increased corporate organization was a factor that contributed to increasing the value of offices like those of notary and procurer, which Doyle reports benefited from rapidly escalating prices. See Doyle, "The Prices of Offices in Pre-Revolutionary France," *Historical Journal* 27 (1984): 831–60.

like the village communities, the guilds, the provincial Estates, and the chancelleries of royal secretaries. The Crown had discovered that traditionally constituted bodies could help contribute to the establishment of sound public credit. To create conditions for the public to have confidence in their financial predictability and solvency, the Crown in many cases expanded the privileges and protected the property belonging to constituted bodies.

For example, giving cities the right to collect taxes on goods entering and leaving their jurisdictions allowed municipalities to sell bonds or annuities for the king, using the anticipated revenues from the taxes (*octrois*) as surety. Here, too, local privilege was reinforced in the collection of local taxes, so that the Crown could expand its fiscal resources.[35] A good example is the right to collect tolls on all traffic using the Saône, given the Estates of Burgundy by the king in exchange for a yearly payment in advance.[36]

Similarly, as we saw in chapter 6, fiscal incentives led the Crown to reinforce guild monopolies over local production. By using state power to protect their monopolies, the Crown guaranteed the solvency of the guilds. In exchange for that protection, the Crown could extract rents from the guilds in the form of forced loans. This, in turn, made it possible for the guilds to borrow money from the public to loan to the king.

## THE FAILURE OF REFORM

The king never explicitly stated his dependence on corporate groups and mechanisms. There is no evidence from memoirs, speeches, or decrees in which the Crown acknowledged the rationality of binding its hands. If the monarch and his advisers did not consciously acknowledge the rationality of what had in effect become practice, it was because that rationality directly conflicted with the official rhetoric of divine right monarchy. In the public rhetoric, the king never admitted responsibility to human institutions and repudiated any contractual theory of kingship.[37] Nevertheless, corporate management of the debt advanced with the king's consent. Bargaining between societal groups and the king defined the structure of the Old Regime's financial institutions. The king could have used his legal authority to challenge or veto the development of corporate rights. The fact that corporate charters were often granted by the king suggests that

---

[35] See Jacques Maillard, *Le Pouvoir municipal à Angers de 1657 à 1789* (Paris: Presses de l'Universite d'Angers, 1984).
[36] AN, H-144 (October 1773).
[37] Michel Antoine, "La Monarchie absolue," in *The Political Culture of the Old Regime*, ed. Keith M. Baker (London: Pergamon Press, 1987), 3–24.

nicipal corporations, professional associations, and guilds that provided revenues for the king during the eighteenth century.

## GOVERNMENT BONDS

The government's *rentes perpetuelles* worked according to the same principles as offices. Just as owners of offices received a yearly *gage*, or salary, from the Crown, the owners of *rentes perpetuelles* or perpetual annuities (to be referred to as perpetuities) were entitled to a permanent revenue. An owner could sell these rights to another individual, but he could not cash them in. The market value of the perpetuities fell when the king did not pay the interest due, just as the value of offices diminished when the king delayed payments of *gages*. A tendency to late payment inevitably diminished the long-term value of both perpetuities and offices, making additional perpetuities or offices harder to sell. There was one important difference between these two fiscal expedients. Although the owners of offices could organize into corporations to protect the value of their possessions, the owners of perpetuities were too scattered to do so. (Perpetuities circulated privately and their circulation is difficult to trace. Moreover, the prices of perpetuities are not available, which makes it difficult to determine their real interest rates.)[33] This difference should help to explain why offices held their value and were generally easier for the Crown to sell than perpetuities. Unable to sell perpetuities, the Crown had to depend on more costly short-term loans or on the sale of life annuities. The annuities proved more marketable but were, in the long run, much more expensive for the king than perpetuities.[34] In light of these difficulties, the factors motivating the Crown to place great value on its relationship with the corporations, which were able to provide funds at lower cost than any of the available alternatives, become more evident. The French Crown's inability to sell perpetual bonds contrasts sharply with the success enjoyed by the Bank of England, which was able to finance an important percentage of the nation's debt through the sale of perpetual bonds that held their face value and carried low interest rates.

## TOWARD MORE PUBLIC FINANCE

As noted, during the reign of Louis XIV (1661–1715), the Crown concentrated on building up the corporate character of already-constituted bodies

---

[33]The perpetuities were often used in business transactions—i.e., the purchase of real estate—which often lacked an alternately defined market price.
[34]M. Morineau has calculated that since 1739 the real interest rate for life annuities had been 10 percent, or double the nominal value of perpetuities ("Budgets de l'état," 306).

their share. When one member was unable to pay, another member could provide the share in exchange for a lien on the office. This way, the king got his money quickly. The corporation could then go out and raise additional capital, if needed, from the public more easily than an individual officeholder. Whereas an individual financier could borrow from his personal network of friends and relations, the corporations could borrow from a much broader segment of the public because lenders had more faith in them than in the king. Bien concludes that corporate organization facilitated borrowing from a wider range of individual citizens, so that corporations could mobilize funds on a far grander scale than could individual financiers or the king. For example, in 1726, the *fermiers généraux* were syndicated, allowing the corporation to negotiate with the king as if it were a single financier. In order to loan the king 25 million livres at an interest rate of 5½ percent in 1741, the Ferme générale, as a corporation, was able to borrow from the public at large.[31] Corporate liability was established, so that the corporation, not specific members, was responsible for outstanding debts.

The corporation could act as an intermediary between the king and the investing public because the public could bring the corporation to court in case of default, which it could not do with the king. Consequently, members of the public who might invest in bonds issued by a corporation had greater assurances that their investments were protected than if they had lent to the king directly, or to an individual financier or officeholder. The ultimate effect of corporate organization was to increase the direct sanctions the king suffered if he defaulted. By organizing into a cohesive unit, the *secrétaires* made it more difficult for the king to default and simply replace them, as he had replaced Fouquet with Colbert in 1661. The institution of the *secrétaires du roi* provides one of many examples of the expansion of corporate privilege by the absolute monarchy. The clergy, perhaps the most important corporate body, gave the Crown an annual "free gift" and, in turn, borrowed heavily from the public. Other prominent corporate groups that had state financial functions were the Ferme générale, the Regie générale, the Administration des domains, the Ferme des postes, the Trésor royale, the *procureurs* of the Chambre des comptes, the *notaires* of Paris, the *huissiers du Chatelet* of Paris, the professors of theology at the Sorbonne and Navarre, and the faculties of law and medicine at the University of Paris.[32] In addition there were hundreds of mu-

---

[31]Morineau, "Budgets de l'état," 305.
[32]See BN, L397053, vol. 2, *Recherches et considerations nouvelles sur les finances* (London: M. le Bon de Cormere, 1779).

office as part of a family strategy to acquire the status of tax-exempt nobles, Bien notes; the offices involved few real governmental functions and could be viewed as useless. As individuals, however, the *secrétaires* were subject to frequent fleecing and revocation of privileges. In fact, from 1701 to 1707 alone, the Crown made four separate requests for additional capital sums from officers. Those who did not pay would lose their privileges and salaries (*gages*). In fear of losing their investments, all paid—sometimes with funds borrowed from networks of friends and relatives. Later, by organizing, they would be able to borrow from the public at large.

In the 1720s, the *secrétaires* began to establish procedures of corporate governance that permitted them to use their collective credit to supplement the credit of individual members. The ability to borrow directly from the public as part of a collective unit protected and enhanced the value of their offices. The members established the principle of limited liability: a member's responsibility for the corporation's debt was limited to the value of his office. Potential office buyers wanted assurances that an officeholder's private property would not be subject to seizure for payment of the corporation's debt and that, when an officeholder's office was sold, his obligations ceased and would be assumed by a new member. Once these assurances could be established, the offices would be worth more and the corporation could borrow from the public at lower interest rates.[30]

The institutions devised to impose corporate liability on the financiers emerged from a bargaining process between the Crown and private groups. The Crown had much to gain from strengthening the corporations. It was easier for the king to ask for funds from the corporation as a group than to attempt to contact and negotiate with individual officeholders or separate family networks, many of whom might be difficult to locate or unable to pay. With corporate responsibility, the group had to provide the sum and it was their responsibility, not the king's, to see that all members paid

---

[30]Determining private interest rates accurately will be very difficult. Since it was a crime to loan above the legal interest rate of 5 percent, businesspeople had to dissimulate in order to contract loans at higher rates. Nevertheless, qualitative sources suggest that interest rates were higher in France, where rates of 10 or 12 percent were not uncommon, than in England. Public interest rates declined significantly after 1720, falling from peaks of 16–20 percent during the War of the Spanish Succession. To determine the interest rates for government bonds, it must be determined how much they were discounted when sold. Because the Crown was legally restricted from increasing the rate over 5 percent, it sold its perpetual bonds at a discount. Discounts of 40 percent were common, bringing the real interest rates up to 6.7 percent. See Herbert Luethy, *La Banque protestante en France de la révocation de l'Edit de Nantes à la Révolution* (Paris: S.E.V.P.E.N., 1959), 2:58. In *A History of Interest Rates* (New Brunswick, N.J.: Rutgers University Press, 1963), Sidney Homer cites only nominal interest rates.

could easily be replaced by rival families.[27] Nor did the king repudiate only his debts to large financiers. The Crown constantly reneged or "held up" small officeholders by demanding additional payments for offices already purchased, threatening, for instance, to discontinue interest payments for the office, to cancel tax exemptions, or to withhold the promised payments of salary or pension due on offices.[28] The Crown would claim it was renegotiating the contracts owing to changed conditions. In addition, the Crown squeezed officeholders by selling new offices, which diminished the value of those that already existed. The new offices might be designated to supersede the functions of existing offices. Current officeholders, then, were often compelled to purchase the new offices to minimize their losses from the creation of additional offices. However, the additional office creation led officeholders to demand collective organization. As collectives, eighteenth-century officeholders presented the state with a new terrain for loans, at interest rates less onerous to the Crown than those required in the direct sale of government bonds or annuities.

## THE DEMAND FOR CORPORATE GOVERNANCE: CONSTRAINING KINGLY DISCRETION

Although, as we have seen, there were few restraints in the seventeenth century that prevented the king from engaging in opportunistic behavior, he nevertheless paid a price. When he reneged on his debts to officeholders, he decreased the value of the offices they often used as surety for loans. The officeholders found it harder to borrow when it was perceived that these offices could easily be confiscated. The possibility of the king reneging on his officeholders by increasing either the supply of offices or his demands for repayment reduced their ability to trade on his behalf.

To protect themselves from the depredations of the Crown and to preserve the value of their offices, officeholders demanded the right to establish public corporations. They wanted to limit their individual liability and, more important, to increase the sanctions against default by the king.[29]

The evolution of corporate liability is examined in David Bien's essay "The *secrétaires du roi*: Absolutism, Corporations, and Privilege under the *ancien régime*." In the seventeenth century, the *secrétaires* bought the

---

[27]By the eighteenth century, however, the scale of operations had become too vast and too centralized for the king to use that strategy.

[28]Those salaries were normally one-eighth of the capital cost of the office a year plus an additional pension.

[29]Bosher, too, has argued that the corporation's efficiency was enhanced by its strong corporate organization (*French Finance: From Business to Bureaucracy* [London: Cambridge University Press, 1970], 76).

propose that the Chambre then in session could save the Crown many millions of livres by confiscating the offices of all the financiers.[22] Nevertheless, the most spectacular example of such prosecutions was that of the *surintendent des finances*, Fouquet, in 1659, resulting in the confiscation of his property and his life imprisonment.[23]

In effect, the courts were created to drum up public support so that the Crown could cancel its debts to private financiers. The prosecutions generally set off a wave of private bankruptcies among financiers. Even the vague threat of punishment for ill-defined crimes could cause an individual financier to lose his credibility among his peers and force him into bankruptcy. The surviving financiers inevitably demanded more favorable rates from the king and more costly guarantees for the future.[24]

Another measure the French monarchy commonly employed to cancel its debts was currency reform. The Crown could repudiate debts by reducing the value of the unit of account in which such debts were denominated. Since coinage (the louis d'or) was written up in terms of the unit of account (the livre), by allowing the value of the unit of account to decline, the Crown somewhat reduced its debt. For example, between 1689 and 1726, the equivalent of a livre in silver declined from 8.33 grams to under 4.45 grams.[25]

In summary, kingly discretion characterized the private arrangements between individual financiers and the Crown. Financiers, as individuals or networks, could do little to protect themselves from repudiations.[26] The king reneged by using devices ranging from devaluation to prosecution to outright default, because he assumed that networks of financial families

---

[22]See J. F. Bosher, "*Chambres de justice* in the French Monarchy," in *French Government and Society, 1500–1800: Essays in Memory of Alfred Cobban*, ed. id. (London: Athlone Press, 1973), 19–40.

[23]See Daniel Dessert, "Finances et société au XVIIe siècle: A propos de la Chambre de justice de 1661," *Annales: Economies, sociétés, civilisations* 29 (1974): 847–71.

[24]Not all of these trials were a product of the Crown's high discount rate; they can be seen as a form of callable debt factored into the price in advance. Callable debt exists to cap the upside return to the security holder. The Crown borrowed at a high rate in wartime, serviced that high rate until peace came, and then reduced the rate unilaterally. The Chambre de justice seemed to target financiers who accumulated particularly large fortunes and posed a threat to the Crown.

[25]See James Riley, *The Seven Years War and the Old Regime in France* (Princeton: Princeton University Press, 1986), 167.

[26]Samuel Bernard loaned Louis XIV 15 million livres in 1703, 20 million in 1704, and 30 million in 1708. When Bernard refused further advances in 1709, he was denied payments on the outstanding debt. Unable to repay his creditors, Bernard went into bankruptcy. After the war he was able to recover what he was owed only after agreeing to a fine of 6 million livres. See Charles P. Kindleberger, *A Financial History of Western Europe* (London: George Allen & Unwin, 1984), 95–96.

legal limit. Creditors were thus unable to find a legal sanction to employ against the king when he wanted to default.

## REPEAT PLAY: THE CREATION OF A MINI-SOCIETY

In the absence of public institutions, the Crown relied on networks of family financiers to organize the complex credit transactions that supported state finances between 1610 and 1661. A mini-society of financiers evolved through intermarriage and worked according to the logic known to game theorists as repeat play. Intermarriage among financial families provided a basis for continuity in trade and reasons to limit opportunism. Since the value of the relationship with a family member exceeded the value of a relationship with a stranger—one expects to trade with a family member much more frequently than with a stranger—the future costs of reneging on credit obligations to one's kin were far greater than those of repudiating obligations owed a stranger.[20] Credit relationships that might be impossible between strangers could exist among family members. Whereas repeat play provided some regulation among family networks, it rarely restrained the king.

## KINGLY DISCRETION

"Discretion" refers to rules adopted or contracts entered into at one point in time that do not restrict the parties' later actions. By this logic, the king was free to do whatever best furthered his subsequent aims.

When it proved convenient, the king used a kind of special court, the Chambre de justice, to prosecute individual financiers. These special court sessions were often spectacles designed to inspire public indignation against financiers. The language used to describe financiers in the edicts announcing the Chambre of 1716 was typical: "the immense and lofty fortunes of those [the financiers] enriched by criminal means, the excess of their luxurious living insults most subjects: it is not surprising that they dissipate with profusion what they have acquired by injustice. The riches they [the financiers] possess are the spoils of our provinces, the subsistence of our people, and the patrimony of the state."[21] In 1629, the principal minister of King Louis XIII, Cardinal Richelieu, had gone so far as to

---

[20] Anthropologists and economists like Pranab K. Bardhan use the term *multi-plex* to refer to multistranded relationships such as those between family members. See Bardhan, *Land, Labor, and Rural Poverty: Essays in Developmental Economics* (Delhi: Oxford University Press, 1984).
[21] "Edit portant etablissement d'une Chambre de justice," cited in Dessert, *Argent, pouvoir et société*, 243. The same words were used in the opening of the edict creating the Chambre of November 1661.

not make unsecured loans directly to the Crown; they insisted on making such loans to the highly placed officials of the state whose personal fortunes secured the loans. At all stages of the financial system, the Crown's credit depended on the personal resources of its intermediaries. These officials thus had to possess substantial monetary reserves, enjoy significant credit, and have reliable networks upon which they could call for funds.[17]

During the years 1610–61, the superintendent of finances was the Crown's chief financial official; the arrangement of credit was his principal function. For instance, financial superintendents like Nicolas Fouquet were appointed because of their ability to attract funds from their networks of clients.[18] There were two bases from which Fouquet operated to mobilize credit. One involved the use of his own property as security for loans intended directly or indirectly for the Crown; the other involved loans he contracted using the state's resources as security. The superintendent's clerks were appointed to help him to extend links with the financial elites by persuading potential investors to lend money against future receipts of the financial system at large. Success depended on their ability to ensure repayment when necessary.[19]

The superintendent's clerks often mobilized funds by arranging interest rates for their clients well above the legal limits set by the Crown. Such arrangements had to be made without the formal complicity of the superintendent of finance. The Crown could nevertheless exploit the fact that its agents (the clerks who worked for the superintendent of finance) had acted illegally. The excessive interest rates paid private investors could be cited later as a justification for the Crown to repudiate loans and to persecute its own agents. The financiers could not protect themselves legally from such persecution since they had agreed to interest rates above the

---

their collateral and are not privy to the debtor's inner workings. The move from intermediated government debt to direct debt is thus part of a more general process. Disintermediation has now spread to corporations (commercial paper) and short-term government debt (money market funds).

[17] See Julian Dent, *Crisis in Finance: Crown, Financiers and Society in Seventeenth-Century France* (New York: St. Martin's Press, 1973).

[18] The office of *surintendent des finances* was abolished in 1661. Colbert became the first *controleur générale*.

[19] This system was very successful in the seventeenth century, providing the French monarchy with financial resources far greater than those of its rivals. According to a contemporary analyst, Gregory King, Louis XIV possessed 175.5 million units of revenue (King does not specify the currency), while England had 43.6 million and the United Provinces 61.7 million. The French fiscal system provided France with the means to dominate European politics throughout the late seventeenth century. See Emmanuel Le Roy Ladurie, "Les Comptes fantastiques de Gregory King," *Annales: Economies, sociétés, civilisations* 23 (1968): 1086–1102.

of funds. Nevertheless, corporations involved in the king's finances provided the Crown with important additional borrowing capacity.[14]

It may be that a causal relationship existed between the decline of government interest rates and the shoring up of corporate institutions by the Crown. The 9 and 10 percent interest rates accorded to certain kinds of annuities under Necker, often deemed responsible for the bankruptcy of 1789, did not come close to the 25 percent interest rates registered at the end of Louis XIV's reign. By strengthening corporate institutions, the king had made royal default more costly in the eighteenth century; lower interest rates reflected the diminished probability of the declaration of royal bankruptcy, so common in the seventeenth century.

## FINANCIERS: PUBLIC CREDIT SUPPORTED BY PRIVATE ARRANGEMENTS

The definition of financiers common during the eighteenth century differed in important respects from what became common in the nineteenth century, when it expanded to include banking and other financial services, both public and private. While the classification of financial activity changed, the functions of bankers remained consistent over time. Many of the royal financiers also financed private projects, and all private financiers had some role in state finance, similar to that of banks in the nineteenth century, which were required to hold government securities as reserves.[15] Since the financiers were essentially private business people who managed state finance, they can be thought of as surrogate royal functionaries. Unlike functionaries in a modern bureaucracy, however, these eighteenth-century financiers used personal property—much of it actually state apparatus given them as collateral by the Crown—to secure loans intended directly or indirectly for the Crown.[16] Smaller investors did

---

[14] The percentage of the Crown's total revenue that was supplied by the new forms cannot be determined, but these new forms were rising and provided fiscal services that enlarged the Crown's capacity to borrow. See Alain Guery, "Les Finances de la monarchie française sous l'ancien régime," *Annales: Economies, sociétés, civilisations* 33 (1978): 216–39, and "Le Roi dépensier: Le Don, la contrainte, et l'origine du système financier de la monarchie française d'ancien régime," ibid. 39 (1984): 1241–69. Guery and M. Morineau are reconstructing the Old Regime budget but have yet to determine the percentages of total revenues provided by corporations or by officeholders in general.

[15] During the eighteenth century, the term *financiers* did not have the pejorative connotation of *traitants* (tax farmers) or *partisans*.

[16] Although the definition of financiers has changed since the eighteenth century, the arrangements resembled what we normally describe as banking. Even today, most investing is done through intermediaries; we do not generally lend to corporations, small businesses, or homeowners, because we do not know the value of

them.[10] Under absolutism, the king was the source of law; this meant he could not be held legally accountable by other human beings for the discharge of his sovereign prerogatives.[11]

Because the reliability of the king's commitments was questionable, his credit was weaker than that of many of his wealthiest subjects. For this reason, the growth of state power during the seventeenth century depended upon the king's cultivation of his wealthy subjects to act as intermediaries in contracting loans needed to support the state's expanding military and bureaucratic apparatus. These individuals constructed networks among themselves through intermarriage and contracted with the king's fiscal agents on a personal basis.

Two new developments characterized the evolution of state finance during the eighteenth century. The general farms, which collected the king's taxes, became more bureaucratic, and officeholders organized into corporations. They were joined by many of the traditional corporations in providing loans to the Crown. However, not all officeholders were linked in corporations, and certainly not all corporations were comprised of officeholders. For example, the *receveurs generaux des finances*, who collected direct taxes, were officeholders until 1716; the *fermiers généraux*, created in 1680 to collect indirect taxes, were not officeholders but did enjoy corporate privileges.[12] The *bureaux des finances* of Lille did not fully succeed in establishing a strong corporate structure.[13] In short, financing by corporations supplemented but did not replace individual financiers as sources

---

[10]For a summary of the extensive literature on sovereign repudiations, see John Hicks, "The Finances of the Sovereign," in *A Theory of Economic History* (Oxford: Oxford University Press, 1969), 81–100. In "Repudiations, Defaults and Confiscations by the Medieval State: The Italian Bankers in England, 1270–1345," *Journal of Economic History* 46 (1986), a significant contribution to that literature, John M. Veitch relates medieval interest rates to the probability of default.

[11]Defenders of absolutism wrote as if the sovereign could have the last say and still be accountable to law. This was wishful thinking; it could not and cannot be both ways. If constitutional law is not binding on those who exercise governmental authority, then the conduct of government is no longer subject to the rule of law.

[12]The Ferme générale, which handled the king's extraordinary financing, had grown from supplying 16.6 percent of royal revenues in 1656 to a height of providing 54.7 percent under Louis XIV, stabilizing during the eighteenth century at about 45 percent of all revenue. See Yves Durand, *Les Fermiers généraux au XVIIIe siècle* (Paris: Presses universitaires de France, 1971), 57–56, or id., *Finance et mécénat: Les Fermiers généraux au XVIIIe siècle* (Paris: Hachette, 1976,), 21–22. I plan to study the evolution of the contracts of the various fiscal groups to determine how corporate responsibility evolved.

[13]See Bossenga, "From Corporations to Citizenship."

pansion of corporate society because corporate institutions enabled him to obtain credit.[7] The increasing control of corporations by the Crown was motivated by the need for credible commitments from a monarch who claimed to be above the law.[8] If the king could credibly commit to honor his obligations, then his credit would be strengthened, thereby increasing his ability to finance his government.[9]

Historians generally argue that a desire to promote economic individualism and a free market economy led the Crown to attack corporate groups and corporate privilege. Because strong corporate institutions gave the king access to credit at a lower cost than would otherwise have been possible with competitive markets, one may doubt the "modernizing intentions" of the Old Regime monarchy. The Crown could not have acted as a champion of competitive markets because the royal government would have been less capable of financing itself in a competitive environment.

That the principal player—the king—was above the law constituted the main obstacle to efficient state finance under the Old Regime. This meant he could not be compelled to honor his debts and often chose to repudiate

---

[7] Not all offices had financial functions; many conferred access to lucrative opportunities connected with the office's function. In this chapter, the focus will be on the offices that provided the Crown with financial services. Many offices had purposes beyond helping the king borrow money.

[8] Corporations did not necessarily originate as devices to raise money for the king, but there is considerable evidence that during the seventeenth century, corporations that could be used to raise funds throve, while those that did not were phased out. James Collins argues that the survival of provincial estates during the Old Regime depended on how effectively they raised taxes or floated loans for the king. Those that failed to do so were eliminated. The king would ask the Estates of Brittany for yearly advances on indirect taxes, for example, and because the Estates had to borrow the entire amount, good credit was necessary for their survival. See Collins, *Fiscal Limits of Absolutism: Direct Taxation in Early Seventeenth-Century France* (Berkeley and Los Angeles: University of California Press, 1987), chs. 1 and 2.

[9] *Commit* here means agreeing to a binding contract specifying in advance the government's possible actions. In "Rules Rather Than Discretion: The Inconsistency of Optimal Plans," *Journal of Political Economy* 85 (1977): 473–91, F. W. Kydland and E. C. Prescott argue that rules can produce higher payoffs in dynamically competitive environments than the exercise of discretion. Interest rates on government obligations demanded by competitive markets may be decreased by governmental commitments that increase either the direct or opportunity costs of debt repudiation. This application of the Kydland-Prescott logic allows us to understand the proliferation of institutions under absolutism that increased the costs to the king of behaving opportunistically toward his creditors. For a recent summary of the literature on time-consistency, see Robert Barro, "Recent Developments in the Theory of Rules versus Discretion," *Economic Journal* 96 (1986 supplement): 23–37.

A century later, the corporate organization of society would similarly be condemned as useless and corrupt by government officials such as Turgot. Today, historians commonly echo these eighteenth-century denunciations by depicting corporate bodies such as the provincial estates, municipal corps, and village communities as vestiges of an archaic and moribund old order. To explain the relationship between the state and corporate bodies during this period, the range of modes of contracting from which the king could have chosen to organize his finances should be considered. An analysis of the contractual problems of credit exchange under the constraint of absolute monarchy suggests a different interpretation of the relationship between absolutism and corporate society. Corporate bodies were far from moribund; moreover, corporations that handled the king's funds prospered. Corporate groups with fundamentally different origins—such as the chancelleries of royal secretaries, the municipal corps, and the village communities—all flourished during the eighteenth century.[5] Why would a monarch claiming absolute power allow the proliferation of intermediary bodies whose rights and privileges reduced the Crown's absolute authority and constrained the king's discretion? This counterintuitive outcome seems to have a firm and rational economic basis. As one eighteenth-century administrator explained, "the credit of the estates, the cities and the guilds is the credit of the king."[6]

## THE ECONOMIC FOUNDATIONS OF CORPORATE SOCIETY: THE EVOLUTION OF FINANCIAL INTERMEDIATION UNDER THE OLD REGIME

One of the most important functions of the corporate institutions that expanded in seventeenth- and eighteenth-century France was the creation of trust among partners involved in state finance. The proliferation of corporate bodies can be linked to the king's reputation for repudiating his promises; corporate institutions evolved, not as methods of enhancing the gains from corruption, but as restraints needed to prevent opportunistic sovereigns from defaulting on their creditors. The king supported the ex-

---

[5]See David Bien, "The *secrétaires du roi:* Absolutism, Corporations, and Privilege under the *ancien régime,*" in *Vom ancien régime zur französischen Revolution: Forschungen und Perspektiven/De l'ancien régime à la Révolution française: Recherches et perspectives,* ed. E. Hinrichs (Göttingen: Vandenhoeck & Ruprecht, 1978), 153–67; Gail Bossenga, "From Corporations to Citizenship: The *bureaux des finances* before the French Revolution," *Journal of Modern History* 58 (1986): 610–42; and Hilton L. Root, *Peasants and King in Burgundy: Agrarian Foundations of French Absolutism* (Berkeley and Los Angeles: University of California Press, 1987).
[6]BN, Joly de Fleury, 2536, no. 53 (unsigned manuscript, March 1770).

nations relied more heavily on credit than on taxation to support the rapidly expanding needs of armies and other state functions.² An instructive example is found in the financial history of Old Regime France. There, credit operations accounted for more than half of the state's revenues by the middle of the seventeenth century, and by the eve of the French Revolution, debt service consumed the greater part of current revenues.³ Nevertheless, policies that were hostile to and destructive of the long-term stability of royal credit were commonplace. Such policies have routinely been condemned by historians as manifestations of the fundamentally corrupt and venal structure of traditional French society.

When describing royal finances in seventeenth- and eighteenth-century France, both contemporaries and historians invoke images of flamboyant corruption. Financiers are commonly depicted as parasites whose capital is the nation's blood, drawn from the lower levels of financial administration (like the collection of the *taille*, or tax on peasant incomes) and then reinvested at higher levels in the form of loans to the state. Daniel Dessert, who has provided the most extensive account that we possess of the world of high finance during the seventeenth century, has vividly described how financiers were viewed by their contemporaries:

> The kingdom dreamed of radical measures against the financiers, whose ostentatious displays of wealth, worldly success, and monopolization of the most lucrative state functions all seemed scandalous. The people, exhausted by misery and war, and the state officeholders, led by the *parlementaires*, were the first to suffer from the increased extraordinary activity [their offices lost value by the multiplication of offices created by the king and sold by the financiers], and finally the nobility, always ready to oppose royal power, nostalgically resumed their mythic role as defenders of the oppressed; all these social groups jointly cried vengeance with wonderful unanimity. . . . here was a demagogic program that was sure to be popular at little cost. At the heart of the crisis, [individual financiers] were designated as scapegoats to channel the discontent. Public opinion, long conditioned by literature passionately hostile to financiers, welcomed the sight of tax collectors disgorging [their illicit gains].⁴

---

²Because the government's expenditures occurred continuously and were unpredictably distributed over time and geography, the king had a consistent need for credit.
³See M. Morineau, "Budgets de l'état et gestion des finances royales en France au dix-huitième siècle," *Revue historique* October–November 1981: 289–337.
⁴Daniel Dessert, *Argent, pouvoir et société au grand siècle* (Paris: Fayard, 1984), 242.

# 8 Tying the King's Hands
## Credible Commitments and Royal Fiscal Policy under the Old Regime

Under the Old Regime, the French king sold offices, which in effect constituted the creation of debt shares in the state. The king sold the shares to avoid the alternative of making his subjects into equity holders by granting them representation. The sale of offices extended the fiscal capability of the French Crown by increasing the kingdom's financial liquidity while preserving the king's role as the kingdom's principal deal maker. The Crown's reputation for repudiating its debts meant that the direct sale of the kingdom's debt by the Crown was never an option.

Episodes of fiscal irresponsibility—debt repudiation, currency devaluation, and the expulsion and persecution of state creditors and financiers—are ubiquitous in both early modern French and English history.[1] This is especially curious, since from medieval through modern times, both

---

This chapter began as a paper prepared for presentation in the Program for the Assessment and Revitalization of the Social Sciences (PARSS) seminar series in Historical Data and Rational Choice on December 4, 1986. An earlier version of this chapter also appeared in *Rationality and Society*. I thank J. F. Bosher, Michel Bruguiere, James Collins, Daniel Dessert, Vivian Gruder, Alain Guery, Dan Ingberman, Robert Inman, Tom Kaiser, Lynn Lees, Margaret Levi, John Markoff, Larry Neal, James Riley, Herbert Rowan, Martin Wolfe, and seminar participants at the University of Pennsylvania, Washington University (St. Louis), and the Washington Seminar for French History at George Washington University for helpful comments. My outstanding debt is to David Bien, whose work inspired me to undertake this project. I also gratefully acknowledge the financial support of the Andrew Mellon Foundation and PARSS.

[1] There were many notorious events linked to repudiations by sovereigns. The Jews were expelled from France under Philip IV and from England under Edward I in 1290. Philip IV dissolved the Knights Templar in 1307. English kings continually repudiated loans made by Italian merchant societies between 1270 and 1345. In 1661 the Chamber of Justice under Louis XIV led to a life sentence for the king's minister of finance, Nicholas Fouquet.

# 4
## THE VERY PRIVILEGED

nopolies for both the government and seekers of monopoly rents. In England, by contrast, the possibility of rival interests outbidding the proposers of monopoly legislation and the practice of multilateral parliamentary negotiating allowed methods of state finance to emerge that were more efficient than the sharing of excessive monopoly profits among private groups and the government.

Differences between the industrial organization and rate of industrial innovation between England and France can thus be attributed to differences in the functioning of political markets. Innovation in both technological and organizational forms was discouraged by the high costs of sharing information and negotiating alterations in rights among French guilds. In England, by contrast, industries expanded their technological frontiers because resource holders could trade rights and privileges with the backing of the court system. Groups represented in Parliament could prevent the creation of privileges at their expense, and the independent judiciary was unlikely to sympathize with the ambitions of would-be monopolists. The differences in the structure of English political markets from those of France underlay the different economic achievements of the two nations. We see again that differences in institutions that determine political choices can produce differences in economic policy outcomes.

In sum, the failure of mercantilism in seventeenth-century England can be primarily attributed to three causes: disputes between competing public authorities (Crown and Parliament), the difficulty of gaining support in Parliament and in the common law courts for monopoly legislation, and the problems of monopoly enforcement—that is, the venality of public officials. Attempts by the Crown to institute monopolies and to regulate industry as a revenue-raising measure failed, as the opposition of Parliament and the common law courts put the legal status of Crown monopolies in jeopardy. Parliament was unreceptive to the efforts of monopolists because of the diffuse and pluralistic nature of its constituency. The variety of interests represented in Parliament made acceptance of a given monopoly difficult, since conflicting economic interests set would-be monopolists against one another. Although broadly defined interest groups such as grain growers were able to obtain their goals, a monopolizer of one industrial product would often impose costs on related industries and on landowners, and, as Ricardo noted, inefficiencies in the economy ultimately result in lower rents. A monopolist would therefore find it difficult to negotiate concessions with neighboring interests or related industries. Economic interests might have responded to the inhospitable environment for monopolies by devoting more resources to production and fewer to rent seeking. Consider Adam Smith's example of the pin makers, who in 1690 opposed efforts to obtain a monopoly on behalf of their industry. It seems the pin makers had decided that the required investment in lobbying Parliament produced results that were less valuable than investments in improving production. Finally, we must add to the rent seekers' calculus the uncertainty of enforcement, which further reduced the possible gains from their considerable investments in lobbying Parliament for a monopoly.

To explain England's precocious development of free domestic markets, scholars sometimes contrast the puritanical, practical, business-minded English with the Catholic, aristocratic French, whose traditional values and preoccupation with spiritual salvation and military prowess distracted them from projects to increase the gross national product. Here, however, rather than arguing that English gentlemen were more culturally receptive to capitalism than their French counterparts, it is suggested that the concentration of financial and industrial discretion in the office of the controller general permitted the French Crown to provide favored business groups with special privileges. The privileges were enforced by a system of administrative courts and law that stood above traditional provincial jurisdictions. The regulatory authority concentrated in the French controller generalship reduced the costs of establishing and protecting mo-

petitive markets was owing to more than policy recommendations and philosophical considerations; it also reflected the inability of the English government to create and enforce mercantilist policies. The discretionary pattern of monopoly enforcement by JPs and the need for the consent of England's competing economic interests to legislation sealed the fate of English mercantilism.

The philosophical argument in favor of a free market took a long time to penetrate the public policies of the British Parliament. For example, Parliament was still trying to control labor mobility in the late seventeenth century. The Settlement Act of 1662 gave JPs the right to order migrants to return to their rural parishes. By 1697, migrants were allowed to move within the country only if they obtained a certificate of settlement from the authorities in the new place of residence. It was not until the nineteenth century that Parliament seems to have converted to a free-trade philosophy. The Bubble Act of 1720, ordering citizens to obtain express authorization before forming a corporation, was repealed only in 1825, and it was not until 1833 that all English people, not just freemen, were authorized to set up shop and trade in the City of London. Not until 1832 was authorization granted to set up a business without a special permit, and only in 1844 was automatic registration granted. Parliament authorized registered businesses to become limited liability stock companies only in 1862. Two centuries earlier, Parliament had attempted to compete with the king for the privilege of establishing an enterprise. This competition was motivated by the bribes and credits that could be generated. In practice, English producers had learned that efforts to invoke restrictive regulations often incurred costs that were greater than the privileges they conferred. As the competition between the courts and the uncertainty of enforcement hindered the application of mercantile regulations, English producers became more dependent on voluntary contracts. Eventually, the English court system decided to enforce them.

The same evolution toward a voluntary regime might have occurred in France had it not been for the rise of absolutism. The French monarchy found in mercantilism an important source of state revenues. Access to these revenues derived from the monarchy's ability to enforce regulations by bypassing traditional local jurisdictions and establishing the supremacy of royal statutes. The autonomy of the English legal system from the political system allowed changes in property rights to be implemented without the intervention of executive authority. The possessors of British monopolies could not appeal to special royal courts to defend their monopolies, but depended on common law courts and juries made up of individuals unlikely to sympathize with those who defended the right to crush low-cost competitors in order to keep prices high.

authorities. The rise of Parliament was the final blow to guild well-being. Parliament constituted an uninviting political target for the seekers of monopoly, because the groups that would bear the costs of monopoly legislation were also represented in Parliament.

The decline of English mercantilism and of government-approved monopolies has traditionally been explained by reference to the influence of a laissez-faire philosophy on Parliament. Yet it seems that there was much more to the decline than that. As C. G. A. Clay points out, opposition to the Crown on religious, constitutional, and foreign policy grounds did not make MPs supporters of economic freedom.[46] The view that the rise of Parliament was responsible for ending governmental monopolies in England oversimplifies the story. The difficulty of gaining support for monopolies in a pluralistic institution such as Parliament was reflected in the large number of monopolies granted by the Crown as compared to the few granted by Parliament. Nevertheless, Ekelund and Tollison's argument—that mercantilism declined because mercantilist rents were dissipated in the competition between Parliament and the king for control of the domestic economy—leaves room for expansion. For Parliament opposed all but a few monopolies, and aside from the one example cited by Ekelund and Tollison, no instance of a monopoly being granted by Parliament without pressure from the Crown is available for the early seventeenth century. The structure of English political institutions—the difficulty of lobbying Parliament and the Crown's dependence on the justices of the peace—provides additional insight into the decay of English mercantilism. Heckscher's examination of the role of the common law courts is valuable, but the jurisdictional autonomy of those authorities who controlled access to the local marketplace must be part of a fuller answer. The JPs enforced policies that catered to local interests rather than policies predicated on the needs of those outside their jurisdiction. One consequence of local jurisdictional competition was an exodus of industry from towns that enforced municipal restrictions on production to the countryside and regions, such as the north, where guild monopolies did not exist.

At every step the absolutist ambitions of the English Crown were thwarted: consent of Parliament was needed for taxes; consent of the law courts was needed for legal enforcement of alternative revenue sources; and, most important, consent of the gentry was needed for daily implementation of monopolies. It seems, therefore, that the expansion of com-

---

[46]C. G. A. Clay, *Economic Expansion and Social Change: England, 1500–1700*, vol. 2, *Industry, Trade and Government* (New York: Cambridge University Press, 1984), 239.

mon law decision went even beyond the Custom of London to specify that certain crafts required no professional skills and were therefore outside the scope of the statute.[42]

To cope with the chaos in guild rights, the Crown often offered regulations tailor-made to a specific guild. Of course, the Crown's motive was consistently the collection of rents. In an example of a guild dispute, the watermen, who controlled boat transportation on the Thames in London, appealed to the Crown to ban coaches. Parliament rejected a proposed bill to ban the coaches, but in 1614 the Crown's prerogative courts limited their use, and in 1634 the Star Chamber banned their use altogether, in return for a payment by the watermen. An appeal of the coachmen to the Crown to allow freedom of transportation, accompanied by an offer of a larger grant to the Crown, prompted revocation of the ban.[43]

After the Restoration (1660), control of the guilds remained in the hands of Parliament, which increasingly granted exceptions to the strict apprenticeship requirements set down in the Statute of Artificers. In 1663, the linen industry saw all apprenticeship requirements removed; in 1666, freedom to practice a trade was granted to all those rebuilding London after the great fire; and in 1667–68 the silk-throwing industry was forbidden to limit the number of spindles and apprentices.[44] Furthermore, the restrictive apprenticeship clauses of the statute were completely disregarded by judges in rural areas during the Restoration period.[45]

## WHY DID COMPETITIVE MARKETS DEVELOP MORE FULLY IN ENGLAND THAN IN FRANCE?

The guilds played an important role in the traditional structure of medieval industry in England by providing insurance and social benefits for their members and by acting as distributional coalitions that used their monopoly power to their members' benefit. Although the early development of national markets broadened the potential for guild goods and services, it weakened the guilds. Once markets developed on a national scale and jurisdiction was given to the JPs, each guild only had a small portion of the total market. Even if local craftspeople could easily lobby the councils of small towns and villages, they were relatively ineffective in the developing national market. The shift of economic power from local to national jurisdiction reduced the opportunities of guilds to influence government

---

[42]Ibid., 292.
[43]George Unwin, *The Guilds and Companies of London* (London: Methuen, 1908), 331–32.
[44]Heckscher, *Mercantilism*, 304.
[45]Ibid., 314.

since the Norman Conquest had the Crown developed so sustained an attack on the established political powers of the aristocracy and major gentry."[38] James II so alienated the English gentry by the purge that it led to his overthrow.

## GUILDS AND THE COMMON LAW

Before concluding, let us consider one further example of how the industrial structures of early modern France and England differed. English guilds traditionally faced substantial limitations on their powers. First, guilds did not exist in many unincorporated cities, not even in such long-established cities as Cambridge. A study by Sidney and Beatrice Webb found evidence of guilds in only one-quarter of cities that existed in 1689.[39] Some cities were incorporated deliberately so that guilds could be established: the 1626 incorporation of Leeds can be identified as an attempt to regulate the wool industry. However, incorporations of this type were uncommon for England, and many cities remained free of guilds.[40]

The guilds in incorporated cities faced substantial limitations in controlling their members owing to the Custom of London, which granted any artisan the right to practice his trade in any guild, as long as he met that guild's standards. The municipal government of London tried unsuccessfully to stop small craftspeople from exercising this right. Just as firms in modern-day America will incorporate wherever corporate laws are most favorable, craftspeople in early modern England granted the right to the Custom of London joined whichever guild was least strict. Heckscher gives two examples of the heterogeneous membership of the London Goldsmith's Company, which was evidently the "Delaware" of guilds: thirty-nine gemstone setters belonged to it in 1671, as opposed to fifty-two in their own guild, and a Newcastle confectioner chose to join the goldsmiths' guild in 1685.[41]

The courts further undermined the ability of guilds to control competition. As early as 1590, the Court of the Exchequer ruled that a seven-year apprenticeship in one trade granted a right to practice all trades, apparently disregarding the limits to participation in crafts imposed by the Statute of Artificers, passed fewer than thirty years before. A 1615 com-

---

[38]J. H. Plumb, *England in the Eighteenth Century, 1714–1815* (Harmondsworth: Penguin Books, 1950), 29.
[39]Sidney Webb, *English Local Government from the Revolution to the Municipal Corporations Act: The Manor and the Borough* (New York: Longmans, Green, 1908), 1:297.
[40]Heckscher, *Mercantilism*, 243.
[41]Ibid., 245.

Second, the system of nominations of JPs by local squires was well entrenched by the time the Stuarts came to power. In the 1590s, Lord Burghley, Queen Elizabeth's principal minister and chief of the Exchequer, had tried to purge the benches, but those removed from the lists soon reappeared. The Crown did not possess the means to conduct a thorough examination of the qualifications of JPs and assize judges. "[By the reign of James I] nomination had become largely decentralized, a matter of pleading and pushing with the right people at the right time."[34] The nomination process contributed to this general pattern of lack of Crown control. The lord chancellor, who appointed JPs, took on trust most of the names offered to him at the local level. Lords lieutenant, who made requests for additional justices for their counties, made most of their nominations on local suggestion. Nominations to the bench by prominent local officials were often made on a patronage basis. Furthermore, attempts at pruning the number of JPs invariably ran into local opposition. In 1625, one of the most effective purges of the century removed almost half of the Sussex commission. The old and enfeebled who had been forced to retire stayed off the lists; but the younger men returned to the commission "following pressure from the shire."[35]

Even during the traumatic political events of the seventeenth century, the combination of local pressure and the vast number of JPs needed to run the administration preserved the hold of the local gentry on the commissions. During the Civil War, Parliament attempted to replace all those suspected of royalist or neutralist sympathies. However, the shortage of qualified members of the local gentry forced the continuance of many royalist judges. A study by John Morrill of Restoration JPs in Cheshire reveals continuity in the selection of JPs: 40 percent of Restoration JPs were the sons of royalists, but 33 percent were moderate Parliamentarians who had been purged in the 1650s, and 27 percent were JPs who had actually participated in the commissions of the 1650s under Cromwell.[36]

The only systematic attempt at the complete remodeling of the JP commissions during the seventeenth century was made by James II. In 1687, every county had its bench revised; 498 new justices were installed, of whom 64 percent were Catholic. Further changes in 1688 completely dispossessed the Anglican squires: turnover of 75 percent or greater occurred in many counties.[37] J. H. Plumb argues that James II's purge of the JP commissions was the fundamental cause of the Glorious Revolution: "Not

[34]Ibid., 6.
[35]Ibid., 7–8.
[36]Ibid., 19.
[37]Ibid., 24–25.

During the Elizabethan era, outright refusals by JPs to enforce monopolies were not uncommon. JPs in Yorkshire in 1588 refused to enforce a 1585 patent that entailed a salt monopoly in Boston, King's Lynn, and Hull. One of the JPs even sold four shiploads of contraband Scottish salt at King's Lynn.[29] To enforce the unpopular soap monopoly, as discussed earlier, an expansion of the royal bureaucracy beyond the JPs was needed. According to Price, "The hostility of local authorities [JPs] was so great that enforcement could not be entrusted to the ordinary magistrates."[30] Heckscher concludes that although JPs had an influence on setting wages and poor relief, they were ineffective in regulating production.[31]

As the seventeenth century wore on, the reliability of the JPs did not improve, and Restoration England did not develop a system of central administration comparable to Colbert's intendants. The JPs' status as unpaid government officials recruited from the prominent local gentry made them a particularly weak tool in the Crown's attempts at enforcing regulation and monopolies. Charles I found himself forced to employ messengers of the Star Chamber to enforce his mercantilist legislation, but Charles II (1660–85) did not have prerogative courts at his disposal. Charles II's best executive agents were the lords lieutenant, whose "general uselessness and particular inefficiency for the purposes of the new state regulation" were widely recognized. As the royal bureaucracy in France was expanding, Heckscher notes, "the administration which had served the older Stuarts was on the contrary breaking down and nothing was being set up in its place."[32]

However, this cannot be the end of the story. For if the JPs were so intransigent, why did the Crown not replace them? After all, they were supposedly Crown officials. The answer lies in the limits of royal discretion in the selection of JPs.

First, the number of JPs needed to run the local administration was substantial by the seventeenth century. Fifty-one English and Welsh counties (two of which were divided into ridings) were served by commissions of JPs, and the number of JPs on the commissions could be substantial. The total number of JPs in 1600 has been estimated at 1,200; by 1714, it had risen to over 3,000.[33]

---

[29] Nef, *Industry and Government*, 106.
[30] Price, *English Patents*, 122.
[31] Heckscher, *Mercantilism*, 247–53.
[32] Ibid., 262–63.
[33] Anthony Fletcher, *Reform in the Provinces: The Government of Stuart England* (New Haven: Yale University Press, 1986), 39.

rounding countryside. James I incorporated companies in the textile-producing areas of Suffolk, Norfolk, and Essex to legally center industry in the towns. In 1625, the "New Draperies," lighter cloth producers, were to be organized into local monopolies. A 1662–63 plan was to organize the woolen industry of Yorkshire around Leeds into one company. Notably, there was the only successful incorporation. Only a 1623–24 incorporation of all the Hallamshire iron industry was enacted by Parliament, and even this was merely a formal recognition of an already-existing organization.[24]

During his personal rule, Charles I attempted to allocate monopoly powers to each of the London trades in exchange for rents.[25] As an example, the makers of playing cards were incorporated into a monopoly if they were within a ten-mile radius of London, thus being obliged to pay the king a rent of 12s. per gross. The 1638 charter of the London Silkweavers' Company extended its control over the whole of England. The prominent Canterbury silk weavers were compelled to join the monopoly, which suppressed the loom as a harmful invention.[26] To circumvent the local jurisdiction that regulated local production, the Crown attempted to create regional or national royal monopolies, but their attempts seem to have failed for lack of enforcement. So far the English Crown's weak control over the kingdom's industrial structure resembles that of France before Colbert. Guilds were also in decline there, inasmuch as industry was moving to the suburbs and to the countryside. As we have seen, the French monarchy developed institutions to assert its economic *dirigisme*. The justices of the peace, a peculiarly English administrative institution, were one reason for the failure to implement similar royal control in England via monopoly rights.

## SELF-INTERESTED ENFORCEMENT

Robert Ekelund and Robert Tollison have already drawn attention to the role of justices of the peace in the decline of English mercantilism.[27] Many contemporary sources also allege that JPs did not perform their duties with either attention or integrity. JPs, who were prominent members of the local gentry, were not paid for their work, so examples of their self-interested approach to the enforcement of regulations are abundant.[28]

---

[24]Ibid., 241–42.
[25]The 1623–24 Statute of Monopolies banned monopolies based solely on the royal prerogative. The statute was intended as an impediment to royal monopolies, but Charles I evaded it during his personal rule by granting monopolies to corporations instead of individuals.
[26]Price, *English Patents*, 39.
[27]Ekelund and Tollison, *Mercantilism*, 35–42.
[28]Heckscher, *Mercantilism*, 247–53.

nopolies and guilds to London and towns corporate, the geographic scope of monopolies had been limited to certain cities.[20]

Before the seventeenth century, the limits of the Crown's jurisdiction over industrial regulation were already apparent. In 1576, the Tallow Chandlers' Guild gained a royal patent to stop the illegal manufacture of tallow in London and the suburbs. This right was negated by a combination of two factors. Not only did the mayor and aldermen of London oppose the patent's enforcement, but the lords who held Courts Leet (local baronial courts) in the suburbs also refused to enforce the search for illegal producers.[21]

In response to the strict regulation within the towns, industrial production shifted to the countryside—a shift already noted during the sixteenth century. Thus much English production escaped the reach of guild and royal regulation. A law of 1557–58 claimed that cloth manufacturers "do not only engross divers farms and pastures into their hands, displeasing the husbandman and decaying the ploughs and tillages, but also draw with them out of the city, burghs and towns corporate all sorts of artificers." In this law, as in others of the sixteenth century, the government attempted to prevent the exodus of industry to the countryside. However, this law allowed the continued existence of already-established rural manufacturers, indicating that this "legislation yielded before a fait accompli." Even this was not enough, and enforcement of the law was deemed so impractical that it was abolished in 1623–24.[22] "If our clothiers were commanded to inhabit in towns, as they do in France, Flanders, Brabant, Holland and other places, we should have as many good towns in England as you have in France and cloth more finer and trulier made, not withstanding your brags," declared Sir John Coke (1563–1644).[23] One important difference between France and England must be stated here. The British Parliament refused to extend guild statutes and jurisdiction to the outlying countryside. By contrast, France's royal courts supported the claims of French guilds to regulate rural production.

Subsequent efforts failed to extend the authority of the guilds beyond the towns and include suburban industrial production in the monopolistic companies of the early Stuarts. During the seventeenth century, the government made a number of attempts, almost all by the Crown rather than Parliament, to extend the geographic control of urban guilds over the sur-

[20]Ibid., 284–85.
[21]Unwin, *Industrial Organization*, 295.
[22]Heckscher, *Mercantilism*, 239.
[23]J. Coke, "The Debate between the Heralds of England and France," *Tudor Economic Documents*, 3:6, 8.

expense of intense political opposition, the Crown's monopolies functioned as a fiscal system independent of Parliament. The revenues they produced were insufficient to meet all of Charles I's fiscal needs, but the outline of an absolutist, rent-seeking monarchy resembling the absolutist state that later came into existence in France was beginning to appear.

Although the sale of offices and most monopolies was abolished by the Long Parliament, the fiscal motive for regulation did not die with Charles I. The soap monopoly, which survived the Civil War, escaped the wrath of the Long Parliament toward monopolies in general. It gained the sanction of Cromwell and in 1656 was the subject of a case heard by the Court of the Exchequer, which ruled in the monopoly's favor. An appeal the following year was quashed by order of Parliament. Price suggests that this monopoly facilitated collection of the excise tax on soap; Parliament preferred to assess charges from one company rather than attempt to collect taxes nationwide from numerous soap manufacturers or from consumers directly.[18] The soap company was a substitute for an administrative structure for collecting soap excise taxes; it was a mechanism to facilitate tax collection.

## COMPETING JURISDICTIONS

Since English kings faced restraints on their ability to create and enforce monopolies, the English Crown profited less than the French from the monopolies it authorized. By the seventeenth century, monopolies based on royal charter alone were considered invalid by the common law courts. A 1599 judgment struck down a guild regulation based on a royal charter on the grounds that "the ordinance although it had the countenance of a charter, was against the common law because it was against the liberty of the subject"; and a 1614 judgment decided that "to make a monopoly . . . is to take away Free-trade, which is the birthright of every subject." Heckscher quotes these cases as typical of the courts' insistence that royal monopolies violated common law.[19] The courts did respect monopolies based on acts of Parliament, but there were few such monopolies. Furthermore, the courts would not respect local monopolies unless these were based on immemorial custom. During the seventeenth century, the common law courts prevented the extension of guilds' privileges; by 1705, the courts prevented newly privileged cities from restricting industrial freedom without the support of an act of Parliament (even within their own local jurisdiction). Since the Statute of Monopolies had also limited mo-

---

[18]Ibid., 126.
[19]Heckscher, *Mercantilism*, 283.

dustrial regulation was farmed out to inspectors (called patentees), who could keep the fines they collected. All too often, according to Eli Heckscher, sales of such regulatory offices were motivated by purely fiscal concerns.[14] The inspectors quickly acquired a reputation for venality and for protecting the interests of those who offered the highest bribes, which often meant that they worked on behalf of the manufacturers they were assigned to regulate.[15]

The Cockayne Project of 1614 is another example of governmental support for regulation containing fiscal benefits for the Crown. The project was proposed as a method of encouraging cloth finishing in England by forbidding the export of unfinished cloth; but only after James I applied considerable political pressure was the project approved in the Privy Council. His enthusiasm is unsurprising if one considers the annual customs revenue that James hoped to gain: £20,000 on dyestuffs and £20,000 on the finished cloth exports. In the end, increased production on the Continent, the inadequacy of the English industry to cope with the sudden increase in demand, and retaliatory trade measures by the Dutch forced the end of the customs on dyestuffs and finished cloth exports. The retaliatory action by the Dutch brings to mind the problems of Bartlett's pin monopoly and reveals the importance of international pressure on English government economic policy.[16]

By the end of the period of Charles I's personal government, the king was receiving substantial revenue from the alum, wine (£30,000 per annum), tobacco (£13,125), and soap (£30,825) monopolies, as well as additional income from such minor sources as playing cards and dice (£750). "In all but name, an excise system had been established, which imposed substantial indirect taxes upon internal trade," Price comments.[17] At the

---

[14] Eli F. Heckscher, *Mercantilism* (New York: Macmillan, 1955), 1:253–55. Nef concurs with Heckscher's assessment and offers the following example: in response to complaints about the quality of coal in London, the Crown created the office of "surveyor of coals" to inspect coal. The king granted this very profitable office to royal favorites on three separate occasions between 1618 and 1637. The position was worth £2,000 a year (the surveyor was entitled to a fee for each chaldron [ = 36 bushels] of coal). But this fiscally motivated response failed to satisfy consumers and producers of coal. In 1618, both the mayor of Newcastle and the lord mayor of London refused to support this position of surveyor; the former was a colliery owner and the latter was influenced by the politically powerful coal shippers. See Nef, *Industry and Government*, 54.

[15] Heckscher, *Mercantilism*, 247–53.

[16] B. E. Supple, *Commercial Crisis and Change in England, 1600–1642: A Study in the Instability of a Mercantile Economy* (Cambridge: Cambridge University Press, 1970), 50.

[17] Price, *English Patents*, 42.

for the king. But in 1646 he surrendered Lundy to Parliament in return for the restoration of the mines. His lease was subsequently renewed by both Oliver and Richard Cromwell. Then, after the Restoration, Bushell petitioned Charles II for repayment of his expenses to Charles I and for his losses owing to "the usurper Cromwell." This case illustrates that Parliament was not opposed to the idea of monopolies that served convenient political ends. However, monopolies submitted to Parliament for approval typically faced substantial opposition from adjacent economic interests.[11]

Another example of a monopoly that had parliamentary support was the soap corporation. Charles I's lord treasurer, the earl of Portland, who died a Catholic, supported the vastly unpopular (and largely Catholic) Westminster Company soap monopoly, against the opposition of Archbishop Laud of the Church of England. After Portland's death in 1635, Laud's support gave a new company, consisting of the chief manufacturers of London, Bristol, and Bridgewater, the opportunity to buy out the Westminster Company and create a more broadly based, cartel-like monopoly.[12] The new monopoly was subsequently able to gain the approval of the Long Parliament and Cromwell, as well as a judgment in its favor by the Court of the Exchequer. Again Parliament was not ideologically opposed to monopoly. "The continuance of this monopoly shows that some even of the most questionable privileges might thrive as well under the Commonwealth as under the monarchy," William Hyde Price comments.[13] Parliament, like the Crown, viewed monopolies as a potential source of revenue.

## MONOPOLY ENFORCEMENT

Because of the shortage of royal revenue and the lack of a royal administrative structure, the early Stuarts were unable to pay their officials. One solution to this problem was to expand the jurisdiction of justices of the peace to include industrial regulation; but for reasons elaborated later, the Crown could not rely upon the JPs to enforce industrial regulation, and James I and Charles I resorted to an alternative that would raise revenue while regulating industry. The office of supervision and inspection of in-

---

[11]For example, in the controversy over a 1690 application by the New Company of White Paper Makers for a grant of monopoly, the paper sellers of London successfully denounced the application as a violation of the Statute of Monopolies. See W. J. Cameron, "Lobbying by the White Paper Makers, 1690," in *Seventeenth-Century Economic Documents*, ed. Joan Thirsk and J. P. Cooper (Oxford: Clarendon Press, 1972), 314.
[12]John U. Nef, *Industry and Government in France and England, 1540–1640* (Ithaca, N.Y.: Cornell University Press, 1969), 122.
[13]Price, *English Patents*, 127.

seventeenth century posed an obstacle to potential monopolists who depended on royal charters. As in the pin makers' case, royal support was not always sufficient to enforce monopolies, since other interest groups could appeal to Parliament. The experience of the starch makers provides another example. Early in the reign of James I, the Starchmakers' Company wanted its charter of monopoly sanctioned by the king, courts, and Parliament. While the starch makers were able to gain royal charters and a tariff against foreign starch, the common law courts refused to sanction the starch makers' monopoly without an act of Parliament, which was not forthcoming. The grocers who retailed starch to consumers protested to both Parliament and the king that the price of starch had doubled. In response, a royal order of 1610 suspended the charter of the royal monopoly and forbade all domestic manufacture. This bizarre decision, while it must have greatly increased Crown revenues from the tariff, displeased the grocers, whose starch costs were still higher than before 1610. A new royal decision in 1622 reinstated the Starchmakers' Company over the protests of the grocers and City of London merchants, many of whom must have been starch users unhappy with the thought of a revived monopoly.[9]

The history of the Cardiganshire mines offers an example of how rent-seeking strategies depended on the incentives created by political institutions.[10] The Society of the Mines Royal, whose members were royal courtiers, was granted a charter in 1604 stipulating sole mining rights for metal in Wales and northern England in return for granting 10 percent of the mineral riches to the Crown. In fact, the society did nothing except collect rents from private prospectors. For example, Thomas Bushell, who restored the broken-down mining works in Cardiganshire in the 1630s, paid for a lease from the society, although it offered him no assistance. The unproductive role of the society and the possibility of extracting higher rents direct from the prospectors came to the attention of the Privy Council, which subsequently deprived the society of its rights over the Cardiganshire mines. Accordingly, upon the expiration of the first lease, Bushell had to pay an increase of rent of £1,000, plus a "gratuity" of £1,000. Interestingly, Bushell attempted to keep the lease to the mines despite political uncertainty during the Civil War and its aftermath (1640–60). Charles I recognized his services to the royal cause in 1643, and in the course of the Civil War, Bushell fled to the isle of Lundy, which he held

---

[9]William Hyde Price, *The English Patents of Monopoly* (New York: Houghton Mifflin, 1906), 37.
[10]Ibid., 50–55.

To gain a monopoly in Parliament, where the arguments of diverse groups could be simultaneously presented, was difficult. The problem for potential seekers of monopoly was that they had to contend in Parliament with the very parties their monopoly would affect. It is easier to create monopolies when the victims are not represented in the negotiations; more parties to the negotiation meant more competitive pricing for economic privilege. Parliament represented a competitive market for the purchase of privilege that did not exist in France.

The pin makers' need to gain the support of both the Crown and Parliament to enforce regulations is highly illustrative of a new reality in English industrial organization. As England became a national market, local guild authorities could not enforce regulation by themselves; they needed the cooperation of some third party with national coercive authority. Earlier guild monopolies were sustained by collusion with municipal or regional governments that could enforce local monopoly conditions. A single guild could much more easily achieve its goals when the only authority it depended upon was the local town council. The coercive powers of a single municipality were not extensive enough to provide enforcement beyond the local marketplace. National recognition, as noted, had to be backed by the coercive authority of a national authority such as the Crown or Parliament. Thus, Parliament's support was needed by any would-be monopolist when it expanded its jurisdiction vis-à-vis the Crown after the Civil War. Securing a majority in Parliament for a particular monopoly, however, was not easy.

## COMPETING PUBLIC AUTHORITIES

Although seventeenth-century English rent seekers could attempt to protect their monopolies at Court through political connections or bribes, the growing aspirations of Parliament might make such protection inadequate. It was much easier to obtain rents from one source—in this case, the English Crown—than from a multiplicity.[8] However, the claims of authority that Parliament and the common law courts were making by the

---

[8] See Robert B. Ekelund, Jr., and Robert D. Tollison, *Mercantilism as a Rent-Seeking Society: Economic Regulation in Historical Perspective* (College Station: Texas A&M University Press, 1981), 17–28. One clarification is necessary. A dictator or an absolute monarchy may have an administrative or decision-making bureaucracy that is just as numerous and complex as a legislative body. Conversely, the number of people and diversity of views in an organization need not necessarily correspond to the number of liaisons needed by an outsider to transact business with that organization, since it may assign one person or office to deal with a particular function or activity. For example, although there may be many different opinions about purchases in a firm, a single person or department usually does its buying.

this time, the proposal was opposed from within the industry by some of the pin makers themselves. The internal opposition noted that the industry was in no need of protection; the export of pins had become a thriving business. In addition, the pin makers opposing the monopoly argued that it might produce the same adverse conditions produced by the card makers' monopoly renewed by Charles II: high prices, poor employment conditions for workers, the perpetuation of costly methods of production, and restriction of output. Abstract economic theory was not the basis of their argument.

Perhaps the pin makers' repeated and dramatic failures to achieve monopoly conditions prompted them to adopt the innovations in the organization of production eventually touted by Adam Smith, who viewed the pin-making industry as a model for the application of the economic laws governing specialization and the division of labor.[7] In fact, the history of the pin makers during the seventeenth century is emblematic of the failure of English mercantilism, a failure that raises a number of questions. Why were the pin makers successful with the Crown, but not with Parliament? Why did the Crown sell its role in the 1640 proposal to reorganize the pin industry? Why did the pin makers' guild seek an independent company charter and the patronage of a courtier rather than remain within the traditional guild structure? Why did Bartlett find himself unable to gain a nationwide monopoly, and why did having a national charter matter? Finally, what led to the failure of Lydsey's monopoly in 1635, despite its royal sanction?

In English industrial history, the pin makers' success in gaining the Crown's support was as common a phenomenon as their failure with Parliament. The competition between Parliament and the Crown for the right to regulate economic activity had resulted in the failure of numerous other efforts to secure monopoly rights. Parliamentary and royal industrial regulation had the same motivation—revenue. However, competing interests within Parliament often prevented it from endorsing private efforts to secure monopolies. Only monopolies that did not challenge already-constituted interest groups were likely to gain parliamentary approval. Despite the difficulties experienced by Parliament in granting monopolies and its consistent anti-monopolistic public stance, however, Parliament did approve monopolies that placed revenues at its disposal.

---

[7]"It is an interesting coincidence to find this practical refutation of mercantilist ideas coming from the industry which was presently to furnish to the greatest of economic theorists [Adam Smith] his most classical illustration of the advantages of free industrial development," Unwin notes (ibid., 171).

profits resulting from foisting inferior English wire on domestic pin producers. George Unwin notes that "the pinmakers, if left to themselves, would have preferred foreign wire, which made better pins."[6] To persuade the pin makers to accept the Royal Battery Works' wire, the Crown was willing to make concessions to them. In March 1640, the king agreed to build the pin makers a hall, supply wire at £8 per hundredweight, and make available £10,000 to buy up foreign pins. In return, the pin makers agreed to buy wire only from the Royal Battery Works. Next, the king contracted with Lydsey to buy wire from him for ten years at £6 12s. per hundredweight and to pay Lydsey 10s. per hundredweight for all imported wire acquired by the king. Finally, in an even more complicated transaction, the king sold his role as intermediary to a man named Halstead, who was granted what we would call a regulated monopoly. Halstead was allowed 8 percent on his capital after management expenses, with the provisions that out of the remaining profits, £1,000 per annum was to be paid to the Exchequer, Lydsey's £7,000 in losses was to be repaid with interest, and any remainder was to be paid to the king. Halstead was also required to provide regular accounts to the Treasury and to return the business to the king at the end of ten years if the king so chose, with the proviso that the king repay the capital with interest. The government of Charles was eager to play this rent-seeking game with would-be monopolists in exchange for a share of the monopoly profits. The costs of all these arrangements were passed along to English users of pins and more generally to wearers of English clothing.

The monopoly was quickly dissolved as a result of the Crown's defeat in the English Civil War (1641–49). The pin makers had to wait until 1664 for their monopoly to be reestablished when Charles II approved an arrangement similar to that of his royal predecessor. However, after the Civil War, Parliament too claimed that it had the right to grant the privilege of establishing an enterprise. Moreover, the elimination of the Crown's prerogative courts and the growing authority of the common law courts made legal acceptance of any monopoly conditional upon Parliament's approval. The haberdashers, ironmongers, and wiredrawers all vehemently opposed the bill in the House of Commons creating a pin makers' monopoly, and their efforts were again thwarted. The persistent pin makers next attempted to renew their proposal in the Privy Council in 1675, promising the king at least £4,000 a year in revenue, but the opposition of the related trades again ruined their chances. In 1690, the pin makers' company made a last attempt to get Parliament to approve a monopoly;

[6]Ibid.

trayed as trying to eliminate the English industry to secure a monopoly.[4] Defenders of the Dutch interests advanced similarly inflammatory arguments, asserting that English pin makers could not satisfy more than one-third of the demand and that excluding imports of Dutch pins would provoke retaliation and create an English monopoly in the uncertain hope of preventing a Dutch monopoly in the future. A compromise was reached by the Privy Council in 1608 that subjected foreign imports of pins to a tariff of sixpence per 12,000.

After another round of lawsuits by the pin makers and failed attempts at mediation by the Privy Council in 1616, Bartlett attempted to organize a pin makers' company in 1618, with the goal of obtaining the sole right to import pins. He successfully obtained a supply of wire for the pin makers and won the unique privilege of importing pins at fixed prices. In return for his pin-importing monopoly, Bartlett had to agree that the price of domestic pins not be raised over the price that had prevailed twenty years before, that the price of foreign pins not be raised over the 1616 price, and that the monopoly include only London and its suburbs; pins made elsewhere in the kingdom were not subject to the agreement. Bartlett obtained a court order against importers who infringed his patent and seemed to have achieved his aim until the government reneged. Anxious not to damage trade relations with Holland, the Crown forbade the implementation of the verdict against the importers. The pin makers were therefore unable to enforce their monopoly, and "Sir Thomas, driven to desperation, made himself so troublesome to the Government that in the end he was committed to the Tower, and shortly afterwards died."[5] This case demonstrates how efforts by a potential monopolist were thwarted by the very government that was the source of his privileges.

In 1635, a second attempt to secure a pin monopoly proved almost as fatal to its advocate as the first. A Mr. Lydsey, who owned an interest in a wire-manufacturing company called the Royal Battery Works and hoped to find a market for its product in pin making, obtained a new grant of monopoly and prohibition of all imports on behalf of Bartlett's heirs in return for an annual payment of £500 to the queen. By 1638, however, Lydsey claimed losses of £7,000 and was involved in a breach-of-trust suit with Bartlett's heirs.

Charles I (r. 1625–49) stepped in directly to manage the pin industry. He discovered a way for the Crown to obtain direct access to the monopoly

---

[4]See George Unwin, *Industrial Organization in the Sixteenth and Seventeenth Centuries* (London: Cass, 1957), 165–71.
[5]Ibid., 168.

attributed to the influence of England's free-trade philosophers on public policy. Yet England's lawmakers and government officials were not better trained in economics than their French counterparts, and public discourse in France was at least as well informed by economic principles as that in England. In fact, the edicts and proclamations of the French king often explicitly professed adherence to the ideas of economists. Nevertheless, the spread of physiocratic and liberal theories did not eliminate the industrial *dirigisme* of the French government. Why did an administration generally well tutored in economic principles apply them less efficiently? An examination of the evolution of economic regulation in England might help us better understand the gulf between theory and practice in France.

Although the English Crown made many efforts to organize seventeenth-century industry into monopolies, competitive markets developed. Scholars sometimes assume that ideological shifts explain the success of laissez-faire and the expansion of competitive markets. Yet the classic eighteenth-century example of Adam Smith's economic thought—the division of labor exemplified by the English pin industry—also illustrates the breakdown of regulation, which in turn fostered a competitive environment. Perhaps Adam Smith, often considered the father of free market theory, can also be seen as the father of a philosophy based on practice.

## THE PIN MAKERS' TALE: FROM ASPIRING MONOPOLISTS TO PROMOTERS OF FREE TRADE

At the time of the accession of James I (1603), in order to raise prices by engineering the prohibition of pin imports, English pin makers sought to separate themselves from the Girdlers' Company, under which they were subsumed. Although pin imports had been prohibited since Edward IV's reign, English demand exceeded domestic supply, and Dutch pins were imported under special exemptions and through illegal shipments. Since pin makers lacked the funds to purchase a guild charter outright, they agreed to pay a courtier fourpence per 12,000 pins manufactured for forty years if he would obtain a charter on their behalf.

After paying £8,000 to buy out a fellow courtier who had previously represented the pin makers, Sir Thomas Bartlett took up their cause by initiating a test case against a pin importer. The controversy pitted the pin makers and their courtier backers against the formidable combined resistance of the Dutch importers, the Haberdashers' Company (the largest organized group of British pin users), and the London City Council, which adjudicated the disagreement. Arguments made on behalf of the 20,000 workers in the pin makers' trade included the accusation that the Dutch were "flooding the country" with subsidized pins. The Dutch were por-

# 7 The Rise and Decline of English Mercantilism in Comparative Perspective

In many historical accounts, capitalist and pre-capitalist cultures broke apart violently during the seventeenth and eighteenth centuries. The separation was presumedly precipitated by the rise of the bourgeoisie, champions of free trade and liberal economics. Christopher Hill believes the English Civil War (1641–49) to be one of the first great bourgeois revolutions. In Hill's account, the Civil War was a clash pitting supporters of a free economy against the Crown and resulted in the deregulation of the British economy.[1] In Hill's account, the Parliamentary party, wanting to prepare the way for capitalism, fought to deprive the Crown of its right to use royal monopolies to gain revenue and patronage. Free national markets occurred in England, we are told, because the British upper classes were more rationally motivated (in the narrow, profit-maximizing sense) than their continental counterparts. Although it is true that the expansion of the English economy during the eighteenth century was characterized by the increased integration of local markets, it may be questioned whether a free domestic market was the intended outcome of a political revolution bringing the "bourgeoisie" to power.[2]

## ENGLISH MERCANTILISM IN CRISIS

While French guilds were being reinforced in the eighteenth century, English guilds were already in sharp decline.[3] The difference is sometimes

---

[1] Christopher Hill, *The Century of Revolution: 1603–1714* (London: Nelson, 1961).
[2] During the sixteenth century, the English government issued legislation regulating industry and commerce, granting industrial monopolies, controlling prices, and prohibiting land enclosure. The government continued to regulate, but the Revolution transformed the goals and the groups that benefited from regulation.
[3] Since mercantilism declined in England at the time when it took off in France, the decline of English guilds in the seventeenth century will be compared with the reinforcement of French guilds in the eighteenth century.

production could be more effectively carried out by a different guild owing to the development of new techniques, it would be very costly for the guilds to negotiate among themselves over how the new technique could be adopted. In this industrial hierarchy, royal officials alone could coordinate the renegotiation of corporate responsibilities and assets. However, the royal officials did not have the sources of information available to determine the optimal structure of industry.[82]

The proliferation of guilds during a period of jurisdictional and political unification arose because the Crown needed to collect revenues from tax-exempt consumers of luxury goods. However, by supporting the inefficient property rights of the trades, the king had foreclosed on many socially profitable investments in the development of craft specialization and interdependence. Unfortunately, the king was constrained by the political structure to maximize the rents he could draw from policing the system of guild production, which led him to ignore the discrepancy between the governmental and social rates of return.[83] The king did not have a choice of the most efficient sources of revenue from all possible alternatives. The transaction costs of assessing and collecting revenues prevented him from acting as a residual claimant who could enjoy the surplus income produced by instituting the most efficient property rights. Many arguments could be made against the state's continued support of the guilds on the basis of the obstacles guilds posed to economic efficiency, but the short-term political and economic cost to the state, and to the kingdom's financial elites, of adjusting the revenue base was the key obstacle to reform. The controller general's office, which also controlled industrial regulation, could not implement changes that would temporarily have disrupted the flow of revenue into the state coffers. Consequently, programs to suppress the guilds faltered.[84]

---

[82]Jan Winiecki's analysis of the various malfunctions endogenous to central management systems seems in some ways analogous to the organizational problems of Old Regime France. Developing and introducing the new technologies that were instrumental during the early stages of the Industrial Revolution required linkages that evolved without a central coordinator, in which enterprises acted as both suppliers of inputs and purchasers of outputs from one another. The early Industrial Revolution was the result of the performances of nonlinear intra- and inter-industry linkages that evolved spontaneously without a central planner. See Jan Winiecki, "Are Soviet-Type Economies Entering an Era of Long-term Decline?" *Soviet Studies* 38, no. 3: 325–48, and "Soviet-Type Economies: Considerations for the Future?" *Soviet Studies* 38, no. 4: 543–61.

[83]For example, he could not raise taxes without the *parlement*'s consent.

[84]I would like to thank members of the Economic History Workshop at Northwestern University and the Social Science History Workshop at Stanford University for their helpful comments.

omists may have believed that monopoly protected the rewards of innovators; the problem was rarely addressed.[77]

The evolution of the regulation of French guilds highlights the importance of transaction costs in affecting the choice of institutional arrangements.[78] It also provides us with an example of how institutions persisted despite their economic inefficiency. Institutional innovation did not occur in a perfectly competitive political arena in which the king could select only efficient innovations.[79] Instead, a marriage of state and industry in the generation and division of monopoly rents accounts in large part for the industrial organization of France under absolutism. Under Louis XIV, the government traded its services, its protection, and its justice in exchange for revenue from the guilds.[80] The Crown explicitly acknowledged this motivation in a declaration of 1709, when it reported "giving relatively certain and suitable rights to each corporation of merchants and crafts, in order that they might find the means to support their financial obligations."[81] In assigning property rights, the Crown assumed that the various guilds operated within segregated markets. Few trades, however, were independent of other trades. As a result, the property rights that the Crown assigned to particular trades often overlapped with rights offered to adjacent trades. Nevertheless, the Crown's revenue imperative led it to ignore the costs these inefficient and artificial barriers imposed on the trades. The numerous conflicts between trades because of disputes over markets were adjudicated at the expense of the consumer.

The centralization of the guild structure by the French monarchy limited the information available among guilds about possible joint economies or production strategies. More frequent mergers and the sharing of information among guilds might have occurred had the Crown not imposed a structure of vertical supervision controlled by royal officials. Under royal supervision, members of various guilds had neither the incentive nor the capacity to share information about markets or production opportunities. Since barriers between trades were predetermined, there was little incentive to explore alternative uses of capital and labor. If a particular type of

---

[77] L. Hilaire-Perez, "Invention and the State in Eighteenth Century France," *Technology and Culture* 32, no. 4 (October 1991): 911–31.
[78] On the importance of transaction costs in determining the choice of institutional arrangements, see Douglass C. North, *Structure and Change in Economic History* (New York: Norton, 1981).
[79] The tactics needed to build a revenue base in the present may limit the choice set available in the future, so that the ruler can rarely get to a point where it is possible to devise the most efficient, welfare-enhancing institutions.
[80] See North's definition of the state in *Structure and Change*, 20–32.
[81] AN, AD/XI/10, "Déclaration du roi" (December 10, 1709).

to legalize informal production in order to tax the informal sector.[75] Another edict in July 1781 gave intendants, already responsible for supervising guild finance, control over admission to the corporations. However, the quarrels and jealousies that sent craftspeople to the courts to litigate against each other's privileges still existed. Ironically, the access provided by Necker's edict to previously closed industries may eventually have inhibited the development of new industries, since workers could more easily become members of the previously closed guilds.

The edict abolishing the guilds was only an exercise in the theory of liberalizing trade, for the guilds were not eliminated. Turgot's edict barely left a trace in the guild archives, for, despite his efforts, many of the provincial archives indicate uninterrupted recruitment of new masters up until 1789. Moreover, guild debt, which Turgot hoped to liquidate, persisted. A number of *parlements* had refused to register the edict creating new guilds until the debts of the old guilds were liquidated. The back payment on *rentes* and the sums produced by the sale of corporate property, while sometimes enough to meet the interest payments owed by the old corporations, were rarely enough to reimburse the capital. The guilds had become so interconnected with other sectors of the economy that they could not be radically altered unless the other sectors were reformed as well. The restoration of the guilds was temporarily lucrative for the monarchy. The edicts creating the new corporations produced 11,050,000 livres for the Crown in payments for admission to the status of master.[76]

Ultimately, royal manufactures were not affected by the legislation abolishing the guilds. They were absent from the controversy over liberalization, despite the fact that many operated at a loss. Even advocates of liberalism generally accepted the exclusive privileges of royal manufacture, despite their deviation from the rules of free competition. Perhaps contemporaries believed that, in the absence of efficient legislation or industrial patents encouraging invention, such privileges were the only way to protect inventors and investors in new technology. Eighteenth-century econ-

---

[75] Between 1779 and 1781, Necker instituted another major reform of the guilds by establishing the so-called intermediate system in the textile industries. While it left the guilds and the formal markets with their royal inspectors operating exactly as before, it made optional the use of these institutions. Producers who did not wish to submit to guild restrictions or royal production regulations simply had to bring the cloth to market and have it stamped "free." Although Necker was seeking a compromise solution between free-trade and pro-regulation factions, the guilds nonetheless complained that they could not compete with nonguild producers.
[76] AN, F/12/750, "Mémoir remis à Mr. Sauvigny, le 20 Février 1787, pour être adressé par lui à M. le comisseur général."

April 20, 1776, that committed the intendants to the liquidation of guild debts prior to the abolition of guilds. Elsewhere the edict was rarely applied because of corporate debts; in many cases it was not even registered.[72] The failure of Turgot's reform legislation was in part owing to lack of support from the intendants, who generally fought with the Crown to protect local industries from competition.[73] With few exceptions, provincial intendants were regulators, not liberators.

Turgot had not anticipated that abolishing the guilds might result in a general financial crisis, a lack of foresight difficult to understand. His short-lived efforts to abolish the guilds came to an end in August 1776, when a new edict essentially restored the guilds with some structural changes.[74] Guild debts were the main obstacle to abolition. (It is unknown whether the abolition of the guilds was an outright default by the Crown in the sense that Crown responsibilities to guild officeholders were annulled.) The efficiency gains of eliminating the guilds could not be accessed in the absence of a fully elaborated system of excise taxes or personal income taxes. The Crown needed alternative sources of taxation to use as a basis for credit. The potential for government credit exists whenever there is a predictable cash flow from taxation; it is anticipated taxation. Viewed from this perspective, corporate forms came into existence to facilitate both present and future taxation. Thus even if credit markets had not existed, the taxation imperative would have preserved corporate forms.

The failure of Turgot's efforts to abolish the guilds led to the attempt of Controller General Jacques Necker to coordinate the regulation of the formal and informal sectors. In an edict of May 5, 1779, Necker attempted

---

[72]On the liquidation of the debts of the suppressed communities, see AN, V7/277 and 297. On the efforts to liquidate communal debts after 1776, see AN, F12/204, 205, and 206.

[73]For instance, Intendant Tourny of Bordeaux was ambiguous about free trade and competition; he believed in the ultimate power of the administration to control and supervise commerce and industry more than the rule of the market and of competition (Passet, *Industrie dans la généralité*, 158–59).

[74]The edict recreating guilds stipulated that masters who belonged to suppressed guilds could join the new guilds by signing up at the subdelegates' office. The cost of entry to the new guilds was reduced for Parisians but increased for provincial craftsmen. Artisans previously outside guilds were required to join the new guilds and also had to pay a *droit* when registering. Those who wanted to register as masters could apply to do so. Those who exercised several crafts were encouraged to register as well. In an effort to reduce court costs, the edict stipulated that disputes over defective work were to be brought before the lieutenant general of police. Decision making in the new guilds after 1776 was done by ten deputies elected by the *confrères*. Lawsuits in progress were terminated.

nating the Crown commission of 1716.⁶⁸ Turgot's edicts separated the debts of corporations into two categories: loans contracted for the purchase of offices, which Turgot hoped would be paid with the aid of *gages* (a yearly interest payment owed to all purchasers of offices) from the royal treasury and all other loans, which he believed could be eliminated by the sale of communal property belonging to the guilds. The surplus from these sales would be divided among existing masters. However, the interest payments on the debts were larger than the Crown's yearly payment of *gages*, and the sale of communal properties of guilds could not generate enough revenue to cover their debts.⁶⁹ Turgot had evidently underestimated the extent of the debt and overestimated the extent of corporate property.

Despite the preparation and the support from within the royal government, provincial resistance to Turgot's edicts was difficult to overcome. The message from the provinces was that abolition would not be possible until the debts were liquidated. The response from the Beauvaisie, emphasizing the insurmountable debt, was typical: "The unhappy creditors of the guilds asked how they could collect outstanding debts."⁷⁰ Local officials reported that the trail of debts the guilds left behind was so vast and complex that their full reimbursement was unlikely, thereby bringing on a local financial crisis. Why not expropriate and suppress the outstanding debt? It should not matter if debt service were larger than new revenues unless the Crown were worried about the effect on its external reputation or the loan holders were politically powerful or had information upon which the Crown depended. Why the Crown did not repudiate the debt is one of those mysteries whose answer has yet to be revealed. In a letter of April 30, 1776, Turgot reported to the intendant of Britanny that the edict of February "could only be definitively applied at a later date once the liquidation of debts was on course."⁷¹ Turgot demanded a complete account of the financial situation of Breton guilds and sent an *arrêt du conseil* on

---

⁶⁸AN, AD/XI/11, "Edit du roi pourtant suppression des jurandes et communautés de commerce, arts et métiers" (February 1776), and AN, AD/11, "Edit du roi pourtant nouvelle création de six corps de marchands, et quarante-quatre communautés d'arts et métiers" (August 1776).

⁶⁹In a series of memoirs on uniting different communities into a single community, the author notes that "the debts of communities will be an obstacle to unification, but if we abolish the communities we must see to it that their debts are reimbursed, since they were contracted to support the Crown." See Georges Ruhlmann, *Les Corporations, les manufactures et le travail libre à Abbeville au XVIIIe siècle* (Paris and Lille: Recueil Sirey, 1948), 45.

⁷⁰BN, Joly de Fleury, 1730.

⁷¹Armand Rebillon, *Recherches sur les anciennes corporations ouvrières et marchandes de la ville de Rennes* (Paris, 1902), 175. AN, AD/I.V., série C, liasses 1452, 1439.

izing rural manufacturing. The new legislation was partly designed to regulate, and thereby tax, rural production. In effect, the Crown was acknowledging that the putting-out system was widespread and seeking a means to tax its continued development.[64] It is misleading, then, to view the legislation as a recognition by the Crown of the informal sector's right to produce according to consumers' demand. The Crown was extending control over nascent industries as had been done with the privileged royal manufactures. Nevertheless, the Crown's recognition and regulation of rural industries seriously compromised the guilds and provided a counterweight to guild power, making even more radical reforms possible.

In 1767, the Crown ruled that workers who were not in guilds must pay a tax for the right to sell their wares. The Crown claimed this tax was warranted by its concern "to increase the activity of commerce and industry." In effect the tax recognized the rights of workers not registered in guilds to dispose legally of their products so long as they conformed to standards that permitted their production to be assessed for tax purposes.[65]

The campaign to limit the guilds that began around 1750[66] concluded with Turgot's edicts of February 1776 abolishing the guilds[67] and termi-

---

[64] AN, AD/XI/11 (September 5, 1762). "The peasants and those staying in each place where there is no patented corporation are authorized to spin every kind of material and to manufacture all kinds of fabrics and finish them, on condition that they conform to current regulations."

[65] AN, AD/XI/11, "Arrêt du Conseil d'état du roi" (October 30, 1767).

[66] By midcentury many of the permanent members of the Crown bureaucracy had been converted to the cause of restricting the guilds. Daniel-Charles Trudaine and Vincent de Gournay were proponents of free trade and promoters of liberal policies. Gournay's disciple and successor, Robert de Cotte, pursued Gounay's work and helped to promulgate free-trade ideas among two generations of government officials. The controllers general Jean-Baptiste Machault d'Arnouville (1745–1754) and Etienne de Silhouette (1758–1759) were more ambiguous, endorsing the expansion of free trade while also strongly supporting economic development under state supervision. Nonetheless, the controller general's office remained the core of the mercantilist economy until the brief ministry of Turgot. See Simone Meyssonnier, *La Balance et l'horloge: La Genèse de la pensée libérale en France au XVIII$^e$ siècle* (Paris: Les Editions de la passion, 1989). Trudaine was *conseiller au Conseil royal des finances* from 1744 to 1756 and a *conseiller au Conseil royal de commerce*. Michel Antoine, *Le Conseil du roi sous le régime de Louis XV* (Paris and Geneva: Libraire Droz, 1970), 239. Gournay was *intendant du commerce* from 1751 to 1759 and *conseiller honoraire au Grand conseil*. See Michel Antoine, *Le Gouvernement et l'administration sous Louis XV* (Paris: Editions du CNRS, 1978), 246.

[67] Turgot's edict of February 1776 was registered by the *parlements* only after a *lit de justice* on March 12, 1776, but Turgot forgot the *deniers comtants*. He did not think of leases or mortgages and had to issue a special *arrêt* of March 16, 1776, calling for the immediate sale of guild property. He also forgot the opposition of creditors (*arrêt* of March 21).

The Crown's fiscal officials, particularly the farmers of indirect taxes, also mistrusted fashion-oriented production. Goods priced according to taste were more difficult to tax. This was one reason the Crown was reluctant to lift the ban of October 26, 1686, on the sale of printed cottons.[61] The value of a printed fabric was in the eyes of the beholder, since what distinguished one fabric from another were design, color, and pattern; taste-specific value was not easily assessed by the tax collector.[62]

## ABOLITION AND REVIVAL OF THE GUILDS

Despite the efforts of the Crown commission to restore guild finances, the guilds were overwhelmed with debt by the mid eighteenth century (for many the years between 1735 and 1745 were the hardest). The cause of this indebtedness was everywhere the same—the excessive number of offices. Of the thirty-nine guilds in Bordeaux, twenty-five were highly indebted by the mid eighteenth century.[63] To prevent additional indebtedness, a declaration of April 2, 1763, again denied guilds the right to borrow. Although the limits stabilized the level of debt, the majority of corporations were still unable to pay off existing debts. As an example of how onerous these purchases could be, in 1750 the *tailleurs* had to raise 6,195 livres to buy twenty offices, while their annual receipts equaled 281 livres 12 sols. Only guilds concerned with military production, like cannon manufacturers, were exempt, although they too could be pressed for funds in times of need.

The covenant between the guilds and the monarchy established under Colbert was broken in the mid eighteenth century. After ruining the corporations, the Crown lost interest in them. The first step in dismantling the guilds came in 1762, when, against the concerted opposition of the wool merchants and the various guilds that used wool in their production, the King's Council permitted the manufacture of cotton linen, "white painted and printed as are those of the Indies." Since the manufacturers involved had previously been outlaws, the legislation was rightly viewed as an attack on the monopoly of the traditional guild masters. A decree of September 5, 1762, broke the handicraft monopoly of the towns by legal-

---

[61]See Edgard Depitre, *La Toile peinte en France au XVII<sup>e</sup> et XVIII<sup>e</sup> siècles* (Paris: Marcel Rivière, 1912).
[62]See Ekelund and Tollison, *Mercantilism as a Rent-Seeking Society*. Product uniformity facilitates regulation. The uniformity of most textile products was well controlled. Printed calicoes allowed product differentiation that permitted competition in areas like taste. Nonprice competition among producers would have dissipated the excess profits of the guild producers, thereby undermining the regulatory apparatus the Crown had constructed.
[63]Passet, *Industrie dans la généralité*, 80.

the guilds' guidance. Was it not the guilds' primary duty to ensure quality and to protect the public from shoddy manufactures? Moreover, guild members believed that consumers should buy either the best or not at all.[59] In effect, the rise of the informal sector had driven the guilds into the portion of the market in which demand was most inelastic—production of luxury goods for wealthy consumers.

The guilds faced a fundamental problem in coming to terms with changing tastes and with market-driven demand. Insistence on guild definitions of quality and durability was often an excuse for perpetuating seventeenth-century industrial standards. A monopoly could best be maintained if all producers were constrained to produce according to the same standards. The regulated trades were unable to adapt to the new demand for mass-produced, standardized, less expensive goods, so the guilds sought to prevent other producers from supplying the public with the simpler, cheaper, more colorful items it wanted. The statutes, in effect, only permitted the production of what was already produced, closing the market to new entrants.[60]

[59]Guild representatives referred to a contract with the public, enforceable by the Crown, to provide the finest quality of goods. AN, F/12/659, "Observation sur la necessité de conserver le régime actuel de la marque et du plomb de controle sur les étoffes nationales, ou d'en supprimer ces caractères" (unsigned, undated [1788 or 1789], 38 pages), calls for a certain degree of liberty but the preservation of seals to protect the better manufacturers and the public from fraud. AN, F/12/659 (August 3, 1778) advocates the position taken by the Corps de commerce de la généralité de Tours against a plan to allow the manufacture and sale of cloth without a guild seal of inspection; the author argues that the public will not be able to distinguish well-made cloth from shoddy and that they will be seduced by the lower price of goods manufactured in bad faith. "The system of regulation was without doubt defective like all human institutions, but that of unlimited freedom is still worse." Picardy merchants similarly argued against the "intermediary regime" between unlimited freedom and complete regulation (AN, F/12/659 [April 28, 1778]). In the absence of regulation, they asked, how were those who produced in bad faith to be isolated and punished? Was the advantage of selling more at a lower price worth the invitation to fraud that would ultimately erode consumer confidence? Worst of all, once the availability of cheap cloth reduced the quality of all cloth, the makers of quality cloth would no longer be careful to use only the best techniques and quality materials. The rules should therefore be updated to keep up with improvements in technique, but they should not be abandoned. The petition of the city of Romans in the Dauphine followed the same reasoning (F/12/659 [1778]). Dijon was also reluctant to accept deregulation but was willing to distinguish peasant production for rural consumption from urban luxury goods (F/12/661/15 [July 18, 1778]). The physiocrats responded that consumers were the best inspectors.
[60]This problem appeared in the economies of eastern European nations under communism, where factories were likely to produce only what they had always produced.

hordes of intriguers, usurers, and servile men without honor."⁵⁷ In the edict to abolish the guilds dated the same year, Controller General Turgot argued that the rules that allowed guild workers to monopolize work were only devices for enriching inspectors and guild masters at the expense of the workers and the public. "In those places where free trade is practiced, like the Faubourg St. Antoine, work is done at least as well as by the guilds."⁵⁸ Advocates of free trade noted that masterships were often for sale and that the only restriction on their acquisition was the ability of would-be masters to pay for them.

Finally, our corporate spokesman invoked the right of property to defend the discriminatory recruitment policies of the guilds. In particular, he defended the fact that the son of a guild master typically paid less to enter a guild than other candidates:

> [He is thus] convinced that he cannot engage in commerce without paying for the rights demanded by the regulation of the guilds that give him the privilege. He submits himself to the law that the sovereign has proclaimed, saying, the money I give today is not lost to me, because I am buying the right to sell cooperatively with all the members of the corps of which I am a member. No other can attach himself to the branch of commerce that nourishes me or submit himself to a law that I obey; if I die, my wife will enjoy my privilege, or can lease it, and my children, if they want, can continue my business. My admission to membership in the guild gives me a real property.

The physiocrats, well-known defenders of property rights, argued differently. In their view, guild members' habit of seeing the barriers placed on industry as a common right to which they were entitled interfered with the rights of other workers and with the right of consumers to hire the workers of their choice. The property rights of the guilds allowed the Crown to capture the maximum revenue at lowest cost.

The rising empire of fashion was one of the guild masters' greatest concerns. They viewed the grip of fashion and novelty over the public's imagination as the source of the informal sector's success. The guilds argued that fashion allowed nonguild producers to exploit the public's credulity by selling shoddy goods. Not being initiated into the mysteries of the craft, and thus unable to make an intelligent choice, the public needed

---

⁵⁷AN, AD/XI/11, piece 42, "Memoir à consulter sur l'existence actuelle des six corps, et la conservation de leurs privilèges" (signed Delacroix, February 1, 1776).
⁵⁸AN, AD/XI/11, "Edit du roi pourtant suppression des jurandes et communautés de commerce, arts et métiers" (February 1776).

ufacture and renders the apprentice equal to the *campagnon* and the *campagnon* equal to the master and finally removes the small obstacles that prevent the gross tastes of the village from entering the city." If these illegal immigrants were not stopped from taking the work belonging to the guilds, "soon you will see hordes of peasants abandon themselves to other work much less useful to humanity." To justify their privileges, guild advocates argued that their trades required great skill, but in fact the manufacture of many products could easily be done by unapprenticed workers.

Above all, our author viewed unregulated production as a threat to the status of guild masters. "Workers are largely ignorant, because they have undergone an apprenticeship that was too short and too superficial," he assures us. However, giving them license to sell their unregulated wares in unregulated markets was the equivalent of confirming their equality to guild masters. "Having been made equal with masters, they think themselves very knowledgeable; they will become con artists, because they have nothing to lose." He was referring to the fact that these unregulated, or "false," workers, as they are called in the documents, had less to lose if caught working improperly, because they did not risk rights gained from years of apprenticeship. Apprenticeship, he believed, functioned as a performance bond, which a guild worker would not want to hazard. Lacking a similar investment in their training, unregulated workers "will cheat the public without fearing their contempt." If the guilds' control over the trades were further compromised, he predicted, "merchants will no longer peacefully and decently attend the consumer, they will become but a collection of Jews, hawkers, and former servants who insinuate themselves into homes to seduce the trusting and the ignorant; but they will sell in false measures because they are no longer subject to the inspectors who verify their weights and measures."[56] By contrast, guild members offer an example of honor and decency, because "they must either fulfill their duty as head of family, help the sovereign who protects them, and honor the magistrates who judge them, or wander into the void confounded with

---

[56] See AN, F/12/657, *Mémoire* dated August 20, 1732, a request to bar Jews from Bordeaux. Jews were accused of buying and selling defective merchandise and of not paying taxes because they bought and sold in cash. They had to buy and sell in cash because, not being entitled to legal rights, they had no means to defend themselves from opportunism. The author concluded that the treatment of Jews by other nations should be a model for the French: "These people are despised not only by Christians but also by more barbarous nations." In 1733 the merchants of Bordeaux objected to the goods sold by Jews on grounds that those goods did not conform to regulations established in 1669.

tions were directed at the King's Council and were published in the course of 1758 when the threat of official action to recognize the informal sector was imminent. The protests emanated from the cities with long-established privileges, such as Amiens, Lyons, Paris, and Rouen. They were intent on preventing greater toleration of the "outlaw" trades. The most frequent complaints were against textile manufacturers in the countryside, who were breaking the monopoly of the traditional masters. The outlawed merchants naturally preferred to remain silent; they depended on the ideological convictions of the king's officials to carry the case for free enterprise. The guild advocates emphasized the need to protect consumers and to ensure equality among guild masters.

One particular memoir submitted to the king in defense of the regulated trades stands out for being forcefully stated.[55] The author champions the segregation of markets and skills: individuals should be forbidden from practicing several trades or from selling various kinds of merchandise, the author insists, "if one sells or manufactures only socks, he will make good socks, since his reputation depends on that alone. The division of tasks offers more certainty for the consumer and greater equality for merchants. Money divides itself into several channels and can help several families instead of running in a single stream that nourishes the richest, while the others languish in misery." A limit on migration to the cities was needed because "there are always too many workers in the cities, and never enough in the country." He seems to have believed that the countryside was becoming depopulated, a perception shared by many of his contemporaries. Like many members of the guilds, he was threatened by additions to the labor force, especially since unapprenticed, nonguild workers were able to perform many of the low-skilled tasks that characterized a large portion of guild work. Our author claims that the apprenticeship system is itself threatened by this influx of cheap labor into the cities. "Dispensing with apprenticeships allows ignorance and incompetence to penetrate man-

---

tilism was very much alive among those who viewed the world from the vantage of the French fisc. In a book he published later, *Principes et observations oeconomiques* (Amsterdam, 1767), Forbonnais included examples of the arguments of the free-trade school. By contrast, Abbot André Morellet (1727–1819) argued for the elimination of the Compagnie des Indes and total freedom of commerce, including the elimination of the protected royal manufactures. "Mercantilist regulations," he argued, "were designed to promote the advancement of manufactures, by weakening a certain fraction of them and not by improving their techniques" (*Réflexions sur les avantages de la libre circulation* [Geneva, 1758]).

[55]AN, F/12/65, "Memoir en consultation d'admistration est préferable d'assujettir les différentes fabriques" (unsigned, undated).

held responsible for its quality. This would also help inspectors and the public identify nonguild products, thus enabling the Crown to find and tax nonguild manufacturers in the countryside.[51] Enforcement would obviously be difficult. The guilds also lobbied for stronger measures to prevent merchants from other districts gaining access to their territory.[52] In addition, they requested stricter measures against merchants and workers who did not go through the system to acquire masterships. The edict that finally abolished the guilds contains a preamble that summarizes the situation:

> The corporations were above all concerned with keeping the work and merchandise of other workers out of their territory. They depend upon their right to ban the sale of merchandise that they consider poorly made. This motive leads them to desire for themselves new regulation prescribing the quality of materials used and the methods of production. This regulation, the execution of which was conferred on the corporations' officers, would certainly be used against nonguild workers, but it would also be used to prevent masters of the same corporation ... from ever separating their interests from those of the corporation, and as a consequence to render them accomplices in all machinations inspired in the spirit of monopoly by the corporation's leaders.[53]

Tensions between the regulated and the unregulated sectors mounted as the success of the informal sector promoted the fear of imminent deregulation. The guilds prepared many elaborate justifications for their continued existence in the face of this danger, and the larger guilds put lawyers on retainer. They also faced the challenge by circulating memoirs to the king's ministers and among the public.[54] Many of the requests and peti-

---

[51] The guilds were not satisfied, for they viewed the *arrêt* as tacit recognition of the right of nonguild producers to openly vend their wares. AN, AD/II, "Règlement pour la teinture des étoffes de laine, et des laines servant à leur fabrication" (January 15, 1737). See AN, AD/II, "Code des manufactures d'étoffes, toiles et toileries," for extracts of all *lettres-patentes* and *arrêts* concerning cloth from 1737 to August 26, 1784, printed in Dijon by J. B. Capel in 1786, by order of the intendant.
[52] AN, F/12/750 (January 10, 1747).
[53] AN, AD/XI/10, "Edit du roi pourtant suppression des jurandes et communautés de commerce, arts et métiers," Versailles, February 1776. Registered March 12, 1776.
[54] One particularly articulate defense of the guilds, on the advantages of continuing guild production of painted fabrics, was François Véron Duverger de Forbonnais, *Examen des avantages et des désavantages de la prohibition des toiles peintes* (Marseilles: Chez Carapatria, 1755). Forbonnais (1722–1800) was largely influenced by fiscal considerations, particularly the loss of revenue if the prohibition on printed fabrics were removed. A defender of his argument reveals that mercan-

indirectly relied, had to be maintained by whatever regulatory means necessary. The reality of the guilds' deteriorating financial condition had to be concealed, especially after 1750, when economic reformers began to militate against the mercantilist system and the guilds.

As guild debts increased during the century, it was rare for corporations to reimburse the capital. They usually resorted to contracting new debts just to pay off the interest already owed.[49] The royal commissioners who supervised guild finances were principally concerned with assuring interest payments on the debts. The commission never achieved its goal of eliminating the debts; instead, by assuring that interest payments were paid, the commission guaranteed the creditworthiness of the corporations, thus allowing them to incur additional debts. The ability of guilds to acquire these additional debts suggests the existence of either good capital markets or overlapping contracts that turned debts into perpetuities.

In the short run, the amount of debt a guild could incur was constrained by the ability of individual members to exit the association with their assets intact.[50] Devices came into being to discourage such exit. To make the defection of capital to other uses more costly, internal guild regulations required that assets be specific to products in which the guild held a monopoly. If guild masters could freely move their assets, both physical and human, from one guild to another, members would defect as individuals shopped for the guild that provided the most favorable conditions, as in England. The guilds with the lowest debts, all else being equal, would therefore be the most popular. There was an additional constraint on mobility in the form of deferred compensation, because guild masters expected to retire on guild annuities. In sum, the incentives to maintain corporate integrity enhanced the creditworthiness of the guild.

## THE INFORMAL SECTOR THREATENS

In the 1730s, numerous guilds demanded the right to regulate merchants' selling goods produced outside the guild structure. The Crown catered to this concern by ruling in January 1737 that manufacturers of cloth must put the first letters of their names on their fabric so that they could be

---

[49]Many questions concerning the guilds' liability structure have yet to be answered. Did their liability structure go from short- to long-term debt? Was much of the debt converted to equity capital? What proportion of guild liabilities was debt and how much was equity? How much was held by masters and how much was owned by outsiders? Did the guild assets take the form of government bonds or loans? What proportion of guild assets were receivables or liquid instruments as opposed to plant and equipment?

[50]In the long run, this constraint would not be binding, because individuals would not make the initial investment in guild membership.

factions within a corporate body to avoid responsibility for a legal outcome by claiming that a decision did not represent the will of the majority and to prevent a faction within the corps from litigating in the corporation's name.

These preliminary efforts to assure guild solvency became more elaborate on March 16, 1716, when the Crown appointed a commission to liquidate the debts of corporations throughout the kingdom.[43] On May 16, 1716, another commission appointed *commissaires* with the right of last appeal over all disputes concerning guild debts. An *arrêt* of September 21, 1724, expanded the commission's tutelage over corporations.[44] The commission had become a tribunal, its *arrêts* sovereign, and its decisions not subject to appeal.[45] Moreover, the introduction of personal liability added weight to the commission's decisions, as the Crown made *syndics* or representatives of the corporation personally responsible to the intendant for expenses incurred while in office.[46] Similarly, the *arrêt* of August 14, 1749, made inspectors personally responsible for their accounts, as well as those of their predecessors.[47]

As we have seen, the simple inquiry of 1716, which only had the authority to inspect the finances of guilds, had evolved by 1749 into the court of last resort for all cases concerning the corporations, inasmuch as it could pronounce judgment without right of appeal.[48] The commission charged with liquidating communal debts was designed to give investors confidence in the solvency of corporations and to add to the guilds' prestige, something they dearly needed as their financial status became more precarious. The Crown needed to give the appearance that guild debts were in the process of being liquidated so that investors would have confidence in the bonds being issued by the guilds. The guilds' credit, upon which the Crown

---

[43] AN, AD/XI/10, "Arrêt du conseil d'état du roi concernant les attributions accordées à la Commission établie pour la liquidation des dettes des corps et communautés d'arts et métiers de la ville de Paris de Mars 16, 1716, à Février, 1740."
[44] AN, AD/XI/10. The office was created in 1693 and noted in *Extrait des Registres du Conseil d'état*, September 21, 1724.
[45] Nigeon, *Etat financier des corporations parisiennes*, 41.
[46] AN, AD/XI/10, "Arrêt du conseil d'état," March 16, 1716–February 9, 1740. This *arrêt* made "syndics, inspectors, and receivers personally responsible for the payment of the 1,000 livres by all reasonable means, and even physical means."
[47] The *arrêts* of the King's Council pertaining to the commission of 1716 can be found in AN, E 716, 766c, 786b, and 882. E 2524 and E 2525, numbers 1, 29, 30, 64, and 140, concern the activities of the commission of 1716.
[48] AN, V7, 420–43. From 1689 onward, the intendants were the last resort for all questions concerning the liquidation of communal debts. In the *procès-verbaux* of the Council for the Liquidation of Debts, this stipulation is reiterated. See AN, AD/10, *arrêt* of September 14, 1728.

guild as a whole. Although some borrowing had already occurred by 1709, the king's declaration of December 10 of that year resulted in much heavier borrowing by the guilds.[37] The Crown still prohibited guilds from issuing bonds to maintain their debts and did not allow the *épiciers-apothicaires* to sell bonds in 1715.[38] Perhaps the king viewed corporate bonds as competing with royal issues. Nevertheless, later in the century guilds commonly borrowed by issuing bonds to raise funds to buy the offices.[39] Generally, the entire company was collectively responsible for the bond issues, which were secured by the company's communal properties, consisting of its buildings and materials.[40]

The growing dependency of the Crown on funds borrowed from the guilds required that financial relationships between the Crown and the guilds become more formal. With the guilds' increasing fiscal burden, the Crown discovered that it had to regulate guild solvency as well. Some preliminary steps to ensure that guild finance was managed in an orderly fashion had already been undertaken by Colbert, who gave intendants the right to visit the corporations, to requisition guild products, and to attend all meetings. In addition, intendants could demand to see guild accounts. One of the goals of this intervention was to control costs that might interfere with a guild's ability to fulfill its financial responsibility to the Crown. One method of controlling costs was to allow intendants summarily to settle disputes between merchants and artisans.[41] Guild corporations were required by a declaration of October 2, 1703, to obtain the intendant's permission to sue.[42] The Crown wanted to make it difficult for

---

[37] AN, AD/XI/10. In order to help communities pay their financial obligations, an *arrêt* of December 10, 1709, permitted communities to receive as many masters as they saw fit and to borrow sums needed to make payments on debts. The Crown had acknowledged that corporations could borrow since 1693, when corporations with more than 9,000 livres of debt were allowed to borrow to pay for the offices of *auditeurs* and examiners of accounts.

[38] They proposed to raise 200,000 livres from the members of the two corporations, distributed proportionally according to the capacities of each. A simple visa from the lieutenant-general of police would permit the *gardes* to prosecute and to constrain the members to contribute.

[39] AN, AD/XI/10, a royal edict of August 29, 1741, seems to have assumed that guilds could issue *rentes*.

[40] AN, AD/XI/10 (May 25, 1700). An *arrêt du conseil d'état* stated that all guild members were personally responsible for guild debts. A debt contract issued by the *tailleurs* of Dijon provides a good example of how this stipulation continued to be observed through the eighteenth century: the entire company was collectively responsible and the debt was secured on the company's goods. AD of Dijon C 28 1/10/1772.

[41] AN, AD/XI/10, declaration of December 7, 1694.

[42] AN, AD/XI/10, declaration of October 2, 1703.

His marriage in 1725 was commemorated by the creation of additional masterships. Not surprisingly, the guilds strongly opposed these *lettres de maîtrises,* since they lowered the value of their previously purchased masterships. Yet the guilds grudgingly purchased the new masterships to prevent competition. The guilds suppressed the new offices, just as they generally bought and suppressed the offices of *syndic* and inspector. When the masterships fell into the hands of individuals, guild inspectors were reputedly harsh in approving the work produced by the new masters. Purchasers of new masterships often found themselves involved in long and expensive court cases to protect their right to practice the trade.

In order to help pay for the new offices, guilds had to increase the cost of existing masterships, usually their most important source of revenue. In turn, the rising cost of masterships had the effect of making the guilds more exclusive.[35] The guilds had become more exclusive in the sense that apprentices were no longer able to save enough to buy masterships. This growing exclusiveness, often noted by contemporaries and historians, was a response to the increasingly heavy fiscal obligations imposed by the Crown.

Not content with the impositions, the Crown also coerced donations from the already hard-pressed guilds. Some of the more spectacular examples of these efforts by guilds to prove their loyalty to the Crown were made by the richest of the Parisian guilds, known as the Six Corps. In 1759, they offered the king 514,000 livres. Only two years later, they offered the king 700,000 livres for the construction of a 72-gun warship. In 1782, the guilds of Paris offered 1,500,000 livres for another warship. In 1788, the corporations of Paris provided 100,000 livres to aid farmers whose crops had been destroyed by the hail of July 1786.[36]

The corporate debt of the guilds began to accumulate on a large scale beginning in the early eighteenth century. In 1694, the Crown had discouraged borrowing; for example, when the Six Corps were unable to come up with the 680,000 livres to buy the offices of *auditeurs* and examiners of accounts, they were able to negotiate for a reduced payment to the Crown of 403,200 livres instead. Rather than borrow, corporations resorted to levies or taxes on members. Perhaps borrowing had been transferred to individual members because their reputations were better than that of the

---

[35]Maurice Garden, *Lyon et les Lyonnais au XVIII$^e$ siècle* (Paris: Les Belles Lettres, 1970), ch. 6. Garden claims that there was a tendency to become more exclusive as the century progressed.

[36]The accounts of the Six Corps are to be found in AN, KK 1341–43. These payments are noted in Edmond-Jean-François Barbier, *Journal d'un bourgeois de Paris sous le régime de Louis XV* (Paris: Renovard, 1847–56), 165, 166, 167, and 169.

and controllers of weights and measures; in 1709, archivists; and in 1710, treasurers.[32] These offices had value to their purchasers because they often carried tax exemptions and allowed the holder to perform banking services. It seems these offices were designed to be responsible to the Crown, so that their creation was a usurpation of local prerogatives. The municipalities were deprived of revenue, while the Crown gained knowledge of monopoly rents. After Louis XIV's reign, new offices were created less frequently: in 1730, inspectors of halls and markets were reestablished; in 1745, the office of inspector and controller of masters and inspectors was created; and on July 3 of that same year, an office was established to supervise merchants and artisans who were not members of guilds. In 1745, when the Crown had difficulty selling offices, it forbade inspectors of guilds to receive new masters, apprentices, or *compagnons* (even sons of masters) until the new offices were purchased.[33] In 1747, to accelerate the purchase of unsold offices of inspectors and controllers, the Crown ordered the merchants and artisans of each profession in which these offices were created to contribute to the purchase price in proportion to their wealth.[34] The creation of offices profoundly altered the nature of the guilds, but it also altered the relationship of the Crown to the guilds, making the Crown dependent on their existence.

By midcentury, however, it seemed that the guilds were saturated; many were too deeply indebted to absorb new offices. In response, the Crown turned to a new method of revenue extraction, the sale of *droits* (licenses). In 1745, the Crown created a *droit* that guild inspectors had to pay upon their election, and guild inspectors charged *droit de visite* when they inspected a guild workshop. Other new licenses included ones for opening a store and selling retail goods, for a wine cellar, for maintaining a *confrèrie*, for the registration of masters, and for a widow to inherit her husband's practice. Guilds were even charged for the right to take on new masters or apprentices.

The sale of new masterships proved to be another effective tactic of raising revenue through the guilds. *Lettres de maîtrises* were created under all kinds of pretexts: marriage of the king, birth of a prince, the naming of the king's brothers or cousins. Under Louis XIV, new masterships were created in 1660, 1661, 1666, 1673, and 1710. In 1722, four letters of *maîtrise* were created in each guild on the occasion of Louis XV's majority.

[32]For a complete list of the offices created by Louis XIV, see AN, AD/XI/10, "Arrêts du Conseil d'état, concernant les attributions accordées à la commission établie pour la liquidation des dettes des corps et commmunautés," 20.
[33]AN, AD/XI/10 (July 3, 1745).
[34]AN, AD/XI/10 (January 10, 1747).

ing hereditary and ensure that they could continue to choose their own officers, guilds would generally purchase the offices. An edict of December 1691 created *syndics* among all merchants and even required that nonguild member artisans and workers register with a *syndic*.[28] In March 1694, the Crown created the office of *auditeurs* and examiners of accounts.[29] In July 1702, the Crown created *trésoriers receveurs* and *payeurs* for the communal properties of all corporations.[30] The pace of office creation continued unabated during the early eighteenth century. Among those established: in 1704, hereditary offices of inspector,[31] or *auneurs de drap;* in 1705, *greffiers* for the registration of letters of apprenticeship; in 1706, registrars

---

rowed the money from twelve merchants, one *commissaire des guerres*, a notary, a *trésorier de France*, a convent, a *maître des requêtes*, and a doctor of the deceased queen. These loans were made at 5 percent. If the figure in the documents is accurate, it was considerably less than the rate of interest paid by the king. René Nigeon, *Etat financier des corporations parisiennes d'arts et métiers au XVIII$^e$ siècle* (Paris: Editions Rieder, 1934), 161.

[28] AN, AD/XI/10, "Edit du roi," December 1691, "Pourtant création des syndics, parmi les Marchands, Artisans et Ouvriers des Villes et Bourgs clos du Royaume, qui n'ont ni Maîtresse ni Jurande; Et de ceux qui prétendent n'être point des Corps et Communautez sujets à icelles." All were required to register with a *syndic*.

[29] AN, AD/XI/10, "Edit de mars 1694." The cost of this office was significant. Nigeon calculated, for example, that in 1695 the guilds of the small town of Abbeville spent 32,786 livres for the office of *auditeur* and *examinateur* of accounts. The sums raised in Paris were staggering according to Nigeon's calculations. The first number is the price of the office of *auditeur-examinateur* of accounts in 1694–96; the second is the amount paid for the hereditary inspectorship: *merciers:* 198,092/300,000; *marchands de vins:* 120,000/120,000; *épiciers:* 76,000/120,000; *drapiers:* 59,000/100,000; *orfevres:* 39,000/60,000; *chandeliers:* 22,000/30,000; *bonnetiers:* 21,000/36,000; *rotisseurs:* 16,667/30,000; *corroyeurs:* 13,000/18,000; *charcutiers:* 10,000/12,000; *bourreliers:* 8,000/10,000; *pelletiers-fourreurs:* 6,178/8,000; *chaudronniers:* 5,000; *chapeliers:* 41,000; *grainiers:* 8,000.

[30] AN, AD/XI/10, "Edit du roi pourtant création pour chacun des corps et communautez d'arts et métiers, tant dans les ville et fauxbourgs de Paris, que dans toutes les autres villes et bourgs clos du royaume, d'un trésorier receveur et payeur de leurs deniers communs," Paris, July 1702, registered August 1702.

[31] The Crown decided to transform its royal inspectors of manufacturers from commissioners into owners of hereditary offices. The edict of October 1704 proclaimed the establishment of two inspectors general in each *généralité* and created special commissioners (*contrôleurs et visiteurs*) and *concierges-gardes* in each workplace. This meant sixty-four inspectors general and hundreds of warehouse guards and controllers. After considerable outcry, a declaration of December 30, 1704, abolished the offices and reinstituted the regular inspectors. That order insisted on the indemnification for the loss of revenue from the sale of the offices. The series of *arrêts* in 1705 and 1706 that finalized the indemnification resulted in an indemnity of over one million livres. See Thomas J. Schaeper, *The French Council of Commerce, 1700–1715: A Study of Mercantilism after Colbert* (Columbus: Ohio State University Press, 1983), 159–61.

tries, factories, or individual entrepreneurs, it caused an uproar among adjacent traders, who demanded similar subsidies. To encourage large enterprises, the government generally had to provide investors with monopolies, subsidies, and tariff protection. Considerable resources were allocated by capitalists to the pursuit of such protection, further diverting capital from more productive applications. As a result of Colbert's policies, the demand for government regulation and subsidies preceded any significant investment of capital.[24] A process that was difficult to control had begun.

## THE COSTS OF PRODUCING WITHIN THE FORMAL SECTOR: THE STATE ESTABLISHES ITS TUTELAGE OVER GUILD FINANCE

Colbert's drive to restore the guilds and ensure the quality of French goods was ultimately subordinated to the revenue imperative. After 1691, the Crown created and sold an impressively long list of offices to raise money from the guilds. By the mid eighteenth century, the fiscal importance of the guilds had become so obvious that the intendant of Bordeaux observed in 1750, "Generally, all the tradespeople are organized into guilds in order that they may pay their taxes."[25] Because the Crown found it easier to raise funds from corporations than from individual tradespeople, it was willing to recognize even those guilds that lacked royal charters and were simply organized under municipal statutes.[26]

One of the chief instruments for raising revenue proved to be the sale of new guild offices. An edict of March 1691 created hereditary *syndics* and inspectors in all guilds.[27] To prevent these inspectorships from becom-

---

[24]Similarly, in many American cities, large building projects are often predicated upon property tax abatements granted by city councils. Such breaks are only available to those with substantial funds to invest. Thus, smaller developers are discriminated against.

[25]René Passet, *L'Industrie dans la généralité de Bordeaux sous l'intendant Tourny: Contribution à l'étude de la décadence du système corporatif au mileu du XVIII$^e$ siècle* (Bordeaux and Paris: Editions Bière, 1954), 88.

[26]It was not until the eighteenth century that guilds needed *lettres patentes* from the king. The *conseillers* of commerce in Bordeaux invoked this rule for the first time in 1725 (Passet, *Industrie dans la généralité*, 83). At that time, it was recognized that only the monarch could issue statutes or rules to the guilds. Nevertheless, of thirty-nine guilds in Bordeaux, only ten had statutes registered by the city.

[27]AN, AD/XI/10, March 1691 edict suppressing the elections of *maîtresse et gardes des corps des marchands et des jurez, syndics ou prieurs des arts et métiers*. To continue to elect their inspectors, the corporations agreed to purchase the office of inspector *syndic* created by the king. In Paris, the edict of March 1691 imposed a charge of three hundred thousand livres on the *mercerie* alone. The mercers bor-

before Colbert. A society characterized by "the courtier and the sycophant, dominated by ambitions for the secure social position conferred by land and offices," needed to be shaken up. "Industry and commerce were at best merely means of purchasing social security, and neither industry nor trade was expanding rapidly enough to inspire much hope or to foster a general spirit of enterprise and adventure. . . . [A]n individual looked for shelter and security rather than for opportunities to do new things or exploit new fields. . . . [Hence the perception] that the state might contribute much to the economic development of this society was shrewd realism" on Colbert's part. By administering the codes "in a different spirit," Usher concluded, Colbert's successors subjected France to "the dangers of state interference." He attributed this failure to "the mediocrity of the bureaucratic mind."[21]

In his two-volume study of Colbert, Charles Woolsey Cole argued that Colbert intended the privileges extended to particular merchants and to particular industries to be temporary measures. Cole believed that Colbert wanted to help French industry catch up to that of Holland and England, and that after an initial start-up period, the privileges were to be rescinded. However, Colbert's followers lost sight of the inspiration of his work by obsessively applying regulations to the letter. Cole concluded that these high-ranking officials lacked foresight and were prejudiced against businesspeople.[22] Usher's and Cole's arguments can be extended by noting that the increase in the demand for regulation was an outcome of the very methods used by Colbert to encourage French industry.

Having fostered an industrial environment of royal patents, monopolies, and franchises, the Crown had to grant additional monopolies in order to develop new industries. A potential investor would not venture his capital without assurances of protection or special concessions similar to those granted to already-existing industries.[23] Entrepreneurs would hesitate to enter a field where they were threatened by established masters who might use their legal powers to restrict competition. In favored new industries, such as calico works and wallpaper manufactures, the Crown subsidized some of the fixed capital costs of large installations. However, each time the Crown granted new rights or subsidies to particular indus-

---

[21]Abbot Payson Usher, "Colbert and Governmental Control of Industry in Seventeenth-Century France," *Review of Economic Statistics* 16 (1934): 237–40.
[22]Charles Woolsey Cole, *Colbert and a Century of French Mercantilism* (New York: Columbia University Press, 1939).
[23]This is a good indication that French rent seeking (i.e., cronyism) did not dissipate all possible rents, as was the case in England. In the French case, there was a significant difference between monopoly and competitive alternatives.

or of new technology inevitably precipitated an industrial crisis, inasmuch as adjustment was obstructed by the legal entitlements of the various competing guilds and royal industries.[18] Inevitably, these restrictions influenced the growth of new industries and the development of new technology.[19] The transference of much of the economy's dynamism to the informal sector was another consequence of the revival of the guilds, thus shifting much production out of the Crown's fiscal grasp.

The mercantilist goal of supporting manufacturing activity continued after Colbert, and subsequent administrations were often more interventionist than Colbert's. Prosper Boissonnade lists 150 decrees and orders regulating industry between 1664 and Colbert's death; between 1684 and 1753, however, there were more than 1,000; and in the period between 1753 and 1789, Boissonnade counts about 500 regulations.[20] Although the granting of titles for royal manufactories remained at a constant rate after 1753, the ten-year average for granting such titles was higher in the later eighteenth century than during the early part of the century. In other words, the spread of physiocratic and liberal theories did not reduce the extent of the state's industrial *dirigisme*, the persistence of which can be related to the course Colbert set for French commerce and manufacture.

In an early study of Colbert's industrial policy, Abbot Usher raised some important issues in defense of Colbert's strategies. He argued that traditional production had reached its height of development in France

---

[18]The introduction of new industrial techniques generally led to fighting with adjacent crafts. For example, in 1736 button makers opposed the manufacturing of *boutons au métier*; plumbers fought for twelve years (1719–31) to use *les plombs laminés*, which were considerably better than *les plombs coulés* but had not been foreseen in the statutes. In another case, to protect guild interests, an intendant refused an inventor, Dallande, the right to apply a procedure he had developed to facilitate the production of paper.

Note that I use the term *corporation* interchangeably with *guild* in this chapter, even though the former term was not employed in the eighteenth century. The terms more frequently used at that time, *corps* and *community*, are less specific for twentieth-century readers.

[19]Ravillon, the inventor of wallpaper, was harassed by several corporations for illegal competition. His opponents included *imprimeurs*, *graveurs*, and *tapissiers*. Overcoming this opposition required governmental intervention and support of the new industry. Occasionally, new guilds were created to accommodate new industrial processes, such as the *baracaniers* (producers of crude woolen fabrics) created by Colbert.

[20]Prosper Boissonnade, "Etude sur les réglements relatifs à la fabrication, sur les inspecteurs des manufactures, sur la police générale des métiers et en général sur l'intervention de l'administration royale dans l'industrie" (unpublished essay), cited in Pierre Deyon and Philippe Guignet, "The Royal Manufactures and Economic and Technical Progress in France before the Industrial Revolution," *Journal of European Economic History* 9 (1980): 611–32.

primarily luxury goods. This meant restricting the sale of nonguild products on the grounds that they were of poor quality, thus protecting guild-produced luxury goods from competition. The state's services did not come free of charge; the guilds paid the government for this policing service, which they could not as efficiently provide themselves. Under Colbert's successors, the payment demanded increased dramatically as the Crown attempted to extract as much revenue as possible from the guilds.

Another element of Colbert's drive to expand France's industrial capacity was import substitution and the establishment of new industries. This drive placed particular emphasis on industries deemed necessary for national defense and on nascent industries. However, the achievement of this goal of autonomy often conflicted directly with Colbert's goal of strengthening guild privileges. In fact, the need to establish state-sponsored monopolies or royal manufactures cannot be understood apart from the rising role of the guilds during this period. New industries had to be protected from the very regulations used to support the guilds. Privilege was needed to overcome privilege.

One instance of the need to circumvent guild privileges can be seen in the example of a fine-quality textile enterprise. Such an enterprise required skills dispersed among several guilds. To embark on such an undertaking, an entrepreneur needed the privilege of being allowed to transcend guild restrictions to combine the various skills needed for production under a single roof. The title of *manufacture royale* was sometimes given to these undertakings.[17] Without such privileges, it would have been difficult to create large-scale, integrated enterprises. To act independently of the corporations, the directors of royal manufactures needed the privilege of devising their own rules and regulations just like the corporations. Because the mandate of the new industries restricted their activities very precisely, royal manufacturers found it difficult to add new capacities and develop new technologies. This meant that the appearance of new trends in fashion

---

[17]Royal manufactures were not all alike. The monarchy sometimes granted, as an honorary title, the status of royal manufacture to all manufacturers and master craftsmen of a city to protect them from local guild regulations. The Crown might also buy a company's assets and assume direct management, especially in cases where the state was the principal consumer. For instance, the monarchy might assume the role of manufacturer in workshops of high artistic quality (Gobelins, Savonnerie, where the court nobility were the principal consumers) or factories producing military supplies. Most royal manufactories remained in private hands and enjoyed support in the form of subsidies, loans, and privileges. These could come in the form of juridical privileges or fiscal exemptions such as exemption from the taxes on raw materials and on finished goods. But by far the most valuable privilege conferred by the Crown was the prohibition of competition in the production or sale of goods.

tion in output was motivated by greater attention to quality, this explanation is incomplete without considering the gains from cartelization, as higher prices could be obtained by restricting the supply of goods.[13]

Despite the efforts of craftspeople to form local guilds in France, as in much of western Europe during the medieval period, many regions and much industrial activity had managed to escape guild control by the sixteenth century. Although the nationalization of the guilds was given the force of law by royal edicts of 1581 and 1597, it was owing to the efforts of Controller General Jean-Baptiste Colbert in the second half of the seventeenth century to establish and maintain national industrial standards that the influence of the guilds revived.[14] Colbert strengthened the guilds by nationwide decrees, enforced by a corps of inspectors directly responsible to the central government.[15]

## COLBERT: THE FATHER OF ECONOMIC NATIONALISM

Colbert believed in encouraging exports, retaining foreign markets by maintaining high standards of quality, and supporting commerce that attracted precious metals. To keep money in the country, he advocated a prohibition of the export of bullion and a reduction of imports by increasing the kingdom's self-sufficiency. Colbert was convinced that a reputation for shoddy goods hurt French manufactures in international markets and that French products would sell better if national standards of quality could be imposed through the guilds. He thus envisioned an important role for the guilds in a drive to increase French exports.[16] The regulations were extended to cover many nonluxury goods, such as cloth.

Merchants had much to gain from Colbert's efforts to increase both domestic and foreign markets. In effect, Colbert's ministry helped guilds maintain their reputations by guaranteeing the quality of guild products,

---

(College Station: Texas A&M University Press, 1981), 18–25. To understand whether rent seeking was efficient, it would be necessary to take into consideration the uncertainty connected with engagements in which the king was a partner.

[13]Guilds might also be understood as methods to reduce transaction costs in markets and to give France a comparative advantage in luxury-goods production.

[14]Nevertheless, Colbert deliberately allowed crafts in the Faubourg St. Antoine to remain unincorporated and outside the control of the Parisian guilds.

[15]F. Bacquié, *Les Inspecteurs des manufactures sous l'ancien régime, 1669–1792* (Paris: Hachette, 1927). These inspectors in turn supervised the inspectors chosen by the guilds.

[16]Colbert's three reasons for regulation were the attainment of uniformity and good order, the protection of the consumer, and the maintenance of quality to win markets. He believed that the guilds could be harnessed to help achieve each of these ends.

security of contracts in the absence of government enforcment. However, when the guilds were reinforced under Louis IV, this reputation mechanism was no longer needed, since government courts had taken over the role of contract enforcer.[11]

The guilds also increased the credit of individual members. If the guild as a whole bought inputs, the creditworthiness of individual guildspeople was irrelevant to the provider, thereby reducing credit restraints. In an age of high information costs and dramatic asymmetries of information, the guilds loosened credit restraints by monitoring the reputations of their members. Aggregation of purchasing loosened the liquidity constraints on individual guild members by allowing members to benefit from the guild's collective credit, so that, during the different stages of their cash flow, individual guild members could still acquire the necessary materials. If every transaction depended on the cash and reputations of individual tradespeople, the total amount of trade would be severely restricted. Aggregation of credit reputations meant that each individual member could bank on the creditworthiness of the guild, which increased craft production by reducing liquidity constraints and lowering the cost of capital.

The positive social benefits of aggregation were counterbalanced by the guild's acquisition of monopoly powers over retail markets. Once granted exclusive access to a particular market, guild members generally agreed to reduce output by restricting membership, as an individual monopolist would have done in order to enjoy a higher price. To prevent guild members from competing away their monopoly profits, guilds further limited the expansion of output by controlling the amount of raw materials that a single guild producer could purchase, the number of apprentices a master could employ, and the number of hours a master's shop could be open each week. Competition within the guild was thus restricted, as was competition in the marketplace.[12] Although the guilds claimed that the reduc-

---

[11]On the advantages of communal reputation mechanisms as compared to bilateral reputation mechanisms, see Avner Grief, Paul Milgrom, and Barry Weingast, "The Merchant Guild as a Nexus of Contracts," *Journal of Political Economy*, forthcoming. Unlike for craft guilds, the volume of trade, rather than the quality of the product, was the critical variable for merchant guilds.

[12]Competition and rivalry did, of course, play a role in the development of guilds. Guilds competed to maintain and extend privileges vis-à-vis their rivals. *Rent seeking* is the term economists find most apt to describe this kind of competition. Rent seeking is the expenditure of scarce resources to capture a pure transfer. More specifically, rent seeking is the collusive pursuit by producers of restrictions on competition that transforms consumer surplus into producer surplus. Nevertheless, resources spent to capture monopoly rents are from a social point of view inefficiently employed. See Robert B. Ekelund and Robert D. Tollison, *Mercantilism as a Rent-Seeking Society: Economic Regulation in Historical Perspective*

cartel."⁶ The expansion of markets and of administrative jurisdictions thus usually coincided with the elimination or weakening of guilds, because establishing a national cartel would have prohibitive lobbying costs.⁷ Olson's framework is useful for understanding the success of guilds in Europe during the Middle Ages, when the unit of effective political jurisdiction was not larger than a city or county.⁸ His observation also neatly coincides with the decline of English guilds during the early modern period when national markets and the national political authority of Parliament were established. Nevertheless, Olson's model does not seem to account for the situation in Old Regime France, where the creation of national administrative jurisdictions intensified the control of guilds over the economy.⁹

## THE ORIGIN OF THE GUILDS

To understand the growth of Old Regime guilds, it is useful to probe their medieval origins. Guilds often began as groups of workers who organized to supervise the quality of work produced by their peers and to offer consumers recourse in the case of disputes, much as the Better Business Bureau does today. A guild also functioned as a trademark designed to establish a reputation for quality among a particular group of craftspeople.¹⁰ These organizations were predicated upon the belief that the public would pay a premium to purchase goods from producers who were members of self-policing organizations, on the premise that "he who buys needs a hundred eyes; he who sells needs only one." To protect the reputation of their products, guilds set up courts where consumers could settle disputes about quality. This self-policing helped a guild sustain its reputation, which in turn allowed its members to charge a premium for their products. The guilds generally featured a communal reputation mechanism: when one guild member reneged on an agreement, other members might refuse to trade with him in the future. This reputation mechanism improved the

⁶Mancur Olson, *The Rise and Decline of Nations* (New Haven: Yale University Press, 1982), 33.
⁷The expansion of administrative jurisdictions and the expansion of markets seem to occur simultaneously with the weakening of the guilds. How could markets become national if guilds were powerful? Other variables that influenced the expansion of markets and made possible larger administrative bodies were lower information costs and reduced agency problems. These forces also sustained larger firms and guilds.
⁸See Emile Coornaert, *Les Corporations en France* (Paris, 1941).
⁹We have much to learn about the process by which guilds expanded during the late seventeenth century. Questions such as whether the initiative came from the Crown or from local producers remain unanswered.
¹⁰Similarly, McDonald's Corporation guarantees the public a predictable level of service and product in its restaurants.

ful" goods or services in question, thus producing a perverse outcome.¹ Similarly, the French Crown's dependence upon the financial support of the guilds led the Crown reluctantly to support the guilds.

The guilds arose during the early Middle Ages, when the authority of the central government was fragmented and the effective unit of governance was the town or province.² Tradespeople eventually found that by organizing they could increase the income of their members through the elimination of competition. However, the cooperation of local government was needed in order for guilds to enforce their monopoly on the services and goods available in the local marketplace.³ In most cases, local governments enforced guild monopolies in exchange for a share of the profits, which were taxed or borrowed. Guilds in this sense supported local governments by providing revenue. In effect, guilds represented a method for local governments to extract rents from the consumers of guild products, primarily the upper classes, by offering monopoly rights to produce and sell luxury goods. The government acquired this revenue for the price of policing the trade.⁴ Of course, whether by accident or design, much production escaped government supervision.⁵

The lobbying process that accounted for the monopolies of local craftspeople and merchants in Old Regime France was analogous to that described in Mancur Olson's *The Rise and Decline of Nations*. He reasons that lobbies of business interests, trades, or cartels are more likely to proliferate within small jurisdictions, such as a modest municipality or a town, than in a large nation-state. It is easy to understand that if a particular line of business in a town were in the hands of only a few firms, and if the town were distant enough from other markets, a relatively small number of skilled craftspeople would be able to create a cartel. "In a big country, the resources needed to influence the national government are likely to be much more substantial, and unless the firms are (as they sometimes are) gigantic, many of them would have to cooperate to create an effective

---

[1] The demand for sinful products is generally inelastic.
[2] Unlike firms, guilds did not market their members' products, but most guilds observed collective regulations in acquiring raw materials (factor inputs), restricting the supply. The number of apprentices was also restricted. Guild officials were elected by all members of the guild. Guilds were not national. A Lyons goldsmith was not recognized in Toulouse.
[3] However, many towns resisted the guilds, finding that introducing guild monopolies prevented free workers from setting up taxable trades in the city.
[4] Luxury-goods producers especially valued such policing since they needed protection from cheap imitations.
[5] While guilds were particularly effective at producing high-end goods that appealed to wealthy citizens, they also produced goods such as cloth for large export markets.

# 6   Rent Seeking and Trade Regulation

THE RESURGENCE OF THE GUILDS

The proto-industrial sector was perhaps the most dynamic component of the French economy. Despite its strength, proto-industrial producers had to struggle under industrial codes limiting their access to capital, to markets, and to technological innovations. The informal proto-industrial sector was unable to obtain the rights of the formal sector. The guilds were unable to trade rights with other guilds with which their production and expertise overlapped. This absence of markets for all possible industrial property rights that could be traded was a political market failure. Again France offers an example—highlighted by the English counterexample—of failure to consummate deals to reduce inefficiencies clearly identified by the groups bearing the costs.

During the seventeenth century, royal policy influenced France's industrial structure in two major ways: the strengthening of guilds and the establishment of state-sponsored monopolies in new industries. Of the two, the role of the guilds began to be questioned by many of the king's administrators during the eighteenth century. Although supported by the King's Council, reforms designed to promote competition by abolishing the guilds were difficult to implement. Reformers quickly discovered that the institutional structure the crown had established to regulate the trades was a formidable obstacle to deregulation, particularly when the proposed reforms conflicted with the fiscal services the guilds provided the crown.

A modern analogy to the difficulty of abolishing the guilds is fiscal reliance upon taxes on goods and services whose consumption is considered harmful, such as alcohol, tobacco, and gambling. Over time, reliance on "sin taxes" often causes government to support the producers of the "sin-

both the army and the large cities, especially Paris, with bread at prices lower than those offered by producers. These agents of the state were thus not willing to accept market allocation when it concerned special consumers. Ironically, the urban work force of nascent capitalism, not the "pre-capitalist peasantry," most forcefully demanded protection from the laws of supply and demand.

crowds. Georges Rudé, E. P. Thompson, Charles Tilly, and George Lefebvre cite eighteenth-century grain riots as evidence that an alliance of state makers and capitalists was attempting to replace traditional, more moral notions of food entitlement with the logic of market relations. Food riots are viewed as a manifestation of cultural, class, and moral conflict, in which consumers tried to maintain traditional communal rights and fight the advent of the market economy, "which diminished human reciprocities to the wage nexus."[70] These arguments, however, may overstate the importance of class in attitudes to the market.

It may not be accurate to characterize French rioters as "representatives" of their class, thereby assuming that the winners and losers were neatly ordered by class structure. Urban consumers of bread were often successful in gaining concessions from the government because they could easily organize to apply active pressure. Employers agreed with their employees on the availability of cheap grain, inasmuch as it would enable them to keep wages low; a similar urban coalition successfully lobbied for lower grain prices during the debate on the repeal of the English Corn Laws. The coalition of urban employees and workers had another advantage: proximity to political power, which enabled towns to gain government intervention.

The mere identification of legislation as benefiting a given class is not sufficient to demonstrate that the legislation was the result of that class's collective action. The benefits that accrue to some members of a representative group may ultimately be paid for by other members of the same class with less visibility or organizational skill. Eighteenth-century urban bread subsidies came at the expense of poor farmers who directly (through expropriation) and indirectly (through smaller supplies of grain and less productive agriculture) had to bear the costs of supplying city dwellers with cheap grain. Although the total costs to the peasantry were greater, they were too diffuse for successful collective action. Ultimately, the inefficiencies induced in agriculture adversely affected the entire nation's welfare. What seems at first to be a simple struggle between poor workers and wealthy urban elites becomes on further inspection an example of a well-organized, politically threatening group extracting benefits that impose larger—although diffuse—costs on an unorganized, and largely unaware, peasantry.

A review of the historical evidence suggests another revision of the way we view pre-industrial crowd action. Clearly, representatives of the national government were willing to interfere with the market to provide

---

[70] See Thompson, "Moral Economy of the English Crowd."

local price movements occurred despite the absence of dramatic variations in the level of national production.[68]

The fluctuations of the seventeenth and early eighteenth centuries repeated themselves in the period 1789 to 1812. The Revolution thus presents an opportunity to test the hypothesis being presented here. Interregional price disparities reappeared because national authorities were not strong enough to keep trade open and free from regional intervention. Before the recall of the intendants, local officials were unable to prohibit access to local markets. The Revolutionary disjuncture was owing to the government's inability to keep channels of trade open at times when regions of abundance closed their borders to traders from regions where prices were higher. Violent disparities in prices resulted from the isolation of regions and their dependence on local resources. The lack of political will needed to keep interregional trade open, rather than a decline in national production, was the critical reason for the price disparities.[69]

## THE PRE-REVOLUTIONARY CROWD AS A DISTRIBUTIONAL COALITION

Assertions that social relations in early modern France and England were guided by a pre-capitalist ethic have often relied upon historical studies of

---

[68]The figures supporting these conclusions come from Dominique Margairaz, "Les Dénivellations interrégionales des prix de froment en France, 1756–1870" (Thèse du 3e cycle, Université de Paris I, 1982). See C. E. Labrousse, "Prix et structure régionale: Le Froment dans les regions françaises de 1782 à 1790," *AHES* 1939: 382, and J. Meuvret, "Géographie des prix des céréales et les anciennes économies européennes: Prix méditerranéens, prix continentaux, prix atlantiques à la fin du 17e siècle," *Revista de economica* 4, no. 2 (1951): 97–104.

[69]In a recent study of the system of food distribution in early modern England, Robert Fogel has put together an impressive body of data showing that reductions in the national food supply of more than 5 percent were extremely rare. Deficits of 4 percent were more frequent and resulted in devastating subsistence crises for the poor. Fogel found the variance in food prices during the Tudor-Stuart period, when the government regulated the grain markets in ways reminiscent of France, to be less dramatic than during the period after the English Civil War, when paternalistic controls were lifted. He argues that public policy, rather than weather or population pressures, determined whether or not small shifts in the quantity of the harvest would reduce a normally poor diet to starvation levels. Devising regulations to alleviate present shortages and increasing incentives to production in order to minimize future shortages are of course two different matters. Food subsidies for preferred cities or the army could exacerbate shortages. Wars and the policies to sustain them, Fogel finds, may have been the single most important cause of famine and famine-related mortality in the premodern period. The period in early modern English history during which famine-related mortality was lowest (1600–1640) was one of limited military activity. See Robert Fogel, Working Paper, University of Chicago, 1990.

broadly across the population, these actions generated benefits that were localized and highly visible. Urban groups often benefited at the expense of the more numerous but geographically diffuse peasantry. The moral economy argument does not account for these macroeconomic outcomes of policies that in effect subsidized grain consumption for town dwellers.

The comparison of England and France does not contrast a free with a regulated grain market; instead, it highlights how differences in the structure of government led to different forms of regulation. In both nations political power determined the course of a highly subsidized commerce, in which narrow interest groups influenced the government to interfere in the market on their behalf. The outcomes were detrimental to the poor of both nations. The negative consequences of France's paternalistic interference were, however, less visible than the more conspicuous injustice caused by the British government's support of large landowners and grain dealers.

Cultural or moral differences alone cannot account for the divergent outcomes of riots in England and France. In both nations government policymakers defined problems and outlined preferences by applying the same values: a belief in the primacy of economic development and in the applicability of market solutions. The popular classes of both nations asserted similar values and employed the same rhetorical strategies in attempting to defend traditional entitlements. Yet the outcomes of collective action by grain consumers varied significantly. Differences in the political process and the access various groups had to the decision-making apparatus of the state were decisive. The critical issue was not the degree of centralization but where political power was located and the nature of the institutions through which it was expressed. Institutional and political developments in France deprived rural groups of the mechanisms and channels to participate in politics, while town-based bureaucratic centralization gave urban crowds significant opportunities to draw attention to their grievances. As far as grain policy was concerned, in France, the rise of central authority meant government by the city, from the city, for the city. In England, by contrast, the rise of Parliament as the voice of the nation gave rural elites avenues for dominating national policymaking.

French grain prices fluctuated less toward the end of the Old Regime than during the seventeenth and early eighteenth centuries. During the late eighteenth century, seasonal fluctuations had lost much of the violence that characterized price movements during the seventeenth and early eighteenth centuries, when it was common to find an increase of more than 50 percent in the same year. These extreme seasonal, regional, and

make their administration seem unsuccessful and would make later relationships with the population more difficult.

The vulnerability of the government to urban disaffection was one of the consequences of France's political centralization. Riots in the capital could bring the government to a halt, just as riots in the heavily centralized and bureaucratic nations of the developing world today pose a threat to their governments and ultimately lead to concessions that benefit cities at the countryside's expense.[67] When faced with popular discontent, both local and central government officials in France consistently backed down from support of free trade, because they did not want to be identified with laissez-faire policies and thus judged responsible for shortages. By backing down from protecting open national grain markets, officials thus allowed the merchants to become the targets of popular resentment.

A similar urban bias did not exist in England, since the loci of real power were the provincial homes and districts of members of Parliament. In consequence, as we have seen, English development in the eighteenth century had a rural rather than urban bias. The agrarian elites were able to secure government regulations that shifted the terms of trade in favor of large-scale agriculture by dominating the primary political institutions and creating alliances with important commercial elements in the towns. Manufacturing interests were powerless against the merchant-agrarian alliance. If MPs were not concerned about riots in London, it was because their base of power was in the countryside. As a result, the expansion of state power and the demographic rise of London were unrelated. Political power rested with the representatives of rural boroughs.

## FOOD POLICY AND COLLECTIVE VIOLENCE DURING THE OLD REGIME

The French policies designed to defend consumer interests produced price distortions that reduced overall income and transferred income from the countryside to the town. The term *moral economy* does not capture this aspect of early modern crowd action. A more accurate description would emphasize the monopolistic character of the policies that crowds were trying to defend and the costs their actions imposed on the population at large. Although crowd actions promoted policies that imposed costs spread

---

[67]See Michael Lipton, *Why Poor People Stay Poor: Urban Bias in World Development* (Cambridge, Mass.: Harvard University Press, 1977); and Robert H. Bates, *Markets and States in Tropical Africa: The Political Basis of Agricultural Policies* (Berkeley and Los Angeles: University of California Press, 1981).

similarly redistributed income to the cities, since the principal recipients of the dues lived in or at least maintained residences in cities. Maintaining policies that benefited city interests at the countryside's expense was essential, since the political and social elites lived in the city. The government also protected urban manufactures from foreign competition and granted monopolies in many key export-oriented industries. The most protected industries were the luxury manufactures, also city activities. Thus the Crown's tendency to protect city industries from competition also favored urban development. The benefits, however, were short-lived, since they produced welfare losses for the nation as a whole.[64]

Pierre-Samuel du Pont de Nemours summed up the French pattern thus:

> Despite thirty years of the efforts of reason, of arithmetic, and of Philosophy, despite the principles of liberty and of equality, the citizens of the urban municipalities are more disposed than ever to treat their fellow citizens of the rural communities as serfs of the soil and to dispose arbitrarily of their labor, their time, their harvests, and their carts. The tendency toward this unjust and dire abuse of power seems increased in the cities since the Sovereignty seems to uphold that the citizens of populous municipalities . . . represent the totality of the Republic.[65]

The proximity of urban interests to the center of political power was what made the French rioters successful and allowed for a distinct policy bias to develop in favor of urban power blocs.[66] Local urban governments could be held hostage to urban populations that demanded cheap food and protection from abrupt fluctuations in the price of grain. The intendants and other representatives of the central government were based in the cities and were reluctant to use force to prevent riots, because that would

---

[64]On how a reduction in the purchasing power of workers provoked a crisis of underconsumption or of industrial overproduction, see C. E. Labrousse, *Esquisse du mouvement des prix et des revenus en France au XVIII*ᵉ *siècle* (Paris: Dalloz, 1933), 2:628.

[65]Pierre-Samuel du Pont de Nemours, *The Autobiography of Du Pont de Nemours*, ed. Elizabeth Fox-Genovese (Wilmington, Del.: Scholarly Resources Inc., 1984), 265.

[66]The concessions made by the Crown to urban constituencies were not costless. Privileges guaranteed by the Crown were generally paid for in the form of forced loans and indirect taxes. Gail Bossenga has argued that, during the eighteenth century, royal officials were transferring the financial burden of the growing state to the urban poor and workers. See Bossenga, "City and State: An Urban Perspective on the Origins of the French Revolution," in *The Political Culture of the Old Regime*, ed. Keith M. Baker (London: Pergamon Press, 1987), 115–40.

tional scale in France was unknown or at best occasional. The bulk of the grain trade was abandoned to a multitude of petty dealers whose commerce was inefficient, unreliable, and "too small" to serve the public needs.[59]

## URBAN BIAS

In his study of popular culture in eighteenth-century France, Daniel Roche emphasizes that security of food supplies was a primary concern of the state. "The problem of grain," he notes, "was a matter of politics, not economics."[60] As long as provisions were affordable, the populace of Paris did not revolt. Similarly, Richard Cobb writes that subsistence during the eighteenth century had become "above all a political problem, as perhaps it had always been, demanding political solutions and involving the reputation of the public authorities up to the highest level."[61] Other historians—Kaplan and Rudé—have emphasized the strategic nature of provisioning towns to safeguard central power from popular protest. Above all, the Crown wanted to prevent dearth in Paris, which was why Turgot's free-trade decree did not apply to the Paris region.[62] Royal officials feared that unrest in Paris might spread to other cities, and they knew that it was easier to contain unrest in the provincial cities if Paris remained calm.

In both France and England, urban employees and employers had much in common when it came to demands for cheap sources of food. Both could agree on government policies that guaranteed adequate supplies of low-cost food. Both preferred export restrictions on grain so that local prices would remain low. Food shortages could thus produce an alliance between urban workers and their employers.[63] Only in France, however, did the fear of riots by this urban coalition lead the Crown to implement policies that unwittingly allocated a large share of the nation's income to the cities.

The structure of taxes in France also had the effect of redistributing income to the cities, since many townspeople were tax-exempt. Feudal dues

---

[59]Kaplan, *Provisioning Paris*, 82.
[60]Daniel Roche, *The People of Paris*, trans. M. Evans (Berkeley and Los Angeles: University of California Press, 1987).
[61]Richard Cobb, *The Police and the People: French Popular Protest, 1789–1820* (London: Oxford University Press, 1970).
[62]In 1776, Turgot issued six edicts, one of which pertained to Paris.
[63]"The urban revolution was the mainstay of the national revolution: the peasantry could regulate the pace of change, accelerating it by revolt as it did in 1789, obstructing it by disinterest or hostility as it did in 1793–94. But without the Parisian Revolution the National Assembly would have been still born, and without the urban revolution in the provinces the national revolution would have died in infancy as it did in 1848 and 1870," Lynn Hunt argues in *Revolution and Urban Politics in Provincial France* (Stanford: Stanford University Press, 1978), 3.

too dispersed geographically for any one to have an influence on the current price, and, like consumers, they were "price takers"—that is, they took the market price as given. With numerous sources of supply, reasonably good transport, and numerous dealers in the market, it was the equilibrium price and quantity that determined the price. In spite of the fears of local *parlements*, no group of grain dealers was powerful enough to set up a cartel. Moreover, the presence of so many merchants and middlemen trying to take advantage of surpluses and shortages by hoarding (i.e., storing) grain tended to stabilize rather than raise grain prices.

## STORAGE

Even though northern France was among the most grain-rich regions in Europe, extreme fluctuations in grain prices were common. France, a nation dependent on a single crop for a large portion of its food supply, had nevertheless failed to develop storage facilities. This inefficiency can be related to government policies designed to win the confidence and cooperation of consumers. The government policies that prevented middlemen from trading freely prevented the development of private granaries. Middlemen were never sure that their investments in granaries would be protected; storage was viewed by the population as hoarding, and grain traders were viewed as dealers in the vulnerabilities of the people. The grain traders experienced social censure and low status as well as real danger. Grain might be seized during times of dearth and its owner prosecuted as a hoarder. Even efforts by the Crown to store grain were mistrusted by the populace and might be viewed as a ploy to drive up the price of grain. The royal government especially did not want to create the impression that it was in league with grain dealers. Since there was no political benefit associated with storage, only liability, the Crown also was reluctant to undertake building facilities.

The prevalence of the "market principle," as defined by Kaplan, contributed to the backward state of France's agricultural economy. In particular it stymied investment by middlemen in storage facilities that could bridge grain crises by providing greater price stability. The overall result of the Crown's inability to provide a secure environment for investment by traders is summarized by Kaplan:

> Only a great banker or a merchant prince could undertake this trade on a grand scale, with its constantly changing loci of surplus and deficit, its need for a vast network of correspondents, its exorbitant risks, and its enormous costs. And such individuals preferred to invest their wealth in other enterprises. The result was that grain commerce on a truly national or interna-

Like most French advocates of free trade in grain, Turgot realized that a system of public relief was needed to prevent chronic malnutrition and famine-related mortality. In his view, public authorities were responsible for ensuring that part of the surplus generated by free markets was put aside to provide assistance to the poor, who needed protection from high prices. As intendant of Limousin, Turgot set an example by giving the poor subsidies to buy supplies at market prices. Turgot envisioned that a free grain trade would be able to provide the surplus necessary to protect the poor from crisis at less cost to the general population than the paternalistic interference of the past.

The essential issue raised by Turgot was that local decision making about the distribution of grain was biased by concessions to rioters. These concessions, he believed, produced welfare losses that reduced the overall efficiency of the economy. The policies that might allay crowds in one city created inefficiencies or externalities for consumers of grain in neighboring towns. Inefficiencies resulted because the officers of a single city considered only those costs of their decisions that were borne by their own community. Turgot believed that vulnerability to urban disaffection, as illustrated by the example of Dijon, resulted in provisioning policies that produced price distortions, resulting in the transfer of income from the countryside to the town. If the grain trade had evolved under competitive conditions, French consumers as a whole would have enjoyed a greater surplus. The intendants had the general responsibility of reducing these inefficiencies. Since they were also responsible for urban tranquility, however, they too had incentives that conflicted with the creation of a free grain market. The intendant's dilemma was that implementing liberal grain policies might increase resistance that would impinge upon the intendant's foremost responsibility of working with local officials to see that taxes were paid. The rioters, local officials, and *parlements* thus prevailed, and the liberal experiment failed. Turgot, not the disobedient Intendant Dupleix, was ousted.

## THE CONSEQUENCES OF INTERVENTION: PRICE DETERMINATION AND GRAIN MARKETS

As we have seen, high grain prices led the authorities and public to suspect a conspiracy among grain dealers. It was assumed that, by collaborating among themselves, dealers could alter the price of grain at their pleasure. In the eyes of the populace, conspiring to manipulate supplies made grain dealers morally responsible for famine.

Grain markets had many participants, however, none of whom could have had a noticeable influence on prices. Dealers were too numerous and

Such methods only alarm the public and intimidate commerce. You are to make no further visits in the future to know the quantity of provisions even at the bakers. If depots or warehouses of wheat belonging to traders existed in the city, they could supply the bakers, who [are] not numerous or wealthy enough to provision the entire city.

It is important to prevent commerce from being repulsed by the prejudices of the people. You told me that the people of Dijon are not persuaded that free trade will increase the circulation of specie needed to produce abundance. That on the contrary, they believe that unlimited freedom will produce shortage in the midst of abundance because of the greed of merchants, who are called *enharreurs*, a most abusive term in Dijon. It is not the people who must lead you; it is the law. Your failure to uphold the law indicates that administration is badly done in Dijon, especially if you allow people to reserve the greatest insults for those upon whom they depend in moments of greatest need. Those who apply such terms to merchants should be punished.[57]

On the subject of public grain purchases proposed by the *parlement* of Dijon, Turgot wrote:

> Do not buy grain on the king's account. I will not even allow the municipal officers to buy on the city's account even if they have the means. Experience has shown that such purchases spread shortages without diminishing prices in those areas they were designed to alleviate. Merchants have no desire to enter into competition with the government or with municipal bodies determined to lose on their supplies, which can only buy and sell in a ruinous manner. All true merchants will withdraw when commerce entails the risk of public censure, and only merchants subsidized by the government will remain.[58]

Turgot did not overlook the poor. In the hope that the comparative advantage of regions would generate surpluses for grain consumers, he advocated free national grain markets to encourage interregional specialization. Prices, Turgot believed, should reflect supply and demand as accurately as possible, so that traders would have the information they needed to make investments and decisions that were socially most useful.

---

[57] AN H-187/116, *contrôleur général* to *le viconte mayeur et échevin* of Dijon, April 24, 1774.
[58] AN H-187/119, *contrôleur général* to M. Perard, *procureur général* of the *parlement* of Dijon, April 22, 1775.

> 2. Once order is reestablished, proprietors must not expect them [merchants] to sell their produce at a loss, as you have imprudently demanded in the past. As for the poor, it is better to put them to work so that they can pay for food than to manipulate the price, because then you will not find any food.

Unlike the intendant, Turgot realized that the rioters and the poor were not the same people. Turgot established another precedent.

> 3. You must not let the rioters go unpunished and you must indemnify those who suffered losses. Otherwise those who have bad intentions and who have nothing to lose will again excite the populace to pillage. In 1770 there were a rather large number of riots and no prosecutions or very light penalties. This was a great encouragement for the riots that followed. The unhappy victims who were pillaged, beaten, and insulted obtained no reparation. By refusing to protect traders, the government contributes to the stigmatization and denigration of grain merchants by public opinion.

He concluded that, once public order was reestablished,

> 4. The leaders of the riots should be punished. It is essential that all those whose wheat and property were damaged should be reimbursed even by a citywide tax. The city in effect should take responsibility for these misdemeanors.[55]

"Wheat is rare throughout Europe this year, since the harvest is bad," Turgot explained to the Elus (a permanent body that managed daily business) of the Estates of Burgundy. Grain prices were high because the harvest had been inadequate and not because of the greed of merchants. Moreover, "the high prices of which you complain" were the best remedy for shortages. "High prices will act as bait to lure inexpensive grain to where there is greatest need."[56] He reprimanded Dijon's mayor, reminding him that requisitions and visits of judges, police, and magistrates were prohibited by the *arrêt du conseil* of July 1773:

> Despite your pure intentions the actions that you took were immediately followed by a riot. I cannot approve the visits you made to all the bakers of the city to know the quantity of grain and flour they possess....

---

[55] AN, H-187/110, *Contrôleur Général* Turgot to M. de la Tour du Pin, April 20, 1775.
[56] Ibid., *Contrôleur Général* Turgot to the Elus of the Estates of Burgundy, April 18, 1775.

The king forbade municipal magistrates from interfering in the provisioning process and decreed that competition would prevent prices from becoming excessive. Unfortunately for Turgot, the controller general who promoted free grain policies, harvests were not abundant during the years 1774 and 1775, and municipal officials disregarded the king's orders to prevent local shortages. The situation in Dijon was typical. Tumult broke out in 1774, and rioters pillaged a number of private homes and even destroyed a mill. Turgot addressed a series of letters to the town's officials in which he announced that the king held the local officials responsible for the outbreaks. He told the Estates of Burgundy that the municipal officers of Dijon and of Beaune were to blame for the shortages. "I am not surprised by the tumult in Dijon," he wrote one local official. "Whenever one shares in the terrors and prejudices of the people there is no excess that is not encouraged." By "their impudent investigations" of bakers' stocks, Turgot insisted, the municipal officials had "precipitated the unhappiness that followed."[51] To the Estates of Burgundy he wrote: "Certainly the price of wheat will continue to increase if the administrators let themselves be ruled by popular terror, which they intensify by interventions that repulse commerce."[52] Turgot believed that there was no better way to create a shortage than to promulgate public ordinances designed to prevent one. The error lay, he wrote, in "permitting visits and *ordonnances* that intensified the fear of the people and intimidated the merchants and farmers from whom alone the city can hope to secure its subsistence. *Taxation* [price regulation] of grain causes provisions to flee."[53] To restore order, he advised to the Burgundian mayor M. de la Tour du Pin:

> 1. One must above all silence the populace. Strength must be used even if it is necessary to have troops. If security is not entirely restored, merchants and farmers will not bring wheat to Dijon. No one is going to expose their property or person to the fury of the populace.

This call to use the army had few precedents in the history of Burgundian grain riots. The contrast with England during this period could not be more striking. If a mill or residence were damaged in England, rioters might be hanged. All members of a crowd were capitally liable for individual acts of breaking and entering, and all were equally liable for the felony.[54] In his instructions to M. de la Tour du Pin, Turgot continued:

[51] AN, H-187/110, *contrôleur général* to M. de la Tour du Pin, April 20, 1775.
[52] AN, H-187/109, letter from the *contrôleur général* to the Elus of the Estates of Burgundy, April 18, 1775.
[53] *Contrôleur général* to the Elus, April 18, 1775.
[54] John Bohstedt, *Riots and Community Politics*, 34.

worried that Renfort would not be the only trader prosecuted as a hoarder and profiteer. "There are more than thirty awaiting prosecution," he notes, which will "only increase the price of bread; but the *parlement* cares only about embellishing its image as father of the people."⁵⁰

The following month the intendant wrote to Paris that enough grain should be available to feed everyone despite the meager harvest. He explained: "The high prices that followed the bad harvest can be attributed to the excessive liberty given exporters, which excited fear of shortage and enticed the merchants to stop provisioning the market." He reported that merchants were holding out for panic prices. The intendant's criticism of trading freedom here suggests that his understanding of and commitment to free trade was ambivalent. We learn that the peasants, too, seemed unwilling to cooperate and were not bringing their grain to market. It had become impossible to find wagons to transport grain; the few owners of carts who were willing to risk attack were asking inordinate prices. In fact, peasants were unwilling to risk confiscation or sabotage of their wares and their wagons. The intendant thought peasants were simply waiting for higher prices. This was why he ordered a *corvèe*, or forced transport, of grain from the countryside. The intendant further argued that the government should distribute food at its own expense, believing that once merchants and farmers learned of the crisis, they would certainly withhold grain from the market in anticipation of higher prices. The intendant did not seem to understand that the reverse was true. Public purchases discouraged traders from bringing their grain to Dijon, since traders did not want to adjust their prices downward in order to compete with those set by the government. Nevertheless, the intendant gave in to local pressures in 1770, just as his predecessor had done in 1759. The concessions he made to local interests may have contributed to a national subsistence crisis.

Intendants characteristically took the same parochial view as local officials, and with few exceptions they were more interested in sheltering their regional supplies than in promoting national distribution. In this regard, they were little different from the *parlements*. There were only a few intendants with liberal inclinations, just as there were only a handful of *parlements* similarly disposed; they were the exceptions and only for brief periods.

In 1774 the King's Council accorded the grain trade complete liberty, including exemption for producers from requisitions and the visits of judges, police, and magistrates. The king wanted to prevent disorders that he believed were encouraged by the intervention of local governments.

⁵⁰AN, H-187/87, unsigned letter, October 11, 1759.

"But most important an annulment of the *parlement*'s *arrêt* will cause a great sensation in Dijon and throughout Burgundy, and we shall have unrest that it would be best to avoid under those circumstances. Do not forget, Monsieur [the controller general], that there are no troops stationed in Dijon, but only 150 *invalides* guarding the Château. It would be necessary to bring a regiment from their winter quarters, which means I shall have to see M. le comte de Tavannes. Feelings are now so inflamed that . . . the appearance of troops in the capital will incite further disruptions." The army was elsewhere and it had other priorities. Besides, it, too, was interested in reduced grain prices.

The controller general responded to the intendant by insisting that Burgundian officials take into account the damage they would do interregional trade if they sealed off the province from outside traders. Finally, as pressures mounted, the controller general authorized Intendant Joly de Fleury to buy grain to be sold beneath the market price.[47] He also told the intendant to extract in secret as much grain as possible from the nearby regions of the Mâconnais, Bresse, and Bugey by contacting royal subdelegates there, so that local officials would not oppose the departure of grain.[48] In conclusion the controller general wrote to the intendant: "If some expense must be sacrificed in order to indemnify those who you will engage to take these steps and sell under the market price, I authorize you to promise and pay out whatever you judge necessary. I give you my trust and am sure that you will neglect nothing to calm promptly the disturbances that will be provoked."[49]

A grain shortage again threatened in 1770, and again traders and free trade were popularly viewed as the culprits. To gain the confidence of the populace, the *parlement* recommended stern measures against dealers. The intendant, Jean-Antoine Amelot (1764–75), reported to the controller general that the mayor of Arny-le-Duc, M. Renfort, had been imprisoned under the *parlement*'s authority for selling grain at a profit. "He was a *monopoleur* who merits severe punishment; one does not hesitate to condemn him to the pillory. No one will take his defense." The intendant

---

[47]AN, H-187 (October 11, 1770).
[48]We only know that Joly claimed he wanted to keep the grain trade free. His later actions in Burgundy, however, belie his statements. Perhaps he was only pandering to the susceptibilities of the central ministry, or perhaps in this affair he believed that the king's *arrêt* did not carry enough weight to force the *parlement*'s hand. Jean-Françoise Joly de Fleury de la Vallette was *procureur général* of the *parlement* of Paris and *maître des requêtes* in 1743, *president du grand conseil* in 1746, *conseiller d'état* in 1761, and later *secretaire d'état*. He died in 1802 at 82. A study of his career could teach us much concerning the politics of the Old Regime.
[49]AN, H-187, *contrôleur général* to Joly de Fleury, Dijon, October 10, 1759.

why the standard type of regional intervention had the long-term result of perpetuating an economy of crises.

In the spring of 1759, rumors of a possible grain shortage circulated in Dijon, the capital of the Generality of Burgundy. In a memoir to the controller general in Paris, the intendant of Burgundy explained that the people had become restless as the price of grain rose and that uprisings had occurred in several cities. The *parlement* responded by forbidding the export of grain from the province and even called for the interception of shipments on the Saône. The intendant, Joly de Fleury (1749–1761), reported that these precautions "produced all the evil that might have been expected. Shortages were intensified, unrest increased, and neighboring provinces were alarmed. Neighbors that might be able to help Burgundy will close their borders to Burgundian traders. The result will be unrest and excessively high prices in a large part of the kingdom."[46]

Despite the intendant's efforts to keep the grain trade free, the *parlement* of Dijon had issued an *arrêt* prohibiting exports, as it had done during the shortages of 1747. "They were touched by the outcry of the people at grain shortages and by the eagerness of merchants, who were hoarding grain everywhere at any price, even before the grain was threshed." The intendant claimed that he had done everything in his power to impress upon the *parlement* the damage that would be caused by its actions: "I even showed him [the president of the *parlement*] a copy of the *arrêt du conseil* of 1754 that ordered free grain traffic from province to province. My efforts were to no avail." The *parlement*'s president insisted upon the legitimacy of the previous *arrêt* of 1747 as the legal basis for preventing the exit of grain from the province.

In his letter to the controller general, the intendant was concerned about the national impact of this regional response: "The people complain not only that there is not enough bread but that the price is excessive, and the price here will certainly be too high if the export prohibitions are removed. Prohibiting export of grain from the province will certainly cause a great sensation in Lyons and Provence, causing prices to increase, which must inevitably put additional pressure on Burgundian prices. I know that we can annul the *parlement*'s *arrêt*, since it is against the laws of the kingdom, but the king's *arrêt* of 1754 [calling for free circulation of grain] was neither accompanied by *lettres patentes* nor addressed to the *parlements*." The intendant further reminded Paris that the King's Council had not annulled the earlier *arrêt* of 1747, which had also been issued after a poor harvest. In his response to the controller general, the intendant reported:

---

[46] AN, H-187 (August 19, 1759).

might deteriorate when crisis came. With the exception of the winter of 1709, France probably grew enough food to feed its population during the eighteenth century. Nevertheless, owing to transportation limits and market imperfections, often caused by local regulations, famine continued to threaten.

## PROMOTING THE FLOUR TRADE

During the middle of the eighteenth century, the French Crown was urged by the physiocrats to pursue policies that would expand the flour trade. Both the Crown and the physiocrats hoped that establishing milling facilities would promote modern techniques and protect Paris and the provincial capitals from future subsistence crises.[44] Stimulating the flour trade would, moreover, increase the availability of supplies for immediate consumption, increase the geographic scope of trade, since flour was cheaper to transport than grain, and eliminate numerous middlemen. By the second half of the eighteenth century, however, only in the Paris region did flour become a more important trading commodity than grain.[45] Efforts to encourage the flour trade throughout the kingdom apparently failed because producers, middlemen, bakers, and above all millers did not want to incur the capital expenditures and risks necessary to develop milling, conservation, and storage facilities for flour. Although millers faced large initial investments, there was an additional reason for the more general absence of storage facilities. Merchants feared that, in moments of high prices, stored merchandise, flour or grain, would be preyed upon by rioters or government officials. Moreover, since the French government tended to protect certain preferred large merchants from competition, individuals were unwilling to undertake major investments unless they could be sure of similar exemptions. Because of these government policies limiting competition, individual merchants were reluctant to develop the extensive milling facilities that the flour trade required on their own initiative.

## BURGUNDY

Whereas the historical literature on grain riots is dominated by accounts representing the side of local consumers, the correspondence between controllers general and the intendants of Burgundy, especially that with Controller General Turgot, provides insights into the imperatives that guided the behavior of producers and merchants during regional shortages. Moreover, the insights provided by the Burgundy example should help clarify

---

[44]See Kaplan, *Provisioning Paris*, 422–26, on the importance of economic milling to the government and the physiocrats.
[45]Ibid., 106–8 (table 5).

kets. To further prevent merchants from circumventing the system, all grain in transports had to carry papers verifying where it had been bought. Grain that was purchased illegally would be subject to confiscation.

During the seventeenth century, shortages could lead to famine and increased mortality. By the mid eighteenth century, however, transportation facilities were greater.[41] In addition, intendants increasingly corresponded about the state of the harvest, so that shortages and abundance could be anticipated and arrangements could be made to avoid crisis. Records called *mercuriales* were kept, which provided a nationwide account of grain prices. Greater market integration, wider markets, and greater trading freedom were by far the most important contributors to the elimination of famines. When shortages were imminent, however, intendants often found that local officials were more concerned with local supplies than with national priorities. In times of dearth, municipal officials, backed by the local *parlement*, would attempt to restrict access to local supplies of grain. Thus, the threat of shortage often pitted regions against each other. By contrast, English local officials could not close their markets to English goods or traders. As defenders of local prerogatives, the local French *parlements* were typically in the forefront of groups aiming to override efforts by the Crown to keep the grain trade as national and free as possible. Often the *parlement's* position was hypocritical: it praised free trade in grain but refused to endorse free-trade legislation written in Paris. The discrepancy between the actions and statements of *parlements* was because of their narrow defense of provincial prerogatives and their opposition to the growth of royal administrative authority.[42] *Parlements* claimed the right to determine access to local markets. In defending the enforcement of trade restrictions, they could claim they were standing up for provincial interests.[43] Since a grain shortage might unite a town's elites with its masses, intendants were likely to concede to local wishes. Hence, the national system of free trade that the Crown attempted to promote

---

[41]Several historians are skeptical of interregional trade and emphasize that France was divided into three distinct zones of provisioning: a southwestern zone, the Paris basin, and an eastern zone dominated by Lyons. Prices in these zones varied significantly. For example, prices tended to be about 30 percent higher than Paris in the zone provisioning Lyons.

[42]Kaplan, *Bread, Politics and Political Economy*, 2:421.

[43]"In certain states of emergency, during periods of famine for example, when feelings ran high amongst the people and the local authorities saw a chance of asserting themselves, the central government allowed the parlements to take charge for the duration of the crisis and to make a great show of beneficent activity" (Alexis de Tocqueville, *The Old Regime and the French Revolution* [1856; New York: Anchor Books, 1955], 58).

sell.[38] This implies that exporters could pay more than local consumers for favorable policies and may account for export licenses being granted during periods of widespread dearth. Justices might have promoted economic development in their jurisdictions by creating an atmosphere friendly to trade: by regulating less, the justices could attract middlemen to their market towns. Although local economic decisions were made by local officials, they could not deny other English products access to the county market.

## PROVISIONING FRANCE

The French Crown, Steven Kaplan suggests, was unable to maintain a consistent course in its grain policies, which wavered between "market principles," or the "free market," and the "marketplace." Market principles implied the private nature of exchange, freedom from police intervention, and freedom to choose the place of exchange. The success of this system can be measured in profits. In sharp contrast, the "marketplace" was public and closely monitored by government agents; it concentrated actors and goods in a specified location where they could be supervised by public authorities. Its success could be measured in public tranquility.[39] In normal times, government intervention was rare, but in times of dearth the principles of paternalistic provisioning returned with a vengeance. The goals of government regulation, Kaplan explains, were "to establish clear-cut lines of supply, and to keep them open at all costs. They aimed at forcing grain into commerce as rapidly as possible, keeping it visible and moving, and directing it to market through the hands of as few middlemen as possible where it could be sold quickly and openly at a reasonable price."[40]

The months of greatest apprehension in the market for grain were April, May, and June. Rumors of possible shortages or of hoarding by dealers could invite protests or cause prices to climb. Trouble was also likely in September, when rumors of a poor crop yield were expected to result in hoarding because of the expectation that towns would view buyers from neighboring towns as rivals and restrict access to their zone of provisioning. This was done first by ruling that all grain sales had to be conducted in the public market; merchants could not buy grain directly from peasants at their farms. Then a town would require merchants to carry passports and would restrict out-of-town merchants' access to local mar-

---

[38] Evidence of venal justices of the peace is provided by Gras, *Evolution of the English Corn Market*, 232.
[39] Kaplan, *Provisioning Paris*, 27.
[40] Steven Laurence Kaplan, *Bread, Politics and Political Economy in the Reign of Louis XV* (The Hague: Martinus Nijhoff, 1976), 1:65.

abandoned after 1672.[34] R. B. Outhwaite has provided a highly illustrative example of this change by contrasting the government's efforts at regulating the grain market in response to the severe shortages of 1590 with its inaction in the face of the shortages of the 1690s. He found that government officials ignored the crisis of 1692–93 and that there was little government action after bad harvests in 1695 and 1698.[35] The lack of government response to the shortages of the 1690s was a prelude to the essentially unregulated internal trade of the eighteenth century.

If authorities did little to protect consumers from high prices, they did much to suppress rebellions without making significant concessions to the rioters. Sustained unrest was put down by troops and rarely resulted in a popular victory, as was so often the case in France. So brutal and deliberate was the enforcement of the laws that it may very well have contributed to the rise in mortality rates in England.[36]

One reason for the new grain policy after 1688 in England was that Crown and Parliament were constantly struggling for power at the top of the government hierarchy. Owing to the Crown's relative loss of power in relation to Parliament after the Restoration, the monarchy was unable to enforce grain policies. With Parliament battling the king, and factions within Parliament fighting one another, the government was unable to legislate unified policies over time. Evidence for this can be found in the many reversals of export laws and in the well-known black market in grain that flourished in the seventeenth and eighteenth centuries.[37] Moreover, sporadic attempts to control imports and ban exports of grain failed in the late seventeenth and early eighteenth centuries because the vast scope of private exchanges could not be monitored by the government's limited number of police agents. Easily corruptible local government officials often had the same interests as local grain dealers. The justices of the peace, upon whom the enforcement of regulations depended, could be bought by local interests and were often local landowners with grain surpluses to

---

[34]Lasting machinery to control the grain trade was never set up in England. The king regulated rural exports in times of dearth but advocated free trade as early as 1361. The English authorities rarely fixed the price of corn, occasionally passing legislation prohibiting purveyance but never resorting to the seizure of corn. See Gras, *Evolution of the English Corn Market*, 132–33.

[35]The grain shortages of 1692, 1693, 1695, and 1698 were not discussed in government papers and involved little government action. See R. B. Outhwaite, "Dearth and Government Intervention in English Grain Markets, 1590–1700," *Economic History Review*, 2d ser., 34 (1981): 389–406.

[36]Ormrod, *English Grain Exports*, 90–91.

[37]See Vincent Ponko, Jr., "Norman Scott Gras and Elizabethan Corn Policy: A Reexamination of the Problem," *Economic History Review*, 2d ser., 17 (1964): 32.

London grain merchant might extend credit to a baker knowing that if the baker failed to pay his debt, the merchant could prosecute him in court and threaten him with debtors' prison. Supported by a system that guaranteed that debts would be paid, it was easier to invest in improved transportation or storage methods. In the long run, such investments would increase the merchant's efficiency and enable him to supply more grain for sale at the market price, possibly at a lower price. In contrast to the British system, the French credit structure was not strongly supported by the coercive power of the state. If a dispute arose between a merchant and a baker over credit, there was little the state would do to help resolve it. It was probably difficult for frugal bakers to distinguish themselves from their spendthrift colleagues; consequently, bakers as a class suffered. Steven Kaplan contends that the French government was hesitant to intervene on behalf of the middlemen because the authorities wanted to "sustain as many bakers as possible."[31] Protecting bakers from the snares of greedy middlemen was not, however, the real problem. Prison terms, property seizure, and other legal means could have been used to help the merchants collect their debts in eighteenth-century France. However, many means were also available to bakers who wanted to stay out of jail or to pay back loans slowly, so that grain merchants often met with little success when they tried to collect outstanding payments. Although 25 percent of French bakers died in debt, these debts were often trivial since, under the circumstances described above, bakers rarely borrowed large sums.[32] In general the lack of a strong state policy to protect creditors from default stifled the ability of French grain traders to take risks and resulted in an undercapitalized trade.[33] Loose enforcement of loan contracts only exacerbated the shortage of bakers and led to their lack of capital resources.

## THE POLITICS OF PROVISIONING ENGLAND

As we have seen, public policies in England were designed to aid grain producers, merchants, and exporters by the late seventeenth century. Earlier measures protective of consumers, although never well enforced, were

---

[31]Steven Laurence Kaplan, *Provisioning Paris: Merchants and Millers in the Grain and Flour Trade during the Eighteenth Century* (Ithaca, N.Y.: Cornell University Press, 1984), 148–51; quotation from p. 150.
[32]Ibid., 149.
[33]Since bakers with large inventories were more likely to become victims of riots, they would be less likely to find credit. South Central Los Angeles, where one finds relatively more small shopkeepers than large supermarkets in riot-free areas, offers a parallel.

## THE EVOLUTION OF THE ENGLISH MARKET: IMPROVEMENTS IN INTERNAL MARKETING

Efficiencies in English grain production seem to have come from improvements in distribution and marketing rather than from gains in productivity. Deregulated trade in England during the eighteenth century resulted in the creation of a large, highly specialized grain market. English economic historians emphasize the increasingly national character of markets and the tendency for prices of basic commodities to become uniform as regions tended to specialize. "The regionalism and provincialism in the home market was breaking down"; by 1750 there was a national market.[28] Improved information about markets, the availability of supplies, and prices stimulated the growth of efficient networks of supply for growing urban populations. Competition intensified among carters and the owners of coastal vessels. London prices were published in the provincial press. The corn factors' exchange was completed in 1751, so that merchants had a place to meet with other specialized grain traders. Middlemen had more freedom than before—they could now trade outside the formal marketplace—and they had more influence on trade. Farmers around London were less likely to visit markets and sold instead to roaming middlemen on the basis of samples. The reduced role played by public markets in the retailing of grain contributed to the elimination of price-fixing by riot. English consumers became dependent on stores for their grain supplies. The scale of operations among English merchants could vary enormously, from small speculative shipments arranged by nonspecialists to substantial quantities of grain handled by the navy victualing contractors (assembling 4,000 quarters of wheat meal alone per month in the 1750s). By the century's end, a handful of merchants dominated the grain trade.[29] One London factor, Thomas Farrer, claimed to have shipped 40,000 quarters in one year. The Coutts brothers of London and Edinburgh established an elaborate network of factors throughout England and Scotland to supply their extensive export trade.[30] Judging from Steven Kaplan's extensive study of the French grain trade, similarly substantial trading operations controlled by a handful of large dealers did not exist in France.

## CREDIT AND THE MIDDLEMAN

The rules regarding credit exchanges in England enabled middlemen to take risks their French counterparts were unlikely to take. For example, a

---

[28]Chartre, "Marketing of Agricultural Produce," 406–502.
[29]Ibid., 501.
[30]The history of the firm has been told by W. Forbes, *Memoirs of a Banking House* (compiled 1803, published in Edinburgh, 1859).

## THE COST OF ENGLISH WHEAT

While the prices of agricultural products were falling throughout Europe, those in England remained relatively constant, largely because dramatic local price disparities diminished. Wilhelm Abel has calculated a relative index of the price of agricultural products from 1650 to 1700. On a base of 100, prices fell to 84 for England, 75 for France, 73 for the southern Netherlands, 70 for the United Provinces, and 60 for Poland during this period.[25] Although the English maintained a high level of exports during this period, it was not a result of the low cost of their agricultural products.[26] Even London prices, which were generally lower than prices in the rest of England for the period 1700–1759, were higher than Danzig prices, except for during the 1740s. How, then, can the competitive position of English wheat be explained? Part of the answer lies in geography. England benefited from being closer to the principal European markets than Danzig, and, in addition, English ports were open during the winter, while the port of Danzig was not. The export bounties, which often covered freight and handling charges, made English grain competitive throughout Europe. Another part of the answer lies in the existence of storage facilities and stocks, which assured relative price stability in England. Despite high average prices for English domestic grain, price stability allowed English merchants to take advantage of the price fluctuations on the Continent.

Because of the government's pro-export policies, the larger English estates had an advantage that they would not have otherwise enjoyed in relation to small peasant farms in France during this period of grain surplus and low continental prices. Farmers of large English estates maintained a larger percentage of the arable land in cultivation than would otherwise have been needed. The grain trade certainly contributed to the well-being of producers and to agrarian prosperity. Nevertheless, the net cost to general economic growth in Britain of subsidizing agriculture is difficult to assess.[27]

---

[25]Wilhelm Abel, *Agrarkrisen und Agrarkonjunktur im Mitteleuropa vom 13. bis zum 19. Jahrhundert* (Berlin: P. Parey, 1966), 152–53.

[26]It seems from the figures given by Braudel and Spooner that England's system of large estates was performing less competitively than France's system of small peasant production. See Fernand P. Braudel and F. Spooner, "Prices in Europe from 1450," in *The Cambridge Economic History of Europe*, ed. E. E. Rich and C. H. Wilson, 4:470–71.

[27]See the discussion among N. F. R. Crafts, Jeffrey G. Williamson, and Joel Mokyr in *Explorations in Economic History* 24 (1987): 245–325; E. L. Jones, "Agriculture 1700–80," in *The Economic History of Britain since 1700*, vol. 1, *1700–1860*, ed. Roderick Floud and Donald McCloskey (Cambridge: Cambridge University Press, 1981), 36–66; and Ormrod, *English Grain Exports*, 70–95.

## EXPORT BOUNTIES IN ENGLAND

English historians, as we have seen, often argue that grain export and the government policies that favored it were the most common inspiration to riot during the eighteenth century. It is therefore remarkable that during most of the period, beginning in the 1680s, the government encouraged merchants to export grain by giving them bounties. Even as early as the 1670s, government policies protected landlords by raising prices through subsidized grain exports. This policy, however, represented a shift from earlier policies designed either to protect or to subsidize consumers.

In the early 1670s, farmers began complaining that grain prices were too low and that they were unable to maintain rent payments. In 1672 an act of Parliament protected the home market by excluding imported grain and encouraged exports by paying bounties on all grain exported overseas. The preamble of the act creating the bounties explained that it would help landowners better support the burden of the new land tax. The bounty was suspended after an experimental period and then reenacted in 1688 on a permanent basis. As a result of the bounty, English grain producers were able to export a considerable quantity of grain during the eighteenth century and pay their taxes.[22]

The impact of the bounty policy was felt in another important area—prices. Generally, less than 3.5 percent of the total domestic output was exported, but at times this figure reached 10 percent. However, exports had a dramatic influence on domestic prices, as the policy of subsidized grain exports raised domestic price levels by 19 percent.[23] It is probable that grain prices in England, that of wheat in particular, were the highest in Europe during most of the years between 1690 and 1760 (excluding the 1740s).[24] This suggests that, had it not been for the bounties, England would not have been as successful at exporting.

---

action does not seem to have been common in France. In England, by contrast, "disturbances over the country as a whole ... were in most instances easily suppressed by military forces" (David Ormrod, *English Grain Exports and the Structure of Agrarian Capitalism, 1700–1760* [Hull: Hull University Press, 1985], 89).
[22]Basing his projections on the statistics of bounty expenditures, N. S. B. Gras estimates that grain exports increased dramatically: between 1697 and 1731 they totaled 353,353 quarters annually, up from 303,925 quarters annually in 1675–77. See Gras, *The Evolution of the English Corn Market* (Cambridge, Mass.: Harvard University Press, 1915).
[23]J. A. Chartre, "The Marketing of Agricultural Produce," in *Agrarian Change*, bk. 2 of *1640–1750*, vol. 5 of *Agrarian History of England and Wales*, ed. Joan Thirsk (Cambridge: Cambridge University Press, 1985), 448, 450–54, 500.
[24]See Ormrod, *English Grain Exports*, 49–52.

were executed and fifty-seven others were convicted of felonies.[17] John Bohstedt has reported that between 1790 and 1810, roughly 6 percent of the grain riots resulted in fatalities, as "one or more rioters were killed in 37 of 617 riots."[18] Depending on the military was a far-from-ideal solution: there were only twelve peacetime regiments available for the task. The troops placed an extra burden on the food supply and occasionally became active in the rioting.[19] Despite the frequency and national scope of the British rioting, it had little effect on national grain policies. Authorities in England might invoke old statutes against market abuse, provide additional poor relief, temporarily suspend exports (usually too late to prevent dearth), and occasionally offer grain at subsidized prices. Dealers might make informal concessions to crowds to avoid confrontations. Unlike in France, however, national and regional export restrictions were never established, and neither was the sale of grain confined to publicly supervised marketplaces in England. English merchants did not need licenses for internal trade. The militia was never sent to large farms to compel the release of grain stocks.[20] It seems that rioters in England were more likely to be severely punished than rioters in France (*taxation populaire* was not tolerated in England), and, despite the greater availability of troops in France, military force was used less frequently against rioters there.[21]

---

[17]"Where frequent large-scale disturbances overmatched the abilities of the magistrates the government sent in troops" (Dale Williams, in Charlesworth, ed., *Atlas of Rural Protest*, 88).

[18]See Bohstedt, *Riots and Community Politics*, 230. "In the various food disturbances [between 1700 and 1800] . . . several food rioters were killed by authorities and a number executed" (Stevenson, " 'Moral Economy' of the English Crowd," 235).

[19]John Stevenson, "Food Riots in England, 1792–1818," in *Popular Protest and Public Order: Six Studies in British History, 1790–1920*, ed. R. Quinault and J. Stevenson (London: George Allen & Unwin, 1974), 47–48; Charlesworth, ed., *Atlas of Rural Protest*, 100.

[20]E. P. Thompson emphasizes that magistrates were often reluctant to impose severe penalties on protesters, and courts could invoke old rules that limited the action of middlemen. However, these magistrates had little influence on public policy, which was dictated by Parliament and enforced by the justices of the peace. Unlike the magistrates, these creators and enforcers of policy did not usually concern themselves with upholding ancient legal traditions that protected consumers. We must distinguish between legal treatment meted out by judicial officials and the formation of policies that suited consumer goals. Thompson also emphasizes the chilling effect that the threat of riots or the memory of past riots would have on the behavior of traders. Again this misses the essential point, which is, which groups determine the formation and implementation of public policy?

[21]Troops were used to quell the massive, nationwide riots of 1775. Hundreds of protesters were arrested, and there were two public executions in the capital. See Rudé, *Crowd in History*, 28–30. Except for the years 1725, 1752, and 1775, troop

policies by fixing prices and regulating supply. In each case, rioting led to the revocation of a government decree deregulating the grain trade. In England, similar disturbances rarely had the same impact. The claims of the French rioters were clearly more threatening to the political authorities than similar claims raised by English crowds.

## RIOTS IN ENGLAND

English grain riots were rarely motivated by acute shortage; rather, they focused on the principle of grain export. For example, the years between 1730 and 1750 were characterized by an exceptional run of favorable seasons and good harvests, yet crowd action against export was common during this period.[14] Exporters and grain in transit were the most common targets. To deter the attacks, legislation was enacted in 1737 that imposed severe penalties—hard labor, public whipping, and transportation—on those who opposed the purchase or shipment of grain. In the 1740s, when actual shortages led to rioting in many parts of England, Parliament still refused to tamper with the legislation encouraging export and instead enforced legislation dating from 1552 against forestalling, engrossing, and regrating. A complete account of English rioting has yet to be completed, but the contributors to *An Atlas of Rural Protest in Britain*, edited by Andrew Charlesworth, provide considerable evidence on the distribution of the riots and the different forms of action taken. Between 1660 and 1737, there were 56 recorded food protests, 84 in 1740 alone; there were over 140 in thirty different counties during the crisis of 1756–1757 and over 170 during 1766. Whereas authorities could do little to prevent nonviolent intimidation of grain suppliers or spontaneous attacks on grain convoys, sustained rioting often resulted in the calling in of troops. The response of municipal authorities tended to be brutal, especially when local mayors were involved in the grain trade.[15] In May 1728, the mayor of Falmouth demanded two detachments of troops from a man-of-war in Falmouth harbor after receiving word of a threatened attack on exports. In the Midland food riots of 1756, magistrates promptly tried and hanged two ringleaders. Military force was later used to quell rioting that continued into Derby and Nottingham.[16] During the riots of 1766, seven men

---

[14]T. H. Baker, *Records of the Seasons: Prices of Agricultural Produce and Phenomena Observed in the British Isles* (London, 1883), 187.
[15]A comparison of French and English local officials, especially mayors, however useful, is not possible with the evidence available at this time.
[16]Jeremy Caple, "North Midlands: August and September 1756," in Charlesworth, ed., *Atlas of Rural Protest*, 112.

discretionary income of urban workers, thus reducing what could be spent on manufactured goods. To avoid disruptions in urban demand, then, the officials of Paris, and of a number of provincial capitals, supported policies to reduce the cost of living in the cities.[12] The grain rioters, primarily townspeople—industrial or proto-industrial employees—seeking cheap bread through market regulation, prompted town officials to assert monopoly privileges over local grain supplies. This included continuing traditional price and market controls, prohibiting exports, restricting sale to local merchants, and limiting the access of local marketplaces to out-of-town merchants. Meanwhile, rural producers bore the costs of these policies designed primarily to lower the cost of food. This urban political coalition, to use Mancur Olson's terminology, shared certain fundamental but selective incentives that made organizing relatively costless.[13] Peasants were dispersed throughout the countryside in villages that were largely independent of one another. Members of the largest group in the nation, the peasantry, although they shared vital common interests, were thus unable to express their needs and to counterbalance the organizational power of workers rioting in cities. Rioters may have claimed that they were entitled to bread at a fair price, but it was their ability to organize that made such claims visible and threatening.

A number of incidents highlight France's vulnerability to consumer disaffection when a rise in prices sparked widespread discontent. French rioters successfully prevented the export of grain, forced market traders to reduce prices, and persuaded government officials to abandon free-trade

---

dwellers. Food riots often occurred in rural areas but involved proto-industrial and industrial workers and artisans. "One of our contentions is that in the main food riots were not staged by agricultural workers," Andrew Charlesworth writes. "Food riots in Britain were in the main the direct collective actions of town artisans and proto-industrial and industrial, that is non-agricultural workers. . . . Food rioting in Britain was mainly a strategy employed by industrial workers in defence of their living standards" (id., ed., *An Atlas of Rural Protest in Britain, 1548–1900* [Philadelphia: University of Pennsylvania Press, 1983], 1, 63). There is less agreement among French historians on this point, but, as noted earlier, that disagreement does not influence the argument presented here.

[12]The emphasis is on local demand because subsidies to urban consumers would shift the location of demand for manufactured goods but would be unsuccessful in raising aggregate national demand for manufactured goods. This and other clarifications of traditional misconceptions about the role of agricultural demand in spurring industrial demand are discussed in Joel Mokyr, "Demand vs. Supply in the Industrial Revolution," *Journal of Economic History* 37 (1977): 981–1008.

[13]The actions with which I am concerned took place primarily in cities even if, as was sometimes the case in France, the actors lived in the countryside. Many of those who participated from outside the city were involved in rural putting-out industries that were part of urban supply and distribution networks.

The harm done by low grain prices to those who work the land is as important as the damage done to owner-producers. Consider that workers are harmed because of reduced employment and lower wages. Similarly, when workers are paid in kind, low grain prices cost them more because the value of their work is reduced. In short, because of the structure of political authority, the savings capacity in France was being transferred from agriculture to the urban economy, and from the production of goods for the large domestic market to the production of luxury goods priced for international markets.[10]

The authors who emphasize the importance of moral perceptions have made a significant contribution to our understanding of popular collective action during the eighteenth century. They have helped us to understand the cultural context in which rioters formulated their grievances, the language they employed, and the symbolism they shared. Their studies concentrate on the aims of the protesters. Taking the language of protest seriously, they have taught that rioters perceived their actions in terms of moral obligations and rights. They have not explained why rioters were more able to determine national grain policy in France than in England.

## WHY GRAIN CONSUMERS WERE MORE LIKELY TO REBEL THAN PRODUCERS

Although French grain producers shared vital common interests, they failed to obtain government policies favorable to rural interests. The costs of the Crown's grain policies were spread out among millions of peasants located in twenty thousand villages, while the benefits were concentrated among a much smaller percentage of the population, concentrated in a few hundred cities. While the total cost to the agrarian population was great, the average cost of the grain policies to each peasant was small relative to the benefits attained by urban workers. Grain rioters, generally representing city and town-based interests (including rural putting-out networks that originated in towns), were able to prevail against the interests of the larger group, the producers, which included a significant segment of the peasantry. As a result, laws in France often restricted exports, limited the freedom of traders, reduced storage, and diminished grain prices.

In both England and France, the strongest pressure in favor of government intervention in the grain trade came from a coalition of the urban worker and the urban employer.[11] An increase in food prices reduced the

---

[10]When the taxation transfers levied by the Crown are factored in, the disparity is lessened.

[11]A consensus exists among historians of England that English rioters were town

such actions were asserting a prior right to consume what was produced locally. Local officials might sanction crowd action taken to prevent exports during periods of dearth; therefore, participants in *entraves* were less likely to be punished than participants in *taxation populaire*. Historians believe that such claims to regional self-sufficiency were sometimes more just or fair-minded with regard to the welfare of the poor than the values fostered by the system of property rights they generally call capitalism.

Did the development of free national markets in grain, in fact, raise a conflict pitting economic efficiency and social equity against each other? This view ignores a point well understood by political economists of the eighteenth century. The practices associated with a moral economy served narrow regional and occupational interest groups at the expense of general welfare. Such practices hastened the exodus from agricultural regions and lowered agricultural productivity as a whole. The result was an increase in urbanization without an efficient reallocation of resources. The belief that such practices were defenses of a system of grain entitlement that was more moral than market-driven allocation represented the position of but one group, the most vocal and best-organized. The benefits of intervention on behalf of urban consumers were more visible than the costs to the many French who earned their living producing grain.

To say that grain policies dictated by the "moral economy" pitted rural against urban interests does not exclude the possibility that some members of the rural community may have preferred such policies. The short-term benefits of such policies must be contrasted with the perpetuation and deepening of rural poverty that resulted. A policy that encouraged high grain prices would have kept more well-paid employment in the countryside. Such employment might not have benefited all peasants equally, but in global terms it would have benefited the country over the city.

---

would invite savage retaliation from the authorities" (John Walter and Keith Wrightson, "Dearth and the Social Order in Early Modern England," in *Rebellion, Popular Protest and the Social Order in Early Modern England*, ed. Paul Slack [Cambridge: Cambridge University Press, 1984], 119). "A substantial proportion of all disturbances took place at ports, market towns or trans-shipment points" (John Stevenson, "The Moral Economy of the English Crowd," in *Order and Disorder in Early Modern England*, ed. A. Fletcher and John Stevenson [Cambridge: Cambridge University Press, 1985], 233). By contrast, John Bohstedt argues in *Riots and Community Politics in England and Wales, 1790–1810* (Cambridge, Mass.: Harvard University Press, 1983) that price-fixing by crowds was part of Devon's "classic" pattern of food riots. Bohstedt calculates that two of every three riots were responses to price.

by a traditional concern for justice."⁶ Since the publication of Rudé's pathbreaking studies, a number of historians have asserted their belief in the moral corruption of capitalism by studying the efforts of crowds to prevent the export and free trade of grain during the eighteenth century.

Charles Tilly is among the scholars who view grain riots as the last efforts of pre-industrial society to thwart the irresistible progress of capitalism. In numerous publications, Tilly has emphasized that eighteenth-century state makers and capitalists joined forces in order to promote a policy of free trade and to develop national grain markets: traditional, more "moral" notions of food entitlement were subjected to the logic of market relations. Those who rioted against high prices or blocked grain shipments were attacking the "system of property relations we now call capitalism."⁷ Rioters attempted to defend traditional notions of the community in which the rights of the collectivity were stronger than the rights of the individual and in which the needs of the local community took precedence over those of the national community.⁸

The moral economy of the poor in eighteenth-century Europe embraced two somewhat different conceptions of equity and was expressed in two different types of collective action designed to reduce food prices. The first of these notions of equity was the belief that grain was too precious to be subject to market forces and that in times of shortage a just price should prevail over the market price. This belief underlay demands for *taxation populaire,* or price regulation, often motivating attacks on merchants, bakers, or wealthy peasants suspected of hoarding food supplies. Such attacks were more common in France than in England. The second belief was that the local community should have primary access to locally raised grain. Collective actions to achieve this goal were known as *entraves* and consisted of attacks on convoys or the transport of grain.⁹ The participants in

---

⁶Ibid., 30.
⁷Charles Tilly, *The Contentious French* (Cambridge, Mass.: Harvard University Press, 1986), 23.
⁸Louise Tilly takes the same position in "Food Entitlement, Famine, and Conflict," in *Hunger and History: The Impact of Changing Food Production and Consumption Patterns on Society,* ed. Robert I. Rotberg and Theodore K. Rabb (Cambridge: Cambridge University Press, 1985). See also Louise A. Tilly, "The Food Riot as a Form of Political Conflict in France," *Journal of Interdisciplinary History* 2 (1971): 23–57; and id., "Food Entitlement, Famine, and Conflict," *Journal of Interdisciplinary History* 14 (1983): 333–49.
⁹Even during the mid seventeenth century, *entraves* were the general form of crowd action in England. "There is an absence of those requisitioning riots in which crowds proceed to the homes of farmers, millers or other wealthy individuals to pillage them and their granaries. A possible explanation for this might be ... that the poor were almost certainly aware that such a clear challenge to the social order

between what are conceived of as two cultures: the capitalist and the pre-capitalist. In a seminal article on the causes of rioting in eighteenth-century England, E. P. Thompson argued that "the grievances were rooted within a popular consensus as to what were legitimate or more generally speaking were rooted in a consistent traditional view of social norms and obligations which, taken together, can be said to constitute the moral economy of the poor. An outrage to these moral assumptions, quite as much as actual deprivation, was the usual occasion for direct action."[3] He claimed that rioters were defending the old moral economy of provisions from the new political economy of the free market: "They were responding to a political economy which diminished human reciprocities to the wages-nexus."[4] Thompson was inspired by the pioneering work of Rudé, who observed that crowd action in France usually led to an unofficial price control known as *taxation populaire*. Local people would take matters into their own hands and compel dealers to sell wheat at a "just price." To Rudé, the concept of the "just price" was a holdover from a pre-capitalist mentality. He believed that food was considered too vital to the welfare of the people in the pre-capitalist world to be left to the discretion of market forces. "Small consumers and producers of town and countryside reacted to the process of change by clinging stubbornly to the old paternalist, protectionist legislation as it was gradually abandoned by the rulers," Rudé observed.[5] The riots, he believed, expressed "the hostility of the small people of town and countryside to the newfangled doctrine that the price of the necessities of life should be regulated by supply and demand rather than

---

[3] E. P. Thompson, "The Moral Economy of the English Crowd in the Eighteenth Century," *Past and Present* 50 (1971): 79. Although grain prices were higher in England than in France, eighteenth-century observers unanimously agreed that the standard of living was higher in England than in France. Part of the higher standard of living was a more varied diet. Nevertheless, it does not follow from Thompson's argument that English riots would have been less intense than those in France. Thompson's point is that the intensity of riots did not necessarily reflect actual need but the perception of injustice.

[4] Ibid. Thompson provided a fundamental insight—that protests occurred without there being any decline in the supply of food; availability was thus not the only factor affecting which groups had food. This insight led him to view the redistributive process in terms of rights or entitlements and the manner in which such entitlements were politically legitimated. In arguing that the grain riots were emblematic of the struggle by the undifferentiated "people" against the "extortionate mechanisms of an unregulated market," he disregarded the assertion of the rights of some poor people at the expense of many other poor people. The crowds Thompson failed to differentiate among represented the interests primarily of industrial workers of certain cities at certain moments. They were far from representative of all cities or of all workers or of the poor in general. See ibid.

[5] Rudé, *Crowd in History*, 226.

illustrate Smith's point. Those grain riots, scholars generally agree, were the most characteristic form of collective action during the late seventeenth and eighteenth centuries. "Food riots formed the vast majority of disturbances in which the pre-industrial crowd in France and England were actively engaged," wrote Georges Rudé, the grandfather of collective action studies.[1] The riots play a large part in the different interpretations of long-term change offered by historians of early modern Europe. Inspired by Rudé, studies have focused on moral and cultural conflict as elites and governments abandoned the pre-capitalist for a capitalist system of values and public policies. The new policies were opposed by the poor, who attempted to defend pre-capitalist institutions and entitlements on moral grounds. Studies by scholars of both nations indicate a similarity in the rhetorical structure of the grievances that motivated crowds in England and France to oppose governmental efforts to establish national grain markets and to restrict local interference in the provisioning process. Their emphasis helps us to understand who thought they benefited and how they justified their actions. These studies, nevertheless, do not address the macroeconomic consequences and costs of successful crowd action; they tend to ignore the divergence between rural and urban interests and make little of the different outcomes and levels of success enjoyed by rioters in the two nations. Despite the sensitivity exhibited in the studies of historians to ethical perceptions, the different outcomes elude explanation. Policy-makers in both nations emphasized market solutions and the need to promote high grain prices in order to provide producers with incentives to expand cultivation and to invest in new technology.[2]

## THE "MORAL ECONOMY" OF THE PRE-INDUSTRIAL CROWD

Studies by historians of crowd response to changing patterns of food distribution often serve as the basis for assertions of the ethical differences

---

[1] Georges Rudé, *The Crowd in History: A Study of Popular Disturbances in France and England, 1730–1848* (New York: Wiley, 1964), 218.

[2] This chapter is about the official grain market but does not presume it to be the only grain market. Unofficial channels of distribution probably coexisted with official networks. These unofficial channels were supplied by peasants who could secretly bring their imports into the city or by town dwellers who owned land in the country. They were allowed to bring in, tax free, for their own consumption grain grown on their farms. One consequence of the French Crown's grain-control policy may have been shadow prices that were higher than the English prices. Grain rioters could outbid suppliers and purchase supplies at below the cost that dealers were willing to charge. But town dwellers who did not riot might have had to purchase grain at shadow prices. Since not everyone could be at the riot, many consumers must have depended on supplies that were smuggled into the city and sold in secondary markets at shadow prices above the official price.

# 5 The Political Economy of Collective Violence
*What Did the "Moral Economy" of Pre-Revolutionary Europe Cost?*

In Old Regime France, grain merchants could not obtain rights to export, while landlords, led by an ancient seigneurial elite, had to sell their grain according to conditions set by urban officials. Why did an alliance of such powerful elements of Old Regime society not obtain property rights that would have increased their wealth as well as that of society? Royal administrators understood that the inefficient regulation of grain markets put the productivity of French agriculture at risk, yet efficiency-enhancing deals did not occur to reduce the costs to the rural sector of grain policies that favored urban consumption.

The property rights that governed the distribution of grain, like those that determined the access of peasants to markets, reflected the institutional nexus in which the decisions were framed. A forum was lacking in which the landlords who would benefit most from higher grain prices could make a deal with the urban consumers who benefited most from low grain prices. France had a tradition of urban autonomy that inhibited the development of institutions uniting the interests of urban and rural elites. By contrast, England had political markets—a national parliament—in which landlords and merchants could meet, negotiate, and trade rights. The creation of political markets that brought the relevant resource-holders to the bargaining table was the institutional innovation responsible for transforming English agrarian property rights and expanding grain exports.

## THE POLITICS OF PROVISIONING

Adam Smith emphasized that even the most basic building blocks of economic analysis depend on ethical convictions and commitments. The grain riots that frequently erupted in early modern France and England clearly

# 3
THE MORE PRIVILEGED

moral economists he inspired usually argue that the monopoly power of elites was an inevitable outcome of markets, but a more likely culprit would seem to be the political structure that determined the social distribution of surpluses generated by markets.

The restrictions on the direct marketing of grain imposed on peasant production in premodern France by lords and towns are examples of political influence, not competitive production strategies. If inequality in market access, not the existence of markets, ultimately led to a deterioration in peasant welfare, then peasant resistance may be reinterpreted as a response to the monopoly of control by elites over the surpluses created by the market. A conflict over equal access to the kingdom's growing market economy, then, put lord and peasant at loggerheads in 1789.[35]

All social groups were affected by the redistributive consequences of mercantilism and absolutism. The peasantry's "moral economy" was a response to the economic risks and uncertainties produced by the institutions that distributed the nation's income away from the countryside and toward the cities, where powerful interest groups could threaten the monarchy's political security. The relative bargaining strength of the peasantry in the context of a particular set of political institutions was the critical variable underpinning the peasantry's economic potential during the Old Regime. Those political structures evolved in response to the incentives, strategies, and choices of well-organized groups in French society.

[35]Rodney Hilton came to the same conclusion about lord-peasant conflicts in medieval England: "The essential quarrel between the peasantry and the aristocracy was about access to the market. It was not that peasants were worried about the impact of the market in a disintegrating sense upon their community; they wanted to be able to put their produce on the market and to have a freer market in land which would enable them to take advantage of the benefits of the market" (Hilton, "Medieval Peasants—Any Lessons?" *Journal of Peasant Studies* 1 [1974]: 217).

gests that peasants were able to use savings and/or to borrow from informal credit markets to pay for higher-priced grain.[34]

There is one major caveat: The growth of markets made it possible for successful peasants to exit the system of collective rights and practices. Tocqueville may have missed the full significance of the defection of the wealthy from the village when he spoke of a countryside deprived by the towns of its most articulate and resourceful members. His point, nevertheless, is critical; the departure of the wealthy peasantry—and their rights, privileges, and properties—created many losers in the countryside. The withdrawal of the wealthy peasantry's production from that of the village reduced the value of those collective goods that remained. Then there was also the effect of their departure on existing social networks, the value of which can never be measured in monetary terms. The net result of the defections was the isolation of the village and the impoverishment of the village's remaining collective rights and privileges. Because the village community is a public good, people who opt out are seen as free riders. The defection of the successful from the communal system, and ultimately from the village, was the underlying cause of the tension within the village that scholars often link to the growth of markets. Although the right to exit the communal system had always existed, the development of a more active market economy made it possible for the most dynamic elements of village society to depart in great numbers. By offering the wealthy greater means to exercise their right of defection, the spread of economic opportunity undermined the value of communal social and economic arrangements.

Lefebvre argued that a pre-capitalist mentality motivated the outbreak of hostilities between lord and peasant. This theme gave coherence to Lefebvre's work and has passed into the broader debates on peasant politics and violence. Lefebvre viewed the expansion of markets and the monopoly authority of elites as interchangeable and mutually dependent. He and the

---

(1946): 643–50, and "Demographic Crisis in France from the Sixteenth and Eighteenth Centuries," in *Population and History*, ed. David Glass and D. E. C. Eversley (London: E. Arnold; Aldine, 1965); and David R. Weir, "Life under Pressure: France and England, 1670–1870," *Journal of Economic History* 44 (March 1984): 27–47. Harvest failures did not result in shortages, because grain could be brought in from the outside, although at higher prices.

[34] A succession of bad harvests such as occurred in 1708 and 1709 would, however, increase mortality. This suggests that successive bad harvests would deplete local savings. On the existence of local rural credit markets, see Jean-Laurent Rosenthal, "Credit Markets and Economic Change in Southeastern France, 1630–1788," *Explorations in Economic History* 30 (April 1993): 129–57.

Economic theory explains peasant behavior in ways Lefebvre and the moral economy school did not anticipate. There is evidence that markets do not necessarily make peasants worse off. The willingness of the peasantry to participate in a market system depends on the character of the incentives rather than on innate cultural predilections. As eighteenth-century peasants came to depend on markets to reduce the probability of starvation, incentives to conform to traditional collectivist norms and communal practices diminished. Peasants might not automatically accept the market and abandon those norms, but they had an incentive to orient their production to markets and diminish their dependence on traditional practices. Markets provided better insurance than traditional norms predicated on the village's ability to provide for its own subsistence.

Once the development of competitive national and international markets gave individuals greater certainty of finding supplies in times of need, the critical concern became an individual's ability to save or to find wage-paying employment. This way the age-old communal traditions were replaced by individualistic norms. Peasants became farmers or wage laborers. Markets evened out peasant food requirements over time. While technological limitations prevented the storage of crops, peasants could sell part of their current produce in exchange for money and use the latter for purchases of food during a bad year. Larger markets prevented a disaster in one town from drastically affecting the availability, and thus the prices, of food in another: the reduced variability diminished the utility of communal practices and properties.

Contrary to Adam Smith's assertions about the effects of royal taxation on peasant behavior, many indirect examples of savings by peasant families have been provided by historians of Old Regime France. Peasants used savings to provide for social mobility and for farm implements, buildings, and schools.[32] The most striking indirect evidence concerns the growing ability of peasants to absorb harvest failures. Generally, during famines, incomes did not increase in proportion to increases in food prices. Yet David Weir offers evidence that harvest failures of one year had little influence on mortality in eighteenth-century France.[33] This evidence sug-

---

[32]See Jean Jacquart, *La Crise rurale en Ile-de-France, 1550–1670* (Paris: Armand Colin, 1974); Gaston Rupnel, *La Ville et la campagne au dix-septième siècle: Etude sur les populations du pays dijonnais* (Paris, 1922); and Pierre de Saint-Jacob, *Les paysans de la Bourgogne du nord au dernier siècle de l'ancien régime* (Dijon, 1960).
[33]See David R. Weir, "Markets and Mortality in France, 1600–1789" (MS, Yale University, 1984), which suggests that the impact of harvest conditions on mortality was considerably reduced after 1715. And see, too, Jean Meuvret, "Les Crises des subsistances et la demographie de la France de l'ancien regime," *Population* 1

The persistence of feudal dues was another disincentive to participating in the market. Predicated on the basis that the lords would provide the peasantry with justice and administration, the dues lacked any justification, since the seigneurie no longer provided such services by the late eighteenth century. When, in a paper titled "The Inconvenience of Feudal Dues," a contemporary advised that dues prevented peasants from enjoying their share of market profits, the president of the *parlement* of Paris responded that such speculation would only arouse unrest and condemned the author for expressing "criminal views," declaring, "this brochure contains . . . a plan that leads to nothing less than the systematic reversal of all the maxims and laws of even the constitution of the monarchy itself, which would shatter the social hierarchy and arm the peasants against the lords, fomenting war in the nation's body between the king's subjects."[30]

The cause of free markets was taken up by a number of reformers and was openly discussed by the political elite, but discussion of the disincentives to market production imposed on peasants by feudal dues was taboo. Since the elite were the principal recipients of the dues, openly articulating a general opposition to the dues was virtually impossible. Instead, the battle against feudal dues was fought in thousands of costly court cases, in which lawyers working for peasant communities disputed the legitimacy of particular dues in complex legal arguments.

Insights from a wide range of literature on peasant politics suggest an explanation of the origins of peasant radicalism that differs from that of Lefebvre and Scott. Subsistence only made sense when peasants were not assured of being able to buy from or sell to distant regions at times of crisis. Because the expansion of markets can potentially provide a better form of security than traditional peasant institutions, subsistence strategies declined. Markets lead to more regular flows of supply, because deficits in one region can be made up for by surpluses in another. Moreover, as Adam Smith recognized, the growth of markets generates specialization, which in turn increases the total supply of food. Thus, given fair opportunities to participate in markets, peasants could in fact defend themselves more effectively against environmental hazards.[31] In choosing markets, eighteenth-century peasants were not any less risk-averse than their ancestors; they were opting for an improved form of insurance.

---

[30]Hagley Library, W2 4594, March 5, 1776. Mentioned in *Oeuvre de Turgot*, ed. Gustav Schelle (Paris: Alcan, 1913–23), 5:270–71.
[31]Often peasants possessing the smallest parcels engaged in some of the most risky forms of cultivation, producing wine, vegetables, and, in the nineteenth century, flowers.

grain in transport could be confiscated at Macon by officials who wanted supplies for local provisioning. As a result, Lyons was forced to buy Italian grain in Marseilles, while the farmers in the Comté were ruined by low prices. The public authorities in both regions blamed their difficulties on free trade, but the problem was that trade was subject to regulations that contradicted economic sense.

Despite efforts by the Crown to keep communication and trade open between regions, local authorities continued to confiscate grain passing through their jurisdictions. The jurisdictions of the various authorities claiming rights to regulate the grain trade overlapped. Royal prohibitions did not prevent the *parlement* of Dijon from taxing all grain destined for markets under its supervision. Merchants from neighboring regions were often imprisoned for exporting wheat without permission. Similarly, grain in transit between Germany and Switzerland could not be sent the shortest distance through Alsace for fear of confiscation by the Alsatian authorities. The *parlements* of coastal provinces such as Rouen similarly restricted trade during local shortages; Rouen typically taxed or confiscated grain headed for higher-priced Parisian markets.

As a result of regional restrictions on the transport of grain, one province could experience a shortage while a neighbor experienced abundance. Not surprisingly, French grain prices fluctuated quite sharply during this period. Thinking of his native Burgundy, one contemporary analyst observed that "the price of wheat will reach 33 livres in bad years but only nine livres during the good years."[29] If free trade were guaranteed, he speculated, warehouses would be organized during the abundant years and the price difference between the good and bad years would be less significant. Being denied a market during surplus years, peasants were less able to save money for difficult years. Even when capable of saving, a peasant was not assured of being able to find supplies during local shortages. If a peasant did have a surplus during years of local shortages, he might be forbidden to sell his grain at prices high enough to allow him to survive the years of low prices.

Individual peasants might respond to unpredictable grain markets by attempting to assure their own subsistence. Peasants often grew a diversity of crops, despite the unsuitability of the soil; for example, wine grapes and hemp were grown throughout the kingdom, even where the soil was inhospitable. Although they reduced overall productivity, these second-best solutions made good sense from the perspective of the individual peasant household.

---

[29]Cited in BN, Joly de Fleury, 2536, 300–301.

upheld the view that any savings to consumers resulting from low-priced grain should not come at the expense of the distributor's monopoly rights. The money from the fine was then given to the corporation in recognition of the damage to its interests.

The control of market officials over access to grain markets encouraged the public's fears of conspiracies among merchants and officials and fueled rumors of famine plots in which the government and the dealers colluded to raise the price of grain. To regulate large movements of grain during a shortage, provincial intendants were entitled to grant exclusive trading permits to a handful of merchants. Although allegedly designed to guarantee a constant flow of grain, this practice made possible the very hoarding that the rules were designed to prevent, while the possession of permits enabled preferred merchants to ruin their competitors.

Although a declaration of May 25, 1763, decreed that grain could freely circulate in the kingdom, there were many ways municipal officials, mayors, and *parlements* could circumvent this order.[28] Tolls were a particularly effective method of preventing grain from moving freely throughout the kingdom. For example, to prevent the shipment to Lyons of grain from the Franche Comté, the city of Gray, through which the grain had to pass, imposed tolls of 20 sols per *septier* of wheat, while the price of a *septier* of grain in Lyons was only 24 sols. Such tolls made it impossible for the Franche Comté to provision Lyons, even during periods when farmers in the Comté had considerable reserves. The tolls were established because Gray's market officials feared that if local grain prices climbed to the level of those of Lyons, the standard of living in Gray would fall. Local unemployment and lower consumption of manufactured goods would result in Gray, they believed, because the higher price of necessities would reduce the surplus available to consume locally produced manufactured goods. Local leaders did not consider that a wealthier peasantry might consume larger quantities of city-made goods.

The monarchy was well aware of the many negative consequences that resulted when local officials isolated local markets from national trends. Unable to influence the decisions made by market officials, peasants were often left with unsold stocks and accumulated debts even in the best harvest years. Moreover, the passage of grain through intermediary jurisdictions made shipments subject to seizure by local officials. For example, even when merchants of Lyons were able to buy additional grain in Gray,

[28]What follows is based upon BN, Joly de Fleury, 2536, "Memoire sur le commerce des blés" (August 4, 1770), 288–306. See also "Memoire sur les lettres patentes concernant le commerce les grains," 260–72; and the *parlement*'s response, 274–87.

low prices during good years. Peasants may have rationally selected greater market participation once presented with the prospect of larger markets. With new market opportunities, the emphasis on subsistence in peasant survival strategies diminished. Conflicts to eliminate feudal dues at the end of the eighteenth century thus reflected a struggle by the peasants to gain access to new and improved forms of insurance provided by the development of a national marketing system. Studies of peasant decisions of what to plant would help illuminate this point. We know, for example, that smallholders were often inclined to take great risks by growing purely commercial crops like grapes. Wheat was also grown mostly with urban markets in mind.[26]

Lefebvre ignores the ability of lords or urban grain consumers to obtain unfair trade advantages through their political position vis-à-vis the state and instead assumes that peasants do not take advantage of markets. Yet seigneurial and urban authorities dictated the time, the place, and the price of grain, because peasants were not allowed to sell grain directly out of their own granaries. Peasants were not even allowed to sell on the basis of samples; instead, they were required to bring their entire stock to prescribed marketplaces so that market taxes called *droits de halle* could be assessed.[27] Seigneurial and urban officials generally reserved the right to requisition, on behalf of local consumers, additional stocks from peasants during times of shortage. Even less tolerable was the apparently innocuous right of town officials to decide which merchants had a right to buy in the marketplace. The urban authorities would entitle certain merchants *accredités* or *assermentés*, effectively establishing an oligopsony on purchases from farmers and a corresponding oligopoly with respect to distribution to consumers. Merchants lacking proper authority risked the confiscation of their produce. For example, the city of Rouen granted a monopsony to a corporation of grain dealers by allowing them exclusive rights to purchase grain in the province's four most important markets. In support of this monopsony, the local *parlement* found a merchant guilty for selling grain at a reduced price during a shortage and fined him. The *parlement*

---

[26] R. Romano, *Commerce et prix du blé a Marseille au XVIII$^e$ siècle* (Paris: S.E.V.P.E.N., 1956). Peasants in Provence put aside a large percentage of their harvest for commerce with the Italian cities. In turn they imported darker, less costly grains, which they consumed.

[27] These *droits* had different names in different regions of France. Sometimes they were referred to as *droits de courtage*, sometimes as *droits de minage* and *droits de leyde*. These were quite unevenly and unequally applied and were sometimes collected twice on the same product in the same parish. Dominique Margairaz, *Foires et marchés dans la France préindustrielle* (Paris: Editions de l'Ecole des hautes études en sciences sociales, 1988), 25–26.

were not interested in increasing their wealth beyond subsistence. The core of Lefebvre's explanation of peasant unrest in the late eighteenth century was his belief that peasants wanted to defend the pre-capitalist nature of peasant culture. He assumes that peasants had initially had a communal economy at some time and that adequate markets for peasants' produce did not exist, or that peasants were unaware of their benefits. However, what if potentially adequate markets for agricultural goods did exist, but peasants were unable to take advantage of them? If peasants could not compete effectively in the marketplace, they would indeed have resorted to localized communal economies out of individual self-interest. Lefebvre's argument is contradicted by C. E. Labrousse's claim that most peasants had to satisfy their basic subsistence needs at the marketplace.[24]

Poor peasants, who typically needed credit and access to markets to pay off debts, were particularly vulnerable to exploitation by lords. Often, poor peasants needed producer credit to buy inputs before a crop could be raised. When poor peasants are able to contract loans, it is usually at higher interest rates than those available to peasants with more collateral. Because interest payments eat up a larger portion of small farmers' output, poor farmers are even more dependent than their wealthier counterparts on fair access to the market for the sale of their produce.

The subsistence ethic Lefebvre emphasizes might have been a rational response to the risky conditions under which peasants lived before adequate market opportunities were available, mainly because regional and interregional markets were not reliable enough to provide supplies at times of local shortage. In the 123 years between 1618 and 1741, there were 65 years in which shortages were registered in some region of France and 20 years during which prices tripled from their norms, causing great hardships. Nevertheless, during none of those years were the harvests as bad as those in 1767, 1768, or 1769, by which time greater liberty trade had eliminated some of the worst discrepancies in price.[25] Markets expanded because intendants prevented local officials, mayors, and *parlements* from closing markets to outsiders during times of difficulty. By the late eighteenth century, peasants in many regions could depend upon broader markets for acquiring goods in times of shortage and selling in times of abundance. Local resources could thus be supplemented to pull peasants through local shortages, and local abundance did not result in disastrously

---

[24]C. E. Labrousse, *Esquise du mouvement des prix et des revenus en France au XVIIIe siecle* (Paris: Dalloz, 1932), and Pierre Goubert, *Beauvais et le Beauvaisis de 1600 a 1730* (Paris: Imprimerie nationale, 1960).
[25]Cited in BN, Joly de Fleury, 2536, "Memoire sur le commerce des blés" (August 4, 1770), 300–301.

into market production.²² This argument, that the struggle against the market was a struggle against feudal rights, has been popular even with revisionist authors like Alfred Cobban. Turning traditional Marxist categories on their head, he suggested that the so-called aristocratic reaction of the eighteenth century reflected the influence of bourgeois values on the behavior of rural seigneurs.²³ Like Lefebvre, he argued that the seigneurs were not traditional and retrograde but forward-looking and capitalistic. Hence, peasant resistance was not anti-aristocratic or anti-feudal but anti-bourgeois and anti-capitalist.

An alternative hypothesis for increased hostility to feudal dues during the Old Regime can be suggested. Prior to the so-called capitalist period, the dues paid by peasants to their lords were less often the subject of contention. The expansion of markets in the eighteenth century changed peasant attitudes toward feudal dues. The dues put peasants at a competitive disadvantage because the structure of dues collection allowed the lords to capture a disproportionate percentage of the gains from trade. For example, the lords claimed monopoly control of capital goods such as ovens, mills, and wine presses, and they collected dues that in some areas imposed taxes of 20 percent on peasant production. The burden of the feudal dues thus seemed less and less fair and was more strongly resented as market opportunities expanded. Relations between lord and peasant were further aggravated because the increases in production earmarked for national market consumption enabled lords to find a monetary equivalent for the feudal dues they had originally collected in kind. The expansion and integration of markets provided the lords with an increased incentive to collect dues vigilantly. In the jargon of economics, as markets expanded, so too did the opportunity costs to peasants denied access to the surplus produced for those markets. Both sides would have benefited if the contract imposing the collection of feudal dues could have been renegotiated. Then the struggle would have been over how the percentages should be divided. But the alternative of renegotiating the original allocation of rights would have been too costly under the Old Regime. A market in which the rights could be traded did not exist.

Lefebvre's description of the majority of peasants in Old Regime France as "semi-subsistence producers" tells us little about their access to markets. Their being "semi-subsistence producers" does not mean that peasants

---

²²W. Doyle criticizes Lefebvre's belief in the link between the seigneurial reaction and the Revolution. See Doyle, "Was There an Aristocratic Reaction in Pre-Revolutionary France?" *Past and Present* 57 (1972): 97–123.

²³Alfred Cobban, *The Social Interpretation of the French Revolution* (Cambridge: Cambridge University Press, 1964).

selling the land and turning the proceeds over to the Crown in exchange for a lower tax rate.

Stronger participation in the market economy was not achieved at the expense of village properties and rights, and those rights did not insulate peasants from the external economy.[19] By treating collective properties as commodities to be leased at peak commercial value, commercialization protected those properties from usurpation and dissolution. There was no implicit contradiction between communal property and production for the market; rather, communal properties sustained market activity.

## THE SUBSISTENCE ETHIC

Theorists of moral economy coming after Lefebvre have attempted to explain the rationale for the emergence of institutions that Lefebvre describes. That rationale is most clearly articulated in the writings of James Scott, who draws heavily on Lefebvre for historical evidence.[20] Scott explains that peasants exist in an environment in which they must constantly struggle for survival: given the caprices of nature, primitive technology results in a state of chronic insecurity. To cope with this insecurity, peasants develop institutions and norms that emphasize safety first.[21] The institutions designed to provide minimum subsistence were built upon a logic that Lefebvre and Scott argue was both moral and egalitarian: moral because all members of the community were guaranteed a subsistence minimum; egalitarian in the sense that an attempt was being made to ensure that no one in the village starved unless everyone starved.

Both authors believe that, left on their own, peasants would have preferred common property to private property and subsistence production to market production. Markets and private property, they tell us, were imposed on peasants by outside forces. These forces might be states or dominant classes whose exactions imposed on peasants a need to produce a surplus and to take it to market. The pressure came from seigneurial capitalists during the late eighteenth century who, under cover of feudal rights, introduced new methods of estate management, forcing peasants

---

[19]Florence Gauthier elaborates on Lefebvre's position by arguing that communal independence was threatened by the leasing of communal properties. See Gauthier, *La voie paysanne dans la révolution française: L'example Picard* (Paris: François Maspero, 1977).
[20]James Scott, Jr., *The Moral Economy of the Peasant: Peasant Rebellion and Subsistence in Southeast Asia* (New Haven: Yale University Press, 1974).
[21]"The small peasant cultivates above all for his subsistence and he was tortured by the fear of dearth [*la peur de 'manquer'*]" (Lefebvre, "La Révolution française et les paysans," 348).

Moreover, membership in the community entitled peasants to use the community's rights and properties. Vagrant workers, the poorest peasants, were denied membership in the community and thus received no benefit from common resources. Furthermore, in crisis after crisis, poor peasants learned that common rights and fields could not protect them from falling beneath the subsistence minimum. Once they began to fall below that minimum, they invariably lost their livestock and could no longer benefit from communal properties. The preservation of common rights could increase inequality and stratification among members of the peasant community. Inevitably, peasant commitments to communal agriculture varied according to the proximity of markets. Nevertheless, common property was not a necessary component of the subsistence ethic.

Although Lefebvre associated the existence and preservation of communal rights with peasant values, in numerous cases, royal policy ensured the survival of communal rights and properties. The Crown, beginning with Louis XIV, attempted to reverse a trend toward the loss of communal rights and properties by prohibiting their sale. To provide communities with regular income, royal administrators encouraged lease auctions of village pastures. Royal officials wanted to protect communities that used their common properties as collateral for loans from the risk of losing their properties outright and ensure that communities would have enough income to pay taxes owed to the king.[16]

Far from being vestiges of a pre-capitalist value system, communal properties played an important part in the commercial economy of the eighteenth century and in the calculations and market strategies of peasants. Even the poorest peasants were able to find important commercial uses for common rights. They often pastured sheep for town butchers and in exchange were allowed to keep some of the profits.[17] As communal rights became commercialized, they provided the capital that guaranteed the existence of communities. Villages had a greater incentive to commit resources to defend those properties as their value increased.[18] This incentive to defend collective rights would not have existed if alternative uses of the capital tied up in the land were possible. However, the Crown barred villages from selling the land and investing the proceeds in alternative assets such as dams, roads, and mills. Villages were similarly barred from

---

[16] See ibid., ch. 1.
[17] See Françoise Fortunet, *Charité ingénieuse et pauvre misère: Les Baux à cheptal simple en Auxois aux XVIII$^{ème}$ et XIX$^{ème}$ siècles* (Dijon: Editions universitaires de Dijon, 1985).
[18] See Root, *Peasants and King*, ch. 4.

poor peasants with a safety net: insurance against the threat of complete destitution. Protecting their communal property, then, was an essential means of securing this entitlement.

Lefebvre argues that one would find much more sympathy for nascent capitalism among the rich than among the peasant masses. The wealthy alone benefited from the spread of markets, because capitalism, which spread inequality and thrived by exploitation, could only result in the inevitable proletarianization of the peasantry. Here, Lefebvre asserts the Marxist claim that capitalism required cheap proletarian labor. The traditional peasant smallholding had to be sacrificed so that the essential separation of labor from the means of production could occur. Thus, the rise of capitalism implied greater political and economic domination of the majority of the peasantry by the capitalist class. A further implication of this argument is that markets invariably reduce peasant well-being by exposing the poor to a greater risk of falling below the subsistence level. Lefebvre backs up his claim by arguing that, during the late eighteenth century, the expansion of market relations resulted in an agrarian crisis and increased rural poverty.

Lefebvre assumed that the majority of the peasants opposed the expansion of private property and preferred communal property, but did common rights play the role he attributes to them? During the Revolution, the poor in commercial regions often clamored for the division of the commons into individual parcels, while the rich worked for their preservation.[15] This anomaly can be explained if we look at the example of Burgundy, a region characterized by a highly commercial agriculture. There, well-to-do peasants had much to gain from the preservation of communal fields and meadows because they dominated those fields with their herds of sheep and cattle. The wealthy were also strong defenders of communal woods when the king ordered during the eighteenth century that they be distributed according to tax payments. Wealthy peasants, then, supported communal rights because of the private benefits they derived from them.

---

Lefebvre reiterates some familiar themes: "Progress in agricultural techniques could only be achieved at the expense of the poor" (36), which explains why "the great majority of rural people wished to uphold the traditional agriculture and time-honored regulations which, in effect, curtailed individual property rights" (38).

[15]On wealthy peasants and common rights, see Hilton L. Root, *Peasants and King in Burgundy: Agrarian Foundations of French Absolutism* (Berkeley and Los Angeles: University of California Press, 1987), 16, 95–97, 125, 138–39, 153, 216–17, 228.

their resources were allocated by values determined by communal, as opposed to market, relationships. Opposition to bourgeois values, then, provided the revolutionary ideology that inspired the peasantry.

By locating the origin of agrarian rebellion in efforts to protect peasant institutions from the corrosive effects of market culture, Lefebvre's analysis raises a number of questions about the desirability of markets. The peasants were "above all profoundly attached to collective rights and to regulation, that is, to pre-capitalist economic and social systems, not only by routine but also because the capitalist transformation of agriculture worsened their living conditions." Since he assumed that the spread of markets threatened peasant welfare, Lefebvre argued that the pursuit of improved social welfare would have led the peasant to reject market solutions. "It mattered little to him that productivity was increased because it was he who would have to pay the price of this progress, while the benefits—at least in the beginning—would be reserved for the large landowners who produce in order to sell to the market. In short, he opposed with all his force the capitalist transformation of agriculture."[12]

Lefebvre argued that the peasantry's common fields and rights, which institutionalized pre-market values, were essential to its pre-capitalist identity. "All the thoughts of the poor peasant tended toward limiting the right of individual property in order to defend collective rights, which allowed him to survive and which he regarded as a property as sacred as the others, and to prevent the supplies necessary to his existence from becoming inaccessible."[13] The agricultural system to which Lefebvre was referring included a mixture of privately and collectively owned land. The arable land was divided into a few large, open fields, with families owning strips in each field. Although peasants possessed fields in each strip, separate, fenced-off parcels were not permitted. The village collectively decided what would be planted in the open fields, which, in northern France, were divided into three. One third was usually planted in wheat, one in spring grain (barley or oats), and the remainder was normally fallow. All villagers had the right to pasture their livestock on common fields, wasteland, and the stubble of harvested fields. Communal restrictions on land ownership, Lefebvre tells us, were designed to ensure a subsistence minimum to all members of the community and were thus especially important for the poorer peasants.[14] Common rights, he believed, provided the

---

[12]Lefebvre, "La Révolution française et les paysans," 344, 348.
[13]Ibid., 348.
[14]Georges Lefebvre, "The Place of the Revolution in the Agrarian History of France," translated and reprinted in *Rural Society in France*, ed. Robert Forster and Orest Ranum (Baltimore: Johns Hopkins University Press, 1977), 36. Here

tional production: they wanted to increase their revenues. The theories of the economists provided them with the pretext of serving the national interest."⁷ A reactionary and archaic peasantry, Lefebvre tells us, united to resist this offensive against their traditional rights and properties. Why were the pre-capitalist institutions and practices so valuable to the peasantry?

Lefebvre explains that the pre-capitalist institutions of the peasantry expressed collective moral values that were threatened by capitalism. The pre-capitalist culture embodied what Lefebvre called the *droit social*. This meant that "superior to property are the just needs of the community, in which all the inhabitants have a right to live. This notion of the '*droit social*,' conserved since the beginning of history in the heart of the rural communities, is what present-day socialism should consider the seed of the contemporary [socialist] movement, and [was something] the peasants had not forgotten when they left the village for the factories."⁸ The communal institutions of the village institutionalized the *droit social*.⁹

By "capitalism," Lefebvre seems to mean a system of resource allocation dictated by markets and characterized by private property. Applying the labor theory of value, Lefebvre explains that capital was accumulated by the separation of labor from the means of production.¹⁰ He thus came to believe that the rise of capitalism was deleterious to peasant well-being, because capitalism by definition turns peasants into a proletariat, denied control over the means of production.¹¹

Lefebvre believed that the norms of country dwellers were incompatible with the culture of possessive individualism, which he associated with the rising bourgeoisie. Elite culture, he assumes, was more open to capitalism and market behavior than was popular or peasant culture. Peasant institutions and norms functioned to preserve basic peasant values: membership, equality, and subsistence. Concerned with production for use rather than exchange, Lefebvre's peasants wanted only to reproduce their families. Market participation was subordinated to reciprocity and redistribution, and

---

⁷Lefebvre, "La Révolution française et les paysans," 350–51.
⁸Ibid., 349.
⁹Lefebvre's theory of peasant political violence is still very much alive. Florence Gauthier and Guy-Robert Ikni endorse Lefebvre's approach in *La Guerre du blé au XVIIIᵉ siècle* (Paris: Les Editions de la passion, 1988), 7–31.
¹⁰Private property and separation of the means of production are not the same. One can have either without the other.
¹¹Lefebvre's successor, Albert Soboul, was even more explicit in applying the labor theory of value to the history of the French peasantry. See "The French Rural Communities in the Eighteenth and Nineteenth Centuries," *Past and Present* 10 (1956): 78–96.

In a revolution that was the culmination of a long social and economic evolution, which made the bourgeoisie the political, social, and economic masters of France, the peasants took another road. According to Lefebvre, peasants tried to find their way back to their pre-capitalist, pre-bourgeois past.

Lefebvre's belief in the pre-capitalist nature of peasant culture led him to account for the initial conditions, origin, and design of rural institutions, characteristic patterns of change, and psychological traits of rural dwellers. His explanation of peasant political violence has dominated most subsequent treatments of the subject and is often cited by theorists of modernization in other fields.[4] Lefebvre's emphasis on "the pre-capitalist tendencies" of peasant revolutions[5] is now open to question, as much has been learned about rural institutions since the ideas that influenced Lefebvre were formulated.[6]

## PEASANTS AND MARKETS

Lefebvre believed that the violence that erupted in the early years of the French Revolution reflected efforts by the peasantry to protect their precapitalist culture from the advance of capitalism. The pre-capitalist institutions of peasant society in France, he tells us, were attacked by a coalition of lords and state wanting to "liberate cultivation from all regulation, allow producers to freely sell their produce, suppress collective rights, especially communal pasture rights, and divide communal property. The royal administration was inclined toward the innovations; no doubt the interests of the privileged tipped the balance. Most of them did not care about na-

---

[4] A good example of Lefebvre's influence is Barrington Moore, Jr., "Evolution and Revolution in France," in *Social Origins of Dictatorship and Democracy: Lord and Peasant in the Making of the Modern World* (Boston: Beacon Press, 1966), 40–108.

[5] See Robert H. Bates, "Some Conventional Orthodoxies in the Study of Agrarian Change," *World Politics* 11 (1984); Samuel L. Popkin, *The Rational Peasant* (Berkeley and Los Angeles: University of California Press, 1979); H. Binswanger and M. Rosenzweig, "Contractual Arrangements, Employment and Wages in Rural Labor Markets: A Critical Review," in *Contractual Arrangements, Employment and Wages in Rural Labor Markets in Asia*, ed. H. Binswanger and M. Rosenzweig (New Haven: Yale University Press, 1984); M. Lipton, *Why Poor People Stay Poor: Urban Bias in World Development* (Cambridge, Mass.: Harvard University Press, 1979); T. Schultz, *Transforming Traditional Agriculture* (New Haven: Yale University Press, 1964); T. Schultz, ed., *Distortions of Agricultural Incentives* (Bloomington: Indiana University Press, 1978).

[6] Lefebvre, in turn, owes much of his vision to the ideas of Jules Guesde, who founded a Marxist workers' party in Flemish Wallone. See Adeodat Constant Adolphe Compere-Morel, *Grand dictionnaire socialiste du mouvement politique* (Paris: Publications sociales, 1924).

peasants to simulate poverty, since signs of wealth invited heavy taxation. Peasants thus had few incentives to improve their lot in the ways advocated by the physiocrats. The negative incentives created by taxes and feudal dues were obvious to a wide range of social critics during the eighteenth century. Comparing the English to the French peasant, Voltaire wrote: "He is not afraid to increase the number of his cattle, or to cover his roof with tile, lest his taxes be raised next year. There are many peasants here [England] who own property amounting to some 200,000 francs, and who do not disdain to keep on cultivating the soil that enriched them."[1] Adam Smith wrote that on account of the personal tax (*taille*), "which is assessed in proportion to the stock which he appears to employ in cultivation," the French farmer is "afraid to have a good team of horses or oxen, but endeavors to cultivate with the meanest and most wretched instruments of husbandry that he can. Such is his distrust in the justice of his assessors, that he counterfeits poverty, and wishes to appear scarce able to pay for any thing, for fear of being obliged to pay too much."[2]

Without taking into account the disincentives facing eighteenth-century French peasants, historians today often argue that premodern peasants preferred subsistence and security to production and individual wealth creation. The belief that moral considerations led peasants to adopt a subsistence ethic and communal property underlies the interpretation of the origins of peasant violence commonest in the writings of present-day historians. Georges Lefebvre was the most influential of the authors working out of this tradition. The economic logic of Lefebvre's explanation of rural protest during the Old Regime sharply contrasts with the notion that the peasantry's participation in a market system depends on the character of market incentives.

Lefebvre's discovery of a peasant revolution within the French Revolution is generally viewed as one of the fundamental contributions to the study of the French peasantry. In numerous publications, he asserted that during the French Revolution "there was a peasant revolution, which possessed an autonomy, its own origins, procedures, crises and tendencies."[3]

---

[1] Voltaire, *Philosophical Letters*, trans. Ernest Dilworth (Macmillan, 1985), 38.
[2] Adam Smith, *An Inquiry into the Nature and Causes of the Wealth of Nations* (London: Adam, Black, & Longmans, 1850), bk. 5, art. 2, p. 386. Both Voltaire and Smith confused two separate phenomena: concealing wealth and producing it. Smith's analysis differs from contemporary economics, which emphasizes the return relative to outlay on the margin.
[3] Lefebvre's views on the peasant revolution are synthesized and forcefully stated in "La Révolution française et les paysans," first published in *Annales historiques de la Révolution française* in 1933, and then again in *Cahiers de la Révolution française* in 1934. It was reprinted in Georges Lefebvre, *Etudes sur la Révolution française* (Paris: Presses universitaires de France, 1963), 338–67, the version quoted here.

# 4 Interpreting Peasant Revolutions

The failure to develop a market for all forms of property rights had consequences for the economic potential of Old Regime France. Rural society was perhaps the single greatest victim of that failure. The access of peasants to local markets was restricted by their lords, who themselves were often denied access to international markets for their surplus grain. Wealthy peasants sought to exit from restrictive communal agricultural practices, while poor peasants generally wanted village common lands divided and, like the rich, demanded freedom from feudal dues. All were locked into property rights structures that prevented the optimal allocation of resources. Although the terms of trade and relative bargaining power had shifted during the eighteenth century, contract renegotiation did not occur. Those who paid for inefficient rights had no forum in which to buy out the rights of those who benefited from the arrangements. Bargaining between groups that held economic rights was restricted by the Old Regime's political structure, which permitted the king alone to redefine property rights. Since there was no possibility of direct bargaining, court cases and civil disobedience were the only venues left for renegotiating agrarian property rights.

To overcome the impasse, eighteenth-century French economic reformers, the physiocrats, attempted to convince the king that renegotiating the terms of the contract could enable even the humblest farmer to contribute to the expansion of the nation's wealth. Their belief that peasants would respond to the proper incentives by growing more and by utilizing more efficient methods contrasted sharply with the administrative and legal traditions of the Old Regime. Peasant production was burdened with seigneurial dues and royal taxes that consumed much of the extra income above subsistence produced by the peasants. In fact, the tax system led

# 2

THE LESS PRIVILEGED

Regime France, while not necessarily the most efficient for the economy, did allow the Crown to capture the maximum revenue at the lowest cost.[82]

The expansion of monopolies and other protectionist practices in France may have produced the deadweight losses that economists expect to find in the exercise of monopolies as compared to competitive industries, but perhaps the choice in the Old Regime was between regulated industries or none at all.[83] The French government's rent seeking provided private business interests with institutional structures that facilitated trade and investment. A relatively stable currency and restrictions on the predatory behavior of its agents resulted, which increased the level of investment by comparison with the standards of previous centuries. Although the French monarchy strategically supplied property rights to selected business people to gain revenue, the investments encouraged had positive spillover effects, benefiting the economy overall.[84] The property rights the French state did offer should help us to understand why France's economic expansion was considerable during this period, surpassing that of many of its European rivals, with the exception of Britain.[85]

---

bridge University Press, 1990). And see, too, Robert Bates, *Markets and States in Tropical Africa* (Berkeley and Los Angeles: University of California Press, 1981). Even in post-colonial Africa, where choices seemed relatively unconstrained by the past, it weighed heavily on the present.

[82]The French Crown's failure to reform agriculture provides an example of transaction costs determining the relative advantage of alternative contractual forms. In the eighteenth century, output-maximizing property rights decreed in royal edicts were blocked by local administrators who feared that the new structures (the abolition of collective responsibility for taxes and the elimination of communal property) would result in distributional losses for the state. The likelihood that the new rules would increase the transaction costs of collecting taxes led these local officials to obstruct the implementation of rules designed to increase the aggregate output of peasant communities. See Hilton L. Root, *Peasant and King in Burgundy: Agrarian Foundations of French Absolutism* (Berkeley and Los Angeles: University of California Press, 1987).

[83]For example, many of the new manufactures (silk, tapestries) created and protected by Colbert might not have been established in France. Of course, the optimal solution would have been to provide anonymous institutions to support anonymous private traders in welfare-enhancing trades.

[84]The property rights created resulted in long-term welfare gains that may have offset in present-value terms the welfare losses arising from short-term rent seeking.

[85]On French growth rates, see Patrick O'Brien and Caglar Keydor, *Economic Growth in Britain and France, 1780–1914: Two Paths to the Twentieth Century* (London: George Allen & Unwin, 1978).

fluence on the political evolution of the two nations. Groups that participated in the negotiating process by which English public law was created were likely to become more aware of how their interests corresponded to those of competing groups. At the least they learned to view their private interests in terms of national or public goals. As a result, England developed a more nationalistic and unified political culture that was less prone to revolution and more capable of cooperation in the face of crisis.

## ECONOMIC EFFICIENCY AND ABSOLUTISM

While redistributing the nation's wealth to preferred clients, the French state provided property rights that increased net output. The weakness of competitive markets limited economic efficiency; nevertheless, output was increased by rules that protected the property rights of large investors. Although the Crown only selectively protected the property rights of its subjects, the protection encouraged investments that were socially useful. The Crown provided special courts to enforce contracts among merchants, albeit giving preference to specially chosen royal clients. The economy also benefited from the reinvestments by financiers of their profits from tax farming in the protected industries and privileged commercial companies sponsored by the Crown. Once such investments were made, the Crown generally resisted reneging on the privileges it had provided. While the Crown's finance ministers were likely to acquire private fortunes during their tenure of office, they often worked closely and reliably with their clients. The need to maintain an ongoing relationship with well-organized private business groups gave the Crown an incentive to defend the property rights of the private sector. Recognizing its dependence on repeated interactions with prominent business interests, the Crown took measures to protect private property rights, stabilize monetary policy, and reduce the frequency of debt repudiations. Had it not been for the hope of revenue from the protection of the property rights of its subjects, the king might have created and enforced less efficient property rights or perhaps even none at all. Had the French Crown acted as opportunistically toward business groups as the Spanish Crown did, less investment, and less commercial and technical progress, would have occurred.

Rulers are rarely able first to devise rules that maximize efficient production and then to negotiate the methods of revenue collection. Property rights that increase the wealth of private groups do not automatically lead to greater revenue for the state.[81] The property rights that emerged in Old

[81]On this point, see Douglass C. North, "The Path of Institutional Change," in *Institutions, Institutional Change, and Economic Performance* (New York: Cam-

difference stands out. In England, broader access to the spoils of government and public service may have consolidated a more heterogeneous elite, who desired to perpetuate the regime. Because the governing elite in Britain represented a wider cross section of the population, government policies could enlist greater social support than could the policies of French kings. As a result, a broader sector of the English elite endorsed the rules and the policies they produced. Parliament provided the English political elites with real distributional benefits through private enclosure acts, grain bounties, and patents for overseas trading companies in which elites held shares. The elite of 250,000 voters were also the beneficiaries of the state's limited extractive capabilities. These benefits did not come at the cost of general political stability because they were not restricted to narrow networks of ministerial cronies. The colonies were, of course, quite another matter. They were managed much the way the French ministries regulated the French domestic economy.

By contrast with eighteenth-century England, it seems that conflict among groups in France became increasingly political and ideological. There, the public interest was articulated in such abstract, substantive, or ideal values and norms as natural law, justice, or right reason. Public interest was articulated in abstract concepts that had no basis in practice, perhaps because no institution emerged that could credibly claim to be an arbiter of the public good. Although the social organs of the dominant elites might have changed during the seventeenth century, the family- or clan-oriented character of the political system remained. Ironically, absolutism throve on and embedded the authority of clans and private networks into the structure of government, yet those who benefited most directly from the spoils of the government's redistributive mechanisms often subscribed to a general criticism of the regime and regarded the privileges of other groups with hostility. In England, the parliamentary practice of negotiation, compromise, and face-to-face bargaining became a political value shared by members of the elite. Parliament provided the elite, which probably constituted 3 percent of the population, with a forum in which to engage in face-to-face dialogue. Bargaining in Parliament contributed to the forging of a national culture shared by a broad segment of the nation's wealthy. A more open realm, in which public knowledge of government decision making was necessary, an emphasis on consensus over command as a method of conflict resolution, and a belief that public law should be based on a shared community of understanding among the nation's representatives distinguished the epistemology of parliamentary politics from the philosophical premises of absolutism. The philosophical differences over how public matters should be resolved may have had a decisive in-

discriminate among shippers but provided all with equal advantages.[78] Proposals by particular industries to exclude rivals were less likely to succeed than in France.

In eighteenth-century England, parliamentary decision making became increasingly public, and by the end of the century, parliamentary debates were even disseminated in the press.[79] The efforts to influence Parliament also became more open as private interest groups often made their case public in an effort to win support for their cause. As a consequence, historians of England consider the rise of lobbies as occurring after 1780. Although lobbies worked more openly and hence seemed to have become more influential after 1780, it was probably in an earlier period, characterized by greater governmental secrecy, when they were more effective. The increasingly public character of influence peddling in England made it still more difficult to use political means to achieve private redistribution of the nation's income. English lobbying gave rise to public knowledge and information, while in France knowledge about who received what from the government remained private, leaving many groups feeling excluded.

## SOCIAL DIVISION AND REDISTRIBUTIVE POLITICS IN EARLY MODERN ENGLAND AND FRANCE

In order to cultivate a pro-government majority in Parliament, the British Crown selectively distributed contracts, honors, and offices.[80] In France, similar favors were distributed by a particular minister to gain a personal network of support in the court. Despite these similarities, one important

---

[78]Meanwhile the British shippers as a group were better able than their French counterparts to deny foreign merchants access to the domestic market. This seems to be one of the surprising conclusions suggested by John Nye's comparison of tariffs in France and England. Nye argues that England practiced less free trade than was previously believed. The level of tariffs was much higher in England than in France during most of the nineteenth century. His research underscores the importance of distinguishing between free exchange in international markets and a liberal internal market. Despite its higher tariffs, England had a more liberal domestic market than France. France's higher level of internal tariffs reduced internal trade. See John Nye, "The Myth of Free Trade Britain and Fortress France: Tariffs and Trade in the Nineteenth Century," *Journal of Economic History* 51 (1991): 23–46. Both Adam Smith and Eli F. Heckscher noted that English foreign trade was more interventionist and mercantilist than its internal trade. See Adam Smith, *The Wealth of Nations*, bk. 5, ch. 2; and Heckscher, *Mercantilism* (New York: Macmillan, 1955), chs. 1 and 2.

[79]Michael Harris and Allan Lee, *The Press in English Society from the Seventeenth to Nineteenth Centuries* (London and Toronto: Fairleigh Dickinson University Press, 1986).

[80]The English Crown could even award pocket boroughs to ensure its control of government.

to royal provisioning policies occurred at Montauban, for example, the intendant was replaced by Terray's twenty-two-year-old nephew. To assure the cooperation of the army, Terray is alleged to have made sure that military salaries and pensions were paid with an exactitude previously unknown.

Turgot broke up Terray's monopoly in an *arrêt* of September 13, 1775, which declared free trade within the kingdom and put the right to regulate grain exports in the king's hands. Although the monopolists could no longer count on the king's protection, they had already made an estimated 1,200,000 livres.[76] The proliferation of the belief in a royal grain monopoly is highly illustrative of differences between the political cultures of England and France. The private character of nationally significant government decisions in France made possible the widespread belief in the plot. The notion that highly placed individuals could conspire with the government to starve the people would have seemed less plausible to the English public.[77] There, a similar plot would have been more difficult to orchestrate. Because many members of Parliament were landowners producing grain for the market, a monopoly giving a few dealers or producers the right to monopolize the trade would not have won wide approval. In fact, during the eighteenth century, Parliament granted producers bounties to export grain, a policy benefiting all large landholders equally. Similarly the British Navigation Acts did not establish particular groups of British shippers with a monopoly over any particular branch of shipping; the acts did not

---

[76]Ln/27/19433. M. L. Chazal, *L'Abbé Terray: Contrôleur Général des Finances* (Paris: Batignolles, 1847), 11. Steven Kaplan stresses that the famine plot rumors clung to Terray's name and were one of the principal reasons why Louis XVI chose to replace Terray with a minister known for his personal integrity. Kaplan discounts the rumors of the plot. "Unlike Laverdy (the previous minister) Terray had no doubts about the wisdom of engaging in public victualing whenever and wherever necessary," he writes. "Like Orry, he supervised all provisioning operations vigilantly, working through a kind of public corporation called a *régie*" (Kaplan, *Famine Plot Persuasion*, 58).

[77]An important exception in English history was the South Sea Bubble in 1721, when it was widely believed that the South Sea Company bribed ministers and other MPs. The company hoped to gain political support for its efforts to acquire the funding of that portion of the national debt not held by the Bank of England or the East India Company. This scandal concerned speculators and bankers but had little impact on the population at large. For more on the South Sea Bubble, see J. H. Plumb, *Sir Robert Walpole: The Making of a Statesman* (London: Creeset Press, 1956), 293–329. The Bubble struck at the interests of the financial elite and was akin to the John Law scandal in France, not the Famine Plots. Laws limiting joint stock companies prevented a repeat of the Bubble. In France, the Famine Plots recurred throughout the eighteenth century and concerned the welfare of the populace at large.

endorsed helped to sustain large estates and make them economically viable during a period of reduced demand and depressed agricultural prices.

The slow and quiet transformation brought about by the piecemeal enclosure of England's countryside thus buttressed the dominant class of landlords without destabilizing political consequences. French landlords were unable to find similarly effective support for their agricultural enterprises through government action. The French Crown was unable to provide enforceable legislation in favor of enclosure, so that small and middle-sized holdings continued to dominate French agricultural production. In addition, unlike the English grain bounties, the French government's intervention on the side of grain producers benefited only particular ministerial favorites, not an entire class of large grain producers.

## THE PERCEPTION OF GOVERNMENT CORRUPTION IN FRANCE: THE FAMINE PLOT

That the use of discretionary powers contributes to the spread of conspiracy theories was explained by Karl Popper, who wrote, "This tendency [the increasing use of discretionary powers by members of the government] must greatly increase the irrationality of the system, creating in many the impression that there are hidden powers behind the scenes, and making them susceptible to the conspiracy theory of society with all its consequences—heresy hunts, national, social, and class hostility."[74] Persistent rumors of famine plots and conspiracies to starve the people circulated in France during the Old Regime. The government's direct or indirect involvement in these plots was a central theme of the rumors. Although the existence of these presumed plots has never been confirmed as historical fact, Steven Kaplan has pointed out, "whether the plots existed or not . . . is less interesting than the belief in their existence."[75] The widespread belief that such conspiracies were possible is emblematic of how contemporaries perceived the political system. One such rumor concerned the ministry of Controller General Abbé Terray, reputed to have been among the most venal of Louis XV's finance ministers, who was thought to have used his position at court to contrive with a small coterie of grain dealers to exploit shortages and to generate panic prices, using legislation in favor of free trade as a means of disguising the operation. In the name of free trade, they were reputed to have caused prices to fall where grain was abundant and to increase where it was in demand. When opposition

---

[74] Karl R. Popper, *The Open Society and Its Enemies* (New York: Harper & Row, 1963), 2:133.
[75] Steven L. Kaplan, *The Famine Plot Persuasion in Eighteenth-Century France* (Philadelphia: American Philosophical Society, 1982), 4.

influence political power on behalf of one's particular interests. Economic *dirigisme* by ministers of the Crown transformed France into a nation of self-centered clans and corporations, each fighting to maintain or expand its privileges. By contrast, the party structure in the British Parliament aggregated and articulated the interests of various social groups.

English-style corruption and clientalism may even have increased the political stability of the state, because a high percentage of those English people whose votes and resources were needed to run the government received direct, positive benefits in return from the government. English voters could feel they had a shot at the spoils of political power, whereas in France only a small coterie around each minister were thought to benefit. The relatively broader sharing of the spoils may have increased support for the government among the English electorate. That the French system emphasized private distribution among particular clans at the expense of others probably had the opposite effect, undermining the regime's support. The differences become especially meaningful when we consider why the French monarchy fell so suddenly when confronted with a fiscal crisis. When a tax increase was needed to avoid a fiscal crisis similar in scope to the French crisis of 1789, Pitt was able to get parliamentary approval for new forms of taxation, but the French ministers could not find support among the nation's wealthy for new taxes or for the elimination of exemptions.[73]

Corruption was the most conspicuous form of government redistribution in England. Beneath the commotion generated by corruption, however, a quiet transfer of income from poor to rich was occurring in England as a result of parliamentary action, which aroused little attention among contemporaries. The enclosure movement and the grain bounties, both achieved through legislative action, are outstanding examples of how politics could be used to transfer income from poor to rich in England. English historians now generally agree that the enclosure movement made great progress during the eighteenth century, when the cumulative effect of numerous private bills was the enclosure of a large percentage of the English countryside, thereby channeling much of the country's agrarian income through large estates. Similarly, the grain bounties that Parliament

---

[73]Between 1783 and 1789, Pitt and the British raised taxes and increased revenues from approximately £13 million to £17.5 million, allowing them to retire some of the debts inherited from the American Revolutionary War. As a result, the amount of money needed to service the national debt was reduced to 56 percent of the annual budget and investors could anticipate further reductions. See J. E. D. Binney, *British Public Revenue Administration, 1774–1792* (Oxford: Oxford University Press, 1958).

The corruption of the spoils system that emerged in eighteenth-century England permitted the governing party and the electorate, which numbered from 200,000 to 250,000, to monopolize public offices. Prior to the younger Pitt's reforms in the 1780s, private bidding for government contracts was not required. As a result, MPs were often rewarded for their loyalty to the government with lucrative provisioning contracts or the right to administer a government loan. Namier notes that thirty-seven of fifty merchants who sat in the Parliament of 1761 were government contractors. Such allocations were technically not corruption prior to the reforms of the 1780s, but the government also maintained a secret fund taken from the Treasury for bribes, pensions, and the election expenses of its friends. In five years, a total of £291,000 in bribes was paid out of the Treasury.[71] The Crown also, of course, acquired supporters by creating and disbursing government jobs, which, although not corruption per se, was nonetheless a way of putting the recipients in a position to collect fees and bribes.[72]

It thus appears that England's public administration could rival that of France in clientalism, but there was one very important difference. Although the British Crown's ministers used nepotism, peculation, and malfeasance to ensure the loyalty of a majority of MPs and to pay their electioneering expenses, the British government's corruption increased its exposure to the play of market forces and did not limit access to the market economy in the same way the bureaucracy did in France. Although patronage was deeply rooted in English political practice, it did not redistribute the nation's surplus income among a select group of clans. Members of Parliament might be receptive to bribes, especially when they came in the form of government contracts, but Parliament could not be effectively manipulated by private parties seeking monopoly rights over a particular industry. Compared to the central authorities of the French government, it was more difficult for Parliament to use its political control to determine who participated in and benefited from the market economy. The English system of redistribution let the market, and therefore economic competition, determine outcomes.

Because of the French executive's more explicit regulation of commerce and industry, success in French society required the ability to seize or

---

[71]Sir Lewis B. Namier, *The Structure of Politics at the Accession of George III* (London: Macmillan, 1929), 45–90, 234.
[72]Nevertheless, John Brewer has concluded that "though there can be no doubt that a small number of individuals fed well from the public trough, the overall cost of their privileges and perquisites does not seem high by contemporary European standards" (Brewer, *Sinews of Power*, 73).

fogel's conception and helps to distinguish it from the more sweeping scope of corruption.

The workings of the finance ministry in France clearly illustrate the importance of drawing the distinction between corruption and cronyism. The finance ministry epitomized cronyism but was relatively free of corruption. The French Ferme générale became a model of bureaucratic administration, known in eighteenth-century Europe for its hierarchical model of command and efficiency. Because its members were highly supervised, corruption was reduced. The king's financial ministers, sometimes reputed to be incorruptible, generally used their power to allocate economic privileges to family members or to favorites, thus developing a powerful and wealthy clientele. Although the intendants of finance and of commerce generally enjoyed a reputation for honesty, a number of practices considered legal provided the pretext for later criticism, which became increasingly widespread as knowledge about the financial system circulated among the public during the eighteenth century. For example, the commission, called a *pot de vin*, that was traditionally taken by the controller general for signing a lease with the Ferme générale became the object of criticism in the late eighteenth century. Additional sums of money were typically offered to the controller general in exchange for appointments sought by would-be *fermiers généraux* (new ones had to be appointed by the Crown). In 1774, Turgot ordered the previous controller general, Abbé Joseph-Marie Terray, to return the *pot de vin* of 300,000 livres he had collected. Turgot's act reflected the public's growing concern about the blurred distinction between private and public finance. Intendants of finance were entitled to pensions or payments from the corporations of financiers whose business they had handled. One first secretary of finance, Intendant Ormesson, received a 1 percent interest in a tax farm the size of Languedoc as compensation for his work.[68] As minister of the Treasury, N. F. Mollien received a pension of 3,000 livres for negotiating the lease of 1784 with the Ferme générale.[69] Tax officials usually received payment both from the Crown and from the financial groups they supervised. Although cronyism was more deeply rooted in the administrative practices of the seventeenth century, during the eighteenth century the public was beginning to expect members of the government to divorce their private from their public activities.[70]

---

[68]Antoine, *Conseil du roi*, 410–11.
[69]Bruguière, *Pour une renaissance*, 446.
[70]On the honesty of the king's financial ministers, see Antoine, *Conseil du roi*, 408–11.

with individuals in power.[64] A controller general's participation in a project was often needed to persuade investors that it had the necessary government support. Shrouding its deals in secrecy became more difficult for the French Crown as the end of the eighteenth century approached. The growth of public opinion, nurtured by a burgeoning underground press, slowly whittled away at the secrecy cronyism thrived on.

The use ministerial families made of their places in government to benefit their private interests can be described as "bureaucratic capitalism," a term coined by Karl Wittfogel to depict Old Regime China.[65] Wittfogel used the term to define a system characterized by (1) tax collectors acting as fiscal agents of the ruling bureaucracy; (2) officials or nonofficiating members of such a bureaucracy who, on the strength of their political position, engage in private enterprise such as money lending and tax farming; (3) private business people acting as commercial agents or contractors who do business for the state; (4) bureaucrats who use their place in government to benefit their economic interests or to buttress those of their political group. The conduct of state business by the ministers of Louis XIII and XIV meets all the criteria of Wittfogel's definition. Mazarin, Colbert, and Pontchartrain (controller general, 1689–99) all maintained patrimonial control over decision making in the economy; the distribution of patrimonial services and prebends allowed them to develop networks of clients. Ministers and their families typically reinvested the funds they collected as state tax officials in royal industries and commercial monopolies.[66] State enterprises were almost always turned over to members of the bureaucratic family or clan. As Dessert puts it, "these ministers lived not only for the state, but of it."[67] The term *cronyism* overlaps with Witt-

---

[64]In Suharto's Indonesia, firms feel compelled to place a representative of the president's family on the board. A member of the president's family is needed on the board before a firm's value can be realized and shares can be traded. Similarly, many firms recognized that J. P. Morgan's participation was essential to the sale of shares to overcome the lack of a market. In the 1980s, some junk bonds could not be placed without the personal involvement of Michael Milken. These individuals used their personal reputations as market makers where otherwise a market for their products might not exist.

[65]Karl August Wittfogel, *Oriental Despotism: A Comparative Study of Total Power* (New Haven: Yale University Press, 1957), 255–56.

[66]Roland Mousnier suggests there is evidence that finance officials invested in commercial and industrial enterprises of public interest on an even greater scale in the late eighteenth century than in the past. Some invested in land and in private firms as well. He was not specifying the role of controllers general, where the pattern of direct investment was diminished. See Mousnier, *The Institutions of France under the Absolute Monarchy, 1598–1789: The Organs of State and Society*, trans. Arthur Goldhammer (Chicago: University of Chicago Press, 1979), 2:210–11.

[67]Dessert, *Louis XIV prend le pouvoir*, 138.

there are no nonprice barriers to market entry. Cronyism allocates property rights according to nonmarket criteria, however, since favoritism is of the essence. As a result, the chance of resources being misallocated is greater. Efficient producers see their advantages confiscated. Cronyism may even allow the costs of inefficient producers to be reduced below those of efficient ones, so that the former may thus be able to drive the latter out of the market.

In sum, greater efficiency results from corruption because it makes resources available to those who have the higher-valued uses. Cronyism, by contrast, excludes many potential users or leaves them without a method of signaling their needs. If the political system is in the same hands as the legal system, bids for the property rights of the king's favorites will not occur. Cronyism thereby reduces production possibilities and prevents necessary adjustments to market forces.[63] Corruption in Britain was the equivalent of an auction market for rents and political favors. That rents could be auctioned to the highest bidder increased the liquidity of the social system by creating a market for privilege. In France, rent-extracting possibilities or favors could only be placed privately, preventing a public market or deals among rent seekers from developing.

Secrecy was critical to the success of French cronyism. By monopolizing the sources of information about political regulations and their effects, the Crown made itself indispensable. A private market for privilege or independent deals among rent seekers were impossible so long as the Crown controlled the sources of information. The political or economic favors the Crown dispersed were highly illiquid; they could not be traded, because no one outside of the governing circle knew what the favors were worth. Even if it was known who held a given right, the amount the rights-holder extracted was not. Cronies must make their information proprietary to avoid confiscation of their rents. Since a right's owner has an incentive to restrict public knowledge of its value, credit is also restricted. Moreover, in France, property rights ceased to be enforceable as soon as they left the hands of the circle of cronies. A public market for favors could not develop when political favors or privilege had no value to someone who was not connected to a particular minister. Cronyism was inherently unstable because individuals and private relationships rather than institutional reputations were critical in maintaining confidence in contracts. Political contracts sustained by cronyism depended on continual secret interactions

---

[63]Cronyism can be coupled with rapid growth as the postwar experiences of South Korea and Indonesia suggest.

the desire to avoid the contamination of English corruption. If the king or ministers wanted to see legislation through Parliament, they literally bought the votes of MPs. A large number of seats in Parliament were owned in fee. Parliamentary elections invariably involved bribing the electorate.

Colonial Americans viewed even lobbies and interest groups with a jaundiced eye and equated their work with corruption. However, there is a substantial difference between corruption and cronyism. Corruption is an informal, illegal method of redistribution, whereas cronyism is a more formal, legal, institutionalized, and socially sanctioned method. Influence peddling and lobbying are not necessarily the consequence of either corruption or cronyism. The distribution of privileges and perquisites was cronyism but not corruption. The success of interest groups in gaining favorable treatment is not by itself corruption unless accompanied by corrupt actions such as bribing an official. Conversely, the ability of economic actors to evade compliance with regulation by bribing the officials responsible for enforcement and the ability of political actors to influence the outcome of elections by buying votes are both forms of corruption, and both were more openly prevalent in English than in French public administration. Cronyism, however, was more visible in France.

Corruption and cronyism thus constitute two politically mandated types of market imperfection: informal contracts in political markets that shape how economic markets evolved over time. Corruption is open to market forces and indirectly allows for the allocation of resources according to a criterion of efficiency that cronyism lacks.[62] Here I am referring to the traditional definition of efficiency in economics: a resource is used efficiently when allocated to the user who has the highest marginal willingness and ability to pay. Thus, the most efficient producer in a world without corruption would be the most efficient in a world with corruption. Corruption provides information about the relative efficiency of different regulations. Corruption's main inefficiency lies in its transaction costs—the price of making deals. It is less discriminatory than cronyism, since

---

who make the most advantageous offers, but to those who have the greatest parliamentary interest; thus, from the minister of state, down to the lowest officer, a combination is formed to plunder the nation. Venality and corruption become one common tie, whereby the various parts of this infamous system of administration are knit together in one common interest" (21).

[62]Cronyism restricts entry and exit from the market while corruption does not. In this sense cronyism is like credit rationing that limits funds to preferred clients and prevents some enterprises from getting funds at any price. Corruption, on the other hand, creates equal difficulties for all parties.

eyes the Crown's venality seemed particularly blatant and pervasive, since the king's direct jurisdiction over the colonies was greater than his control over domestic policies. As Sir Lewis Namier sums up the king's role: "In reality, George III never left the safe ground of parliamentary government and merely acted the Primus inter pares, the first among the borough-mongering, electioneering gentlemen of England. While the Stuarts tried to browbeat the House and circumscribe the range of its actions, George III fully accepted its constitution and recognized its powers and merely tried to work it in accordance with the customs of the time."[59]

The authority to control entire industries and to dominate the nation's finances was not vested in royal officials as it was in France. The reason for this difference was simple. The English Crown's ability to offer privilege was dramatically circumscribed by the powers of Parliament, which determined the chief financial and commercial questions. Increases of the national debt, changes in the rate of interest, the advantages of a sinking fund, the existence of bounties and protective duties for trade, the extent of excise taxes, the weight of land taxes and of the continental subsidies—all were subjects of parliamentary rather than royal discretion.

## THE MARKET FOR POLITICAL FAVORS: THE DISTINCTION BETWEEN CRONYISM AND CORRUPTION

An analysis of income redistribution in England would not be complete without a discussion of the role of corruption, a form of income transfer for which eighteenth-century Britain was especially renowned.[60] Government in eighteenth-century England seemed to be driven by corruption, especially to American colonials.[61] One of their often-stated concerns was

---

[59]Sir Lewis Namier, "The Social Foundations," in *Aristocratic Governance and Society in Eighteenth-Century England*, ed. Daniel A. Baugh (New York: New Viewpoints, 1975), 204–43.
[60]For more on English corruption, see Joel Hurtsfield, *Freedom, Corruption and Government in Elizabethan England* (Cambridge, Mass.: Harvard University Press, 1973); and Linda Levy Peck, "Corruption and Political Development in Early Modern Britain," in *Political Corruption: A Handbook*, ed. Arnold J. Heidenheimer, Michael Johnston, and Victor T. Levine (New Brunswick, N.J.: Transaction Publishers, 1989).
[61]In *Observations on Government, Including Some Animadversions on Mr. Adams Defence of the Constitutions of Government of the United States and of Mr. De Lolme's Constitution of England, by a Farmer of New Jersey* (New York: W. Ross in Broad Street, 1787), a book translated into and commented upon in French, John Stevens wrote: "In a government so systematically venal as that of England at present, when administration can expect to be supported in their measures by pecuniary motives alone, an unbounded dissipation of the public revenues becomes unavoidable, nay it becomes absolutely necessary; abuses are not only winked at, but the authors of them, at all events, supported. Contracts are given, not to those

The claim that the British Parliament was the functional equivalent of the French controller general's office where economic regulation was concerned may surprise students of English politics accustomed to viewing the Crown as the center of eighteenth-century British administration. In fact, the duties of the English king's ministers were limited to diplomacy and patronage—the dissemination of offices needed to keep Parliament in line. As J. H. Plumb notes: "The king controlled an immense field of patronage. Every civil servant was the king's own servant, appointed by him and paid out of the royal pocket. The entire administration of the country was carried on by the royal household."[56]

There was nothing to prevent the king from using the entire government work force for patronage. Offices generally provided sinecures, obligating their recipients to the Crown, which helped sway the loyalties of MPs and weakened the party basis of politics. Moreover, as electioneering became more expensive during the eighteenth century, gaining a lucrative office became increasingly desirable. Emphasizing the centrality of royal patronage to the political system, Plumb notes that in consequence, although "the country was essentially left to govern itself as best it could, any increase in the government's power, any extension of its activity, was bitterly resented."[57]

The English Crown's authority fell primarily in the areas of state administration, foreign affairs, and in the management of the army and navy. In other words royal administrators in England did not have means similar to those of their French counterparts to regulate the economy and divide the nation's commercial and industrial wealth. "Patronage in all its complexity became the dominant theme in [English] political life," Plumb observes,[58] but it was a patronage limited to the dissemination of perquisites and had little real impact on the structure of the economy. To American

---

[56]J. H. Plumb, "Robert Walpole's World: The Structure of Government," in *Aristocratic Governance and Society in Eighteenth-Century England: The Foundations of Stability*, ed. Daniel A. Baugh (New York: New Viewpoints, 1975), 116–55.

[57]Ibid., 151.

[58]The authority of the lord lieutenant, England's principal disburser of local privilege, Plumb emphasizes, arose from the fact "that it gave [his] local friends and clients . . . a spokesman at the court, the center of patronage. Thus, he could keep an eye on all appointments including those of justices of the peace and sheriff" (ibid., 122). This patronage was used to secure a corps of loyal MPs. The lord lieutenant's powers were ill suited to the task of closely regulating the nation's industrial and financial development. In fact, some of that patronage had to be dispensed to members of the opposition, which suggests restraints on the lord lieutenant's discretion. Above all, a successful lord lieutenant had to be a manager, not a regulator.

Although only well organized and substantial groups like the Bank, the Royal Assurance Company, and the East India Company could hope to influence Parliament directly, the Board of Trade offered an avenue for smaller groups to gain concessions from the government. The Board, generally viewed as a failure by historians, does seem to have been influential where colonial matters were concerned.[53] Created in 1696, the Board of Trade reviewed colonial laws, prepared instructions for colonial governors, helped settle emigrant groups in the colonies, and nominated members to the colonial councils. The Board developed a relatively comfortable relationship with a number of colonial interest groups, but by catering to relatively small interests that did not risk alienating the major players in English politics. The Board was accessible to Anglo-American interests largely because Parliament tended to allow executive independence on colonial matters, but even there the Board would not act if it risked domestic opposition. Although the Board was particularly successful at meeting the needs of small groups involved in foreign trade and colonization, its authority in domestic affairs was extremely limited. Parliament's crucial role is underscored by the absence of a board for granting domestic favors. It was possible to create new privileges in the colonies and allow them to be governed by an autonomous body because there were no prior interests in Parliament that were infringed upon.[54] For groups desiring major changes in domestic policy, there was no alternative to the slow and costly lobbying of Parliament.[55]

In short, the path to economic advantage in England through the manipulation of government regulation and parliamentary statute was long. In France, a single minister could often push through whatever legislation he wanted in a comparatively short time. This should perhaps make us appreciate why those who wanted to reform French society did not welcome the development of parliamentary institutions. The reformers did not realize, however, that legislation enacted by the British Parliament was more likely to be viewed as legitimate by the public and was more likely to be reinforced by the common law courts than the decrees of French ministers were to be enforced in local courts or *parlements* claiming overlapping jurisdictions.

---

[53] Alison G. Olson, "The Board of Trade and London-American Interest Groups in the Eighteenth Century," in *The British Atlantic Empire before the American Revolution*, ed. Peter Marshall and Glyn Williams (Totowa, N.J.: Frank Cass, 1980), 41–42.
[54] The same lack of infringement on vested interests also underlies the creation of patents or patent law, which in effect mandates the creation of monopolies.
[55] Olson, "Board of Trade and London-American Interest Groups," 36–39.

to issue more legislation in an average four months than Parliament could during the entire reign of George I, more legislation in one year than during the entire reign of George II, and more legislation in any four years than the British Parliament accomplished during the entire sixty-year reign of George III.[51]

| REIGN | Public | Private | Session No. |
|---|---|---|---|
| William III (1689–1702) | 343 | 466 | 58 |
| Anne (1702–1714) | 338 | 605 | 78 |
| George I (1714–1727) | 377 | 381 | 58 |
| George II (1727–1760) | 1,447 | 1,244 | 81 |
| George III (1760–1820) | 9,980 | 5,257 | 254 |

One shortcut was available to English interest groups seeking to bargain with political authority to improve their positions. Lobbyists could hope to influence government policy by appealing directly to ministers of state. The executive ministers of the government could make recommendations and submit legislation to Parliament, thereby exercising a certain degree of agenda control in policymaking. However, the ministers were generally careful not to take a position that might antagonize substantial portions of the electorate. Moreover, the support of the executive ministers did not necessarily guarantee the passage of legislation in Parliament, as the cases of the Anglo-French trade treaty of 1713 and the tobacco excise bill of 1733 both clearly demonstrate.[52] The opponents of the Anglo-French trade treaty successfully lobbied Parliament, bringing about the defeat of the treaty despite ministerial support. Even with high-level connections, merchants or manufacturers wishing to form new companies or effect a change in commercial regulations still had to obtain a charter from Parliament. Their French counterparts, by contrast, needed only a royal decree. The executive shortcut could reduce the lobbying costs incurred by English interest groups; still, it was necessary for them to exert pressure in Parliament in order to secure passage of their legislation.

---

[51]Peter D. G. Thomas, *The House of Commons in the Eighteenth Century* (Oxford: Oxford University Press, 1971), 63.
[52]For more on the defeat of the 1713 trade treaty with France, see D. C. Coleman, "Politics and Economics in the Age of Anne: The Case of the Anglo-French Trade Treaty of 1713," in *Trade, Government and Economy in Pre-Industrial England*, ed. D. C. Coleman and A. H. John (London: Weidenfeld & Nicolson, 1976), 187–213. On the proposed excise scheme of 1733, see Jacob M. Price, "The Excise Affair Revisited: The Administrative and Colonial Dimensions of a Parliamentary Crisis," in *England's Rise to Greatness, 1660–1763*, ed. Stephen Baxter (Berkeley and Los Angeles: University of California Press, 1983), 257–322.

## MAKING LAW IN THE BRITISH PARLIAMENT

Unlike their French counterparts, British lobbyists had to operate on two levels and confronted substantial obstacles. First, they had to develop private relationships with the appropriate officers of state. Whatever the issue, to succeed in Parliament required the support of the minister whose province it was, or at least assurances that he was not hostile. Even with the support of the minister, however, interest groups faced open public debate in Parliament.

The procedure that led to placing a new law on the statute book was long and circuitous. A member of the House of Commons had to submit a petition, risking possible obstruction by MPs who disapproved. Once a petition had been presented, a second reading could be postponed, effectively killing it. Members were not allowed to peruse its contents privately; only the approval of a motion made by an MP could bring a petition out of obscurity. Petitions by lobbies against taxes were allowed only after their enactment. Once read, a petition might have to be vigorously defended from hostile forces. A lobbying campaign tied up in committee might have to be renewed the following year. Lobbying Parliament was time-consuming, expensive, and required considerable organization to succeed.[48]

By contrast, the King's Council in France issued legislation by decree practically without limit (which is not to say that it could ensure enforcement), allowing the executive to regulate the economy to an extent unequaled in England. Consider the amount of legislation generated by the King's Council in the form of *arrêts*. Michel Antoine has observed that "by way of *arrêts* or *lettres patentes*, by the orders transmitted by the ministers or by the intendants, the many decisions made by the king in his council were diffused daily through the kingdom and the colonies."[49] Approximately four thousand *arrêts* were issued each year during the reign of Louis XV, a slightly smaller quantity than under Louis XIV.[50] Many of these *arrêts* were similar in scope to what the British called private bills: legislation in response to a petition from a member or members of the public, authorizing the construction of a bridge or a road, or granting permission to enclose one's fields. The King's Council in France was able

---

[48] Private bills could originate in either house. For the procedures of introducing bills in the House of Lords, see Sheila Lambert, *Bills and Acts: Legislative Procedure in Eighteenth-Century England* (Cambridge: Cambridge University Press, 1971); and Michael McCahill, *Order and Equipoise: The Peerage and the House of Lords* (London: Royal Historical Society, 1978).
[49] Antoine, *Conseil du roi*, 598.
[50] Ibid., 371.

of Colbert's outstanding achievements as minister was the ability to hide personal gain under the cloak of service to the state. It was an illusion so well maintained that until very recently it has gone practically unchallenged by historians. Colbert's ministry began by purging the groups that could oppose his domination of the nation's financial system. Nicolas Fouquet, the previous finance minister, was denounced and imprisoned for initiating a system of clientelism, for creating a corps of parasites who consumed the nation's resources; he was accused of lèse-majesté for having usurped the Crown's authority. The kingdom's finances were turned over to Colbert's cronies, who were also awarded the management of the Crown's great economic enterprises: maritime commerce, the colonial trade, and the new state manufactures. Colbert's family and cronies constituted what Dessert has called the best-organized lobby in the history of the French monarchy. As Dessert explains, it was not Colbert who made his family but rather the family that made Colbert; it held on to power long after the death of Jean-Baptiste.[45] The last ministry of Louis XIV's 54-year reign was that of Nicolas Desmaretz, Colbert's nephew, whose reputation for being unable to distinguish his private purse from that of the king was established long before he was appointed to the office of controller general. Desmaretz had been involved in a scheme for reminting the nation's money in which the gold and silver content of coins was reduced and he pocketed the difference. Nevertheless, his reputation did not prevent Desmaretz from becoming finance minister. Nor did the desperate economic condition of the nation during the War of the Spanish Succession prevent Desmaretz from adding to the fortune he had already illicitly acquired.[46] Because Desmaretz also allowed his cronies to make considerable fortunes, he was often praised as a reliable business partner. Like Colbert, Desmaretz provided needed assurance to other investors by taking a share in a project. The participation of the controller general was needed to overcome information asymmetry and the threat of confiscation, which inhibited private sector investment.[47]

---

chette, 1981), 317–18. See, too, Antoine-Jean-Baptiste Robert Auget de Montyon, *Particularités et observations . . . depuis 1660 jusqu'en 1791* (Paris: Le Normant, 1812), 38–40.

[45]Dessert, *Louis XIV prend le pouvoir*, 124.

[46]See Montyon's account of Desmaretz's ministry (*Particularités*, 88–90). See also M. le Chevalier Hennet, *Théorie du crédit public* (Paris, 1816), 157.

[47]During the last years of Louis XV's reign, power was effectively exercised "not by a monarch in decline; it was in the hands of two ministerial families—the Colberts and the Phelypeaux [Pontchartrain]," comments Claude-Frédéric Lévy, who has conducted the most extensive study of contemporary French business (*Capitalistes et pouvoir*, 2:10).

their favorites was one of the causes of the Civil War, which English historians sometimes describe as a conflict between the ins (those who benefited from royal favors) and the outs (those who did not). After the Restoration, Parliament attempted to limit the Crown's means of rewarding royal favorites: the granting of pensions and favors probably diminished, as did the royal share of the national budget. The purpose of governmental rewards and methods of bestowing them changed significantly from the Stuart model. Unlike the Stuarts, the Whig oligarchy employed patronage primarily to ensure political security, not fiscal survival. They did not, for example, grant monopolies in exchange for short-term fiscal assistance. The duke of Newcastle became infamous for his patronage; however, the recipients were members of Parliament or employees of the administration, not Crown favorites or moneylenders. The rise of Parliament made it more difficult for the Crown to offer favors to particular merchants or nobles. The policies of Parliament may have privileged the economic pursuits of the landed gentry as a class, but it did not reward individual gentlemen at the expense of their peers or individual ministerial families at the expense of the aristocracy more generally.

The venality of seventeenth-century ministers of the French Crown far surpassed that of their English counterparts. Richelieu became one of the wealthiest men in Europe serving the Crown, and Mazarin acquired a fortune without precedent in the history of the French monarchy.[42] Mazarin abandoned management of the Crown's fiscal and financial resources to a hierarchy of relatives and cronies, and his venality was often invoked by those who led the Fronde in 1648. The political grievances underlying that rebellion have received much attention from historians, but Daniel Dessert asserts that it was not only a conflict over the exercise of political authority but also a reaction to what he calls the new "feudalism" of a state eager to enrich itself at its subjects' expense.[43]

Colbert, who began his career as a personal agent of Mazarin's, continued the tradition of ministerial venality associated with his mentor, acquiring a fortune surpassed only by those of Richelieu and Mazarin.[44] One

---

[42]See Joseph Bergin, *Cardinal Richelieu: Power and the Pursuit of Wealth* (New Haven: Yale University Press, 1985), and Daniel Dessert, "Pouvoir et finance au XVII$^e$ siècle: La Fortune du cardinal Mazarin," *Revue d'histoire moderne et contemporaine* 23 (1976): 161–81.

[43]Daniel Dessert, *Louis XIV prend le pouvoir* (Paris: Editions complexe, 1989), 33. Dessert speaks of the "extreme greed tainted by the abject baseness that Mazarin puts into his frantic quest for wealth, [which] explains in part the defensive postures of the 'Grands' confronted by an extremely hungry shark little inclined to share his sources of profit."

[44]Mazarin's fortune is estimated to have been 36 million livres, Richelieu's, 22 million livres, and Colbert's, 5.1 million livres. See Meyer, *Colbert* (Paris: Ha-

ities.[38] Once transformed into courtiers, the nobility directed much of their activities toward gaining shares in short-term loans to the Crown and trying to persuade the government that the projects of their clients were best suited to national priorities. One hidden cost the mercantile economy had to bear was the extravagant court and social life of Paris, which by the time of Louis XVI consumed almost 6 percent of the state's revenues and an equally significant, but difficult to measure, proportion of private revenues.[39] The calculation scarcely captures the full economic costs of the competition for privilege.

Louis XIV's goal was to control the social success of aristocratic French families. Analyzing this process in *Court Society*, a classic of historical sociology, Norbert Elias writes:

> It is possible, within the framework of such a social system, to control and direct the rise of certain families from the royal perspective, even as the king can within certain limits, control and direct their fall. Thus, he could slow or even prevent the impoverishment of an aristocratic family by personal favors; he could save it by the granting of an *octroi* at court or by a military or diplomatic appointment. He could give the family a gift of money in the form of a pension. The benevolence of the king is thus one of the most important opportunities of which noble families dispose in order to escape the vicious cycle provoked by their court related expenses.[40]

The transformation of the nobility into revenue seekers marked the beginning of their alienation from the rest of society. Once the nobles had lost their role as provincial leaders, their remaining privileges came to seem gratuitous and earned the contempt of the peasantry and local bourgeois.

Whereas favoritism flourished in France, it aroused strong resentment in England and created political problems for the monarchy.[41] The Stuarts' attempts to develop a system of awarding monopolies and sinecures to

---

[38] This need to locate in Paris applied to the arts as well as to industry. Musicians, playwrights, and artists similarly vied for the king's support. The provinces ceased to be centers of artistic or economic activity.

[39] The amount was 5.67 percent according to F. Braesch's recreation of the budget of 1788 reprinted in Florin Aftalion, *L'Economie de la Révolution française* (Paris: Hachette, 1987), 47.

[40] Norbert Elias, *La Société de cour*, trans. Pierre Kanntzer (Paris: Calmann-Lévy, 1974), 54.

[41] Consider the impeachment by Parliament of Charles I's favorite George Villiers, 1st duke of Buckingham. One of the reasons Queen Elizabeth I was so successful as compared to James I and Charles I was that she made every effort to avoid favoring only one individual or group.

exported to Louisiana, and 100 to 200 percent on the goods he brought back to France,[36] but his management did little to encourage long-term growth or attract settlers. The profits of the Louisiana Trading Company, which was put under Crozat's leadership in 1712, came at the price of suffocating the colony.

From a fiscal point of view, the Crown's mercantilist policies worked relatively well as a source of revenue during the reign of Louis XIV. However, mercantilism's success prevented the development of public institutions to support commerce on a wider scale. The major commercial transactions were restricted to a small coterie of families in a few cities. The commercial history of this period is one example of how the administrative structure of France allowed leading merchants to benefit from redistributional play. The same institutional structures provided benefits to the nobility. While attempting to limit the old landed families' opportunities to exercise independent political authority, the king offered the nobility many opportunities to share in the redistribution of the nation's income at court.

## THE NOBILITY JOINS IN REDISTRIBUTIONAL PLAY

During the reign of Louis XIV, competition for access to the spoils of government transformed the character of the French aristocracy. The great families of the realm had to establish residences in the capital or the court itself because the political and factional struggles between the king's courtiers often determined both major and minor economic decisions. Because seeking out royal patronage was more highly rewarded than staying in the provinces to oversee the local economy and local affairs, nobles moved to Paris and devoted themselves to competing for the unearned income handed out by the king. However, nobles needed to invest time and money to acquire the political information that would win them sinecures, posts in the Church, access to commercial or industrial patents of monopoly, or shares in tax farms (often using a false name or straw man).[37] Like firms in the highly centralized nations of present-day Latin America, they had to move their offices to the capital at the expense of their provincial activ-

---

[36]Ibid., 120.
[37]A nobleman from Languedoc, for example, might use his connections at court to secure a royal monopoly to produce porcelain in Languedoc, but he would turn the actual management of the operation over to a local bourgeois. It should be noted that even the protection offered by such monopolies could not guarantee the industrial concerns of nobles against poor management and bankruptcy. Freedom from the discipline of the market often did as much harm as good.

One merchant financier, Antoine Crozat, emerged as the dominant figure in French commerce during 1710–15. As the principal director of numerous trading companies—Guinée, Asiento, Saint-Dominique, Mers du sud, Indes orientales, and the Compagnie de Louisiane—he was the master of almost all French maritime traffic.[34] This status allowed Crozat to acquire the funds needed during difficult moments without going outside his family. Moreover, with his large standing accounts with merchants and banks in London and Amsterdam, he could rapidly transfer funds when and where they were needed. Most important, Crozat could pay the Crown more for the rights to overseas commerce than could any combination of rival merchants who did not enjoy the monopoly rents derived from the king's favor.

The efforts to organize the Guinée company are an example of Crozat's monopoly power and influence. The Crown had envisioned a company representing a number of the commercial capitals: La Rochelle, Bordeaux, Marseilles, Saint-Malo, and Nantes. Crozat argued that the plan was impractical; if the company were to succeed, he believed, "it should be in the hands of a few people, those who would lead it soberly, and who, being devoted to the orders of the ministers, would carry them out without having to make them public."[35] As a result, the Crown chose eight directors for the company, all of whom had performed other duties for the king and held financial offices. The Crown thus instituted a commercial policy based on the principle of allowing a small group of individual merchants with connections to the financial system to work closely with the government officials handling foreign affairs and finance. Although this policy culminated in the disastrous union of finance and foreign trade under the leadership of John Law, it continued on a reduced scale throughout the eighteenth century.

Initially, the profits of the trading companies were considerable. Crozat's monopoly on trade earned him 100 to 300 percent on everything he

---

or the whole of their shares without the consent of the other members. In fact, early in the reign of William III, put and call options, bear sales, and bull accounts were well known, so that before the end of the seventeenth century, an open, organized stock market existed in London. See W. R. Scott, *The Constitution and Finance of English, Scottish, and Irish Joint Stock Companies to 1720* (Cambridge: Cambridge University Press, 1910–12), 1:442–43.

[34] See Lévy, *Capitalistes et pouvoir*, 417. According to Lévy, Crozat controlled nearly all of the principal maritime commerce at the end of Louis XIV's reign.

[35] "Il faut qu'elle soit entre les mains de peu de gens qui la conduisent sans éclat et qui, étant dévoués aux ordres (du ministre), les exécuteront sans qu'il soit besoin d'en instruire le public" (Nogaret, *Financiers de Languedoc*, 110).

ciers whose assets partly consisted of advances to the Crown and offices purchased from the Crown. Merchants had greater bargaining power relative to rulers than financiers; the mobility of their assets made tax avoidance easier and confiscation more difficult. One of the reasons Louis XIV feared the Dutch Republic was that the Dutch merchants had acquired great control over state policies in exchange for tax revenues. The French Crown feared that because they could defect with their assets, independent business groups might come to exert a disproportionate influence on government policy. Financiers could not threaten as easily as merchants or bankers to defect from the market, because their assets were relatively immobile.[30] Their wealth was tied up in advances to the king, and they depended on the Crown's support for the collection of taxes. Moreover, participation in tax farms, which offered profits surpassing those of alternative investments, depended on the Crown's approval. Handing foreign trade over to these groups gave the Crown greater control over economic policy. The financiers acted, then, not only as farmers general but as entrepreneurs general, further concentrating wealth in a few hands.[31]

Because France did not have a central bank that held and disbursed funds from a wide group of sources, French merchants were more dependent on the resources of family members than English or Dutch merchants. As a result, the principal commercial affairs of the kingdom were in the hands of a small elite group of financial families.[32] The English companies, by contrast, evolved into joint stock companies combining the wealth of many individuals, who might represent a plurality of political interests.[33]

---

[30]After one of the most prestigious traders of the late eighteenth century, Etienne Berthelot de Pleneuf, whose family had important interests in the *domains d'occident* and in the manufacture of gunpowder for the army, had gone abroad (*levé le pied*), the duc de Noailles, acting in the name of the Regency, seized his papers. When Berthelot was later seen in Genoa, the regency council announced it was prepared to take drastic measures to prevent people leaving the kingdom where they had made their fortunes. The council was acting on the assumption that it had the right to forbid export of profits earned in service to the king. See Lévy, *Capitalistes et pouvoir*, 2:85.
[31]Not even the wealthiest of France's merchants reached the heights of great financiers and court bankers like Samuel Bernard and Antoine Crozat, Fernand Braudel notes (*L'Identité de la France* [Paris: Arthaud & Flammarion, 1986], 336).
[32]What Braudel calls "dormant capital"—hoarded reserves of gold and silver—was another consequence of France's failure to develop modern banking facilities (ibid., 349–55).
[33]The incorporation of the Bank of England in 1694 permitted it to gradually take over management of the long-term national debt and the chartering of the second East India Company and the South Sea Company. Even before the creation of the bank, shares in English companies could be bought and sold with a considerable degree of freedom. In the smaller companies, shareholders could dispose of a part

ment. The ministers, however, were not as powerful as their French counterparts. For example, their accounts were subject to parliamentary review, and they could be impeached by Parliament in extreme cases. At the very least, the ministers (who were often members of Parliament) needed the support of Parliament to effect major legislation, which meant that they, too, had to lobby Parliament. English ministers had to walk a very fine line, plying Parliament with favors while trying very hard not to appear to be cultivating favorites or cronies.

## THE GREAT TRADING COMPANIES OF FRANCE

The redistributive character of the great French trading companies illustrates the links between state finance and commerce. All the great trading companies were dominated by financiers, and almost all were created by direct government action and held strict monopolies.[27] Colbert started the tradition of allowing financiers to direct the trading companies, but it continued well after his death until the end of the Old Regime.[28]

Colbert preferred the leadership of financiers to that of merchants in the chartered companies for two reasons. First, financiers had their networks of family and personal contacts, enabling them to come up with needed funds in the absence of other subscribers, an obligation of their appointment.[29] Second, he feared merchants would act more independently of the royal will than would financiers, who depended upon the king's favor for their role as court bankers. Because the Crown did not want the groups who possessed the most mobile assets to gain control over policy, it turned over the operation of lucrative commercial companies to finan-

---

[27] Under the Stuarts, a similar pattern was emerging of bankers combining loans to the monarch with tax farming and the operation of monopolies granted by royal fiat. Resentment against this combination was mobilized in Parliament.

[28] As an example of the controller general's continual encroachment on commerce, Antoine records Maurepas's complaint in 1745 that the controller general had "appropriated the government of the India Company," to the dismay of the royal navy (Antoine, *Conseil du roi*, 405). Calonne appointed the financier Jean-Baptiste de Boullongne de Magnanville, nephew of Louis XV's mistress Madame de Pompadour, *trésorier de l'extraordinaire des guerres en survivance* (1772–79), as the king's commissioner of the new Compagnie des Indes. He was appointed *fermier général* in 1787. See Yves Durand, *Les Fermiers généraux au XVIIIe siècle* (Paris: Presses universitaires de France, 1971), 84.

[29] The large financiers could farm out or licence smaller companies to carry out some of their activity. In a memoir written in favor of giving financiers leadership in commercial ventures, the author argues that they alone have access to the capital to sustain the company through difficult periods. Arguments like this could always be used against the smaller businessmen in a world where access to banking and credit facilities depended on personal relationships. See Guy Chaussinaud-Nogaret, *Les Financiers de Languedoc au XVIIe siècle* (Paris: S.E.V.P.E.N., 1970), 106.

the Council of Finance met less frequently, it issued the same number of *arrêts* as it had in the past. One can therefore assume that a smaller proportion of *arrêts* were products of the deliberation of the full council.[24] Jacques Necker, controller general in 1777–81 and again in 1788–89, claimed that a number of *arrêts* were never even presented before the Council, and that the decisions of the Council of Finance were simply decisions of the controller general.[25] Council members often simply approved without discussion and signed a prepared edict read by the controller general. In short, the Council of Finance had become a fiction, with the controller general exercising full discretion.[26]

Administrative autonomy of the various royal ministers was another characteristic of the system Louis XIV created. During his reign, he regularly attended council meetings to provide general direction to his government. Autonomy increased after Louis XIV's death, especially as subsequent kings had little interest or competence in finance and allowed the controller general almost total independence. Despite their own infrequent attendance of council meetings, neither Louis XV or Louis XVI appointed a prime minister to oversee the actions of the finance minister or to give overall direction to governmental policy.

In addition to being all-powerful in the Council of Finance when it came to matters of general policy, the controller general was also able to award favors to particular individuals or groups. *Arrêts* issued by the Council of Finance treated such minutiae as maintaining village churches or cemeteries and exemptions from transport taxes for selected products of individual merchants in particular regions. Controllers general like Calonne might distribute favors to develop a clientele at court. Terray is reputed to have issued lush sinecures to army officers so that they would not interfere with his grain monopoly. Without having to account to any superior authority, the office of the controller general could offer monopolies or subsidies to preferred industries and favored merchants.

Industrial licenses originating in the British Parliament had a much more circuitous path to follow, adding costs to the legislative process of creating economic regulation. Except for private bills, British lobbyists had to attempt to influence the king's ministers as well as members of Parlia-

---

[24]See Antoine, *Conseil du roi*, 378, 384.
[25]Jouvencel, *Contrôleur général des finances*, 81.
[26]This fiction was to have significant long-term consequences; because the Conseil d'état du roi had originated and was often identified with royal justice, its decisions seemed less arbitrary than those of a single minister acting on his own. The legitimacy of the government's decision making could be questioned once legislation came to reflect the discretionary authority of a single minister acting on his own.

could organize and form a lobby, but they could not influence a representative body as easily as a single minister of the king.[20]

## INTEREST-GROUP PENETRATION AND MINISTERIAL DISCRETION

As previously noted, the Council of Commerce was subordinate to the King's Council, just as the intendants of commerce were subordinate to the controller general. In theory, the king decided all issues, whether or not he attended the council meetings; in practice, however, the controller general's role in these councils was paramount.[21] Michel Antoine notes that although the composition, convocation, meetings, discipline, etiquette, and procedure were at the king's complete discretion, the controller general was the real master of the council and often determined the decisions and *arrêts* coming from the royal council.[22] Most important, the royal officials who represented the king in the provinces, the intendants, reported to the controller general.

In principle, the Council of Finance should have met every week (under Louis XIV it met twice a week) and the Council of Commerce every two weeks; however, during the course of the eighteenth century, the Council of Finance met less frequently, and the Council of Commerce did not meet at all. In 1736, the only year for which we possess complete records, the Council of Finance met twenty-eight times and the Council of Commerce registered no formal meetings. By the end of Louis XV's reign, the Council of Finance met not more than eight or twelve times annually.[23] Although

---

[20]Whereas in France the chambers of commerce unified the voices of specific cities, in England there were many voices and no official spokesman for reaching the government. The collapse of the General Chamber of Manufacturers revealed no homogeneous business interest. John Brewer notes that although "the younger Pitt, like Henry Pelham before him, showed an unusual degree of solicitude for commercial opinion, [he] would not bow to the collective pressures of the General Chamber of Manufacturers." Brewer tells us that Pitt "was glad to collect, from all parts of the kingdom, a just representation of the interests of all the various branches of trade and manufacture but he would not, as the association founder Samuel Garbett hoped, allow the Chamber to contribute actively to the formulation of policy" (Brewer, *The Sinews of Power* [New York: Knopf, 1989], 233).

[21]Antoine, *Conseil du roi*, 377. Whereas the controller was only a participant in the Conseil des dépêches, he was all-powerful in two of the councils, finance and commerce; there the other councillors had no real power. By the time of Turgot, four of the members of the Council of Finance were intendants of finance, who worked for the controller. The controller general could only enter the councils if he also possessed the title of *ministre d'état*, which most controller generals did, with the notable exception of Necker.

[22]Ibid., 30.

[23]Jouvencel, *Contrôleur général des finances*, 83.

responses to their questions and needs, and government decisions in large part determined how and where they would invest when the opportunity arose. But much had changed. No longer did they share ideas and values with those in power. Unlike the king's intendants of commerce, the deputies of the Assembly did not subscribe to the belief that the interests of large merchants were those of the nation as a whole. The deputies claimed to be concerned with recreating the nation on the basis of egalitarian ideals. They believed themselves to be less dependent on the privileged merchants as sources of revenue. Moreover, the new institutional arrangement changed the lobbying process. "Since the entire new edifice was based on the principle of popular representation, the Assembly needed a small group of appointed deputies who would overcome the opposition of those new members who disapproved of this pressure group," Deveau explains.[19] The Assembly organized a committee of thirty-five deputies to examine all issues pertaining to commerce and agriculture. From Nairac's letters we learn that the Assembly was planning to withhold 600,000 livres in bonuses for commerce formerly dispersed by the Crown to its merchant clients, indicating how successful the chambers of commerce had been as pressure groups before the Revolution. It is unlikely that the extent and frequency of these bonuses were known to the public, as subsidies were allocated on an individual basis. One group of merchants was not privy to the special arrangements its rivals secured, just as tax exemptions in today's complex tax codes are known generally only to the groups that benefit from them.

During the early days of the Revolution, the merchant representatives met incessantly, publishing reports, responding to reports from the Assembly, and addressing it. Committee meetings of five hours a day, followed by more specialized work and correspondence with the home office, were common. Despite unrelenting efforts, representatives like Nairac achieved few results. The legal rights of Africans and the morality of the slave trade dominated the debates in the Assembly. Accustomed to quick results, the home offices of chambers of commerce, including Nairac's, sent letters conveying their impatience to their representatives.

Before the Revolution, French commerce depended upon working privately with the intendants of commerce; afterward, the merchants had to lobby an assembly that represented a broad set of interests. The new situation the merchants faced was similar to the one their British counterparts faced throughout the eighteenth century. The British merchants

---

[19]Deveau, *Commerce rochelais*, 72.

without a chamber of commerce asked that one be created. The prevalence of this desire in the *cahiers* suggests that the chambers were perceived by their authors as sources of important benefits for those cities lucky enough to have them. Especially revealing was that these same *cahiers,* which condemned the commercial privileges of rival towns, also requested the privilege of having a chamber of commerce. Each group or city clamored for the suppression of privileges enjoyed by other groups while advocating the preservation or extension of its own special rights.

The Constituent Assembly abolished all of the chambers of commerce on October 16, 1791. The chambers were viewed as part of the apparatus of Old Regime privilege because they allowed a small coterie of urban merchants to dominate commercial relations with the king, pass off their interests as those of the majority, use formal channels to cultivate personal networks, and vie for royal favors and contracts. In suppressing the chambers, the Assembly evoked the same principles that led it to suppress the guilds.

The Revolution also brought about the end of the intendants of commerce and the dismantling of the King's Council, leaving the large commercial concerns without an official voice in the new government. Commercial concerns then had to lobby the Constituent Assembly directly to achieve their goals. Jean-Michel Deveau provides an illustrative example of the change in *Le Commerce rochelais face à la Révolution,* a book based on the letters of Jean-Baptiste Nairac, a merchant who was sent to Paris to represent the commercial interests of the town of La Rochelle and report back on the activities of the Constituent Assembly. Nairac's frequent correspondence with the merchants of La Rochelle reveals the loss of access to power that accompanied the rise of the representative assembly. From these letters we learn that the lobbying process, too, was dramatically altered. Nairac was quick to understand and adjust to this change, but his colleagues in La Rochelle were not. His efforts to relate the changes to them and their resistance to the changes are instructive.

Retaining the right to deal in slaves, subsidies encouraging long-distance trade, and a guaranteed monopoly on colonial trade were of particular concern to the merchants of La Rochelle, as was suppression of the commercial operations of other cities.[18] Before the Revolution, the merchants of privileged ports like La Rochelle had been accustomed to quick

---

[18]La Rochelle was the only port between Guyenne and Brittany that lay in a duty-free zone, called the Cinq grosses fermes. This meant that goods sold by La Rochelle to consumers within the zone were duty-free. Earlier, La Rochelle also had the exclusive right to trade in slaves, a privilege ended in 1716 when the triangular trade was opened up to Bordeaux, Nantes, and Rouen.

diplomatic objectives. Expanding the economy and increasing the wealth of his subjects were secondary goals.

In 1710, a royal edict created twenty new jurisdictions that could entertain cases concerning merchants who were members of the king's companies. The *parlements* opposed these new jurisdictions. The Crown was so concerned about the issue in 1711 that it polled intendants of all generalities in order to determine their opinions; it went even further in 1715, ordering that the civil bankruptcy of merchants who did business for the king could not be subject to the rulings of ordinary jurisdictions. Privileged members of the commercial classes thereby had direct access to government ministers, and judges in their cases were given the authority to defy the *parlements*.[15]

A number of economic and political rationales concentrated redistribution of commercial and industrial profits upon preferred clients and sites.[16] First, monitoring the economic activities of a select group of elite merchants in a restricted geographic area was easier than dealing with a large number of less prominent merchants. An industry run by a multitude of small producers was difficult to control and difficult to tax. Second, as recipients of government privilege, established merchants could be called upon for loans and sometimes political favors. That the king might call upon privileged business groups for additional sums was well understood and openly admitted. "This group was chosen because it could render service to His Majesty when he might have need of funds," Samuel Bernard declared in choosing twenty individuals to create a new commercial company.[17] Supporting a handful of large capitalists was by far the most cost-effective solution to collecting the Crown's revenue, but it was less effective in encouraging economic development and general prosperity. In particular, small merchants and the industries in which they clustered were put at a competitive disadvantage because they rarely benefited from royal favors. Nevertheless, the high prices, low consumer incomes, great contrasts in the distribution of income, and intensification of rural-urban divisions that resulted did not deter the Crown from continuing these practices.

The value of the privileges accorded favored towns is most obvious when we consider the response they elicited during the Revolutionary period. In the *cahiers de doléance* written in 1789, many of the cities

---

[15]Claude-Frédéric Lévy, *Capitalistes et pouvoir au siècle des lumières* (Paris: Mouton, 1969), 2:60.
[16]For instance, only twelve ports were authorized to trade with the French American islands.
[17]Lévy, *Capitalistes et pouvoir*, 1:72.

nity. Although the principal concern of the local chambers was the protection of local trading privileges, the deputies defended the liberty of trade whenever they stood to gain by it. They also shared with the finance ministers a strong belief in the basic tenets of mercantilism and in the need to regulate manufacturers. Much of the royal legislation of industry resulted from the deputies' consultation with the merchant community represented in the chambers. The establishment of an identifiable group of exclusive and influential merchants suited the state's efforts to control industry and the sources of revenue.[13] It was in the king's interest to have the chambers act as vehicles for favors from individual merchants and for him to grant some favors to those merchants. Thus the Crown encouraged the chambers to allow a select group of merchants to lobby for regulations, subsidies, and intervention to benefit their regions or themselves. Especially privileged were merchants in industries designated as essential to national defense.[14] This structure did not, however, give the merchants from different chambers the means of negotiating or trading privileges among themselves.

The chambers of commerce generally served larger commercial interests, often at the expense of smaller groups. Instead of attempting to encourage the development of a broad entrepreneurial class, French policy was designed to coordinate the needs of the business elite with the fiscal needs of the government. Small merchants tended to cluster in industries where government protection was lacking, and which therefore failed to attract credit and capital, among them the grain trade, leather-working, and metallurgy. All three made little technical progress relative to the same industries in Britain, where local capitalists could find loans to invest in new technology and to increase the scale of their operations. Because they benefited proportionally less from government policy, small merchants were less likely to be loyal to the king. In fact, independent merchants were often viewed as potentially unpatriotic and were depicted as more concerned with the egotistic pursuit of profit than with national interests. The king, of course, defined national interests in terms of his military and

---

[13]This was one reason why the Protestant merchants became loyal to the king after the signing of the Edict of Nantes. The Crown had essentially bought their loyalty by lavishing upon them monopoly rights of all kinds, especially with regard to international trade.
[14]Pierre Dardel has commented on how even in a major commercial center like Rouen, the city's commerce was dominated in 1779 by an elite of sixty-one *marchands armateurs* (Dardel, *Commerce, industrie, et navigation: Rouen et Havre au XVIII*ᵉ *siècle* [Rouen: Société libre d'emulation de la Seine-Maritime, 1966], 141). Also of interest is that during the same period, Rouen could only count four bankers (ibid., 159). Even Paris at that time had only a hundred bankers.

A 1701 edict established councils of commerce in eight more cities—Lille, Rouen, Bordeaux, La Rochelle, Nantes, Saint-Malo, Bayonne, and Montpellier.[10] Thomas Schaeper notes:

> virtually the only thing that every locality had in common was royal supervision. From the very beginning, the controller general and the secretary of state for the navy rigorously supervised the operations of the chambers of commerce and the elections of the deputies of trade. The royal provincial intendants were authorized to preside over the local bodies whenever they wished, and it was up to them to ensure that qualified persons were chosen to attend the council in Paris. The Crown did not impose its own choices on the localities, but it did reserve the right to reject a candidate if it found him unacceptable.[11]

Membership in the councils was generally limited to an elite group of prominent local business people who usually had considerable prior influence over local town councils and governments.[12] These municipal chambers of commerce were responsible for forwarding correspondence from the city's merchants to the king. The chambers, though, were more than just letter boxes: no opinion was passed on to the controller general without the authorization and comments of chamber members, who designated the deputies sent to the national Council of Commerce. The archives of the local chambers of commerce, preserved at the Bourse, reveal a steady increase in activity over the course of the eighteenth century. While the archives contain material on problems of interest to the merchant community at large, maritime and colonial problems were especially frequent topics of consultation between the government and the business commu-

---

[10] Schaeper, *French Council of Commerce*, 73–76. Both Marseilles and Dunkirk already had chambers in 1700, and Lyons established a chamber in 1702 under a different edict. Although authorized by the Crown to organize chambers, Saint-Malo and Nantes did not have any chambers of commerce during the eighteenth century.

[11] Ibid., 74.

[12] See Jean-Michel Deveau, *Le Commerce rochelais face a la Révolution: Correspondance de Jean-Baptiste Nairac* (La Rochelle: Rumeur des âges, 1989), 65–66. The major cities not only supported a permanent representative in Paris but typically sent a special delegation to the capital when matters of special concern arose. The royal *arrêt* that acknowledged the Chamber of Commerce in La Rochelle was typical. It called for thirty of the town's business leaders to choose a director and four syndics; however, Louis XIV reserved the right to make the original thirty appointments. Allowing the king to approve the original membership was an essential element in gaining formal recognition of local chambers. The original members were given the right to co-opt future members, thus assuring that the membership was restricted to those groups or networks of merchants that had ties to the Crown.

extent that decisions had to be made by individual members of the council; yet government efforts to control the economy had not diminished. In 1787, the Commerce Council was reabsorbed by the Council of Finance, illustrating again the subjugation of French commercial policy to royal financial imperatives.

Throughout the Old Regime, the controller general appointed the intendants of commerce; they owed their loyalty entirely to him. In fact, contemporaries viewed the Council of Commerce as a front for the controller general, through which he directly supervised nonmaritime commerce (maritime commerce was under the auspices of the secretary of state and marine).[6] Thus, the controller general, whose primary concern and responsibility was augmenting royal revenues, also directed France's economic development. It should come as no surprise, then, that the revenue imperative took priority over general prosperity. The fiscal orientation of the regime did not escape the notice of contemporaries. In his analysis of the political economy of the Old Regime, the marquis d'Argenson wrote that "the intendants of commerce were agents of the controller general or at least his clients; they knew only him. Finance and commerce identified with each other and rotated on the same axis."[7]

After the controller general acquired the means to control commerce at the national level through the appointment and domination of intendants of commerce and by absorbing the King's Council of Commerce,[8] controllers acted to gain control over commerce at the local level. To accomplish this, the controllers general put themselves in charge of the chambers of commerce in the major commercial cities. Since municipal leaders viewed the chambers as potential threats to local autonomy, with few exceptions, royal prodding was needed to prompt cities to create chambers.[9]

---

[6]A *règlement* of 1699 however divided the responsibility between the secretary of the navy and the controller general. On the Council of Commerce, see Thomas J. Schaeper, *The French Council of Commerce, 1700–1715: A Study in Mercantilism after Colbert* (Columbus: Ohio State University Press, 1983).

[7]René-Louis d'Argenson, *Loisirs*, 1:37–38, quoted in Jouvencel, *Contrôleur général des finances*, 71. In 1769, Maupeou similarly exclaimed, "The dignity of the chancellor is but an empty title since politics on one side and finance on the other have become the two axes upon which all administration rotates" (quoted in Antoine, *Conseil du roi*, 425). The chancellor was the first of the great officers of state. He presided at all tribunals and sat in the *parlement* above the *premier président*. In short, he embodied all justice under the king. Maupeou's statement indicates how justice was also subordinated to finance.

[8]By the ministry of Desmaretz, the Council of Finance included sixteen intendants of finance and six intendants of commerce. The intendants of finance were suppressed during the Regency and were reestablished by a royal edict of May 31, 1724. See Antoine, *Conseil du roi*, 404.

[9]The first one appeared in Marseilles in 1599; this achieved little, and in 1664 the merchants of Marseilles created a new chamber.

this arrangement in place, the Great Council of Commerce was easily subsumed under the Council of Finance. The influential role played by financial imperatives in the regulation of commerce is further highlighted by controller generals who named tax farmers (members of the Ferme générale) to serve on the Council of Commerce.[4]

The Council of Commerce changed its name and structure several times, alternately appearing by royal command and disappearing into the Council of Finance. The Council of Commerce operated out of the Council of Finance until 1664, when Louis XIV reinstituted the Council of Commerce and ordered that it meet every two weeks. Two of the four members of this council were also members of the Royal Council of Finance.

Controller General Jean-Baptiste Colbert (intendant of finance, 1661–65; controller general, 1665–83) invited closer collaboration with provincial business people when in 1673 he recommended that the principal commercial cities each send representatives to Paris to discuss how to compete with the merchant fleets of France's commercial rivals. In 1676 the Council of Commerce disappeared when its functions were again subsumed by the Council of Finance.

The commerce council reappeared in 1700, this time as the Bureau of Commerce.[5] An *arrêt* of June 5, 1708, reoutlined the functions of the intendants of commerce and stipulated that four of them meet as a council once a week. Each of the four intendants was assigned responsibility for specific provinces and branches of industry. Their powers were both broad and specific: they could create industrial regulation to govern an entire industry and grant exemptions to loyal or preferred businesses. Even the smallest favor to a particular firm could be accommodated if the intendant was well disposed. In an *arrêt* of June 22, 1722, the Bureau of Commerce was officially renamed a Council of Commerce. This new council issued its decisions interchangeably as *arrêts* either of finance or of commerce, suggesting the subordination of commercial regulation to fiscal policy. Michel Antoine notes that after 1750, meetings of the Council of Commerce were less frequent because its activities had multiplied to such an

---

[4]Henri de Jouvencel, *Le Contrôleur général des finances sous l'ancien régime* (Paris: Larose, 1901), 85.

[5]Antoine reports that finance had definitively taken commerce back in hand in 1724, when M. Le Peletier des Forts, *conseiller d'état et conseil royal des finances*, assumed control of the Bureau of Commerce. The intendants of commerce were created so that the controller general "would be immediately informed of all business that combined the concerns of commerce and finance, which at heart are the same and which at present are not as well united as they could be" ("Memoir présenté au roi le 31 mai 1724 en vue du rétablissement des intendants du commerce" [AN, E 3656], cited in Antoine, *Conseil du roi*, 404).

Second only to the Conseil d'en haut, which defined the broad policy outline for the many individual councils that formed the King's Council, was the Conseil royale des finances, headed by the controller general. It was the engine of finance and the general administration of the kingdom, and emerged as the most powerful and dynamic organ of central government. About half of the personnel of the royal bureaucracy reported to the controller general, and roughly half of the legislation issued by the Council of State came directly from the Conseil royal des finances. Six ministers (intendants of finance), 300 administrators and 35,000 agents of the Ferme générale, 32 provincial intendants, and 400 subdelegates, as well as inspectors of manufactures, were under the authority of the controller general in 1789.[3] The Conseil royal des finances fixed the sum of direct taxes, farmed out the taxes, and established the sum of the impositions of each generality and each election. This council also decided upon monetary policy, the creation or suppression of offices, the payment of *rentes*, and the increase of *gages*. In addition, it supervised all projects concerned with the distribution of funds and verified the accounts of the Treasury's receivers, and therefore had a central role to play in the kingdom's industrial organization. It also authorized the licensing of industrial and commercial activity.

Because the authority that redistributed wealth in France emanated from the executive branch, the King's Council, political officials could control participation in the growing market economy. Paris and Versailles were transformed into elaborate centers of distributional play, since court politics determined what would be produced and who would benefit. The political judgments creating the rules and quotas became the result of private negotiation, not the subject of open debate. Economic regulation in France was the prerogative of bureaucratic discretion. Regulations, subsidies, taxes, and licenses were granted to favored producers and consumers so that the government could take a share of the excess profits created by the regulation.

In 1607, Henri IV created the Great Council of Commerce to deal with ocean commerce. Rather than appointing business people to the council, however, Henri appointed members of the *parlement*, as well as members of the fiscal courts, who reported to the minister of finance. The Ministry of Finance, led by the controller general, thereby played the dominant role in regulating economic activity, while intendants of commerce, direct subordinates of the controller general, regulated industry and commerce. With

---

[3]Michel Bruguière, *Pour une renaissance de l'histoire financière XVIII<sup>e</sup>–XX<sup>e</sup> siécles* (Paris: Comité pour l'histoire économique et financière de la France, 1991), 156.

harto are all examples of cronyism analogous to the patterns of Old Regime France. Outside observers often underestimate the political stability of corrupt regimes and overestimate the stability of nations in which governmental cronyism dictates development. Comparison of eighteenth-century France and England suggests that the difference between corruption and cronyism is crucial in several regards. Whereas in France individual clans and favorites clustered around particular ministers enjoyed monopoly rents not available to other members of their class, in England a much broader segment of the population benefited from regulation and enjoyed the spoils of government. The English upper classes were also more likely to view the decisions of Parliament as legitimate, making them more acceptable and easier to enforce than those of French ministers, who acted on their own. As a result, while using political and legal institutions to redistribute the nation's income, the English did not pay the high price in stability that the French regime ultimately paid.

## THE REGULATION OF COMMERCE AND INDUSTRY IN FRANCE

In seventeenth-century France, the monarchy did not want the government to be ruled by the interests of narrowly defined social groups. To insulate the government from interest-group penetration, the French kings created an exceedingly simple administrative structure. Its central organ was the Council of State, the King's Council, which Michel Antoine refers to as the soul of the monarchy; the word "council" thus became synonymous with government under Louis XIV.[2] The kings endowed their councils with a high degree of discretion in order to insulate them from the impact of interest groups and, in particular, to reduce their vulnerability to pressures from the old landed nobility. The council's most effective tool was the *arrêt*, an order in the king's name. *Arrêts* were the expression of the king's absolute authority and could not be tested by any other body. Although an *arrêt* had to be signed by the king, many *arrêts* issued in the king's name pertained to issues too trivial to have ever been brought to the king's direct attention. *Arrêts* were often signed in the king's name by lesser ministers.

---

[2]Antoine, *Conseil du roi*. The King's Council consisted of several individual councils: the Conseil des dépêches, responsible for the police or administration of the interior of the kingdom; the Privy Council, dealing with suits between private parties, especially those concerning the king's finances; the Council of Finances; the Council of Commerce; and the Council of Conscience, which dealt with religious matters. These different councils were, however, simply different manifestations of one and the same council.

knowledge, the administrative and political process that allowed the French government to pursue its mercantilist programs was private. Furthermore, the rules in France changed according to ministerial whim. As one historian puts it, public law was a forbidden domain, "a mystery reserved to the king and his ministers,"[1] permitting select members of privileged clans, rather than broadly defined interest groups, to enjoy the benefits of government patronage. Although the creation of sophisticated interests and competitive lobbies allowed the British Parliament to do special favors for particular industries during the eighteenth century, unlike the French executive, neither Parliament nor the English executive was able to distribute monopoly rents to particular ministerial or royal favorites. In England the government's distribution of spoils followed procedures more open to the English political elite as a whole; still, corruption was more pervasive in English public administration than in France, where executive supervision of central government agents was more comprehensive.

The greater discretionary powers of the French ministers allowed select groups of preferred clients to receive the benefits of economic regulation, but those powers were diluted by the rise of the interest groups they created. Legislation aimed at the wholesale liberalization of agriculture and industry thus failed. By contrast, the British government used political and legal methods over the course of the eighteenth century to restructure the economy in ways that made substantial agricultural and industrial change possible. The resulting redistribution of the nation's income was more dramatic in eighteenth-century England than in France despite the French ministers' greater discretionary powers.

The essential institutional element of the French government's redistributional capability was the office of controller general, whose functional equivalent in England was Parliament. Differences between these two decision-making structures can explain why interest groups with similar preferences could not always influence policy in the same way or to the same extent in each country. A comparison of these differences suggests important links between stability and the patterns of redistribution produced by variations in the political structure. The corruption of early modern England has its parallels in the early stages of the development of democratic institutions in a number of nations. Twentieth-century India and Israel and nineteenth-century America are well-studied examples. Iran under the Shah, the Philippines under Marcos, and Indonesia under Su-

---

[1] G. Chevrier, *Remarques sur l'introduction et les vicissitudes de la distinction du "jus privatium" et du "jus publicum" dans les oeuvres des anciens juristes françaises* (Paris, 1952), quoted in Michel Antoine, *Le Conseil du roi sous le régime de Louis XV* (Paris: Libraire Droz, 1970), 2.

# 3 The Redistributive Role of the State

Parliament's deal-making capabilities were to have unforeseen consequences for England's ability to adjust to economic opportunities. The ease of making political deals, in turn, had a direct influence on governability. England's unified legal system allowed contracts negotiated in Parliament to attain an objective market value in part because they were enforceable by the legal system. Shares in the French economy that derived from cronyism were, by contrast, largely unmarketable, since they constituted contracts founded on confidence in the private portfolios and stability of regime officials. In addition, local courts in France could always be used to dispute rights derived from deals with the king's officials. The inability of different groups to trade rights and privileges prevented necessary reforms in the property-rights structure of France. The notable disparities in political stability between France and England mirrored differences in the system of economic redistribution—in the negotiation and enforcement of political contracts allocating shares of the nation's economic pie.

The lobbying activities of private groups had an important redistributive influence on national economic policies in both England and France; however, the different organization of government in the two nations gave a distinctive shape and structure to the redistributive character of national politics in each case. In England, Parliament's role in the legislative process made gaining economic concessions from the government long and difficult. Over the course of the eighteenth century, the British government's role was increasingly limited to adjudicating, under the restraint of law, the claims of influential but conflicting groups. In France, by contrast, the government's economic decisions were subject to neither parliamentary scrutiny nor open public discussion. Whereas the rules of the redistributional game in eighteenth-century England were increasingly public

evolved in France. Nonetheless, despite this ultimately fatal flaw, absolutism provided the basis for relative domestic stability that endured for more than a century. This great victory for the French Crown had redistributive and economic consequences.

This book examines the origin of absolutism's economic institutions by exploring the political incentives that produced those institutions, as well as their possible and probable costs. One implication dominates: the system persisted because of its political logic; that is, the economic institutions of absolutism were consistent with rational political behavior despite their economic inefficiency.[12]

[12]Although economists have yet to reach a consensus on a precise definition of rationality, they do agree on some general characteristics. By "rationality," they do not mean consistent thinking, but something closer to trying to get what you want with the least effort or lowest cost. Calculations of rationality by economists are usually broken down into three components: preferences, likes, or dislikes; costs, the amount of time, money, or effort needed to achieve a goal; and utility, a measure that reconciles costs and preferences. Given two equally preferred goals, the one with the least cost has the greatest utility. To an economist, to be rational is to maximize utility. For an excellent discussion of rationality in economic analysis, see William H. Riker, "Political Science and Rational Choice," in *Perspectives on Positive Political Economy*, ed. James E. Alt and Kenneth A. Shepsle (New York: Cambridge University Press, 1990), 172–74. For a critique of how little is known about economic rationality, see Reinhard Selton, "Evolution, Learning, and Economic Behavior," *Games and Economic Behavior* 3 (1991): 3–24.

that it was able to expand provincial taxes if it did not incur the hostility of the nobility. The magnates were even able to appropriate royal tax money for their own uses.[7]

Although it helped the French monarchy wield national power, the creation of privilege had long-term consequences that were detrimental for the Crown. When it involved the creation of offices, privilege created a component of the bureaucracy beyond the control of the Crown. When it involved exemptions from future taxes, privilege impoverished the Crown by reducing revenue in the long run. By the late eighteenth century, the Crown had compromised much of its control over the tax system, diminishing its ability to cope with crises. The Crown failed to develop an institution that would facilitate the renegotiation of the privileges or political assets created over the course of centuries.

After the Fronde (1652), the provincial estates, the most vigorous upholders of local autonomy in France, were mostly paid off or subdued.[8] They were transformed into revenue-collecting devices to enrich both local elites and the Crown. Those estates that did not become revenue providers were eliminated.[9] With the estates subdued, the king's representatives, the intendants, became the intermediaries between the local elites and the Crown. Domestic political stability was achieved once the kingdom's notables recognized the Crown as the indispensable guarantor of privilege and status. Having emerged as the most important single source of spoils, the Crown also became the arbiter that stood above social groups.[10]

Since the Crown was the only organization empowered to speak for the entire realm, there was no institution in which a consensus among the various elites could develop. When Louis XVI requested the renegotiation of exemptions and privileges on the eve of the French Revolution, the means to undertake and to enforce such negotiations did not exist.[11] No forum in which groups could trade privileges among themselves had

---

II, 1356–1370 (Philadelphia: American Philosophical Association, 1976); id., *Royal Taxation in Fourteenth-Century France: The Development of War Financing, 1322–1356* (Princeton: Princeton University Press, 1971).
[7]Local notables in Languedoc consumed 33 percent of taxes. See William Beik, "Etat et société au XVII$^e$ siècle: La Taille en Languedoc et la question de la redistribution," *Annales: Economies, sociétés, civilisations* 39 (1984): 1270–98.
[8]During the eighteenth century, the *parlements* were protectors of provincial liberty; earlier that role had been played by the provincial estates.
[9]See Collins, *Fiscal Limits*, 3–4, 18, 23, 38–42.
[10]As Turgot was later to point out, too much government activity depended on royal initiative, leaving too little to societal effort ("On the Municipalities," in *Oeuvres de Turgot*, ed. Gustave Schelle [Paris, 1913–23], 4:568–628).
[11]Even the Estates General had not been in session for over a century and a half.

The absence of a centralized consultative assembly from which the government could receive grants of taxation made it necessary for the French Crown to bargain separately with each constituency. As a result the form and level of taxes varied from region to region. For example, sales taxes were levied on regions with commercialized areas, while communities living near war zones had to pay taxes specifically designated for defense. Had a central parliament existed, similar negotiations between central authority and the localities in which one locality received rights denied another would probably not have been approved. Thus, differences between the rights of various regions tended to be effaced through the English Parliament, whereas in France variations were often intensified, as each province negotiated with the Crown to protect its particular exemptions without regard for the costs consequently imposed on neighboring regions. Within the British Empire, relations with America were in many regards analogous to the relationship of the French Crown with the regions of France. When trading rights and privileges for revenue, the French Crown did not have to consider whether the costs of such exemptions were spread unevenly among the population and throughout the kingdom. However, the long-term consequences of such an uneven distribution of fiscal concessions were detrimental to both political stability and economic development. The resulting labyrinth of tariffs and tolls impeded trade, while the prevalence of regional tax privileges prevented the development of a national tax policy. The polarities in administrative traditions between England and France were sustained throughout the medieval and early modern periods.

To maintain the cooperation of well-organized elites, the French Crown allocated favors of various kinds, including pensions, patronage, special legal treatment, exclusive commercial rights, and special courts. The dispersal of privilege was guided by the Crown's intention to make it more advantageous for powerful groups to cooperate rather than resist the growth of central authority. The fiscal exemptions held by the nobility were an example. Nobles were not exempt from levies collected in the middle of the fourteenth century. However, a weak king, Charles VI, granted exemptions in the hope of winning the nobility's support in the war against England.[6] As the king's fiscal needs increased, the Crown found

---

[6]For a summary of the evolution of the tax system, see James B. Collins, *Fiscal Limits of Absolutism: Direct Taxation in Early Seventeenth-Century France* (Berkeley and Los Angeles: University of California Press, 1988), 18–64; Pierre Chaunu, "L'Etat," in *Histoire économique et sociale,* ed. Fernand Braudel and C. E. Labrousse (Paris: Presses universitaires de France, 1977), 9–228; J. B. Henneman, *Royal Taxation in Fourteenth-Century France: The Captivity and Ransom of John*

result, while Tudor-Stuart monarchs attempted to expand paternalistic guidance of the marketplace, implementation was not necessarily achieved. A much higher correlation between legislation and enforcement probably existed after the Glorious Revolution of 1688, when policymakers and enforcers tended to be like-minded individuals—sometimes relatives, or at least members of the same party.

One of the consequences of the cooperation of local authorities with the Crown in England was the cataloging of land ownership in the entire kingdom. Beginning with the Doomsday Inquiry, surveys of individual property became a characteristic of English government; examples include the Hundred Rolls, the Quo Warranto survey of 1272, the valuation of church lands in 1291, Edward III's ministerial inquiries of 1340, and Henry VIII's Valor Ecclesiasticus. The English Crown established records of property holdings, placing ownership under royal supervision. By contrast, one consequence of the fragmentation of political authority in France was that the French Crown never possessed a comprehensive record of land ownership in the kingdom. Even in the eighteenth century, the French Crown did not possess equivalent measurements of the distribution of wealth and property, because local authorities in France, particularly the *parlements*, resisted such inquiries.

Both England and France recognized limits to the powers of the Crown, and the differences in how those limits were established may help explain the differences in political stability and economic development between the two countries. The medieval Crown's principal weakness was the threat of not being able to contain recalcitrant groups and bind the entire kingdom to one will, and the expansion of the role of the English JPs coincided with the rise of Parliament as a body that could make laws for the whole nation. Members of Parliament could commit their local communities to Parliament's decisions, and English kings could therefore bind the nation's political class to upholding the decisions reached by Parliament. The English nation could thus keep its conflicts with the king centered on a single institution, and the Crown was able to reduce the costs of bargaining with national elites.

Organizing a consensus in the French Estates General was more difficult. During the early Middle Ages, French provinces had passed almost entirely out of the king's control and into the hands of great local families, who exercised authority independently of the Crown. As a result of negotiations that varied significantly from province to province, different regions came under royal control at different times. Lacking uniform interests, the various provinces were not inclined to endorse laws that applied to the whole nation.

municipal independence by curtailing the rights of cities to name their own mayors.[5]

English monarchs did not have to struggle to bring local institutions under Crown authority, since those institutions had never completely slipped away. Because local jurisdictions did not possess autonomous authority over local governance, local elites ruled through institutions within royal jurisdiction. Not having to worry about claims of local liberty or autonomy, the English Crown had less reason to be suspicious of local elites. The justices of the peace were neither in a position to oppose the king in the name of provincial liberty themselves nor had to contend with groups, like the French *parlements,* that could. In the absence of independent regional governments that offered local leaders an alternative source of legitimacy, the local elites appointed to represent their communities did not have to be bought off by the English Crown.

The reason why English counties did not possess rights other than those of the nation can be traced to the Norman invasion, when counties were created, with sheriffs appointed as intermediary between the locality and the Crown. Contrary to what might be expected, the sheriffs were not necessarily the great Norman barons. The sheriffs, rather than the barons, executed the major judicial powers of levying troops and raising taxes, making them important for the maintenance of royal authority. The Crown was strong enough to prevent this critical public office from becoming hereditary, thereby keeping provincial administration under royal supervision. Later, to prevent the sheriffs from becoming too independent, the Crown created justices of the peace (JPs), representatives of the local community chosen by the Crown to supervise the sheriffs. The JPs' local governing authority was established in 1349 after the Great Plague, and they were given wide powers to implement the Statute of Laborers (1349–51). Gradually, the powers of the justices were expanded at the expense of those of the sheriffs; by 1494 the justices were empowered to entertain complaints against the sheriffs and even to convict sheriffs of misdemeanors.

While the system of JPs was inexpensive to organize, from the Crown's point of view it had one serious flaw: it would be difficult to get these country gentlemen to implement policies not in their own interest. As a

---

[5] An example of this process is provided in Robert A. Schneider, *Public Life in Toulouse, 1463–1789: From Municipal Republic to Cosmopolitan City* (Ithaca, N.Y.: Cornell University Press, 1989). In *Representative Government in Early Modern France* (New Haven: Yale University Press, 1980), J. Russell Major has argued more generally that curbing the autonomy of local governing officials was critical to the expansion of royal authority.

To hold together these diverse provinces, the French king often had to grant concessions that compromised the uniformity of his rule. In effect, the Crown had to buy off the loyalties of key local groups by supporting local institutions and acknowledging local privilege. For instance, Burgundy was granted a *parlement* in the fifteenth century as part of the agreement by which that province was reunited with the French Crown. Royal proclamations were not law in Burgundy without review and registration by its *parlement.*

Another royal concession was recognition of the rights of local guilds and prominent local merchants. The support of these well-organized groups was needed if the Crown were to assert its rule over the kingdom's prosperous trading centers.³ Moreover, these political concessions facilitated revenue extraction, as the Crown could call upon the guilds and the privileged merchants for financial support.

The search for local leaders who would be loyal to the king did not end there. The Crown attempted to establish an independent bureaucracy through the sale of offices. However, this strategy proved ineffective, because once secure in the possession of their offices, many officeholders pursued their own objectives rather than those of the Crown. The king was thus soon forced either to increase the supply of offices or to subject officeholders to increased control.⁴ As its power, wealth, and territorial domain increased in the seventeenth century, the French Crown was able to extend its control by sending salaried bureaucratic commissioners, or intendants, to the provinces, often against the opposition of local groups and existing officeholders. France was divided into thirty-four administrative districts, called generalities, with one intendant dispatched to each district. The cost of paying for an expanded independent bureaucracy, however, greatly delayed the emergence of central authority in France.

Lacking the means to maintain an extensive network of salaried administrators, the French kings continued to depend on local elites, who occupied positions generally established by charters guaranteeing provincial or municipal rights. When unable to substitute royal for local institutions, the French Crown sometimes attempted to control the recruitment of individuals who performed the functions of local government. For example, during the late sixteenth century the Crown attempted to limit

---

³In France, the international economy was never sealed off, but access was restricted to select groups of merchants. For example, the merchants of Marseilles were allowed to dominate trade with the Levant, and only four cities could enter the slave trade.

⁴Roland Mousnier, *La Vénalité des offices sous Henri IV et Louis XIII* (Paris: Presses universitaires de France, 1945).

# 2 Rivals in Modernization
## *Creating National Communities in France and England*

In undertaking the centralization of political authority, French state makers had to resolve a set of problems significantly different from those faced by their English counterparts. The French had to overcome obstacles of language, geography, institutional diversity, and strongly traditional local sovereignty, while maintaining a large standing army to defend their country's long frontiers. By contrast, few national histories offer examples of greater continuity in the establishment of central state authority than that of England.[1] There, neither the tax system nor the legal system had ever completely slipped out of the central government's control. The institutions that were to characterize the English state until the twentieth century had their origins in feudalism, but it was a feudalism in which every piece of land was a tenement of the Crown, and the king was the lord of all lords.[2] England had a more unified economy, dominated by a central city, London, and a staple export, wool. Levying excise taxes and tariffs was thus much easier in England than in France, where numerous products were traded in often autonomous local or regional markets. An even greater obstacle to the unification of the French nation was the fragmentation of political power. France was a mosaic of conflicting and overlapping jurisdictions, added piecemeal during several hundred years of conquest, marriage, and inheritance.

---

[1] Although the French Revolution would seem to negate the state-building achievements of French absolutism as a model of modernization, French state-construction has much to offer the developing world. The political starting point of most new nations resembles Old Regime France more closely than eighteenth-century England.
[2] See Joseph R. Strayer, *On the Medieval Origins of the Modern State* (Princeton: Princeton University Press, 1970).

rights are liquid and can be freely traded. Whereas the literature in economics assumes that deals to allow resource holders to sell their rights are possible at all levels of the political system, the economic history of France and England suggests that the allocation of rights to participate in the market system is one of the principal variables that explains differences in the economic and political performance of regimes.[26] Eighteenth-century interest groups deliberately fashioned market imperfections in order to profit from them. In fact, transaction costs were often the outcome of groups using their political bargaining power to pursue economic advantage.

[26]Mark Gallagher has argued that parliamentary government increased the amount spent by private groups on rent seeking (*Rent-Seeking and Economic Growth in Africa* [Boulder, Colo.: Westview Press, 1991]). Neither the British Parliament's dramatic redistributional legislation nor the differences between the English and French systems can be explained in terms of commitment to social equity. In both cases, rents were the institutional motivation. The outcomes of parliamentary redistribution were not necessarily the most economically efficient ones. The main difference between the two regimes was that social and economic transformation was achieved in one case without revolution. England's system of parliamentary control over rent distribution resulted in a two-party system that diffused the pressures for radical or revolutionary change.

Groups in the British Parliament bargained out of self-interest for benefits often denied unrepresented groups, such as the peasantry, whose ultimate dispossession was the consequence of exclusion from the deal-making apparatus. By contrast, those at the bargaining table could prevent deals that would be at their expense. A parliament of gamblers will not give one of its members a monopoly to produce playing cards. (If there were no gamblers in a parliament, it might agree to create such a monopoly, since none of the members' interests would be threatened.) Similarly, the British Parliament, a parliament of landlords, would not support industrial monopolies because the economic wisdom of the day assumed that industrial profits ultimately came at the expense of land rents. A commitment to free trade thus need not be invoked to explain why a parliament dominated by agrarian interests opposed industrial monopolies. Members simply believed that low prices for manufactured goods would allow them to collect higher rents. (Ricardo, in fact, taught that high prices for manufactured goods came at the expense of rents.)

A comparison with today's legislatures may help illustrate the peculiarities of early parliaments. The public choice literature explains why interests groups do not cancel each other out in today's U.S. Congress. The committee system, not the full legislature, sets the agenda, with the goal of getting the votes needed to pass a given law. Laws are written so that representatives do not have to choose between one project and another. Projects are added to bills to win the necessary votes. Logrolling and omnibus legislation allow committees to pack bills so that they please as many senators as are needed for passage. Absent the committee system, much of the redistributional activity of the U.S. Congress would be eliminated.[25]

The framework suggested in this chapter is an alternative to the assumption in much economic theory that trades will be consummated until all gains are exhausted. Reaching the point where all feasible trades are consummated requires the existence of institutions designed to maximize the liquidity of all economic rights and assets. This assumes that all privileges and property rights are tradable commodities. However, societies rarely develop political markets in which all social and economic assets and

---

[25]See, e.g., David Mayhew, *Congress: The Electoral Connection* (New Haven: Yale University Press, 1974). Committees in the U.S. Congress can acquire agenda control, veto power, and the resources needed to develop alternative proposals to those offered by the executive. Congress can thus contribute positively to the policy-making process to a greater extent than the British Parliament. See Kenneth Shepsle, "Representation and Governance: The Great Legislative Trade-Off," *Political Science Quarterly* 103, no. 3 (1988): 461–84. A committee structure facilitating logrolling did not exist in post-1688 England. Even today the British attempt to reduce pork-barrel legislation by randomly assigning MPs to committees.

enclosure, price supports that encouraged high grain prices, the decline of guilds and urban trade monopolies, the creation of a highly efficient bureaucracy to collect excise taxes,[19] and the shift of capital-intensive manufacturing to the countryside[20] and to regions in which guild restrictions were weak.[21] Venal though it was, English officialdom helped tilt the economy toward more efficient allocations, since bribe taking shifted resources to those who had the highest-valued capabilities.[22] Parliament played a key role in bringing about these changes, which were all consequences of political trades negotiated in pursuit of private economic interests.

The British Parliament's deal-making capacity is illuminated by the criteria suggested here. Parliament was a market for rights to control the economy: rights could be negotiated and traded, with the result that users with the highest-valued needs were able to buy out those holding traditionally allocated entitlements. In post-1688 England, the parties whose interests were represented, not the king and his agents, became the deal makers.[23] Eighteenth-century England was thus closer than Old Regime France to the ideal of efficient market allocation that assumes that there are no barriers to trade.[24] Theory, however, does not specify the critical role of the institutions that make the economist's assumptions plausible.

---

[19]These innovations are well described in John Brewer, *The Sinews of Power: War, Money, and the English State, 1688–1783* (New York: Knopf, 1989).

[20]French merchants put work out to peasants in order to profit from lax guild restrictions in the countryside, but since rural manufactures could be confiscated, wholesale investment in machines and plants did not occur. The jurisdiction of English guilds did not extend into the countryside, presumably because the common law courts would not uphold those rights.

[21]This is discussed in Barry R. Weingast, "The Economic Role of Political Institutions" (MS). See, too, T. S. Ashton, *An Economic History of England: The Eighteenth Century* (London: Methuen, 1955), 94.

[22]Regional rivalry also contributed, since local officials in the north of England attracted capital and labor by not enforcing restrictive regulations.

[23]The British Parliament had more direct access to information about economic opportunities than did the ministers of the French king's centralized command structure.

[24]Yoram Barzel hypothesizes, for example, "that the structure of rights is designed to allocate ownership of individual attributes among parties in such a way that the parties who have comparative advantage in managing those attributes ... will obtain rights over them"; he believes "people choose to exercise rights when they believe the gains from such actions will exceed the costs" (Barzel, *Economic Analysis of Property Rights* [Cambridge: Cambridge University Press, 1989], 49, 65). This ignores the link between the definition of rights and the political system. One cannot define rights if the political and judicial system does not stand behind the definition. Barzel assumes the existence of a market for property rights, when often a market must be created. The interest of the individual who claims rights may not be sufficient to sustain the costs of creating a market for those rights.

the French Old Regime, embodied in the Estates General. However, the Estates were not called between 1614 and 1789.

Why did the French administration resist the obvious solution of convoking the Estates General? One answer may be that the convocation of a national assembly able to reassign politically defined economic rights would have severely restricted the king's authority as deal maker; once the buyer and seller are brought together, the middleman is no longer needed. The French case teaches us that a ruler may choose *not* to create a market for rights, because in so doing he reduces his power and in effect ceases to rule. The desire to exercise power may ultimately override the wish to do business and remain solvent. In other words, the desire of power brokers to remain in power cannot be measured in monetary terms.[17]

To maintain the discretion of the king's agents, political markets in Old Regime France were based upon private deals or private placement—that is, cronyism. Deals based on cronyism are not tradable, however, since the rights cronies hold are based on their relations with a member of the regime. Many of the potential users of such rights or privileges had no means to signal, either by purchase or bribe, the value such rights represented.

To get access to the rents produced by property rights, excluded groups had to focus on gaining political favor. Gaining political favor in Old Regime France, however, was no different from winning power in a one-party state. If the executive branch of the government is the source of all economic privileges (which is equivalent to the state owning all the enterprises or firms in the economy), one must be a member of the ruling party to receive rights (and the ensuing rents). Since one party, the king's, monopolized rights in Old Regime France, those in opposition had to overthrow the government to gain access to them.[18] Thus when all economic rights are owned by the state, political instability is inevitable. In a parliamentary system, by contrast, the opposition does not have to advocate revolution in order to gain power.

The poor performance of France's political institutions in extending economic and social frontiers is highlighted by the dramatic transformations that occurred simultaneously in England. Among the most notable adjustments were the expansion of large English estates resulting from

---

[17]Colbert warned Louis XIV that war against the Dutch would strain France's fiscal well-being. The debts of the Old Regime essentially originated in the king's willingness to pay any price to achieve his diplomatic and political goals.

[18]The monarchy in Old Regime France was in effect a one-party system (for the term *party* it might perhaps be appropriate to substitute *clientele* or *network of clans*).

enabling himself to collect the additional surplus revenue created by the increased productivity of his subjects?[15] In answering this question, one has to bear in mind that the transaction costs of revenue collection and the king's limited ability to monitor the wealth of his subjects often reduced the benefits to him of more efficient property rights. In addition, a particular set of rights might be more costly to abolish than to reform. For example, if rights became collateral for loans, the difficulty of finding new guarantees might make their abolition impossible.

The Crown could not, in fact, wipe the slate clean of inefficient rights without jeopardizing its political and financial support. The holders of loyalty-based rights could not adjust to economic change. They possessed assets in the form of rights that could not be renegotiated. And these assets gave them the political leverage to prevent the Crown from making the necessary adjustments in the kingdom's property rights structure to reduce inefficiencies. The property rights that ensured the regime's social support were thus a constraint on how much revenue the system ultimately provided and resulted in the king's eventual loss of power; the failure of the Old Regime in France to generate the political markets needed to implement alternative social and economic arrangements underlay the regime's collapse in 1789.

The overall efficiency of the French economy would have been increased if the ease of making deals had been improved; however, that would have involved redefining the king's role. Much of the institutional rigidity of the French Old Regime can be directly attributed to the king's role as principal political deal maker and his monopoly in defining political rights. Consider the market for privilege. Many important economic privileges were held by individuals because of their special relationship with power brokers within the regime. These privileges could not easily be traded, since the king's favor determined their value. One alternative to the disbursement of privilege by the king would have been the creation of a representative body empowered to determine how the economic pie would be sliced.[16] This function existed in embryonic form in the constitution of

---

[15]In terms familiar to economists, the question is, why didn't the king view himself as the residual claimant of all surplus income created by his subjects? The king would then be expected to create the most efficient property rights, knowing himself to be entitled to some of the surplus income created.

[16]Another alternative would have been the creation of deliberative councils in which all the relevant interest groups could sit at the same bargaining table with the Crown to determine policy jointly. If all decisions had been the result of such deliberations, private rent seeking by independent groups would have been diminished.

Another explanation can, however, be suggested: Old Regime France failed to generate political markets to facilitate the trading of property rights among owners of goods and services. Political markets determine how the marketplace is structured and who can trade there; they thus stand above economic markets for goods and services.[13] It is significant, too, that political markets are most efficient when they enable a maximum number of property rights to be openly traded as commodities.

Deals were not made to reduce inefficiencies in Old Regime France because there were no markets to clear such deals. Information about political regulations and their effects on economic activity was monopolized by the king and his agents, preventing independent deals. Access to the market—that is, the right to trade both domestically and internationally—was regulated by the king. The king granted and protected property rights to the extent that they contributed to royal revenue. If the king benefited from the sale of a right, its exercise was likely to receive the protection of the king's courts and military; if there were no rights to sell, the king's protection was likely to lack zeal. The king would not bear the costs of institutional innovation, including the creation and protection of property rights, unless he could capture the benefits. For example, the king might be willing to defend against piracy only those merchants who had purchased royal charters offering exclusive trading rights. If a particular institutional innovation compromised the king's interests (for example, revenue), deadlock was the most likely outcome. The rules needed to achieve an agricultural revolution fell into this category.[14]

Why did the king not simply replace the existing property rights with the most efficient rights, given the available industrial technology, thus

---

[13]Note that the assumption here is not that governments are markets or that a market clearing price for policies can exist based on the supply and demand for a particular policy. On viewing governments as political markets, see Robert H. Bates, "A Critique by Political Scientists," in *Politics and Policy Making in Developing Countries: Perspectives on the New Political Economy*, ed. Gerald M. Meier (San Francisco: International Center for Economic Growth, 1991), 261–72. Among the landmarks in the literature on political markets are James Buchanan and Gorden S. Tulluck, *The Calculus of Consent* (Ann Arbor: University of Michigan Press, 1962); George Stigler, "The Theory of Economic Regulation," *Bell Journal of Economics and Management Science* 2 (Spring 1971): 211–40; Richard Posner, "Theories of Economic Regulation," ibid.: 3–21; Sam Peltzman, "Toward a More General Theory of Regulation," *Journal of Law and Economics* 19, no. 211 (1976); and Gary S. Becker, "A Theory of Competition among Pressure Groups for Political Influence," *Quarterly Journal of Economics* 98, no. 371 (1983).

[14]Negotiations applicable to market makers differ from those that apply among traders within markets. Markets providing relatively free conditions of trade are public goods, while people participating within markets engage in the exchange of private goods and services.

Confiscation was easily justified, since many common business practices, such as loans above the legal interest rate of 5 percent, were illegal. Economic operators could never be sure they had not violated some administrative ordinance or decree. During periods of social unrest, charges of hoarding, speculation, and profiteering led to the fining, imprisonment, and even execution of capitalists.[12] Persecution and confiscation was the fate of Louis XVI's financiers during the Revolution. Many were sent to prison; twenty were guillotined. The royal guilds were suppressed. Even the surplus grain of peasants was confiscated.

Some of the social and economic arrangements in Old Regime France defy the criteria of efficiency upon which modern economic theory is based. Rich peasants could not separate their production and property from that of the village; wealthy *seigneurs* were unable to acquire the property rights necessary to create large estates by enclosing their own property or by engrossing village lands; grain merchants could not obtain the rights to export; a large rural population, led by an ancient and once powerful seignorial elite, had to sell its grain according to restrictions imposed by urban officials.

Assuming that users with higher-valued needs will necessarily buy out the rights of those who stand in their way (even taking transaction costs into account), economists will ask why those who paid the costs did not buy out those who benefited. Why, for example, did efficiency-enhancing deals not occur to reduce the costs to the rural sector of the Crown's grain policy? Why were powerful and well-informed members of traditional elites unable to gain access to markets in which they possessed comparative advantages both in scale of production and in access to information? French economic reformers of the eighteenth century asked these same questions.

In the discussion that follows, I compare a number of redistributional arrangements in Old Regime France with their counterparts in Georgian England in an effort to explain why deals like those made in Britain to reduce economic inefficiencies were not made in France.

To explain the failure of Old Regime French society to consummate trades that would have enhanced both social welfare and the wealth of powerful private groups, scholars often argue that members of Old Regime society were unable to identify their interests in economic terms. They were motivated by pre- or anti-capitalist values, we are told; for example, by a desire to display prowess or achieve salvation, as opposed to profits.

---

[12]In many of today's developing nations, entire ethnic groups live under the threat of expropriation and expulsion. Like the Jews in Old Regime Europe, Indian and Chinese minorities in parts of Africa and Asia cannot disclose the value of their enterprises and must keep their capital hidden in foreign banks.

quasi-legal; capricious officials, barriers to market entry, and legislation hostile to profit caused economic competitors to break the law. To ensure trust, business partners had to be chosen from among family members or friends sharing multiple overlapping ties.[10] The threat of confiscation made it necessary to hide profits. As a result contemporaries were likely to know who had a right, but not how much rent could be extracted. This secrecy created information asymmetries that limited the development of markets for a wide range of products and services. The absence of public information, in turn, reduced credit opportunities and restricted the market for economic rights.[11]

In France, independent rural industries functioned in the shadow of the law. Independent craftspeople were legally barred from competition with urban guilds. Goods produced in the countryside could be confiscated. Conflicting laws and jurisdictions also created uncertainty in markets. Merchants inevitably broke some law or decree of a local *parlement* or town mayor, and during shortages they faced interrogation, expropriation, and imprisonment. Which side the king's representatives would take was unpredictable.

Inventors of new products or production methods thus faced conflicts and sanctions. They could not raise capital without a royal charter granting monopoly rights and assuring Crown protection from guild inspectors. Inventors, merchants, and craftspeople faced the continual risk of confiscation on grounds that they had encroached upon some other party's property rights. The greatest risks were faced by financiers who lent to the state, who needed to take every possible precaution to conceal their role from public view and from condemnation by *parlements* and publicists. Nobles who invested in tax farming generally did so under false names. Because they needed to keep their books private, the credit available to financiers was based on personal reputation rather than ascertainable assets, which ultimately reduced both the liquidity and the depth of financial markets.

Instability within the government posed another set of risks. Personnel changes in the Conseil d'état du roi, or King's Council, could mean the expropriation of the rights and profits of one cohort of cronies by another.

---

[10] When a legal framework to enforce contracts is missing, networks of personal relationships will substitute for contracts to enforce promises and coordinate reciprocal favors.

[11] Today a bank will not give a firm a good interest rate without seeing its books. Organizations like the Securities and Exchange Commission were created to make information widely available, so that a thick liquid market could exist. There was no equivalent of the SEC in Old Regime France.

in allocating and enforcing rights. In autocratic regimes, cronyism can be maintained because the rulers both allocate and enforce rights.⁶ If the legal system is not distinct from the political system, contracts may not be enforced. There is therefore little incentive for more efficient producers to attempt to outbid the ruler's cronies.

Dominating the distribution of rights allowed the French Crown to claim the loyalty of a large clientele.⁷ Although distribution of loyalty-based property rights helped create social support for the regime, economic inefficiencies resulted.⁸ The threat that loyalty-based property rights might be withdrawn limited their market to users favorable to the king, and the inability to trade them more widely reduced their liquidity. The economic value of such rights therefore declined, while the value of being a crony increased.

Since premodern rulers were likely to extend rights to individuals with whom they had multiple overlapping contracts, sanctions against the random diffusion of economic rights were available. Such sanctions included denying the original right holder future deals, denying the buyer adjacent rights or essential information, and refusing to buy goods or services from an unwanted interloper.

These limitations of loyalty rights became especially salient during periods of abrupt economic change. When shifts in wealth among individuals occur, those who benefit from the shift have no way of signaling their newly acquired ability.⁹

Rights holders in an absolute monarchy must always worry about confiscation. In Old Regime France, much routine economic activity was only

---

⁶The common law has been an important component of England's institutional structure, providing incentives suited to long-term investment (see R. M. Hartwell, *The Industrial Revolution and Economic Growth* [London: Methuen, 1971], 244–61). Neither state-granted monopolies nor cartel agreements were sanctioned under common law, and competition, or new entrants into an industry, was not recognized as a tort. Freedom of contract under common law sanctions any terms of exchange that are mutually beneficial and conform to standards of consideration, mutual assent, and absence of fraud, incapacity, or duress. Significantly, common law is bound by precedent, so, unlike with statutory law, one legislature, political party, or king cannot undo the laws of a predecessor. British commercial law developed within this common law tradition.

⁷In the same way the privileges held by members of *nomenklatura* in the Soviet Union created rents that could not be bid away, because the rights could only be used by another member of the Communist party.

⁸Ronald Wintrobe, "The Tinpot and the Totalitarian: An Economic Theory of Dictatorship," *American Political Science Review* 84, no. 3 (September 1990): 849–71; on loyalty-based property and dictatorships, see 866–67.

⁹For example, in the fiscal crisis at the end of the Old Regime or the oil crises of the 1970s.

of products and services, and rights to participate in the international economy were distributed as property by governments seeking revenue.[2] Transaction costs were erected to reduce the range of possible exchanges to those that produced revenue for the state and its clients.

Bringing buyers and sellers together commonly requires the services of a market maker, and the history of investment banking in the twentieth century shows that when the costs of creating a market are high, the reputation of the market maker is crucial.[3] The benefits of creating a market cannot always be captured by those who would bear the costs of collecting and classifying information about potential buyers and sellers and the monitoring expenses associated with market management. A market maker will not emerge unless assured of some profit.[4] As a result, not all possible markets for property rights are created.

Moreover, contracts to assure payment for the transfer of rights are not always easy to write and enforce once an owner has agreed to give up a portion of the shares. If future income from the exercise of rights such as stewardship over the local market, feudal dues, or the liberation of slaves were to be surrendered, guarantees were needed that future payments would be maintained. Writing contracts to buy out present holders of rights could, therefore, be highly problematic.[5]

Premodern rulers often granted access to property rights in exchange for political loyalty. By contrast, open bidding for property rights might compromise the system of patronage, so rulers commonly restricted market access to their chosen clients regardless of considerations of efficiency

---

[2] Property rights determine the way particular resources will be used and assign the resulting costs and benefits. Property rights—or what people believe to be the relevant rules of the game—determine how the process of supply and demand will work.

[3] See, e.g., J. Bradford De Long, "Did J. P. Morgan's Men Add Value?" in *Inside the Business Enterprise*, ed. Peter Temin (Chicago: University of Chicago Press, 1991), 206–36.

[4] "To explain the origins of rights . . . we must look for self-interested motives for grantors as well as petitioners" (William H. Riker, "Civil Rights and Property Rights," in *Liberty, Property, and the Future of Constitutional Development*, ed. Ellen Frankel Paul and Howard Dickman [Albany: State University of New York Press, 1990], 49–64).

[5] The French Revolution might have been avoided if a credible or enforceable contract could have been written allowing the monarchy to buy back the tax exemptions of privileged individuals. Similarly, the American Civil War might have been avoided if a contract could have been written allowing the North to reimburse the South for the liberation of slaves. Japan, Taiwan, and Korea, three of the great success stories of recent economic history, offer examples of the rights of traditional elites being bought out rather than confiscated. The traditional elites were given equity shares in the new regime, enlisting their cooperation in the modern economy.

# 1 The Market for Property Rights

Historically, participation in a market system was a politically allocated right. Markets often originated as grants to privileged individuals in the political hierarchy: not just anyone could open or participate in a market. In their unending search for funds, medieval governments banned all kinds of profitable activities and occupations in order to sell exemptions from those restrictions. A dominant theme of medieval politics was competition for licenses granting lucrative perquisites from which everyone else was excluded.[1]

When property rights are clearly specified, it should not matter to whom they were originally allocated. This simple proposition is a staple of contemporary economic thinking on the evolution of property rights. It is based on the assumption that, in a market system, those who can more effectively use a right will be able to bid for its acquisition. In other words, as long as markets exist that allow those who can realize the value of a right most effectively to obtain it from those to whom it was originally allocated, efficiency will result. Only when the transaction costs from the subsequent transfer of the right exceed the potential benefits of its exploitation will the original allocation prevent efficient utilization.

Observations of the historical evolution of markets suggest a different explanation of why the many privileges and liberties unequally distributed among the populations of early modern states were not freely traded. Usage rights, tax exemptions, judicial prerogatives, manufacturing monopolies, privately owned government offices, rights to buy and sell all kinds

[1] See A. R. Bridbury, "Markets and Freedom in the Middle Ages," in *The Market in History*, ed. B. L. Anderson and A. J. H. Latham (London: Croom Helm, 1986), 79–121, and Henry Clifford Darby, *An Historical Geography of England before A.D. 1800* (Cambridge: Cambridge University Press, 1936), 79–119.

# 1
# THEORETICAL AND HISTORICAL BACKGROUND

student of historical explanations has observed, among historians 'under-researching is frowned upon, under-explaining is not,' and it is tempting to argue that exactly the reverse is true of economics."[5]

The conventions of argument adhered to in this book are those most typical of comparative politics, history, and historical sociology. The issues raised, and their sequence, are determined by major interpretative debates among scholars who have attempted to understand the transition to an open society and economy. Some readers may be puzzled by the fact that, although this is not a survey, new evidence is often presented side by side with material from the work of other scholars. The goal has been to provide an interpretation of the old material in the light of new findings. Many of the debates in social history do not raise issues that engage economists. Economists may be frustrated by discussions of methodological issues that they believe have been resolved. Conversely, since much of the book's theoretical material can be found in technical discussions difficult for the nonspecialist, scholars of social history and politics may be unfamiliar with the relevance to their usual field of inquiry.

As this book seeks to establish a basis for critical discussion across the various frameworks used by the social historian, historical sociologist, and political economist, tolerance is required from all three groups. If we are to communicate across paradigms, we must be able and willing to take seriously the methods of discourse as well as the perceptions of other disciplines. Those perceptions are consistent with the development of a particular intellectual framework. I do not propose to conduct or interpret research without a conceptual framework; however, I hope to show that there are many potential points of contact and comparison among these neighboring fields, allowing scholars of each to escape their particular frameworks. Even if one wants to remain within a specific framework, one can learn to master or translate the criteria of the other. The result should be roomier, better-equipped frameworks for all. As Karl Popper has noted, "The difficulty of discussion between people brought up in different frameworks is to be admitted. But nothing is more fruitful than such a discussion; than the culture clash which has stimulated some of the greatest intellectual revolutions."[6]

---

[5] A. W. Coats, "Explanations in History and Economics," *Social Research* 56 (1989): 345–46.
[6] Karl Popper, "Normal Science and Its Dangers," in *Criticism and the Growth of Knowledge*, ed. Imre Lakatos and Alan Musgrave (New York: Cambridge University Press, 1970), 58.

In this book, privilege is considered alongside other possible means available to rulers to contract with the private groups upon whose cooperation the government depends. Privilege may have been disbursed by state builders in order to make it easier to enforce collective decisions. The access of social groups to privilege followed avenues that varied significantly among the Old Regime states of western Europe. Those differences may have been decisive in determining which regimes survived.

The research presented here may also have contemporary relevance, since the issues involved—particularly the question of how political institutions facilitate the transition from pre-market to market societies, and the role of parliaments in securing political stability during the transition—closely resemble those currently faced in many developing Third World and eastern European nations.

One of the book's missions is to test the accuracy of the social historians' paradigm, based on macrosociology, against the economists' paradigm, based on microeconomics, for predicting the motivations for institutional innovation in early modern Europe.[4] A range of both implicit and explicit assumptions of familiar interpretations have been subjected to scrutiny from the perspective of the two paradigms. Bridging the economist's insistence on finding rational grounds for choice and the historian's concern for demonstrating connections among social structure, institutions, and culture is the objective. Traditionally, economists focus on the individual and view economic development as the aggregate of individual behavior, while social historians focus on groups and view change as the result of the interrelationships among different groups. Combining these two perspectives will, I hope, bring together the ideas of scholars concerned with the interconnections among politics, institutions, and economic systems, regardless of discipline and ideological conviction.

The book requires that the reader tolerate modes of explanation that may at first seem unfamiliar, and it risks offending the tastes of both social historians and political economists at certain margins. While both fields treat overlapping subjects, practitioners often ignore expanding research frontiers in neighboring disciplines. Moreover, the conventions of argument and proof in the two fields are vastly different. "Whereas economists highly value simplicity, elegance, precision, rigor, and system, historians are more concerned with accuracy and, if possible, completeness in the discovery, presentation, and interpretation of evidence—matters on which many economists are notoriously lax," A. W. Coats notes. "As one

---

[4] By *paradigm* I mean not so much a single dominant theory as a research program or mode of explanation that is generally accepted within a discipline.

provided a forum in which competing groups could voice their demands and negotiate compromises. The trade-off between greater political participation and economic development is nevertheless complicated. An active legislature does not eliminate rent seeking but makes it more competitive; it may even increase transfers of wealth directly related to rent seeking.

In Old Regime France, the concentration of political authority encouraged the concentration of wealth among a small number of individuals. This concentration divided French society into three groups according to the extent of the wealth and privilege they enjoyed as a result of their relationship to the state. The peasants, the majority of the population, benefited least. Urban grain consumers, workers, and merchants in privileged industries obtained some advantages. The greatest redistributive benefits by far went to the third group, individuals involved in state finances; not surprisingly, the financiers had the greatest stake in the rise of central authority. While examination of these social categories will provide the overall structure and sequence of this book, I shall also attempt to understand the costs and benefits to the economy of the privileges enjoyed by each group. I do not intend to suggest that these categories are sufficient in themselves as a basis for a social analysis of Old Regime France. Nor do I suggest that one can imagine a state in which there is only distribution and no redistribution. This nonconventional division of French society into groups according to the extent of privileges they hold will illustrate a relationship between the form of government, the type of redistributive policies that are produced, and the stability of the regime.[3]

Scholars of Old Regime societies are caught in a dilemma of overabundance. They possess a literature rich in empirical cases describing the circumstances of particular social groups and institutions. But how does one sift through this empirical work to reach conceptual or theoretical conclusions? A way out of this embarrassment of riches is needed. We need an encounter with deductive theory that can help to bring the disparate literature together. The deficiencies of particular French institutions are well known, but the abrupt, coordinated failure that caused the Old Regime to collapse is quite another matter. The literature on that collapse often emphasizes the corrosive influence of privilege on the body politic, but we still lack a satisfactory account of the political and economic rationale behind this society of privilege.

---

[3]Fernand Braudel was the first to suggest this division; see his *L'Identité de la France* (Paris: Arthaud-Flammarion, 1986), 307–8.

ferent situations among rights-holders, are outcomes the same or similar? Are the rules of the game subject to rapid change or reversal? Are the procedures for changing rules arbitrary or whimsical? Are the rules of the game clear? Is the playing field level for all players? How available is information about economic opportunity and about political decisions? What is the extent of bargaining between groups that possess economic or political privileges? Are regime officials accountable? Are regime officials able to make credible commitments? What sanctions exist to ensure that the government lives up to its obligations? What degree of autonomy or independence from the political system does the legal system enjoy?

Distributive consequences of public policies often determine the success or failure of strategies and tactics for reform. I therefore attempt to analyze the benefits and the costs incurred by the government or by the general population as a result of typical public policies. These costs were often indirect and are not usually discussed in other histories. For example, the beneficial effects of the French policy of privileging urban grain consumers are lauded by modern historians, for that policy seemed to produce only winners. Policies that reduced the cost of living in the cities, despite their popularity, may, however, have had a negative impact on the economy and on the welfare of the many.

Rent seeking was the principal motor of institutional innovation in both nations; however, competition among organized groups for rents was more open in England than in France.[2] In France a monopolistic pattern of rent seeking evolved in which redistributive benefits were based on clientelism or personal relationships with regime officials. Using journalistic jargon, I call this pattern *cronyism*. Cronyism is the allocation of rents to elites according to their loyalty to individuals in power. Greater political risks and uncertainties may result from cronyism than from competitive rent seeking, because cronyism can undermine the legitimacy of a regime. Those denied access to rents may withdraw their loyalty or even allocate resources to discredit the regime. Finally, the comparison between the political development of Georgian England and Old Regime France suggests that a weak legislature (vis-à-vis the executive branch) creates the preconditions for cronyism. Conversely, a legislature whose power was on par with that of the executive branch would induce more competitive rent seeking. British political institutions extracted rents that were allocated across a wide spectrum of interest groups primarily because Parliament

---

[2]*Rent seeking* refers to activities that consume resources to achieve a pure transfer of wealth from one sector, group, or individual to another. These activities are wasteful because they use up resources without creating additional value for society at large. Lobbying for a monopoly is a good example.

# Introduction:
# Speaking across Paradigms

During the early modern period, important segments of the populations of both France and England shifted their allegiance away from small local units of government and informal associations toward large organizations with impersonal rules. The institutional changes that accompanied the shift had the potential to alter the distribution of income and the efficiency of resource use within the economies of both nations. By influencing the objectives of rulers and the collective action of social groups, the changed institutional matrix also altered the degree of political stability enjoyed by the two regimes. To relate the success or failure of policy reform to the constitutional rules that governed collective action, this book compares the Whig ascendancy in England with the Old Regime's collapse in France.[1]

In comparing the principal laws, institutions and political processes that made trade and investment possible in England and France, I have sought to link political and economic development in a common analytical framework. Analyzing the qualitative data we possess on the legal structures and administrative practices of the two governments may perhaps improve our understanding of the transition from a premodern, mercantilist economy to a more modern and open one. Contrasting English and French institutions may shed light on the arrangements that produced inefficiencies in economic and political markets, as well as on those that facilitated structural change and institutional innovation.

Particular attention is paid to the following qualitative attributes of the institutional environment: Given the same or similar circumstances in dif-

---

[1]*Constitutional* includes the institutions and rules governing political decision making. In this sense, all societies possess constitutions, even those, like early modern France and England, that lack explicitly written constitutions.

xi

kin, Filipo Sabetti, Tademi Suzuka, Herman Van der Wee, Barry Weingast, and Marty Wolfe gave generously of their time and insights. Pat Nolan and the staff of the Hagley Library generously shared their expertise and its resources. Several anonymous readers also offered counsel. I was blessed, throughout the writing of this book, by the intelligence, humor, and companionship of Nancy Overholt. To her my gratitude and love.

To all these institutions and individuals, who helped transform this book from concept to reality, I extend my gratitude. Needless to say, I take full responsibility for any errors and miscalculations that have persisted despite advice.

H.L.R.<br>
January 28, 1993<br>
Palo Alto

# Acknowledgments

Financial support for this study was provided by the Program for Revitalizing the Social Sciences at the University of Pennsylvania, Penn Faculty Grants, an NEH Mellon Grant administered by the Hagley Library, and a fellowship from the John B. Olin Foundation.

Robert Bates, James Coleman, Mancur Olson, and Douglass C. North are the four authors whose work has most directly influenced the perspectives adopted here. My co-authors over the past few years—Ed Campos, Dan Ingberman, and John Nye—have also influenced my thinking on a number of critical issues. As they know, it is not always possible to distinguish my ideas from theirs. Moreover, my research assistants and students at the University of Pennsylvania have played an indispensable role; in particular, I would like to single out the efforts of Shannan Clark, Griff Green, Keith Noreika, Todd Rosentover, and Chris Taylor. Greg LaBlanc read with great care and commented on the entire manuscript. I wish them the best in their future endeavors. The uncompromising intellectual standards of three colleagues, Robert M. Hartwell, Alan Charles Kors, and Robert P. Inman, made it possible for me to have strength in my convictions as well as the resolve to finish this book. Florin Aftalion's curiosity to see what a combination of public choice economics and comparative early modern European social history would bear helped me to overcome the many obstacles that typically interfere with the publication of interdisciplinary research. Pierre Deyon, François Furet, and Emmanuel Le Roy Ladurie all provided me with the encouragement to stay with the project until the end. Gary Becker, William Brustein, James Collins, François Crouzet, Leonard Liggio, Giles Postel-Vinay, Jack Goldstone, Margaret Levi, John Markoff, Donald McCloskey, Vincent Ostrom, Sam Pop-

5  HYPOTHESES AND CONCLUSIONS                              211
   10  Modernization, Revolution, and the State           213
   11  Caveat Emptor: Markets and History                 241
       *Works Cited*                                      247
       *Index*                                            271

# Contents

|   |   | *Acknowledgments* | ix |
|---|---|---|---|
|   |   | *Introduction: Speaking across Paradigms* | xi |
| 1 |   | THEORETICAL AND HISTORICAL BACKGROUND | 1 |
|   | 1 | The Market for Property Rights | 3 |
|   | 2 | Rivals in Modernization: Creating National Communities in France and England | 14 |
|   | 3 | The Redistributive Role of the State | 21 |
| 2 |   | THE LESS PRIVILEGED | 59 |
|   | 4 | Interpreting Peasant Revolutions | 61 |
| 3 |   | THE MORE PRIVILEGED | 79 |
|   | 5 | The Political Economy of Collective Violence: What Did the "Moral Economy" of Pre-Revolutionary Europe Cost? | 81 |
|   | 6 | Rent Seeking and Trade Regulation | 113 |
|   | 7 | The Rise and Decline of English Mercantilism in Comparative Perspective | 140 |
| 4 |   | THE VERY PRIVILEGED | 161 |
|   | 8 | Tying the King's Hands: Credible Commitments and Royal Fiscal Policy under the Old Regime | 163 |
|   | 9 | The Fiscal Origins of Democratic Revolution | 179 |

*In Memory of*
*James Allen Vann III*
*friend and teacher*

University of California Press
Berkeley and Los Angeles, California

University of California Press, Ltd.
London, England

© 1994 by
The Regents of the University of California

Root, Hilton L.
    The fountain of privilege : political foundations of markets in Old Regime France and England / Hilton L. Root.
    p. cm.—(California series on social choice and political economy : 26)
Includes bibliographical references and index.
ISBN 0-520-08415-2 (alk. paper)
    1. France—Economic conditions—18th century. 2. France—Politics and government—18th century. 3. Great Britain—Economic conditions—18th century. 4. Great Britiain—Politics and government—18th century. I. Title. II. Series.
HC275.R587    1994
330.944'034—dc20                                             93-5066
                                                                                     CIP

Printed in the United States of America
9 8 7 6 5 4 3 2 1

The paper used in this publication meets the minimum requirements of American National Standard for Information Sciences—Permanence of Paper for Printed Library Materials, ANSI Z39.48-1984. ∞

# The Fountain of Privilege

*Political Foundations of Markets in
Old Regime France and England*

HILTON L. ROOT

*University of California Press*
BERKELEY    LOS ANGELES    LONDON

# California Series on Social Choice and Political Economy

Edited by Brian Barry (1981 to 1991), Robert H. Bates, James S. Coleman (from 1992), and Samuel L. Popkin

1. *Markets and States in Tropical Africa: The Political Basis of Agricultural Policies,* by Robert H. Bates
2. *Political Economics,* by James E. Alt and K. Alec Chrystal
3. *Abortion and the Politics of Motherhood,* by Kristin Luker
4. *Hard Choices: How Women Decide about Work, Career, and Motherhood,* by Kathleen Gerson
5. *Regulatory Policy and the Social Sciences,* edited by Roger Noll
6. *Reactive Risk and Rational Action: Managing Moral Hazard in Insurance Contracts,* by Carol A. Heimer
7. *Post-Revolutionary Nicaragua: State, Class, and the Dilemmas of Agrarian Policy,* by Forrest D. Colburn
8. *Essays on the Political Economy of Rural Africa,* by Robert H. Bates
9. *Peasants and King in Burgundy: Agrarian Foundations of French Absolutism,* by Hilton L. Root
10. *The Causal Theory of Justice,* by Karol Edward Soltan
11. *Principles of Group Solidarity,* by Michael Hechter
12. *Political Survival: Politicians and Public Policy in Latin America,* by Barry Ames
13. *Of Rule and Revenue,* by Margaret Levi
14. *Toward a Political Economy of Development: A Rational Choice Perspective,* edited by Robert H. Bates
15. *Rainbow's End: Irish-Americans and the Dilemmas of Urban Machine Politics, 1840–1985,* by Steven P. Erie
16. *A Treatise on Social Justice, Volume 1: Theories of Justice,* by Brian Barry
17. *The Social Origins of Political Regionalism: France, 1849–1981,* by William Brustein
18. *Nested Games: Rational Choice in Comparative Politics,* by George Tsebelis
19. *Information and Organizations,* by Arthur L. Stinchcombe
20. *Political Argument,* by Brian Barry
21. *Women and the Economic Miracle: Gender and Work in Postwar Japan,* by Mary Brinton
22. *Choosing Justice,* by Norman Frohlich and Joe A. Oppenheimer
23. *Legislative Leviathan: Party Government in the House,* by Mathew D. McCubbins and Gary W. Cox
24. *The Political Logic of Economic Reform in China,* by Susan L. Shirk
25. *Politician's Dilemma: Building State Capacity in Latin America,* by Barbara Geddes
26. *The Fountain of Privilege: Political Foundations of Markets in Old Regime France and England,* by Hilton L. Root

*The Fountain of Privilege*